애프터스쿨 리스닝 level 2

After School Listening Level 2

지은이 안천구, 넥서스영어교육연구소
펴낸이 임상진
펴낸곳 (주)넥서스

출판신고 1992년 4월 3일 제311-2002-2호 ㉑
10880 경기도 파주시 지목로 5
Tel (02)330-5500 Fax (02)330-5555

ISBN 978-89-6000-822-9 58740
978-89-6000-820-5 (SET)

가격은 뒤표지에 있습니다.
잘못 만들어진 책은 구입처에서 바꾸어 드립니다.

www.nexusEDU.kr
NEXUS Edu는 넥서스의 초·중·고 학습물 전문 브랜드입니다.

중학 영어듣기
한 방에 끝낸다

안천구·넥서스영어교육연구소 지음

NEXUS Edu

After School Listening is ...

최신 기출문제 유형을 공부합니다.

지난 5년간 출제된 〈전국 15개 시, 도교육청 공동 주관 영어듣기능력평가〉의 출제유형을 철저히 분석하여 시험에 자주 나오는 최신 문제유형을 제공합니다.

_모의고사 16회 + dictation

_실전모의고사 2회

듣기 시험에 자신감을 심어줍니다.

실제 시험보다 난이도와 속도가 향상된 모의고사를 풀어봄으로써 실전에 대한 적응력을 높이는 것은 물론 평소보다 어려운 문제가 나왔을 경우에도 당황하지 않고 문제를 해결할 수 있는 능력을 키워줍니다.

체계적으로 공부합니다.

전국 15개 시, 도교육청 공동 주관 영어듣기능력평가를 분석하여 가장 많이 출제된 유형을 정리하여 부록으로 제공합니다.

_미니북 : 유형별 학습

영어실력을 한 단계 향상시킬 수 있습니다.

유형분석뿐만 아니라 각 유형과 관련된 단어와 표현 등을 집중적으로 학습하여 듣기 능력뿐만 아니라 전체적인 영어 실력을 향상시킬 수 있습니다.

Constitution

영어듣기모의고사 16회

최근 5년간 출제된 문제유형을 철저히 분석하여 출제 가능성이 높은 16회분 총 320문제의 최신 유형 문제들만 실었습니다.

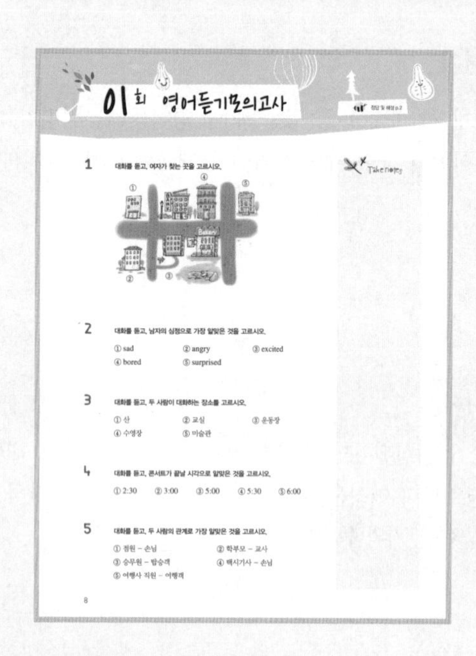

01회 영어듣기모의고사

정답 및 해설 p.2

1 대화를 듣고, 여자가 찾는 곳을 고르시오.

2 대화를 듣고, 남자의 심정으로 가장 알맞은 것을 고르시오.

① sad ② angry ③ excited
④ bored ⑤ surprised

3 대화를 듣고, 두 사람이 대화하는 장소를 고르시오.

① 산 ② 교실 ③ 운동장
④ 수영장 ⑤ 미술관

4 대화를 듣고, 콘서트가 끝날 시각으로 알맞은 것을 고르시오.

① 2:30 ② 3:00 ③ 5:00 ④ 5:30 ⑤ 6:00

5 대화를 듣고, 두 사람의 관계로 가장 알맞은 것을 고르시오.

① 점원 – 손님 ② 학부모 – 교사
③ 승무원 – 탑승객 ④ 택시기사 – 손님
⑤ 여행사 직원 – 여행객

Take notes

8

Dictation

한 회가 끝날 때마다 지문을 다시 한 번 들으면서 놓치기 쉬운 주요 표현들을 받아쓰고 학습할 수 있도록 구성하였습니다.

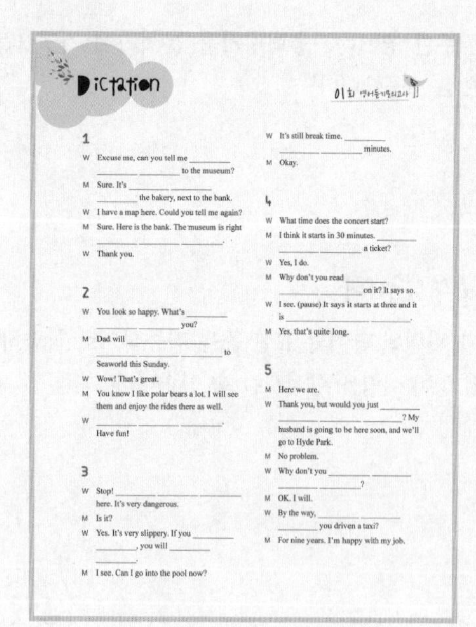

Dictation

01회 영어듣기모의고사

1

W Excuse me, can you tell me ________ ________ ________ to the museum?
M Sure. It's ________ ________ ________ the bakery, next to the bank.
W I have a map here. Could you tell me again?
M Sure. Here is the bank. The museum is right ________ ________ ________.
W Thank you.

2

W You look so happy. What's ________ ________ ________ you?
M Dad will ________ ________ ________ ________ ________ to Seaworld this Sunday.
W Wow! That's great.
M You know I like polar bears a lot. I will see them and enjoy the rides there as well.
W ________ ________ ________. Have fun!

3

W Stop! ________ ________ ________ here. It's very dangerous.
M Is it?
W Yes. It's very slippery. If you ________ ________, you will ________ ________.
M I see. Can I go into the pool now?
W It's still break time. ________ ________ ________ minutes.
M Okay.

4

W What time does the concert start?
M I think it starts in 30 minutes. ________ ________ ________ a ticket?
W Yes, I do.
M Why don't you read ________ ________ ________ on it? It says so.
W I see. (pause) It says it starts at three and it is ________ ________ ________.
M Yes, that's quite long.

5

M Here we are.
W Thank you, but would you just ________ ________ ________ ________? My husband is going to be here soon, and we'll go to Hyde Park.
M No problem.
W Why don't you ________ ________ ________ ________?
M OK. I will.
W By the way, ________ ________ ________ you driven a taxi?
M For nine years. I'm happy with my job.

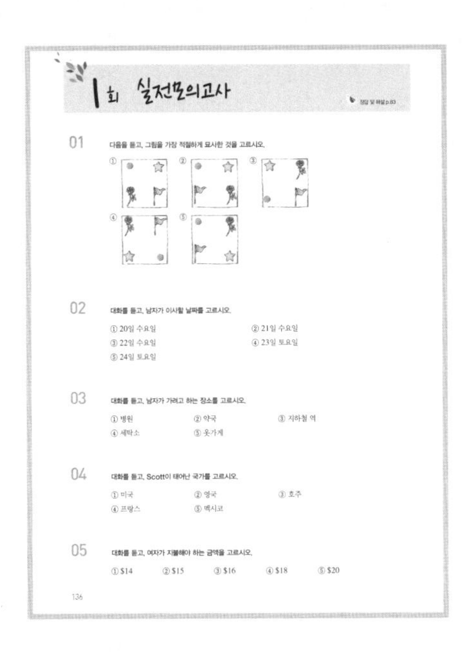

실전모의고사 2회

영어듣기모의고사 16회를 통해서 갈고닦은 영어듣기 실력을 최종 실전모의고사 2회를 통해서 점검하고, 실전에 대비할 수 있습니다.

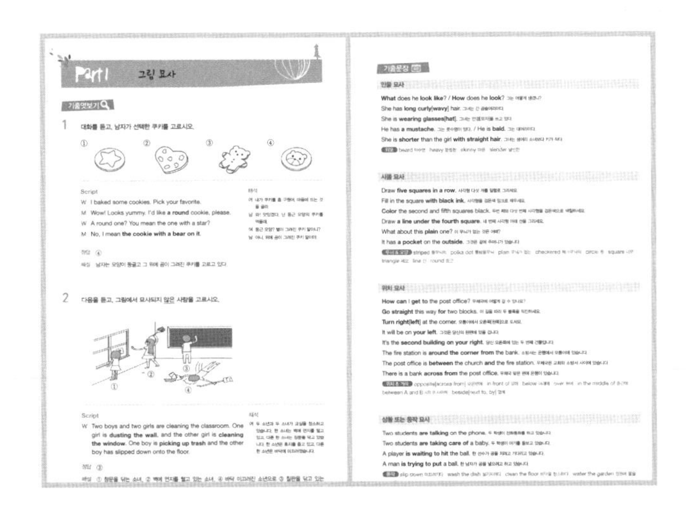

Mini book - 유형별 학습

부록으로 포함된 미니북에는 자주 출제되는 기출 유형과 이에 따른 단어, 숙어, 표현들을 정리하였습니다.
유형과 표현 학습을 끝내고 나서 기출문제를 풀어봄으로써 유형별 문제 풀이 능력을 향상시킬 수 있습니다.

Contents

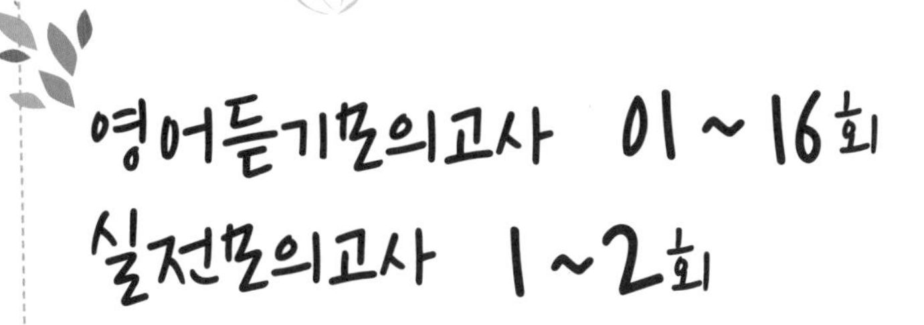
영어듣기모의고사 01~16회
실전모의고사 1~2회

01회 영어듣기모의고사

정답 및 해설 p.2

Take notes

1 대화를 듣고, 여자가 찾는 곳을 고르시오.

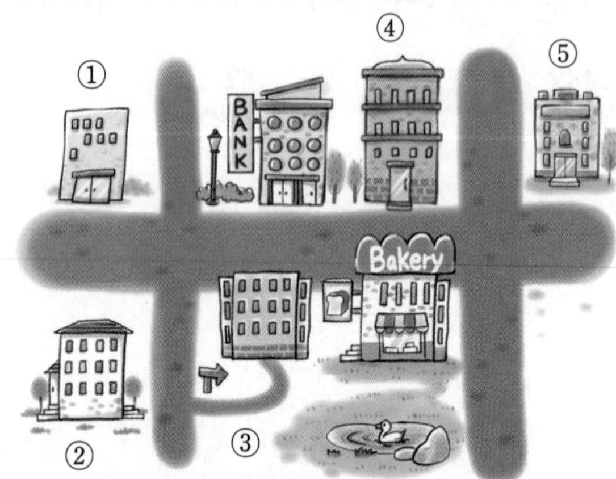

2 대화를 듣고, 남자의 심정으로 가장 알맞은 것을 고르시오.

① sad ② angry ③ excited
④ bored ⑤ surprised

3 대화를 듣고, 두 사람이 대화하는 장소를 고르시오.

① 산 ② 교실 ③ 운동장
④ 수영장 ⑤ 미술관

4 대화를 듣고, 콘서트가 끝날 시각으로 알맞은 것을 고르시오.

① 2:30 ② 3:00 ③ 5:00 ④ 5:30 ⑤ 6:00

5 대화를 듣고, 두 사람의 관계로 가장 알맞은 것을 고르시오.

① 점원 – 손님 ② 학부모 – 교사
③ 승무원 – 탑승객 ④ 택시기사 – 손님
⑤ 여행사 직원 – 여행객

6 대화를 듣고, 여자의 장래희망으로 알맞은 것을 고르시오.

①   ②  ③ 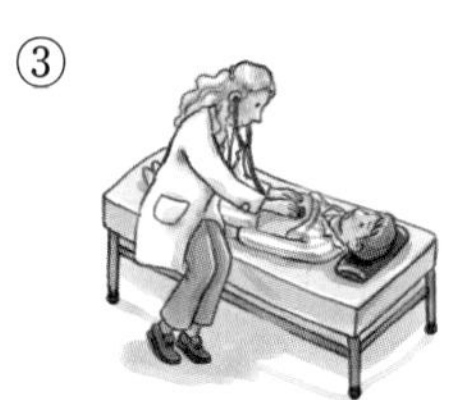

④  ⑤ 

7 다음을 듣고, 무엇에 관한 설명인지 고르시오.

① 경로석 ② 줄서기 ③ 정차 벨
④ 대중교통 ⑤ 교통카드

8 대화를 듣고, 남자가 한 마지막 말의 의도를 고르시오.

① 거절 ② 승낙 ③ 조언 ④ 제안 ⑤ 항의

9 대화를 듣고, 경기에서 우승한 사람을 고르시오.

① John ② Mark ③ Kevin
④ Jason ⑤ Mike

10 다음을 듣고, 탑승권에 대한 설명으로 알맞지 않은 것을 고르시오.

BOARDING PASS		
NAME: PAUL ALLEN FROM: SEOUL	TO: TOKYO	
FLIGHT: GF12	DATE: 17 July	TIME: 11:30
GATE: 30	BOARDING TIME: 11:00	SEAT: 34H
GOODFLYING AIRLINE		

① ② ③ ④ ⑤

Take notes

11 대화를 듣고, 여자가 사야 하는 물건이 아닌 것을 고르시오.

① 감자 ② 양파 ③ 배추
④ 당근 ⑤ 시금치

12 대화를 듣고, 남자가 전화를 건 목적을 고르시오.

① 사과를 하려고
② 약속시간을 정하려고
③ 좋아한다고 고백하려고
④ 여자친구를 소개해 달라고
⑤ 친구가 화난 이유를 물어보려고

13 대화를 듣고, 남자가 이용할 교통수단을 고르시오.

① bus ② taxi ③ subway
④ bicycle ⑤ car

14 다음을 듣고, 내용과 일치하지 않는 것을 고르시오.

① Jim은 졸린 것처럼 보인다.
② David는 오늘 학교에 늦었다.
③ Joshua는 선생님만큼 키가 크다.
④ Olivia는 지금 창문을 닫으려고 한다.
⑤ Jessica는 선생님께 칭찬을 받았다.

15 대화를 듣고, 여자가 서점에 가려는 이유를 고르시오.

① 책을 사기 위하여
② 책을 교환하기 위하여
③ 책을 환불받기 위하여
④ 친구를 소개받기 위하여
⑤ 좋아하는 남자를 보기 위하여

16

대화를 듣고, 남자의 집에서 가장 키가 작은 사람을 고르시오.

① 여동생 ② 엄마 ③ 본인
④ 아빠 ⑤ 형

17

대화를 듣고, 내용과 가장 관련 있는 속담을 고르시오.

① It's a piece of cake.
② Clothes make the man.
③ Don't judge a book by its cover.
④ A little knowledge is dangerous.
⑤ Get angry at other's for one's own mistakes.

18

다음을 듣고, 두 사람의 대화가 어색한 것을 고르시오.

① ② ③ ④ ⑤

19-20 대화를 듣고, 남자의 마지막 말에 이어질 여자의 응답으로 가장 알맞은 것을 고르시오.

19

① As soon as possible.
② Tomorrow is a holiday.
③ I will bring it tomorrow.
④ Thank you for your advice.
⑤ Dave is coming next week.

20

① You must be happy.
② I'm sorry to hear that.
③ They did it to save energy.
④ How could you finish it so fast?
⑤ You can have another chance.

1

W Excuse me, can you tell me __________ __________ __________ to the museum?

M Sure. It's __________ __________ __________ the bakery, next to the bank.

W I have a map here. Could you tell me again?

M Sure. Here is the bank. The museum is right __________ __________ __________.

W Thank you.

2

W You look so happy. What's __________ __________ __________ you?

M Dad will __________ __________ __________ __________ __________ to Seaworld this Sunday.

W Wow! That's great.

M You know I like polar bears a lot. I will see them and enjoy the rides there as well.

W __________ __________ __________. Have fun!

3

W Stop! __________ __________ __________ here. It's very dangerous.

M Is it?

W Yes. It's very slippery. If you __________ __________, you will __________ __________.

M I see. Can I go into the pool now?

W It's still break time. __________ __________ __________ minutes.

M Okay.

4

W What time does the concert start?

M I think it starts in 30 minutes. __________ __________ __________ a ticket?

W Yes, I do.

M Why don't you read __________ __________ __________ on it? It says so.

W I see. (pause) It says it starts at three and it is __________ __________ __________.

M Yes, that's quite long.

5

M Here we are.

W Thank you, but would you just __________ __________ __________? My husband is going to be here soon, and we'll go to Hyde Park.

M No problem.

W Why don't you __________ __________ __________ __________?

M OK. I will.

W By the way, __________ __________ you driven a taxi?

M For nine years. I'm happy with my job.

6

W What would you like to be ________
________ ________?

M I'm interested in science, so I'd like to be a scientist. ________ ________
________?

W I want to be an actress.

M You must ________ ________
________ movies, right?

W Yes. I usually see a movie twice a week.

M I guess you will be a great actress.

7

M These are the seats ________ ________
________ ________. Young people don't usually sit there. These are for elderly people. Some young people sit there, but when an elderly person ________
________, they ________ ________
and offer the seat to the person.

8

M Did you do your homework?

W Yes, I ________ ________ ________
it.

M Then, why don't you ________
________ ________ and watch TV?

W What are you watching?

M I'm watching the news.

W My favorite drama ________ ________
now. Can I watch it?

M Why not?

9

W I heard the game was ________
________ ________ last year's.
Did Jason win the game?

M No. Jason won the game last year, but
________ ________ ________.

W How about Mike?

M He ________ ________ ________.
No one expected John to be the winner.

W He finally made it. I knew he would.
He ________ ________ every day.

10

W ① Boarding is at eleven.

② Paul ________ ________ ________
thirty.

③ The seat number is 34H.

④ This flight ________ ________
Seoul.

⑤ GF12 is the airline and ________
________.

11

M Where are you going?

W I'm going to ________ ________
________.

M For what?

W My mother told me to buy some vegetables like um… I ________ ________
________ somewhere. I got it. Onions, carrots, potatoes, and spinach.

M You are a ________ ________.

12

[Telephone rings.]

W Hello.

M Kathy, it's Richard.

W Hey, __________ __________?

M I have something to ask you. __________ __________ Susie never talks to me? She __________ __________ with me. Why?

W It's because you __________ __________ __________ her in class.

M Really? I didn't know that.

13

W How are you going to get to the flea market?

M I'm __________ __________ __________ my bike.

W Isn't it too far from here? I think it will __________ __________ __________ an hour.

M Then, I will take the subway.

W But there is __________ __________ __________ there.

M Then, I will just take the bus.

14

W This is John's class. David was __________ __________ __________ today. Olivia is trying to open the window. Joshua is __________ __________ __________ __________ the blackboard. He is as tall as our teacher. Jessica looks happy because our teacher __________ __________ for good scores on the test. Jim looks sleepy.

15

W Let's go to the bookstore. I __________ __________ __________ some books about India.

M OK. Why do you need books about India?

W Well, actually, I'm __________ __________ __________ __________ to see some guy.

M Which guy?

W He works there __________ __________ __________, and he is really handsome.

16

W Ross, are you __________ __________ your mother?

M Of course. I'm even taller than my father. But my elder brother is the tallest __________ __________.

W I think your sister is pretty tall __________ __________.

M That's right, but she is shorter than my mother.

W I see.

17

M Oh my god! Mom, it's __________ __________ __________ seven.

W You finally got up!

M Why didn't you __________ __________ __________?

W Don't you remember? I woke you up five different times already, but you didn't get up.

M If I'm late for school, it's __________ __________ __________.

18

① W Which club do you __________
__________ __________?
M I had a really good time.

② W Why don't we take the bus here?
M Okay.

③ W Are you __________ __________
__________?
M I'm not sure. Why?

④ W What will you do after school?
M I'll go to the gym.

⑤ W Will you have __________ __________?
M No, thanks. I'm full.

19

W Joey, can you lend me your digital camera?

M Dave borrowed it, and he __________
__________ __________ to me yet.

W Can you tell him that I __________
__________ __________ it?

M Sure. When do you need it by?

W __________ __________ __________
possible.

20

W How are you doing?

M Not so good.

W You __________ __________. What's wrong with you?

M Well, while I was writing a report on the computer, the power __________
__________. I have to do it all over again because it wasn't saved.

W I'm __________ __________ __________
that.

02회 영어듣기모의고사

정답 및 해설 p.7

Take notes

1 대화를 듣고, 여자의 삼촌을 고르시오.

① ② ③ ④ ⑤

2 대화를 듣고, 두 사람이 만나기로 한 시각을 고르시오.

① 7:00 ② 8:00 ③ 9:00 ④ 9:30 ⑤ 10:00

3 대화를 듣고, 여자의 직업으로 알맞은 것을 고르시오.

① 의사 ② 교사 ③ 승무원
④ 통역사 ⑤ 관광 가이드

4 다음을 듣고, 도표의 내용과 일치하지 않는 것을 고르시오.

이름	목적지	만날 장소	시간
Linda	dance festival	Boston Hall	6:00
Cathy	the movies	box office	5:00
Mark	baseball stadium	main gate	1:30

① ② ③ ④ ⑤

5 대화를 듣고, 여자가 한 마지막 말의 의도를 고르시오.

① 배려 ② 제안 ③ 사과 ④ 경고 ⑤ 거절

6
대화를 듣고, 두 사람이 대화하는 장소를 고르시오.

① hospital
② station
③ restaurant
④ movie theater
⑤ department store

7
대화를 듣고, 남자가 지불해야 할 금액을 고르시오.

① $150
② $300
③ $450
④ $700
⑤ $800

8
다음을 듣고, 무엇에 관한 설명인지 고르시오.

① echo
② song
③ sound
④ dance
⑤ gesture

9
대화를 듣고, 여자가 사려고 하는 일기장을 고르시오.

10
대화를 듣고, 여자가 남자에게 충고하는 내용이 무엇인지 고르시오.

① 시간을 지켜라.
② 과식을 하지 마라.
③ 공부를 열심히 해라.
④ 시간을 낭비하지 마라.
⑤ 좀 더 주의를 기울여라.

Take notes

11

대화를 듣고, 남자가 이번 주말에 할 일을 고르시오.

① camping ② swimming
③ shopping ④ watching TV
⑤ playing tennis

12

대화를 듣고, 남자의 고민이 무엇인지 고르시오.

① 외모 ② 성적
③ 게임 중독 ④ 이성 문제
⑤ 부모님과의 갈등

13

대화를 듣고, 여자가 병원에 가는 이유를 고르시오.

① 다리가 아파서
② 자원봉사를 하려고
③ 친척을 방문하려고
④ 아르바이트를 하려고
⑤ 정기검진을 받으려고

14

다음을 듣고, 내용과 일치하지 않는 것을 고르시오.

① 하루에 12시간 영업한다.
② 큰 주차장을 보유하고 있다.
③ 지금 연말 세일을 하고 있다.
④ 세일은 12월 26일에 시작한다.
⑤ 모든 상품을 50% 세일하여 판매한다.

15

대화를 듣고, 여자가 가져온 물건이 아닌 것을 고르시오.

① rice ② pillow ③ tent
④ vegetable ⑤ flashlight

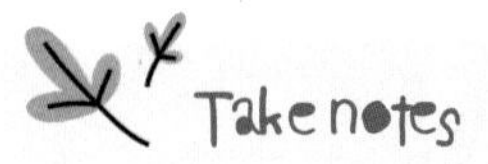

16 다음을 듣고, 두 사람의 대화가 어색한 것을 고르시오.

① ② ③ ④ ⑤

17 다음을 듣고, 무엇에 관한 내용인지 고르시오.

① 절약
② 정직함
③ 청결의 중요성
④ 학업의 중요성
⑤ 화목한 가족 관계

18 대화를 듣고, 내용과 가장 관련 있는 속담을 고르시오.

① Walls have ears.
② Bad news runs fast.
③ Like father, like son.
④ No fire without smoke.
⑤ Kill two birds with one stone.

19-20 대화를 듣고, 남자의 마지막 말에 이어질 여자의 응답으로 가장 알맞은 것을 고르시오.

19

① That's a good idea.
② Sorry, but I can't do that.
③ My mother won't agree with me.
④ Okay, bring your textbook, first.
⑤ Please don't tell my mother about that.

20

① To visit my aunt.
② Please, I'm in a hurry.
③ Here is my passport.
④ Thank you. Have a nice trip.
⑤ I will leave my son here for a moment.

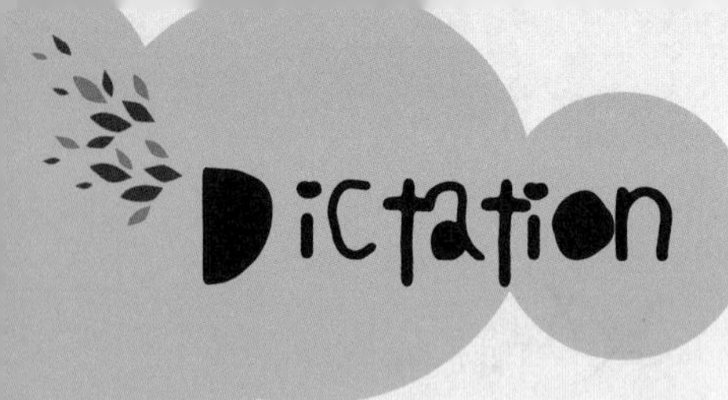

1

W I came here with my uncle __________ __________ my father.

M Where is he?

W He's over there. He is wearing a white shirt and __________ __________ __________.

M Is he wearing glasses?

W No, he is __________ __________ the man wearing glasses.

2

M Is it too early if we meet at seven?

W Yes, that's too early. I usually __________ __________ on Sundays.

M I usually get up at nine __________ __________. But I think we should go to the amusement park early.

W What time does it open?

M Nine o'clock, but it takes an hour and a half to get there.

W OK. I will __________ __________ __________ this time.

3

M How was your flight to London?

W It was fine.

M Your job __________ __________ __________. Because you work long hours standing in the airplane.

W Sometimes it is __________ __________, but I'm happy with my job.

M What __________ __________ __________?

W I enjoy traveling to different countries and meeting lots of people.

4

M ① Cathy is going to __________ __________ __________.

② Mark is going to the baseball stadium.

③ Linda is going to the __________ __________ at six.

④ Cathy is going to meet someone at the __________ __________ at five.

⑤ Linda is going to meet someone at the main gate.

5

W Why did you __________ __________ __________, Bill?

M School finished late.

W Carrie came home early, and she even finished her homework. Did you __________ __________ the Internet cafe again?

M Sorry, Mom. I was going to get home early, but....

W If you lie one more time, I will tell your father. You know __________ __________ __________ next.

6

M I'd like to __________ __________ __________.

W Is something wrong?

M Actually, my mother bought this shirt for me, but I don't like the design.

W Then, why don't you __________ __________ __________ you like?

M I just did, but I didn't __________ __________.

7

M I want to buy a __________ __________ with a big screen. How much do I need?

W A big __________ __________ 300 dollars, and a computer costs 500 dollars.

M That's a lot. __________ __________ a medium sized screen?

W It's 200 dollars, and a small one is 150 dollars.

M Okay. I'll buy a computer __________ __________ __________ screen.

8

W You hear this __________ __________ __________ near a mountain or a big wall. When you __________ __________ something, your voice __________ __________ and hits against a mountain or a big wall, and then comes back to you. This sounds very interesting and sometimes even __________ __________ __________ __________.

9

M Are you looking for something?

W Do you __________ __________?

M Yes, there are many diaries here. How about this diary __________ __________ __________ __________?

W No, I just want a black one.

M Okay, we have two types. You can buy one with or __________ __________ __________.

W I'll take the one with a lock.

10

W John, can I give you a __________ __________ __________?

M What is it?

W Why don't you be more careful? You made __________ __________ __________ again this morning.

M I tried not to, but....

W I know, but you __________ __________ __________.

11

W I'm going camping this weekend.

M That __________ __________ __________.

W I usually have a violin lesson on Saturdays, but I __________ __________ to go camping. How about you?

M Well, on weekends I usually play tennis with my brothers.

W I see. But you're __________ __________ __________ me this weekend, right?

M Of course, just tell me what I have to bring.

Dictation

12

M How ________ ________ in a day do you play computer games?

W I don't play computer games. I think it's a ________ ________ ________.

M Really? I spend too much time playing computer games these days. I even ________ ________ ________ at around one o'clock last night.

W Did you stay up until one playing computer games? Why don't you ________ ________?

M I've tried, but it's not easy.

13

M Where are you going?

W I'm going to the hospital near the park.

M Are you ________ ________?

W No, I work there doing ________ ________ ________ holding patients and cleaning things.

M You mean you have a part-time job?

W No, it is ________ ________. I just go there twice a week.

14

W Attention Shoppers! We are having a ________ ________ from December 26th to December 31st. Everything is ________ ________ for 50% off. So don't miss out on this chance. We open at 8 in the morning and ________ ________ ________ 10 p.m. We also have the ________ ________ ________ in town.

15

M Did you ________ ________?

W Sure. I brought some rice, a flashlight, a tent, and a ________ ________.

M OK. I brought some fruits and vegetables.

W Did you bring ________ ________ ________?

M Sure. It's in the bag.

16

① M How did you ________ ________ ________?

W My big brother helped me.

② M Why don't we clean the park?

W Because it is very dirty.

③ M I ________ ________ ________ in the contest.

W Wow. Congratulations!

④ M Will you carry this bag?

W Okay, I will.

⑤ M Where ________ ________ ________ all day?

W I went to Ryan's house.

17

M My father always tells me not to waste anything. After he ________ ________, he uses the water for flushing the toilet. He still wears the clothes he bought ten years ago. He wants me ________ ________ bottles and paper ________ ________. I really respect my father and ________ ________ ________ his ways.

18

M How is your knee now?

W It's OK. I don't feel pain __________ __________.

M That's good. Did you __________ __________ __________ __________?

W No, I felt pain because I weighed too much, so I started walking a lot. Now it's gone.

M Wow, you have __________ __________.

W Yeah. I lost a lot of weight, maybe ten kilograms.

19

M I __________ __________ __________ on the test. How about you?

W I __________ __________ __________ before, but still low.

M I see. I'm going to study math for one hour every day.

W Why?

M Because I'm __________ __________ __________ it.

W That's a good idea.

20

M How long will you __________ __________ __________?

W Two weeks.

M Okay. Is the boy __________ __________ your son?

W Yes, he is.

M What's the __________ __________ __________ __________?

W To visit my aunt.

03회 영어듣기모의고사

정답 및 해설 p.12

Take notes

1 다음을 듣고, 그림을 가장 적절하게 묘사한 것을 고르시오.

① 
② 
③ 
④ 
⑤ 

2 대화를 듣고, 기차가 떠나는 시각을 고르시오.

① 5:00 ② 5:10 ③ 5:20 ④ 5:30 ⑤ 5:40

3 대화를 듣고, 내일 남자가 학교에 가져갈 것을 고르시오.

① 도화지 ② 컴퍼스 ③ 가위
④ 붓 ⑤ 자

4 대화를 듣고, 두 사람이 대화하는 장소를 고르시오.

① 극장 안 ② 버스 안 ③ 비행기 안
④ 박물관 안 ⑤ 도서관 안

5 대화를 듣고, 여자가 주로 읽는 책의 종류를 고르시오.

① 역사에 대한 책 ② 인물에 대한 책
③ 자연에 대한 책 ④ 지구에 대한 책
⑤ 우주에 관한 책

6

대화를 듣고, 여자가 지불해야 할 금액을 고르시오.

① $6 ② $8 ③ $9 ④ $10 ⑤ $12

7

다음을 듣고, 그림의 내용과 일치하지 않는 것을 고르시오.

① ② ③ ④ ⑤

8

다음을 듣고, 무엇에 관한 설명인지 고르시오.

① nail ② glue ③ scissors
④ stapler ⑤ hammer

9

대화를 듣고, 여자가 남자에게 부탁하는 것을 고르시오.

① 조용히 해 달라고
② 진도를 물어보려고
③ 같이 극장에 가자고
④ 시험 준비를 도와 달라고
⑤ 수학 문제를 풀어 달라고

10

대화를 듣고, 남자가 주문한 음식이 아닌 것을 고르시오.

① cheeseburger ② french fries ③ orange juice
④ coke ⑤ salad

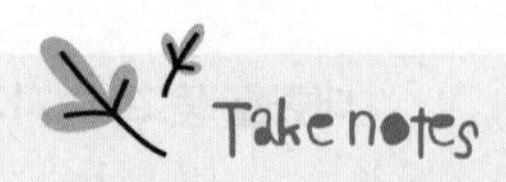

11 대화를 듣고, 여학생이 음악회에 가는 이유를 고르시오.

① 수행평가를 위해
② 공짜 표가 생겨서
③ 문화생활을 즐기려고
④ 부모님이 같이 가자고 해서
⑤ 클래식 음악을 좋아해서

12 다음을 듣고, "I"가 무엇인지 고르시오.

①

②

③

④
⑤

13 대화를 듣고, 이번 여름방학에 남자가 할 일을 고르시오.

① 신문 배달
② 보충 학습
③ 해외여행
④ 농촌 활동
⑤ 봉사 활동

14 대화를 듣고, 남자의 문제로 알맞은 것을 고르시오.

① 게으르다
② 이기적이다
③ 무례하다
④ 낭비벽이 심하다
⑤ 너무 성급하다

15 다음을 듣고, 남자의 심정으로 가장 알맞은 것을 고르시오.

① 우울한
② 창피한
③ 행복한
④ 자랑스러운
⑤ 만족스러운

16 대화를 듣고, 이어지는 질문에 가장 알맞은 답을 고르시오.

① jogging ② walking
③ swimming ④ eating less
⑤ riding a bicycle

17 대화를 듣고, 내용과 일치하는 것을 고르시오.

① 소년은 제시간에 왔다.
② 소년은 집 열쇠가 없다.
③ 소년은 거짓말을 하고 있다.
④ 소년의 엄마는 지금 집에 있다.
⑤ 소년은 엄마가 올 때까지 기다렸다.

18 다음을 듣고, 두 사람의 대화가 어색한 것을 고르시오.

① ② ③ ④ ⑤

19-20 대화를 듣고, 남자의 마지막 말에 이어질 여자의 응답으로 가장 적절한 것을 고르시오.

19

① That's great.
② No thanks, I'm full.
③ It's a piece of cake.
④ You shouldn't cook.
⑤ Let me make them for you.

20

① You can help me, too.
② I'm happy to hear that.
③ They are too new for me.
④ I can give you many things.
⑤ I need money for a new phone.

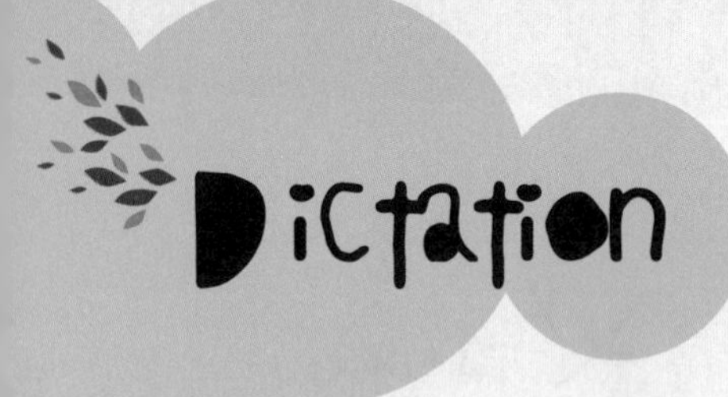

1

W This is a picture my little daughter drew. It is ______ ______ ______, but I decided to hang it on the wall. In the picture, there are ______ ______ ______, a small star between the two big stars, and a full moon ______ ______ ______ the small star.

2

W It's ______ ______ ______.

M Already?

W Yes, it's 5 o'clock.

M Let's have something to eat. I'm hungry.

W I'm OK. You ______ ______, but make it fast. We only have 20 minutes. If we miss this train, the next one isn't for another two hours.

M OK. I'll ______ ______ in 10 minutes.

3

M Do you remember what our teacher ______ ______ ______ ______ tomorrow?

W I wrote it down here. ______ ______ ______. I need scissors, a ruler, and a compass.

M What about me?

W Um, you need ______ ______ ______ and a brush.

M OK. I left some drawing paper in my locker at school, so I only need one thing.

4

W When do we get off?

M We have two more stops.

W ______ ______ ______?

M Don't worry. I've been there before.

W You told me ______ ______ ______ when we went to the museum, but we ______ ______.

M Believe me this time.

5

W What's your hobby, David?

M I like ______ ______, especially basketball and bowling.

W Now I see why you are so ______ ______.

M Thank you. What about you?

W I like reading books, especially ______ ______ ______.

M I like reading, too, and I usually read books on nature and space.

6

W The price tag says it's ten dollars, but can you ______ ______ ______ ______?

M I'm sorry, but I can't.

W But you always give me ten percent off.

M I know, but __________ __________ __________. Instead, I will give you this __________ __________. It's worth two dollars.

W Really? Thanks.

7

W ① There is a vase __________ __________ __________.

② A lamp is __________ __________ the vase.

③ There is a teddy bear on the bed.

④ The cat is sleeping __________ __________ __________.

⑤ A bookcase is between the table and the bed.

8

W This is something that __________ things __________. If something breaks, you can __________ __________ __________ __________ by using this. People usually use this for small things like __________ __________ __________ or a broken piece of plastic. Some people also use this to put something on the wall.

9

W Hello, Jamie. This is Ashley __________ __________.

M Oh, hi, Ashley. What's up?

W I __________ __________ __________ to ask you.

M Go ahead.

W I'm studying for a math test, so I'd like you to __________ __________ __________ __________, please.

M Sorry for bothering you.

10

W Hello, how can I help you?

M I'll have two cheeseburgers with french fries and a salad.

W What would you __________ __________ __________?

M A coke without ice and a vanilla milkshake, please.

W __________ __________?

M That's all.

W For __________ __________ __________ __________?

M Here, please.

11

M Wow! Look at you. Why did you __________ __________?

W I'm going to a concert with my family.

M That's great. Do you __________ __________ often?

W Sometimes. Actually, I don't like to go to them, but my parents like classical music. So they tell me to __________ __________.

M I see. If you __________ __________ __________, try to enjoy it.

12

W People enjoy me in the summer, and I'm __________ __________. Actually, I'm the brother of a watermelon. I have __________ __________ __________. My outside is yellow, and my inside is white. I have lots of seeds. Some people just eat them, while others just __________ __________ __________. What am I?

13

W What are you going to do this summer, Daniel?

M I'm __________ __________ __________ some volunteer work.

W What do you mean?

M Well, I'm going to __________ __________ __________.

W Where?

M At __________ __________ __________ in our neighborhood.

14

W Did you __________ __________ __________?

M No, I didn't, but I will before I go to bed.

W How about __________ __________ __________?

M Should I clean my room?

W I told you this morning.

M I'm sorry. I forgot.

W Oh, you haven't __________ __________ __________ yet, either.

15

M I took my girlfriend to a nice Korean restaurant today. When we arrived, there were __________ __________ __________. So we had to wait. A waitress called me, and we __________ __________ __________ a room that didn't have chairs. As soon as I __________ __________ my shoes to enter the room, I found that my socks were not the same. One was black, and __________ __________ was red.

16

W You seem to __________ __________ so much weight.

M Yes, I __________ __________ about seven kilograms in a month.

W How is that possible?

M I have no idea. The doctor said I should __________ __________.

W Why don't you go jogging every day? I think it's the best way.

M Is it? I'm swimming every morning __________ __________.

Q What is the man doing to lose weight these days?

17

W You are __________ __________ __________.

M I'm sorry. I didn't have the key to my house, so I __________ __________ __________ until my mom came.

W You mean your mom is __________ __________ now?

M Yes, she is at home.

W __________ __________ to me. Your mother is in my kitchen now.

18

① W Brian, can you __________ __________ __________ __________?

M Of course.

② W Carl, what do you see? Can you tell me?

M Yes, I will buy it

③ W I bought __________ __________ __________.

M Show it to me.

④ W I read this book last night.

M __________ __________ __________?

⑤ W Do you understand it now?

M Aha! I get it.

19

M Will you have __________ __________?

W Yes, thanks. Where did you get them?

M I __________ __________ __________. My mom taught me __________ __________ __________ them.

W Really? __________ __________ can you make?

M Pancakes and donuts.

W That's great.

20

M You are getting all of your __________ __________ __________.

W Yes, I'm planning a yard sale.

M You mean __________ __________ __________?

W Yes, it is the same thing.

M What __________ __________ __________?

W I need money for a new phone.

04회 영어듣기모의고사

정답 및 해설 p.17

Take notes

1 다음을 듣고, 그림의 상황에 가장 알맞은 대화를 고르시오.

① ② ③ ④ ⑤

2 대화를 듣고, 여자의 마지막 말의 의도를 고르시오.

① 감사 ② 칭찬 ③ 비판 ④ 책망 ⑤ 위로

3 대화를 듣고, 남자가 가보지 않은 나라를 고르시오.

① China ② America ③ Germany
④ Spain ⑤ Italy

4 대화를 듣고, 여자가 좋아하는 집의 형태를 고르시오.

① 정원이 있는 집 ② 창문이 많은 집
③ 나무가 많은 집 ④ 주위가 조용한 집
⑤ 작은 연못이 있는 집

5 대화를 듣고, 남자가 병원에서 퇴원할 날짜를 고르시오.

① 15일 ② 16일 ③ 17일 ④ 18일 ⑤ 19일

6

대화를 듣고, 여자의 심정으로 가장 알맞은 것을 고르시오.

① angry ② joyful ③ bored
④ nervous ⑤ excited

7

대화를 듣고, 여자가 사려고 하는 물건을 고르시오.

8

대화를 듣고, 여자가 받아야 할 거스름돈의 액수를 고르시오.

① \$2.50 ② \$3 ③ \$5 ④ \$7 ⑤ \$7.45

9

대화를 듣고, 남자가 저녁을 먹지 않는 이유를 고르시오.

① 맛이 없어서 ② 배가 불러서
③ 너무 바빠서 ④ 설거지를 해야 해서
⑤ 다이어트 중이어서

10

대화를 듣고, 여자의 문제로 알맞은 것을 고르시오.

① 매우 이기적이다.
② 남의 말을 듣지 않는다.
③ 언어 구사력이 떨어진다.
④ 어른을 공경할 줄 모른다.
⑤ 한국 문화에 대해 잘 모른다.

11 다음을 듣고, 내용이 가리키는 손 모양을 고르시오.

① 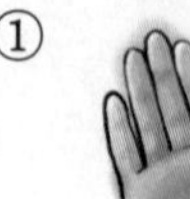 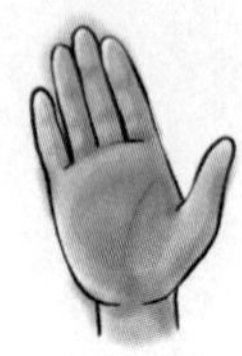
② 
③ 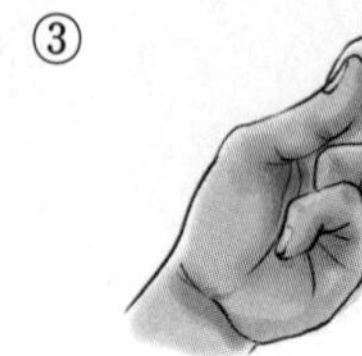
④ 
⑤ 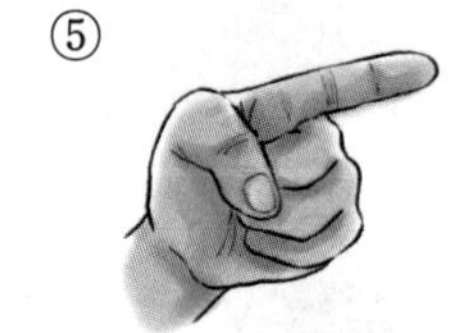

12 대화를 듣고, 남자가 저녁에 할 일을 고르시오.

① 영화 감상
② 집 안 청소
③ 동생 돌보기
④ 부모님과 외식
⑤ 깜짝 파티 계획

13 대화를 듣고, 두 사람이 대화하는 장소를 고르시오.

① 운동장
② 미술관
③ 낚시터
④ 동물원
⑤ 놀이공원

14 대화를 듣고, 남자의 충고로 알맞은 것을 고르시오.

① 운동을 해라.
② 커피를 줄여라.
③ 걱정을 하지 마라.
④ 따뜻한 우유를 마셔라.
⑤ 차분한 노래를 들어라.

15 다음을 듣고, 무엇에 관한 내용인지 고르시오.

① 각 나라의 신화
② 숫자에 관련된 미신
③ 여러 나라의 풍습
④ 다양한 나라의 전설
⑤ 한국과 미국의 미신

Take notes

16 다음을 듣고, 두 사람의 대화가 어색한 것을 고르시오.

① ② ③ ④ ⑤

17 대화를 듣고, Jake가 말한 내용과 다른 것을 고르시오.

① Kevin은 나의 가장 친한 친구 중 한 명이다.
② Kevin이 나를 험담을 하고 다녔다.
③ 나는 Kevin 때문에 무척 화가 난다.
④ Kevin이 내가 이기적이라고 말했다.
⑤ 나는 Kevin에게 돈을 빌렸다.

18 대화를 듣고, 두 사람의 관계로 가장 알맞은 것을 고르시오.

① 남편 – 아내
② 경찰 – 용의자
③ 의사 – 환자
④ 장교 – 사병
⑤ 교장 – 교사

19 다음을 듣고, 마지막 질문에 가장 알맞은 답을 고르시오.

① Have we met before?
② Where are you going?
③ What time shall we get off?
④ Do you know where we are?
⑤ Is this bus going to the National Museum?

20 대화를 듣고, 여자의 마지막 말에 이어질 남자의 응답으로 가장 적절한 것을 고르시오.

① Never mind.
② Sounds great.
③ It's next week.
④ I'm too shy to go there.
⑤ I like your present the most.

1

① M This shirt _____ _____ _____ the pants.

W Can I try it on?

② M Will it hurt a lot?

W Don't look. You probably _____ _____ _____ it.

③ M Can I borrow a needle?

W No, you can't. I have to use it now.

④ M I'm _____ _____ _____ the dog.

W Don't worry. It won't bite you.

⑤ M Is it comfortable?

W Yes, you will feel wonderful, too.

2

W Hi, Mike. What's up?

M We had a soccer game yesterday, and we lost _____ _____ _____ again.

W Oh, no. I thought you would win this time. _____ _____?

M I think I made too many mistakes.

W Maybe you weren't ready, but next time you _____ _____ _____.

3

W Have you ever been to the United States, Sammy?

M Yes, I have been there _____ _____ _____.

W How about other countries?

M I _____ China, Spain, and Germany.

W Wow. You have been to _____ _____. I have only been to Italy.

4

M I heard you are going to buy a new house next year. Do you _____ a house _____?

W I like houses with many windows.

M You do? I like houses _____ _____ _____ _____.

W You _____ _____, right?

M Yes, that's my hobby, but my wife doesn't like it.

5

W Harry, are you okay now?

M Not yet, but I'm _____ _____.

W Sounds good. When will you _____ _____ _____?

M What day is it today?

W It's Saturday the 15th.

M I will be leaving the hospital _____ _____ _____ _____.

6

W Can I use your computer now?

M Sure. What happened to yours?

W My computer was very slow. So Robert __________ __________ __________ to make it work faster.

M And?

W After that, it didn't work at all, so I took it to __________ __________ __________.

M What did Robert say?

W He said it was __________ __________.

7

M May I help you?

W Yes, I'd __________ __________ __________ a desk lamp for my son.

M I see. How about this one?

W That __________ __________. How much is it?

M It's 50 dollars.

W OK. I __________ __________ __________.

8

W How much is this?

M It's 7 dollars and 25 cents.

W Is it __________ __________ __________?

M Of course. We always __________ __________ __________ __________ in town.

W Here is 10 dollars.

M Thank you.

W Wait a minute. I __________ __________ __________.

M OK. Here is __________ __________.

9

W Tom, __________ __________.

M Mom, can I skip dinner? I don't __________ __________ __________.

W I made your favorite. Why don't you __________ __________ __________?

M Thanks, but I had a big lunch, and I'm still full now.

W OK. I will leave some for you.

10

M You always sit with your __________ __________ when talking to my parents. That is rude in Korea.

W Really? __________ __________ you tell me before?

M I thought __________ __________.

W How could I know? I've been in Korea for only one month. You need to tell me Korean __________ __________ __________.

11

M We make this hand gesture to __________ __________ __________ __________ or success. To make this gesture, you __________ __________ your middle finger over your index finger. You can make this gesture to your friend who has a test, saying "__________ __________ on your test," or make it for yourself when you hope your __________ __________ __________.

Dictation

12

W The new Harry Potter movie __________ __________ __________. Ann and I are going to see it tonight. Will you join us?

M I don't think I can. I __________ __________ __________ my brother.

W Aren't your parents at home?

M They are __________ __________ __________ __________ tonight because it's their wedding anniversary.

W You're not going with them?

M Well, I can, but my little brother is too young.

13

M Wow, there are __________ __________ __________ __________.

W Why don't we ride that one?

M Look at the __________ __________. It looks so scary. Let's just ride the merry-go-round instead.

W Come on! Look how many people are __________ __________ __________. It must be exciting.

M Okay, okay!

W You __________ __________.

14

M You look so tired. What's wrong?

W I can't sleep well these days. I was up until three in the morning.

M Is something __________ __________?

W No, not at all. I even __________ __________ coffee.

M Why don't you exercise then? It will help you to __________ __________ __________ __________.

W Okay, I will try that.

15

M There are stories about numbers in some countries. __________ __________, Koreans avoid using the number four because they believe __________ __________. In America, people think the number thirteen is __________ __________. The Chinese like the number eight because they think the number brings lots of money.

16

① W Mike, can you __________ __________ __________ __________?
M No, thank you.

② W What are you interested in?
M I'm interested in basketball, but I'm __________ __________ __________ it.

③ W Thomas, how old is that TV?
M It's eight years old. It still works well.

④ W What are you planning?
M I'm preparing a concert.

⑤ W __________ __________ __________ __________! How have you been?
M Good, I've just been busy with work.

17

M Hi, my name is Jake. I'm very __________ __________ one of my best friends, Kevin. He __________ __________ __________ me to other classmates. He said I was selfish. I __________ __________ __________ he said something like that. I guess it's because I didn't lend him money when he wanted to borrow some from me before.

18

W Why did you steal this ring?

M I told you I didn't steal it. I found it __________ __________ __________.

W That's __________ __________ __________. Where were you last night?

M I was __________ __________ watching TV.

W Oh, yeah? You said you found it on the street. But someone __________ __________ __________ this lady's home last night. How about that?

M I don't know. I was at home.

19

W There is __________ __________ __________ next to you on a bus. You think his face is very familiar. You try hard to think __________ __________ __________ you met him, but you have no idea. You are __________ __________ who the boy is. To ask if you know him, what would you say?

20

W Hey, Sam. You got a new MP3 player.

M Yes, my father bought me one last weekend.

W Why? Was it your __________ __________ __________?

M Yes. It was last Saturday.

W Sorry. I __________ __________ your birthday.

M __________ __________.

05회 영어듣기모의고사

정답 및 해설 p.22

Take notes

1 다음을 듣고, 그림에 대한 설명으로 바르지 않은 것을 고르시오.

①

②

③

④

⑤

2 대화를 듣고, 두 사람이 대화하는 장소를 고르시오.

① 병원 ② 온천 ③ 공원
④ 실험실 ⑤ 수영장

3 대화를 듣고, 여자가 일한 대가로 받을 액수를 고르시오.

① \$40 ② \$60 ③ \$80 ④ \$100 ⑤ \$120

4 다음을 듣고, "this"가 가리키는 것을 고르시오.

① 협동심 ② 자신감 ③ 인내력
④ 정직성 ⑤ 창의력

5 대화를 듣고, 여자가 가장 중요하게 생각하는 것을 고르시오.

① money ② health ③ friends
④ family ⑤ work

6 대화를 듣고, 여자가 만날 사람을 고르시오.

7 대화를 듣고, 남자가 가야 하는 곳을 고르시오.

① 성형외과 ② 정형외과 ③ 피부과
④ 안과 ⑤ 치과

8 대화를 듣고, 남자가 한 마지막 말의 의도를 고르시오.

① 금지 ② 충고 ③ 허락 ④ 제안 ⑤ 불평

9 대화를 듣고, 남자가 처음 Rachel을 만난 요일을 고르시오.

① Wednesday ② Thursday ③ Friday
④ Saturday ⑤ Sunday

10 대화를 듣고, 여자가 남자에게 부탁하는 것을 고르시오.

① 숙제를 같이 하자고
② 선생님이 오시는지 봐 달라고
③ 수학 숙제 범위를 알려 달라고
④ 틀린 문제가 있으면 고쳐 달라고
⑤ 진도가 어디 나가는지 알려 달라고

Take notes

11 대화를 듣고, 남자의 심정으로 가장 알맞은 것을 고르시오.

① pleased ② scared ③ excited
④ disappointed ⑤ satisfied

12 다음을 듣고, 광고문의 내용과 일치하지 않는 것을 고르시오.

Family Restaurant
Lunch: 11:00 a.m. to 2:30 p.m. Mon~Fri
Dinner: 5:30 p.m. to 9:00 p.m. Mon~Sat
Salad: $3-$5 / Main course: $15-$25
Credit cards accepted
Chairs for children available

① ② ③ ④ ⑤

13 다음을 듣고, 두 사람의 대화가 어색한 것을 고르시오.

① ② ③ ④ ⑤

14 대화를 듣고, 내용과 일치하는 것을 고르시오.

① 여자는 공포 영화를 좋아한다.
② 남자는 내일 집에 있을 것이다.
③ 남자는 혼자 연주회에 갈지도 모른다.
④ 남자는 여자와 함께 영화를 볼 것이다.
⑤ 여자에게 연주회에 갈 수 있는 표가 있다.

15 대화를 듣고, 두 사람의 관계로 가장 알맞은 것을 고르시오.

① 아빠 – 딸 ② 이웃 – 이웃
③ 미용사 – 손님 ④ 점원 – 손님
⑤ 운전기사 – 경찰

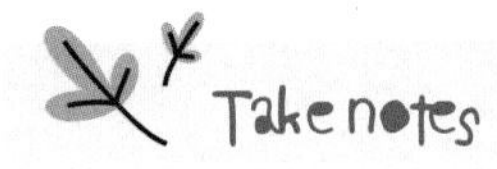

16 대화를 듣고, 이어지는 질문에 알맞은 답을 고르시오.

① police ② doctor ③ scientist
④ teacher ⑤ firefighter

17 대화를 듣고, 남자가 지하철역에 가는 이유를 고르시오.

① 자원봉사를 하려고 ② 가방을 두고 와서
③ 도서관에 가려고 ④ 친구를 만나려고
⑤ 집에 가려고

18 대화를 듣고, 내용과 가장 관련 있는 속담을 고르시오.

① Slow and steady wins the race.
② Two heads are better than one.
③ No news is good news.
④ Out of sight, out of mind.
⑤ Time flies like an arrow.

19-20 대화를 듣고, 남자의 마지막 말에 이어질 여자의 응답으로 가장 알맞은 것을 고르시오.

19
① It opens at nine.
② They are dancing.
③ From May 5th to 12th.
④ In New Hyde Park.
⑤ You can take the subway.

20
① I'll go there by plane.
② Where are you going?
③ Now I'm with you.
④ OK. I will follow you.
⑤ I told you it's not right.

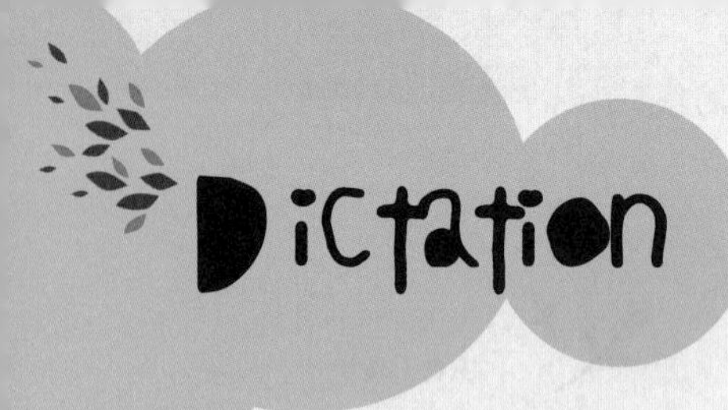

1

M ① Stand on one leg.

② Raise your arms out ______ ______ ______.

③ Stand with your ______ ______.

④ Put your hands to your waist.

⑤ ______ ______ ______ to the sky.

2

W Look at ______ ______ ______. It's 41 degrees. I can't stay here any more.

M Come on. It's good for our bodies.

W I can't bear it any longer.

M OK. You go out and ______ ______ ______. I'll stay here for ten more minutes.

W Sounds good. Enjoy the hot spring ______ ______ ______ you want, but I'm getting out.

3

W ______ ______. Can you tell me how much I am getting?

M Let me see. You ______ ______ ______ from Monday, right?

W That's correct.

M You have worked for five days and I ______ ______ ______ you twenty dollars a day.

W Wow! I will get a lot of money.

4

M This is the ability to ______ ______ ______ for something. When we have to do something that we don't like, we need this. Without this, students can't stay at their desk for very long or easily ______ ______ on something that they are ______ ______ ______.

5

W If you had to choose ______ ______ in your life, what would those three things be?

M That's a very difficult question. Um… family, health, and friends.

W What about money?

M You know money ______ ______ ______. What about you?

W I think the most important thing is health. You know if we lose our health, we ______ ______.

M ______ ______ you exercise every day.

6

W I'm ______ ______ Mr. Johnson.

M He's right over there.

W Which one?

M The __________ __________ __________ wavy hair.

W Is he wearing a striped shirt?

M No, that is Mr. Hopkins. Mr. Johnson is __________ __________ __________ __________.

W I see. Thank you.

7

W What's wrong? You __________ __________ __________.

M I have a terrible toothache. I think I have __________ __________.

W That's too bad.

M I __________ __________ __________ __________ last night.

W I can tell. Did you put some ice on your jaw?

M Yes, I did, but it didn't work.

8

W Dad, what time are you going to __________ __________ __________?

M Around eight. Why?

W I want to practice a song with my friends at home if you are __________ __________ __________.

M For what?

W We are having a contest at school next week.

M OK. I will __________ __________ __________ your friends home.

9

W Mark, did you meet Rachel?

M Yes, I did. I met her the __________ __________ __________. We had a great time.

W What did you do?

M We went to the __________ __________.

W I see. Are you going to meet her again?

M Sure, we __________ __________ __________ because tomorrow is Saturday.

10

W Did you do your math homework?

M Yes, I did. How about you?

W I did, but I __________ __________ __________ of some of my answers. Can you __________ __________ __________?

M Sure.

W If you find any wrong answers, please __________ __________.

M No problem.

11

M What time __________ __________ __________ tomorrow?

W What are you talking about?

M Don't you remember? We are going to go snowboarding tomorrow.

W I __________ __________ about that. Um… I really want to go with you, but I have __________ __________ __________ __________. Can we go another time?

M Oh, no. You can't go with me?

12

M ① Salad is five ________ ________ ________.
② Lunch won't be served after 2:30.
③ This restaurant ________ ________ ________.
④ This restaurant is open from Monday to Friday.
⑤ The restaurant ________ ________ ________ before 5:30 p.m.

13

① W I'm sorry for being late.
M Thanks for coming early.
② W Why don't you ________ ________ ________ ________ with us?
M That would be great.
③ W Can I have ________ ________ ________ cold water?
M Sure. I'll get one for you.
④ W Have you ever been to New York?
M No, but I'd like to go.
⑤ W ________ ________ to the food.
M Thank you.

14

W Chandler, I can't go to the concert tomorrow. There are ________ ________ ________.
M What will you do then?
W I'm not sure. I ________ ________ ________ ________ at all. I'll probably stay home and watch movies.
M What film are you going to watch?
W I don't know. I'll probably ________ ________ some horror movies. I like them.

15

W Hi, I'm Susie Collins. I just ________ ________.
M Hi, I'm John Baker. Please call me John.
W ________ ________ ________ here long?
M Yes, I have lived here for more than ten years. ________ ________ ________, what do you do?
W I'm a police officer.

16

W Hello, Mr. Brown. Jim said you wanted to see me.
M That's right. Because you are ________ ________, I have a few things to ask you.
W Go ahead.
M ________ ________ ________, what do your parents do?
W My father is a teacher ________ ________ ________, and my mother is a scientist.
M Okay. You went to San Jones Middle School, right?
W Yes, I did.
Q What does the woman's father do?

17

W Where are you going?

M I'm going to __________ __________ __________.

W Are you __________ __________?

M No. Actually, I left my bag in the subway.

W That's too bad. Do you want me to __________ __________ __________?

M That's OK. Actually, the man __________ __________ has it now.

18

W Who won the race? You __________ __________, right?

M Yes. How did you know?

W I thought you would. You __________ __________ __________ __________ and try to reach it every day.

M Thank you.

W I've seen you __________ __________ __________ while you deliver newspapers.

19

W This is great! Look at this poster.

M What __________ __________ __________?

W The mask festival will be held __________ __________ __________.

M That sounds very interesting. Where is __________ __________?

W In New Hyde Park.

20

W Can you __________ __________ to me again?

M Sure. Jacob said it took one and a half hours to get to New York, but Carl said it took him ninety minutes.

W So, were they __________ __________ __________ from New York? How?

M Well, ninety minutes is the same as one and a half hours. Do you __________ __________?

W Now __________ __________ __________.

06회 영어듣기모의고사

정답 및 해설 p.27

Take notes

1 다음을 듣고, 그림의 상황에 가장 알맞은 대화를 고르시오.

① ② ③ ④ ⑤

2 다음을 듣고, 예상되는 일요일의 날씨를 고르시오.

① hot ② snowy ③ sunny
④ foggy ⑤ rainy

3 대화를 듣고, 남자가 떠날 날짜를 고르시오.

① 6월 13일 금요일 ② 6월 30일 토요일
③ 7월 3일 토요일 ④ 7월 13일 금요일
⑤ 7월 30일 토요일

4 대화를 듣고, 두 사람이 이용할 교통수단을 고르시오.

① 택시 ② 버스 ③ 도보
④ 전철 ⑤ 자전거

5 대화를 듣고, 여자가 남자에게 부탁하는 것을 고르시오.

① 데리러 와 달라고 ② 짐을 들어 달라고
③ 택시를 불러 달라고 ④ 도착 시각을 알려 달라고
⑤ 방에 난방기를 켜 달라고

6 대화를 듣고, 두 사람이 대화하는 장소를 고르시오.

① bank　　② bookstore
③ library　　④ post office
⑤ coffee shop

7 대화를 듣고, 남자의 장래희망으로 알맞은 것을 고르시오.

①
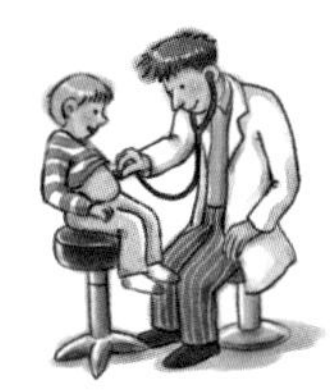
②

③

④

⑤

8 대화를 듣고, 여자가 같은 음악을 계속 듣는 이유를 고르시오.

① 매우 감미로워서
② 고향 생각이 나서
③ 인기 있는 곡이라서
④ 친구 생각이 나서
⑤ 친구가 만든 곡이라서

9 대화를 듣고, 여자가 방문했던 나라가 아닌 것을 고르시오.

① Japan　　② America　　③ Sweden
④ France　　⑤ Greece

10 대화를 듣고, 남자가 지불해야 할 금액을 고르시오.

① $10　　② $15　　③ $20　　④ $25　　⑤ $30

Take notes

11 대화를 듣고, 여자의 심정으로 가장 알맞은 것을 고르시오.

① 즐거운 ② 긴장한 ③ 흥분한
④ 낙담한 ⑤ 만족한

12 대화를 듣고, 여자가 선물로 받은 것이 아닌 것을 고르시오.

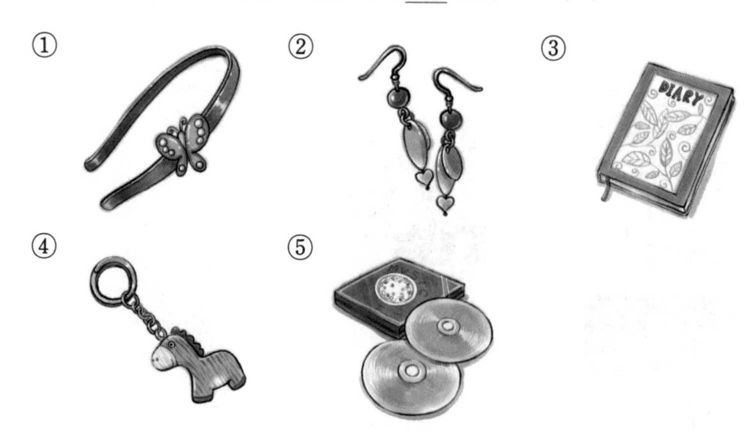

13 다음을 듣고, 무엇에 관한 안내 방송인지 고르시오.

① 지연 안내 ② 탑승 안내
③ 결항 안내 ④ 티켓 안내
⑤ 분실물 안내

14 대화를 듣고, 내용과 일치하지 않는 것을 고르시오.

① Kelly는 지금 사무실에 없다.
② Mark는 서비스 부서에서 일한다.
③ Mark는 Kelly와 통화하고 싶어 한다.
④ Helen이 Kelly에게 온 전화를 대신 받았다.
⑤ Mark는 자신의 번호를 Helen에게 남겼다.

15 대화를 듣고, 영화가 끝나는 시각을 고르시오.

① 6:30 ② 6:40 ③ 6:50 ④ 7:00 ⑤ 9:00

16 다음을 듣고, 무엇에 관한 설명인지 고르시오.

① 추석 ② 광복절 ③ 삼일절
④ 제헌절 ⑤ 한글날

17 대화를 듣고, 남자의 누나에 대해 알 수 없는 것을 고르시오.

① 키가 꽤 큰 편이다.
② 대학에서 영어를 전공하고 있다.
③ 긴 곱슬머리를 가지고 있다.
④ 영어 선생님이 되고 싶어 한다.
⑤ 주말에 종종 관광가이드로 일한다.

18 다음을 듣고, 두 사람의 대화가 어색한 것을 고르시오.

① ② ③ ④ ⑤

19-20 대화를 듣고, 남자의 마지막 말에 이어질 여자의 응답으로 가장 적절한 것을 고르시오.

19

① It's a free meal.
② It's New York steak.
③ I will bring some soup.
④ That's a good choice.
⑤ Yes, today is a very special day.

20

① We call it Dooly.
② It's not expensive.
③ We keep it at home.
④ Not even a month.
⑤ I went to the animal hospital.

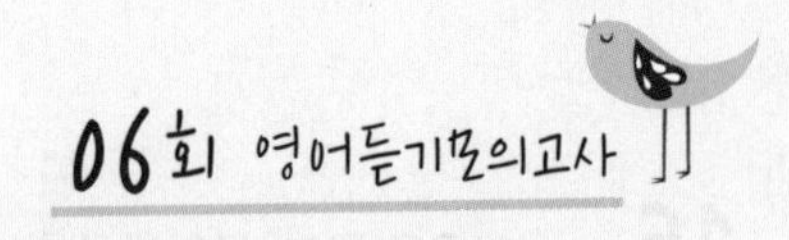

1

① W Dinner's ready! Are you coming?

M I'm __________ __________, Mom.

② W I like spicy food a lot, but this is __________ __________.

M Why don't you have some water?

③ W Did you see who ate my cake?

M No, I wasn't there.

④ W __________ __________! We will be late for the show.

M I'm almost ready!

⑤ W How many times do I have to tell you?

M Sorry, I __________ __________ with my food again.

2

W Good evening, this is the __________ __________ for the weekend. Tomorrow will be cloudy with a very __________ __________ __________ snow, with a temperature down to __________ __________. On Sunday, it will be __________ __________. The high will be around ten degrees, and the low will be about four degrees.

3

W Jason, I will miss you.

M Me, too.

W Anyway, __________ __________ __________ leave on Saturday? If you leave then, I will __________ __________ __________ you off.

M I can't. There are __________ __________ __________.

W I see. That's why you are leaving one day earlier.

M That's right. I'm leaving on the 13th of July.

4

W How are we getting to the gallery, Seth?

M The best way is to __________ __________ __________, but it costs too much.

W You're right. Taking the bus is __________ __________ __________ way, but it takes too long.

M Taking the subway is fine, but we have to walk a lot.

W Why don't we just take a taxi and __________ __________ __________ fifty-fifty?

M That's a good idea.

5

[Telephone rings.]

M Hello.

W Dave, this is Kelly. __________ __________ __________ Seoul tonight at nine.

M Oh, do you want me to __________ __________ __________?

W No, you don't need to. I will just take a cab home.

M OK, then is there something you want me to do?

W Yes. Could you go into my room and __________ __________ __________ on?

M No problem.

6

W What can __________ __________ __________ you?

M I'd like to send this letter to New York.

W Would you like to send it __________ __________ or surface mail?

M Airmail, please.

W Okay. Would you put it __________ __________ __________?

M Yes, here.

W __________ __________ three dollars.

7

M What do you want to be?

W __________ __________ __________. But I think teaching children is interesting. How about you?

M I'm very __________ __________ the universe, so I want to study stars and planets.

W I see, but you are still __________ __________ __________, and you are really good at it.

M Yes, but it's just a hobby.

8

M Susan, why don't you stop playing that music?

W Why? __________ __________ __________ you?

M I think listening to music is okay, but you keep playing the same music __________ __________ __________.

W I'm sorry, but this music __________ __________ __________ my special friend, Sue.

M I understand that, but you're not __________ __________ person here.

9

M Where did you __________ __________ __________ __________ last summer?

W I went to Hawaii, and I spent a lot of time on the beach.

M I see. __________ __________ have you been?

W I've been to France, Sweden, and Greece. What about you?

M I went to Hong Kong and Japan last year.

W Really? How was your trip to Japan? __________ __________ __________ go there.

10

M Excuse me, __________ __________ is a ticket?

W Do you want a children's ticket or an adult ticket?

M __________ __________ __________. I'd like to buy one ticket for an adult and another for a child.

W Okay. Tickets are 10 dollars __________ __________ and 5 dollars __________ __________.

M Thank you.

11

W How did you do on the test?

M Not bad. I mean I did __________ __________ than I did before. How about you?

W I __________ __________ __________ the test. I thought I had enough time, but I was wrong. I couldn't answer __________ __________ six questions.

M That's too bad.

12

M What did you __________ __________ __________ __________?

W I got a hair band from Paul and a key chain from Kelly.

M What else?

W I __________ __________ __________ __________ CDs from Grace.

M And __________ __________ a diary for you.

W Oh, thank you.

13

W May I __________ your __________, please? Flight 101 to Paris is now __________ __________ boarding at Gate 32. Passengers please proceed to Gate 32. Please have your __________ __________ __________ __________ ready. We will begin boarding with business class passengers.

14

[Telephone rings.]

W Hello. Helen speaking.

M Hello. May I __________ __________ Kelly, please?

W Sorry, she's not in the office. Can I __________ __________ __________?

M This is Mark from the Service Center. Please tell her to call me.

W Sure. By the way, does she know __________ __________?

M Yes, she has my number.

15

W The movie starts in a minute. How long __________ __________ __________?

M I think it runs for 120 minutes.

W It's almost five o'clock now. So it will be dinner __________ __________ the movie ends.

M I'm a bit hungry already. Let's __________ __________ __________ as soon as the movie __________.

W Sounds good.

16

M This day is a __________ __________ that always __________ __________ August 15th. On this day in 1945, our country __________ __________ from Japan. To celebrate our independence from Japanese rule, we hang our national flag __________ __________ __________ the house and have some parades.

17

M Hey, Susan. The woman with the __________ __________ __________ is my sister.

W Really? She is pretty tall. Is she a __________ __________?

M Yes, she is __________ __________ English.

W Then, she must be good at English.

M I think so. She often works as a __________ __________ on weekends.

18

① M What time can you __________ __________?

W __________ __________ 2 p.m.

② M What is your father like?

W He is funny, but sometimes very strict.

③ M Can I speak to Isabella?

W Speaking. __________ __________ __________?

④ M Can I get you something cold to drink?

W I'd better put on a jacket.

⑤ M How would you like your steak?

W __________ __________ __________, please.

19

W Hello! It's been a long time. Where __________ __________ __________?

M I've been in London for three months.

W I see. Anyway, __________ __________ __________ like to have?

M What's __________ __________?

W It's New York steak.

20

M What a __________ __________!

W Thanks.

M Look at its small feet! I wish I __________ __________. Where did you get it?

W My aunt gave it to me.

M I see. __________ __________ is he? How many months?

W __________ __________ a month.

07회 영어듣기모의고사

정답 및 해설 p.32

Take notes

1 다음을 듣고, 설명과 일치하지 않는 표지판을 고르시오.

①  
② 
③  
④ 
⑤ 

2 대화를 듣고, 두 사람에게 필요한 재료가 아닌 것을 고르시오.

① 감자 ② 양파 ③ 당근
④ 후추 ⑤ 참기름

3 대화를 듣고, Carl의 나이로 알맞은 것을 고르시오.

① 14세 ② 15세 ③ 16세 ④ 17세 ⑤ 18세

4 대화를 듣고, 학교에서 축구를 가장 잘하는 학생을 고르시오.

① Adam ② Sam ③ David
④ John ⑤ Peter

5 대화를 듣고, 남자가 한 마지막 말의 의도를 고르시오.

① 바람 ② 격려 ③ 재촉 ④ 충고 ⑤ 비판

6 대화를 듣고, 남자의 심정으로 가장 알맞은 것을 고르시오.

① worried ② pleased ③ lonely
④ disappointed ⑤ interested

7 대화를 듣고, 여자가 남자에게 부탁하는 것을 고르시오.

① 전등 끄기 ② 창문 닫기
③ 봉투 사오기 ④ 집에 일찍 오기
⑤ 정원에 물주기

8 대화를 듣고, 두 사람의 관계로 가장 알맞은 것을 고르시오.

① doctor – patient ② coach – player
④ mother – son ③ waiter – customer
⑤ teacher – student

9 다음을 듣고, 무엇에 관한 설명인지 고르시오.

① 
② 
③ 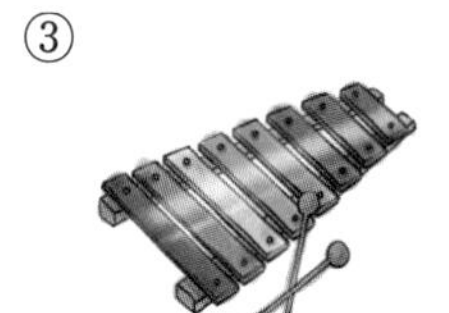
④ 
⑤ 

10 대화를 듣고, 두 사람이 대화하는 장소를 고르시오.

① 미술관 ② 박물관 ③ 방송국
④ 놀이 공원 ⑤ 면접 사무실

11 다음을 듣고, 내용과 일치하지 않는 것을 고르시오.

① 화재가 난 가게는 13층에 있었다.
② 119 구조자들이 사람들을 모두 구조했다.
③ 가게 안에는 13명 이상의 사람들이 있었다.
④ 가게 안에 있던 사람들은 겁에 질려 있었다.
⑤ 잭슨 가에 있는 작은 가게에서 화재가 발생했다.

12 대화를 듣고, 라디오의 가격으로 알맞은 것을 고르시오.

① $20　② $25　③ $30　④ $35　⑤ $40

13 다음을 듣고, 각 도시별 날씨가 바르게 연결된 것을 고르시오.

① London – rainy
② New York – foggy
③ Sydney – windy
④ Beijing – cloudy
⑤ Seoul – sunny

14 대화를 듣고, 여자의 문제로 알맞은 것을 고르시오.

① 낭비벽
② 이기심
③ 무례함
④ 게으름
⑤ 주의력 부족

15 대화를 듣고, 남자가 늦게 일어난 이유를 고르시오.

① 보충수업이 없어서
② 엄마가 깨우지 않아서
③ 수업이 늦게 시작해서
④ 늦은 시간까지 깨어 있어서
⑤ 알람시계가 작동하지 않아서

Take notes

16

다음을 듣고, 바람직한 수업 자세를 가진 학생을 고르시오.

① ② ③ ④ ⑤

17

대화를 듣고, 여자가 제일 먼저 해야 할 일을 고르시오.

① 보고서 쓰기
② 동생 돌보기
③ 봉사활동 하기
④ 도서관에 가기
⑤ 친구 도와주기

18

다음을 듣고, 두 사람의 대화가 어색한 것을 고르시오.

① ② ③ ④ ⑤

19-20 대화를 듣고, 남자의 마지막 말에 이어질 여자의 응답으로 가장 알맞은 것을 고르시오.

19

① Count me in, too.
② You are wasting money.
③ OK. I can start it tomorrow.
④ I went on a picnic last week.
⑤ I have something to show you.

20

① Help yourself!
② It's my pleasure.
③ Don't worry about me.
④ Yes, that's so expensive.
⑤ Some food is really delicious.

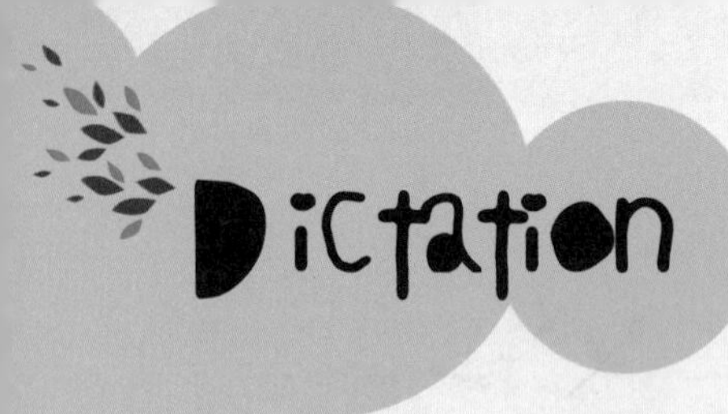

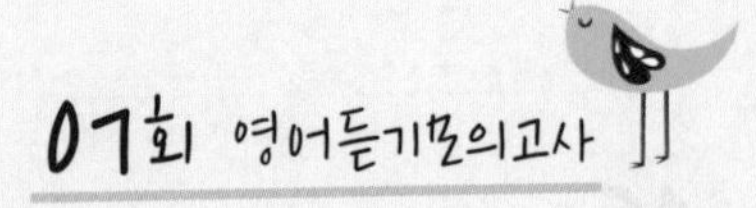

1

M ① No animals allowed.
② No __________ __________.
③ No __________ __________.
④ No swimming allowed.
⑤ __________ __________ __________.

2

W Do you have all the ingredients?

M I think I have them all. Onions are here __________ __________ __________, and potatoes and carrots are in the refrigerator.

W I see, but I don't __________ __________ sesame oil here.

M It's __________ __________ __________, and I even bought some pepper yesterday.

W I don't think we need it today.

3

W Do you know how old Sarah is? She doesn't look older than us, but she __________ __________ __________ high school students.

M I think she is three years __________ __________ __________.

W You mean she is 17 years old?

M Yes. __________ __________, Carl is her brother, and he told me Sarah is three years older than him.

4

W Hey, Adam. David said you are __________ __________ __________ player in the school.

M No, there are many better players like John and Peter. And Sam __________ __________ __________ than me.

W But you are the fastest player.

M That's true, but speed is __________ __________. Sam plays the best, and he __________ __________ __________ today.

W You're right. Anyway, I'm happy we won the game.

5

W I know you read a lot of books. Do you have __________ __________ __________?

M No, I don't. I just like fantasy books.

W I've tried to read fantasy, but they were too long. So I __________ __________.

M You should read them. They are amazing books.

W Okay. By the way, I heard another Harry Potter book is __________ __________ __________.

M I know. I'm __________ __________ __________ it.

6

W Did you have a good weekend, Ian?

M Not really. My grandmother is __________

__________ __________, so I visited her with my brother.

W Sorry to hear that. Is she sick or something?

M It was just a bad flu at first, but it has __________ __________. Now she is staying in the hospital.

W Cheer up! I'm sure she will __________ __________.

M Thank you. But I'm __________ __________ her health.

7

W Ryan, did you __________ __________ the lights and lock the door?

M I sure did.

W Okay, let's go. By the way, when are you __________ __________?

M School finishes at around four. I'll probably get home at about four thirty.

W Can you buy me some envelopes __________ __________ __________ __________?

M No problem, Mom.

8

W What __________ __________ __________ the problem?

M My throat hurts, and I have a __________ __________.

W I see. How long has it been like that?

M For two days.

W I think you caught a cold. Do you __________ __________ __________?

M Yes, I think so.

W OK. Let me __________ __________ __________.

9

M This musical instrument has __________ __________ __________ bars. To play it, you hit them with __________ __________. Some of them come with a different color on each bar. Many people think it is __________ __________ __________, but you can see people playing it in an orchestra.

10

M I'm __________ __________.

W Don't worry. You'll do fine.

M There are so many cameras in the studio. I don't know which camera __________ __________ __________.

W Just look in front of you. Try to relax and __________ __________.

M OK.

W When the director __________ __________ __________, we will start.

11

M There was a big fire in a small store on Jackson Street. When the fire __________ __________, there were more than ten customers and three clerks inside. The store was __________ __________ __________ __________, and the people inside were frightened. But 119 rescuers got there __________ __________ and saved all of them.

Dictation

12

W Are you having a garage sale?

M Yes, I am. Are there any things __________ __________ __________?

W Let me see. How much is that bike?

M It's thirty dollars. It still __________ __________.

W I see. How about that radio?

M It's five dollars more than the bike. If it's not working, I will __________ __________ __________ __________.

13

W Good morning. It's Monday, August 14th. This is today's __________ __________ __________. London will be foggy, and New York will __________ __________ __________. Sydney will be cloudy and cold, but Beijing will be __________ and __________. Finally, it will be sunny in Seoul.

14

M Is this your bag?

W Yes, it is.

M I thought __________ __________ __________, not red.

W I bought a pink one yesterday.

M But they are __________ __________ __________.

W I know, but the colors are different. And I also have another color, too.

M You should __________ __________ __________ on useless stuff.

15

M I'm very upset that Mom didn't __________ __________ __________.

W So you were late for school. Come on, you're not a child __________.

M But she promised that she would.

W Don't you have __________ __________ __________?

M No, I don't. Mom always wakes me up. Why do I need one?

16

M ① Susan is __________ __________ __________.

② Jacob is reading a comic book.

③ Ross and Rachel are __________ __________.

④ Anne sitting in the back seat is listening to music.

⑤ Christine is __________ __________ __________ the teacher.

17

W I have so many things to do, but __________ __________ __________. I should finish my report, do some volunteer work, and go to the library.

M __________ __________ __________. Sometimes I feel the same way. What is the most important thing to do?

W Well, the report has to __________ __________ __________ tomorrow, so it is the most important thing!

M Then, do it first.

18

① M I think it's true.
W Why do you think so?

② M She lost the game.
W ________ ________ ________.

③ M He's much better now.
W I'm ________ ________ ________ that.

④ M Can you go shopping with me?
W I'd love to, but I can't.

⑤ M Will you come to my house?
W Sure, I ________ ________ ________.

19

W What are you doing?

M I'm ________ ________ the weather forecast for this weekend.

W For what?

M Mike, Grace, and I are planning to ________ ________ ________ Mount Forest this weekend.

W ________ ________ ________, too.

20

W Happy birthday to you, Alex! Here is ________ ________ ________ for you. I hope you will like it.

M Thank you. Can I open it now?

W Sure, ________ ________.

M Wow! It's a baseball cap. I really like it. ________ ________ ________.

W It's my pleasure.

08회 영어듣기모의고사

정답 및 해설 p.37

Take notes

1 다음을 듣고, 여자가 설명하는 사람을 고르시오.

① 
② 
③ 
④ 
⑤ 

2 대화를 듣고, 남자에게 필요한 것을 고르시오.

① towel ② toothpaste ③ toothbrush
④ socks ⑤ underwear

3 대화를 듣고, 남자의 장래희망으로 알맞은 것을 고르시오.

① 교수 ② 의사 ③ 발명가
④ 사회 활동가 ⑤ 자원봉사자

4 다음을 듣고, 무엇에 관한 설명인지 고르시오.

① 슈퍼맨 ② 배트맨 ③ 드라큘라
④ 해리 포터 ⑤ 스파이더맨

5 대화를 듣고, 여자가 지불해야 할 금액을 고르시오.

① $30 ② $ 50 ③ $60 ④ $80 ⑤ $90

6 대화를 듣고, 남자가 시험을 치를 요일을 고르시오.

① Monday ② Tuesday ③ Wednesday
④ Thursday ⑤ Friday

7 대화를 듣고, 여자가 화난 이유를 고르시오.

① 성적이 좋지 않아서
② 친구와 말다툼을 해서
③ Jacob이 비밀을 말해서
④ 문제를 잘 풀지 못해서
⑤ Bella가 계획을 취소해서

8 대화를 듣고, 대화의 내용과 메모가 일치하지 않는 것을 고르시오.

Memo

① To: Mr. Brown
② From: Jennifer
③ Message: She wants to talk about the design.
④ Call her back at home.
⑤ Phone Number: 555-1234

9 대화를 듣고, 여자가 관심을 가지는 분야를 고르시오.

① 곤충 ② 식물 ③ 동물 ④ 기후 ⑤ 환경

10 대화를 듣고, 여자가 e-mail을 쓰는 목적을 고르시오.

① 감사 ② 사과 ③ 초대 ④ 추천 ⑤ 의논

11 대화를 듣고, 남자가 한 마지막 말의 의도를 고르시오.

① 경고 ② 충고 ③ 반박 ④ 제안 ⑤ 동의

12 대화를 듣고, 두 사람이 이용할 교통수단을 고르시오

①

②

③

④

⑤

13 다음을 듣고, Jake의 문제로 알맞은 것을 고르시오.

① 이기적이다.
② 건강이 좋지 않다.
③ 낭비하는 습관이 있다.
④ 친구들과 사이가 좋지 않다.
⑤ 남의 말에 귀를 기울이지 않는다.

14 대화를 듣고, 이어지는 질문에 가장 알맞은 답을 고르시오.

① 키가 작아서 ② 몸이 느려서
③ 어깨가 아파서 ④ 시험공부 때문에
⑤ 더 이상 선수가 필요 없어서

15 대화를 듣고, Amanda에 대한 설명과 일치하지 않는 것을 고르시오.

① She has blond hair.
② She is Jimmy's sister.
③ She is twenty eight years old.
④ She works for a hospital as a doctor.
⑤ She and Jessica went to the same high school.

16 다음을 듣고, 알 수 없는 것을 고르시오.

① 3일 동안 100킬로미터 이상을 하이킹할 것이다.
② 개인 소지품은 최소한으로 줄여야 한다.
③ 일이 생기면 인솔 교사에게 알려야 한다.
④ 서로 돕고 다치지 않아야 함을 강조했다.
⑤ 하이킹하면서 물을 계속 마셔야 한다.

17 다음을 듣고, 두 사람의 대화가 어색한 것을 고르시오.

① ② ③ ④ ⑤

18 대화를 듣고, 두 사람이 무엇에 관해 이야기하고 있는지 고르시오.

① 외식
② 저녁 식단
③ 편식의 단점
④ 좋아하는 음식
⑤ 각 나라의 음식 문화

19-20 대화를 듣고, 여자의 마지막 말에 이어질 남자의 응답으로 적절한 것을 고르시오.

19

① Maybe next time.
② Are you ready to go?
③ You had a really good time.
④ I've been there three times.
⑤ But I'm afraid it won't stop.

20

① He may catch a cold soon.
② He's not very good at the piano.
③ We should give him a big hand.
④ I will tell him not to do that again.
⑤ He should spend less time playing sports.

1

W Someone just __________ __________ __________. I was too scared to __________ __________ __________. He is wearing a striped shirt and blue jeans. And he has short hair with __________ __________. Please find him.

2

W Did you __________ __________?

M Um... I have my toothbrush, socks, and underwear. I just __________ __________ a towel. How about you?

W I __________ __________ __________ yet.

M Let me help you then.

3

M What do you want to be __________ __________ __________?

W I want to be a doctor, but my parents want me to be a professor.

M You can be both when you become a doctor.

W That's __________ __________ __________. How about you?

M I want to invent something for handicapped people.

W __________ __________!

4

M He has __________ __________ __________ and usually wears a long black coat. He appears __________ __________ and sucks human blood. People believe that he hates sunlight and silver and he __________ __________ __________ them. There have been a lot of books and movies about him.

5

M Good morning, madam.

W Good morning. I'm __________ __________.

M OK. Can I have your key?

W Sure. __________.

M Thank you. Let me see. You __________ __________ three nights, right?

W That's right. I believe it's thirty dollars __________ __________.

M That's correct.

6

M I didn't take the test today. Our teacher got sick and __________ __________ __________ __________.

W So are you taking it tomorrow?

M No.

W __________ __________?

M We have class __________ __________ __________ on Tuesday and Thursday.

Tomorrow is Friday, so we don't have class until next week.

W I see.

7

W Sean, I'm very upset with Jacob.

M Did he __________ __________ __________?

W I told Jacob not to tell Bella about our plan, but he did.

M Oh, no. We __________ __________ __________.

W We have to __________ __________ __________ a good excuse for her.

8

M I'm back, Melissa. Did anyone call for me while I was out?

W Yes, there was, Mr. Brown. __________ __________ Jennifer called. She wants you to call her back at work. Her number is 555-1234.

M Did she say __________ __________ __________ __________?

W She said she has something to tell you about the design.

M Thank you. __________ __________ __________ her right now.

9

M Eeek, it is a grasshopper. Do you __________ __________ __________ your house?

W Yes, I'm very interested in insects.

M It is __________ __________ __________ that a girl likes insects. Even some boys like me don't like them.

W I know. Some people hate insects. But if you __________ __________ __________ __________, you'll find them to be amazing.

10

M What __________ __________ you so long? I need to use the computer, too.

W I'm sorry, but will you __________ __________ __________ __________?

M What are you doing? Are you writing a report?

W No, I'm writing an email to my __________ __________ __________.

M What for?

W I want to invite him to our school concert. He is the one who taught me __________ __________ __________ the violin.

11

W Does your mother __________ __________ __________?

M Yes, she is a nurse. How about your mom?

W She is a reporter, and she is always busy. Even after work, she cleans the house, cooks, and __________ __________ __________.

M Does your father help your mom?

W No, he is busy watching TV and reading newspapers. That's __________ __________.

M You can __________ __________ __________.

Dictation

12

W What time are we going to the library?

M Eight __________ __________.

W How do you want to get there?

M Let's __________ __________ __________.

W There are too many people on the subway around that time. How about __________ __________ __________ two feet?

M Sounds good.

13

M I have a son, Jake. He never __________ __________ __________. When someone tells him something, he __________ __________ something else. Later, he says nobody told him about it. For example, one week ago I said we would visit his grandparents __________ __________, but he didn't listen. And yesterday he asked me to __________ __________ on that day.

14

W I can't believe that you didn't join the basketball club. You are definitely __________ __________ __________ __________. Don't they need any more players?

M No, that's not it. Actually, I still have pain __________ __________ __________.

W Still?

M Yes, I thought I was OK, but when I __________ __________ __________, it hurt.

W That's too bad.

Q Why couldn't the man join the basketball club?

15

M Jessica, who is the woman with the __________ __________? She is talking to Jimmy now.

W She is Amanda, Jimmy's twin sister.

M I didn't know he had __________ __________ __________ __________. Can you tell me more about her?

W She is 28 years old, and she is a nurse at Saint Jones Hospital. She and I went to __________ __________ __________ __________.

16

M We are going to hike 100 kilometers over a three-day period. Here are a __________ __________ __________ hiking. Please drink a lot of water while hiking. Helping each other and __________ __________ __________ are two of the most important things on our trip. So help other students. If anything happens, please let your teacher know __________ __________.

17

① W Where are you going for summer vacation?

M My vacation starts from next week.

② W ________ ________ ________
________ of a koala?

M Yes, it lives in Australia.

③ W Would you give my puppy a bath?

M Sure, where is the puppy?

④ W Let's ________ ________
________ ________.

M Okay. I won't tell anybody.

⑤ W Are you ________ ________
________?

M I'd like a tuna sandwich.

18

W When are we ________ ________
________ dinner?

M As soon as your brother ________
________.

W Are we going to the same restaurant that we went to last time, Dad?

M No. We are going to a Japanese restaurant this time.

W ________ ________.

M Here he comes. Let's go.

19

W It's raining outside.

M Is it? Oh, no.

W You're ________ ________ ________
________ to Disneyland, right?

M Yes. If it ________ ________, we are not going.

W ________ ________. I'm sure it will stop.

M But I'm afraid it won't stop.

20

M Where is John?

W He is sleeping in his bed.

M ________ ________ ________ so tired?

W Well, he spent all day ________
________ ________.

M Was it part of his school activities?

W No, it wasn't. He said he just wanted to do it.

M We should give him ________ ________
________.

09회 영어듣기모의고사

정답 및 해설 p.42

Take notes

1 대화를 듣고, 현재의 날씨로 알맞은 것을 고르시오.

② 
③ 
④ 
⑤ 

2 대화를 듣고, 두 사람이 대화하는 장소를 고르시오.

① library
② cinema
③ park
④ restaurant
⑤ hospital

3 대화를 듣고, 두 사람의 관계로 가장 알맞은 것을 고르시오.

① 교사 – 학생
② 의사 – 환자
③ 친구 – 친구
④ 학부모 – 교사
⑤ 학부모 – 학부모

4 대화를 듣고, 두 사람이 박물관에 도착할 시각을 고르시오.

① 9:00 ② 9:15 ③ 9:30 ④ 9:45 ⑤ 9:50

5 대화를 듣고, 여자가 남자의 제안을 거절한 이유를 고르시오.

① 돈이 없어서
② 시간이 없어서
③ 이미 다녀와서
④ 같이 갈 사람이 없어서
⑤ 좋아하는 가수가 아니어서

6 대화를 듣고, 여자의 아빠를 고르시오.

① ② ③ ④ ⑤

7 대화를 듣고, 남자가 집에 가서 할 일로 알맞은 것을 고르시오.

① 샤워 ② 휴식 ③ 식사 ④ 숙제 ⑤ 청소

8 대화를 듣고, 여자가 한 마지막 말의 의도를 고르시오.

① 제안 ② 칭찬 ③ 비판 ④ 책망 ⑤ 위로

9 대화를 듣고, 여자가 사려고 하는 물건을 고르시오.

① 벽지 ② 연필 ③ 도화지
④ 크레파스 ⑤ 복사 용지

10 다음을 듣고, 도표의 내용과 일치하지 않는 것을 고르시오.

Job Survey		the total number of students : 100	
Job	Number of students	Job	Number of students
writer	5	artist	13
programmer	15	lawyer	3
singer	8	teacher	20
businessman	5	others	14

① ② ③ ④ ⑤

Take notes

11 대화를 듣고, Lisa가 주말에 한 일이 아닌 것을 고르시오.

① 방 청소
② 하이킹
③ 케이크 만들기
④ 피아노 레슨 받기
⑤ 할머니 생신 파티

12 대화를 듣고, 여자가 지불해야 할 금액을 고르시오.

① $1.25 ② $2 ③ $2.50 ④ $3 ⑤ $4

13 대화를 듣고, 남자가 여자에게 부탁하는 것을 고르시오.

① 차를 태워 달라고
② 돈을 좀 달라고
③ 일찍 깨워 달라고
④ 아침을 준비해 달라고
⑤ 준비물을 챙겨 달라고

14 대화를 듣고, 남자가 찾는 선물 상자로 알맞은 것을 고르시오.

① 
② 
③ 
④

⑤ 

15 대화를 듣고, 남자가 언급한 시골의 장점이 아닌 것을 고르시오.

① 조용해서
② 안전해서
③ 사람들이 친절해서
④ 공해가 없어서
⑤ 식물을 재배하기가 용이해서

16 다음을 듣고, 두 사람의 대화가 어색한 것을 고르시오.

① ② ③ ④ ⑤

17 대화를 듣고, 내용과 일치하지 않는 것을 고르시오.

① 마을에 많은 외국인이 있다.
② 3D업종은 주로 대도시에 많이 있다.
③ 많은 외국인들은 3D 직업에 종사한다.
④ 한국인은 3D업종에 종사하길 싫어한다.
⑤ 3D업종은 더럽고 힘들고, 위험한 직종이다.

18 다음을 듣고, 무엇에 관한 설명인지 고르시오.

① dragon ② snake ③ pig
④ lion ⑤ tiger

19-20 대화를 듣고, 여자의 마지막 말에 이어질 남자의 응답으로 적절한 것을 고르시오.

19
① I will go with you.
② I'd love to, but I can't.
③ I don't think it is right.
④ Thank for your calling me.
⑤ I hope we will meet again soon.

20
① It sounds great.
② No one knows.
③ That's not a good idea.
④ I saw her at school.
⑤ She is with our teacher now.

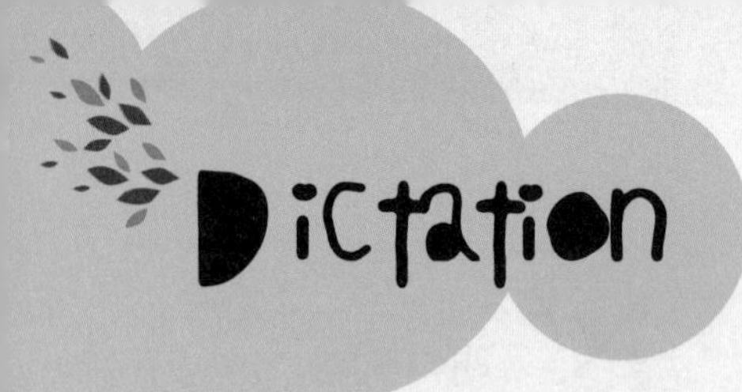

1

M Jenny, let's go to the beach.

W I'm afraid we can't. Did you hear __________ __________ __________?

M No, I didn't.

W Look at __________ __________ __________ in the sky. It may rain soon.

M Do you want me to check the weather?

W I think __________ __________ __________. Let's go next time.

2

M Excuse me. I'm looking for __________ __________ __________ *Oliver Twist.*

W You mean the book written by Charles Dickens?

M Yes, that's right.

W Okay, let me __________ __________ __________ for you. (pause) I'm afraid that the book has already been checked out.

M Then, when would I __________ __________ __________ check out the book?

W It says it will be __________ __________ next Monday.

3

W Carl, I talked to your mother __________ __________ __________ yesterday.

M Did my mother call you?

W Yes, because you are a new student, she is __________ __________you. Do you have any problems with school life?

M No, not __________ __________.

W Great. Have you __________ __________ __________?

M Yes, I have a few friends. They are very friendly.

4

W James, the museum opens at ten o'clock, doesn't it?

M Yes, how are we __________ __________ __________ there?

W If we take the bus, it takes thirty minutes, but if we take the subway, it takes twenty minutes.

M I see. __________ __________ __________ the bus.

W Sounds good to me.

M The bus leaves at nine twenty, so let's meet at nine fifteen __________ __________.

W OK. See you then.

5

M I have two tickets to a concert, and I'll give them to you __________ __________ __________.

W Sorry, but I don't want them.

M Why? You like the singer. You don't have the time?

W No, I just don't want them.

M _________ _________ _________ _________ why. Are they still too expensive?

W No, I just don't want to _________ _________.

6

W I _________ _________ _________ my father. Do you want to meet him?

M Of course. Where is he?

W He is over there next to the man _________ _________.

M He is _________ _________, right?

W That's not him. My father is not going bald. He has short hair.

M Okay. I know _________ _________.

7

W Daniel, here is your notebook.

M Thanks. I actually needed it today.

W Where have you been? I _________ _________ _________ you.

M I was playing soccer with my classmates.

W I see. You _________ _________ _________ dirt from head to toe.

M I know. That's why I'm going home now.

W OK. _________ _________ _________.

8

W What's wrong? You _________ _________.

M I really studied hard, but I didn't _________ _________ _________ _________. My mom will be angry at me.

W Was it worse than the last test?

M No, it is better but not _________ _________.

W Hey, John. Try to look on the _________ _________ _________ things.

9

M Look at that wall. Oliver has drawn many things on it.

W It _________ _________.

M What do you want to do about it?

W I think we should _________ _________ _________

M Since we have guests this weekend, we'd better do it now.

W I'll _________ _________ _________ _________. What color do you want?

10

W ① A writer is _________ _________ _________ a businessman.

② A singer is more popular than an artist.

③ A teacher is _________ _________ _________ job.

④ Eight students would like to be a singer.

⑤ Fifteen students _________ _________ _________ a programmer.

11

W I had a busy weekend.

M What ________ ________ ________ ________, Lisa?

W I went hiking with my family on Saturday.

M What about Sunday?

W I ________ ________ ________ ________ in the morning. After that, I cleaned my room and ________ ________ ________ with my mom. It's for my grandmother's birthday.

M Wow, you did lots of things.

12

W I'd like to ________ ________ from page 10 to 19.

M How many pages ________ ________ ________?

W 10 pages.

M It's 20 cents per page.

W Okay. Please ________ ________ ________.

13

M Mom, I need to ________ ________ ________ tomorrow.

W For what?

M I need to practice basketball.

W I see. Do you want me to ________ ________ for you?

M No, that's OK.

W How about some money? You can buy something to eat.

M I have some. I just need you to ________ ________ ________ ________.

14

M Mom, there are five boxes under the Christmas tree. ________ ________ is mine? Is it the striped box?

W No, it's not. That one is for your elder sister.

M How about the ________ ________?

W That one is for Dad.

M Now I know which one is mine. It has a ________ ________ ________, right?

W You got it.

15

W Do you like your new life in the country?

M Yes, I think it's one of ________ ________ ________ in the world.

W What makes you think that?

M Because there's ________ ________. And people are so nice here.

W I agree. What else?

M We can ________ ________ more easily, and it's very quiet.

16

① W Do you like cats?

M No, I ________ ________ ________ to cats.

② W __________ __________ do you want?
M I want the black one.
③ W How did you know that?
M My sister told me about it.
④ W Have you seen any movies lately?
M Yes. I saw __________ __________ __________ yesterday.
⑤ W What do you think of this picture?
M Wow, it's beautiful. Where __________ __________ __________ __________?

17

W There are a lot of foreigners in our town.
M That's true. __________ __________, many of them do 3D jobs for us.
W What do you mean by 3D?
M 3D means ________, ________, ________ __________. And most Koreans don't want to do 3D jobs.
W I see. That's a __________ __________.

18

W This is an __________ __________ that is common in stories and legends. It has wings and a long tail, and it can __________ __________. Koreans believe if they see it in a dream, it will __________ __________ __________ __________.

19

M It's time to go already.
W Oh, is it? __________ __________ by so quickly.
M That's right. Time flies so fast when we are __________ __________.
W I wish I had more time to talk to you.
M I hope we will __________ __________ __________.

20

W How was the test, Ethan?
M It was very difficult, and I think I __________ __________ __________
W That's too bad. Anyway, I haven't seen Jenny all day. Have you?
M No, in fact, she didn't __________ __________ __________.
W Do you know why __________ __________ __________?
M No one knows.

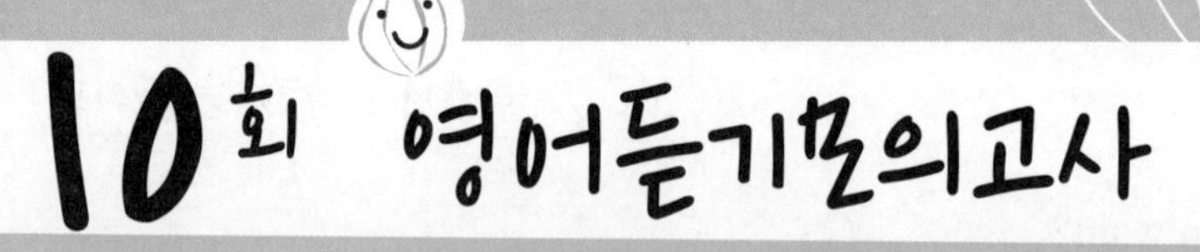

1 대화를 듣고, 두 사람이 언급하지 않은 표지판을 고르시오.

① 
②
③ 
④
⑤ 

Take notes

2 대화를 듣고, 남자가 방문하려고 하는 국가를 고르시오.

① the UK
② Germany
③ Australia
④ France
⑤ Switzerland

3 대화를 듣고, 여자가 한 마지막 말의 의도를 고르시오.

① 비판 ② 제안 ③ 격려 ④ 칭찬 ⑤ 충고

4 대화를 듣고, 여자가 할 일을 고르시오.

① 빨래 ② 설거지 ③ 바닥 쓸기
④ 정원 돌보기 ⑤ 유리창 닦기

5 대화를 듣고, Linda가 도착할 시각을 고르시오.

① 2:00 ② 2:30 ③ 3:00 ④ 3:30 ⑤ 4:00

6 다음을 듣고, 그림의 상황에 가장 알맞은 대화를 고르시오.

① ② ③ ④ ⑤

7 대화를 듣고, 여자의 성격으로 알맞은 것을 고르시오.

① 친절한 ② 관대한 ③ 공손한
④ 이기적인 ⑤ 사려 깊은

8 다음을 듣고, 무엇에 대한 설명인지 고르시오.

① 전통 음식 ② 토속 음식
③ 슬로푸드 ④ 패스트푸드
⑤ 퓨전음식

9 대화를 듣고, 여자의 심정으로 가장 알맞은 것을 고르시오.

① angry ② pleased ③ sad
④ scared ⑤ proud

10 대화를 듣고, 남자가 여자에게 충고하는 것을 고르시오.

① 재활용을 하자. ② 낭비를 줄이자.
③ 자연을 보호하자. ④ 가난한 이웃을 돕자.
⑤ 올바른 예절을 익히자.

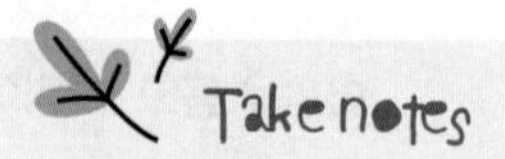

11 대화를 듣고, 현재 여자가 가지고 있는 돈의 액수를 고르시오.

① $60 ② $70 ③ $80
④ $90 ⑤ $100

12 대화를 듣고, 남자가 약속 시간에 늦은 이유를 고르시오.

① 차가 막혀서 ② 전철에서 졸아서
③ 장소를 찾지 못해 ④ 지갑을 두고 와서
⑤ 도중에 친구를 만나서

13 대화를 듣고, 남자의 직업으로 알맞은 것을 고르시오.

① 정비사 ② 경찰관 ③ 공항 직원
④ 여행사 직원 ⑤ 택시 운전사

14 대화를 듣고, 내용과 일치하지 않는 것을 고르시오.

① 아들은 내일 생선을 먹을 것이다.
② 아들은 야채를 먹는 것을 지겨워한다.
③ 엄마는 생선이 신선하지 않아 사지를 않았다.
④ 아들은 오늘도 저녁으로 야채를 먹을 것이다.
⑤ 엄마는 아들에게 야채가 건강에 좋다고 말하고 있다.

15 대화를 듣고, 여자가 전화를 건 목적을 고르시오.

① 숙제를 물어보려고
② 숙제를 같이하자고
③ 진도를 물어보려고
④ 시험 날짜를 알아보려고
⑤ 시험 범위를 알아보려고

Take notes

16

다음을 듣고, 설명과 일치하는 단어를 고르시오.

① divide ② advice ③ choice
④ behind ⑤ honest

17

대화를 듣고, 두 사람이 대화하는 장소를 고르시오.

① garden ② hospital
③ museum ④ playground
⑤ police station

18

다음을 듣고, 두 사람의 대화가 어색한 것을 고르시오.

① ② ③ ④ ⑤

19

다음을 듣고, 마지막 질문에 가장 알맞은 답을 고르시오.

① Wish me good luck.
② Good luck to you on your test.
③ The test is going to be very hard.
④ Did you study hard to prepare for it?
⑤ I knew you were able to pass the test.

20

대화를 듣고, 여자의 마지막 말에 이어질 남자의 응답으로 가장 적절한 것을 고르시오.

① No, I didn't do it.
② I need a lot of help.
③ I can finish it by myself.
④ I know nothing about the project.
⑤ I did it little by little every day.

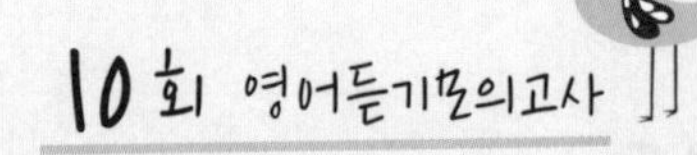

1

W There are many signs around here. Do you know _____ _____ _____?

M I think the one behind you says not to _____ _____ _____, and the one next to you is for handicapped only.

W Wow, you are good. How about these?

M It means you cannot park here, and that one says animals _____ _____ _____.

W That's correct.

2

W Where are you _____ _____ _____ this time?

M Well, I've been to Germany and France, so I think I will visit some _____ _____ _____ like Switzerland or Austria.

W You're a lucky man. You travel so much because you are a tour guide.

M Actually, it's a _____ _____ _____ _____.

3

W Don't _____ _____

M Is it really safe?

W _____ _____ _____ have I told you?

M I know, but I'm a little scared.

W Don't worry. I've never _____ _____ _____ _____.

M OK. Let me try.

W I'm sure you can do it.

4

W What a mess! When did you _____ _____ _____?

M About two weeks ago. I've been so busy.

W Do you want me to help you?

M Why not? I'll _____ _____ _____ the garden after doing the laundry. Will you do the dishes?

W Okay. Is there anything else that I can _____ _____ _____?

M No, I think I can do the _____ _____ the chores myself.

5

M What time is Linda _____ _____ _____ _____?

W She said she _____ _____ _____ at 2 o'clock.

M How long does it usually take?

W About 2 hours.

M I see. Let's _____ _____ while we wait.

W Sounds good.

6

① **W** How often do you _____ _____ _____ _____?

M Three times a week.

② W Is this your book?

M Yes, where did you find it?

③ W Mark, _________ _________ _________ your classmate.

M But I don't know what the homework is.

④ W Please check your _________ _________.

M I forgot to write my name on it.

⑤ W Shh... will you _________ _________, please?

M Oh, I'm sorry.

7

M Excuse me. It really _________ _________.

W What do you mean?

M Because you keep _________ _________ _________ _________, I can't concentrate on the movie. Please don't use your cell phone.

W I'm sorry, but it's a really important call.

M Then, you need to _________ _________ to the lobby.

W Then, I will miss some parts of the movie.

8

W This is a kind of food that can be _________ _________ _________ _________. You can enjoy this at popular restaurant chains that serve this. And you can buy this even at convenience stores these days. This has _________ _________. If you eat this for a long time, you could _________ _________ _________.

9

M Mom, havc you seen my cell phone?

W Yes, I have. It's _________ _________ _________.

M Why did you put it in there?

W Because your teacher called and said that you often use it _________ _________. So I will keep it in my drawer _________ _________ _________.

M I'm sorry, Mom.

10

M Hold it, Jenny! What are you doing?

W What are you _________ _________?

M Don't you recycle? How can you just _________ the bottles _________?

W Don't get so upset. I was only trying to....

M If we recycle, we can _________ _________ and _________ _________.

W Okay, I'll put these bottles into the recycling box.

11

W Do you _________ _________ _________ _________ that Mom gave you?

M No, I _________ _________ _________ on games.

W You mean you already spent 100 dollars?

M Yes, I did. How about you? Do you still have your 100 dollars?

W I wish, but I spent 20 dollars _________ _________ and 10 dollars _________ _________.

Dictation

12

M Sorry __________ __________ __________.

W I've waited for about an hour. Didn't you __________ __________ __________?

M Yes, I did, but I had to go back home.

W How come?

M I left my wallet on the desk.

W I'll __________ __________ __________ __________. Never be late again.

13

W Excuse me, I brought my car for an engine check yesterday. When can I __________ __________ __________ __________?

M May I have your name, please?

W Jenny Parker.

M I think it will __________ __________ tomorrow.

W Thank you. And could you __________ __________ __________, too?

M No problem.

14

M Are we having vegetables for dinner again? I'm __________ __________ __________ these kinds of dishes every day.

W I was going to buy some fish, but I couldn't. It wasn't fresh. And vegetables are __________ __________ __________ __________.

M I know, but I don't think I have to eat them every day.

W All right. I will __________ __________ __________ tomorrow.

15

[Telephone rings.]

W Hello, __________ __________ __________ to Dylan?

M Speaking.

W This is Kelly. I __________ __________ __________. We had English class together this afternoon, right?

M Yes. Why?

W I __________ __________ during the class, and I don't know where __________ __________ __________.

M I see. Let me get the book, and I will let you know.

16

W This is a six-letter-word. The __________ __________ in the word is "d", and the last is "e". __________ __________ __________ it? Okay. I can give you one more clue. The letter "c" is the __________ __________ __________. I guess that is enough.

17

W Look! The man in this picture __________ __________.

M Yes, it's amazing. It took ten years for the painter to __________.

W Wow, that's incredible.

M Look at this crown. It __________ __________ __________ diamonds.

W It says King Edward used to wear it.

M There are lots of things to see. We need at least two hours to __________ __________.

18

① M What's the matter?

W I __________ __________ __________ today.

② M Will she come here?

W She said __________ __________.

③ M I bought this necklace for you.

W Oh, __________ __________ __________ you.

④ M I'm fifteen years old.

W David is __________ __________.

⑤ M Writing the same thing every day is boring.

W Right. It really makes me happy.

19

M Your friend, Abigail is going to __________ __________ __________ __________ today. You know she has studied very hard to prepare for it. You're sure that she will __________ __________ __________. You want to __________ __________ __________ __________. In this situation, what would you say to her?

20

W Mike, I heard that you finished your __________ __________.

M Yes, I did.

W How could you do that in __________ __________ __________ __________ of time?

M I did it __________ __________ __________ every day.

11회 영어듣기모의고사

정답 및 해설 p.52

Take notes

1 대화를 듣고, 남자가 원하는 버클의 모양을 고르시오.

① 
② 
③ 
④ 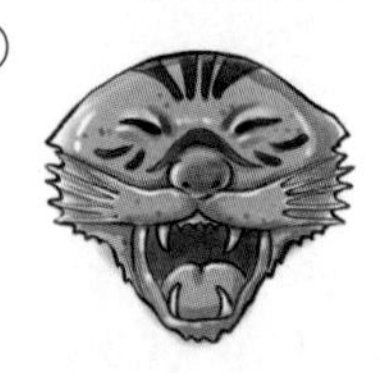
⑤ 

2 대화를 듣고, 여자의 심정으로 가장 알맞은 것을 고르시오.

① 화난　　② 고마운　　③ 슬픈
④ 우울한　　⑤ 행복한

3 대화를 듣고, 남자가 사게 될 셔츠의 색깔을 고르시오.

① brown　　② white　　③ black
④ red　　⑤ yellow

4 다음을 듣고, 지하철에서 지켜야 할 예절이 아닌 것을 고르시오.

①　　②　　③　　④　　⑤

5 대화를 듣고, 여자의 직업으로 알맞은 것을 고르시오.

① 이웃　　② 청소부　　③ 우편배달부
④ 신문 배달부　　⑤ 부동산업자

6 대화를 듣고, 두 사람이 대화하는 장소를 고르시오.

① 병원　② 호텔　③ 교실　④ 도서관　⑤ 박물관

7 대화를 듣고, 여자가 사려는 우산을 고르시오.

①
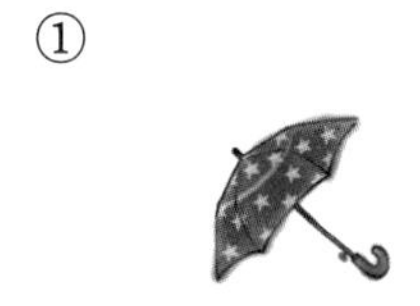
②

③

④

⑤

8 대화를 듣고, 현재 시각을 고르시오.

① 1:30　② 1:40　③ 1:50　④ 2:00　⑤ 2:10

9 다음을 듣고, 메뉴의 내용과 일치하지 않는 것을 고르시오.

MENU			
Hamburger	$3.50	Coke	$1.00
Cheeseburger	$4.00	Coffee	$1.00
Chicken burger	$3.00	Milkshake	$1.50
French fries	$1.20	Salad	$3.00

①　②　③　④　⑤

10 대화를 듣고, 여자가 한 마지막 말의 의도를 고르시오.

① 비난　② 격려　③ 칭찬　④ 동의　⑤ 경고

Take notes

11

대화를 듣고, 남자가 전화를 건 목적을 고르시오.

① 예약하기 ② 예약 취소
③ 예약 확인 ④ 예약 변경
⑤ 위치 확인

12

대화를 듣고, 여자가 지불해야 할 금액을 고르시오.

① $30 ② $35 ③ $40 ④ $45 ⑤ $50

13

다음을 듣고, Joseph에 대한 내용으로 일치하지 않는 것을 고르시오.

① 과학을 좋아한다.
② 책 읽기를 싫어한다.
③ 수학 대회에서 상을 많이 탔다.
④ 물건을 종종 분해하고 조립한다.
⑤ 시계나 자전거를 자주 잃어버린다.

14

대화를 듣고, 남자의 고민을 고르시오.

① 함부로 말하는 것
② 돈을 낭비하는 것
③ 할 일을 뒤로 미루는 것
④ 너무 신중하게 생각하는 것
⑤ 이기적으로 행동하는 것

15

대화를 듣고, 내용과 가장 관련 있는 속담을 고르시오.

① No pain, no gain.
② Two heads are better than one.
③ Don't judge a book by its cover.
④ Too many cooks spoil the broth.
⑤ Don't put all your eggs in one basket.

16 다음을 듣고, 무엇에 관한 설명인지 고르시오.

① 열 ② 땀 ③ 눈물 ④ 상처 ⑤ 탈모

17 다음을 듣고, 두 사람의 대화가 어색한 것을 고르시오.

① ② ③ ④ ⑤

18 대화를 듣고, 남자가 마라톤에 참가하지 못한 이유를 고르시오.

① 자신이 없어서
② 발을 다쳐서
③ 연습이 부족해서
④ 신청을 늦게 해서
⑤ 엄마가 못하게 해서

19-20 대화를 듣고, 남자의 마지막 말에 이어질 여자의 응답으로 가장 알맞은 것을 고르시오.

19

① This is speaking.
② Can I take a message?
③ He is not here right now.
④ It will be ready in two hours.
⑤ I think you've got the wrong number.

20

① I got a part-time job.
② I found it on the street.
③ I sold my digital camera.
④ My father showed it to me.
⑤ My sister borrowed some money.

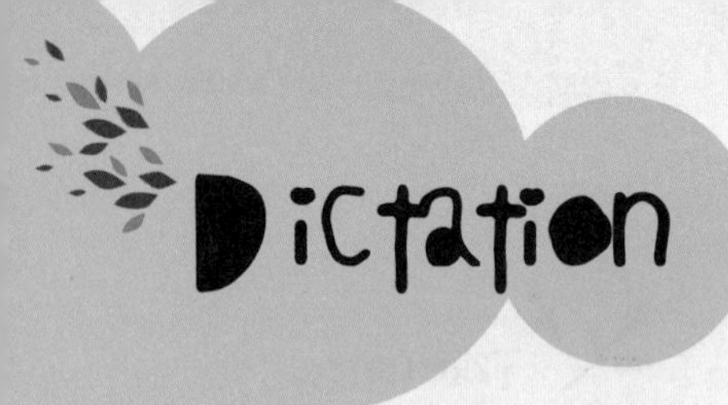

1

W Patrick, I _____ _____ _____ for you and your brothers.

M What are they?

W They're buckles for your belt. You can _____ _____ _____ you like.

M I want the one with the star. No, I mean the one with the eagle.

W OK. I think you _____ _____ _____ _____.

2

M Excuse me, but there's _____ _____ _____ on your card.

W I thought there was.

M You need to _____ _____ _____ instead.

W But I don't have any money right now.

M Then, you have to _____ _____.

W Oh, no. Can you just give me a free ride, please? I will pay you back next time.

M Okay, I will give you _____ _____ _____ just this once.

3

W How about this brown shirt, Mark?

M I don't like it, Mom. I like that red one.

W Mark, brown is a _____ _____ _____ _____.

M But red _____ _____.

W Let's do it this way. Today I'll buy you what you want. But next time, you will _____ _____ _____, okay?

M Okay.

4

M ① Do not run or _____ _____.

② Do not _____ _____ more than one seat.

③ _____ _____ people to get off before you get on.

④ Put your cell phone on vibration mode.

⑤ _____ _____ _____ as wide as you can while sitting.

5

W Excuse me, does Mrs. Smith _____ _____?

M Yes, she is my wife.

W There is no Mrs. Smith in this address book.

M We have _____ _____ _____.

W I see. Here is some mail for her. Could you sign here, please?

M _____ _____.

6

[Telephone rings.]

M Good morning, this is ________ ________, how may I help you?

W Good morning, this is room 707. Could you ________ ________ ________ ________ to my room?

M Sure. What would you like?

W I'd like to have two fried eggs, toast, and some fresh orange juice.

M ________ ________ ________ ________ you would like?

W No, that's all.

7

M May I help you?

W Yes, I'd like to ________.

M We have a few here, and the prices are ________ ________ ________.

W I want to buy a medium-sized one.

M How about the black one?

W No, I'll just take the white one with ________ ________ ________.

8

W Let's go. The concert starts at two o'clock.

M But Brian ________ ________ ________ ________.

W I know, but we are going to be late.

M Let me call Brian again.

W ________ ________ ________. The concert starts in ten minutes.

M Okay, let's do it this way. We leave his ticket at the box office ________ ________ ________ on it.

9

W ① If you have 5 dollars, you can have a hamburger ________ ________ ________.

② If you have 7 dollars, you can have a cheeseburger with a salad.

③ If you have 4 dollars, you can have a chicken burger with a coffee.

④ If you have 6 dollars, you can have ________ ________ ________ a milkshake.

⑤ ________ ________ ________ 5 dollars, you can have a hamburger with a salad.

10

M I missed the movie because you ________ ________ ________!

W What are you talking about? We were supposed to meet at 3:30, weren't we?

M That's right. I arrived ________ ________, but you weren't there.

W ________ ________ ________ me? I was there until 3:50. You're the one who didn't show up and didn't answer my calls.

M Did you call me?

W Yes, I called you three times. You are to ________ ________ ________.

Dictation

11

[Telephone rings.]

W Hello, Happy Life Dentist, how may I help you?

M Hi, my name is John Ford. I ________ ________ ________ at 10.

W John, Ford. Um, yes. That's right. ________ ________.

M I just ________ ________ ________ my appointment.

W Okay, we'll see you then.

12

M Here is ________ ________ ________.

W Thank you. How much is it?

M It's 50 dollars.

W I'm ________ ________ ________ here, so I can get ten ________ ________, right?

M Sure. May I see your membership card?

W Here it is.

13

W My brother, Joseph is really good at math, and he has ________ ________ ________ from math contests. Joseph really hates reading books, but he is very interested in science. He also likes putting things together and ________ ________ ________, so he often breaks things ________ ________ watches or bikes.

14

M Melissa, I think I have a problem.

W What is it?

M I often ________ ________, and it hurts ________.

W I think sometimes you talk so rudely. I'm your close friend, so I understand you, but ________ ________.

M How can I change my bad habit?

W ________ ________ ________ before you speak.

15

W May I ask what you ________ ________ ________ ________?

M Sure, I'm an English teacher.

W You are?

M Yes. It's hard to believe, isn't it? I've ________ ________ ________ ________. Many people think I'm a coach or a policeman or something.

W Is that true?

M Yes, but ________ ________ ________.

16

M This is clear, salty liquid that ________ ________ our skin when we are hot or when we exercise. When our body gets hotter than 37 degrees, our body ________ ________ by making this. But some people get this when they are ________, ________, ________ ________.

17

① W What did you do last weekend?
M I went to the beach with my family.

② W Did you watch TV yesterday?
M No, I didn't. I had ________ ________ ________ ________ TV.

③ W How was the movie?
M It was long and boring.

④ W I ________ ________ ________ on my math exam.
M Sorry to hear that.

⑤ W A young boy ________ ________ the Han River.
M Really? That's amazing.

18

W Hey, Jonathan. I didn't see you ________ ________ ________. What happened?
M I couldn't run.
W Did your mother ________ ________ ________ ________?
M No, she didn't. I ________ ________ by dropping a cup on my foot.
W That's too bad.

19

[Telephone rings.]
W Hello.
M Hello, this is Will. I dropped some ________ ________ ________ yesterday. When will it be ready?
W Who are you calling?
M Isn't this Jim's Laundry? Is Jim there?
W No, it's not. And there is no one here ________ ________ ________. What number are you calling?
M Uh... I dialed 777-4567.
W I think you've got ________ ________ ________.

20

W Hey, Brian. Do you have a digital camera?
M Sure, my parents ________ ________ for me for my birthday.
W I ________ ________. I bought one with money I ________ ________ for three months.
M How did you save the money?
W I ________ ________ ________ job.

12회 영어듣기모의고사

정답 및 해설 p.57

Take notes

1 대화를 듣고, 여자의 남동생을 고르시오.

2 대화를 듣고, 남자에게 필요한 것을 고르시오.

① eraser ② scissors ③ pencil
④ paper ⑤ glue

3 대화를 듣고, 여자가 남자에게 충고하는 것을 고르시오.

① 숙제를 해라.
② 자습서를 봐라.
③ 노트를 검토해라.
④ 교과서를 검토해라.
⑤ 문제를 많이 풀어봐라.

4 대화를 듣고, 남자의 엄마 나이로 알맞은 것을 고르시오.

① 35세 ② 36세 ③ 38세 ④ 39세 ⑤ 40세

5 대화를 듣고, 두 사람이 대화하는 장소를 고르시오.

① 파티 ② 음악회 ③ 영화관
④ 결혼식장 ⑤ 음반 가게

6 대화를 듣고, Amanda가 떠난 시각을 고르시오.

① 12:30 ② 12:40 ③ 1:00
④ 1:20 ⑤ 1:40

7 대화를 듣고, 여자가 사려고 하는 물건을 고르시오.

① 
② 
③ 
④ 
⑤ 

8 대화를 듣고, 남자의 심정으로 가장 알맞은 것을 고르시오.

① 슬픈 ② 화난 ③ 안심한
④ 우울한 ⑤ 짜증나는

9 다음을 듣고, 무엇에 관한 설명인지 고르시오.

① 수저 ② 국자 ③ 나이프
④ 주전자 ⑤ 젓가락

10 대화를 듣고, 다음 중 알 수 없는 것을 고르시오.

① 여자는 고양이 두 마리를 기른다.
② 고양이는 미국에서 가장 인기 있는 애완동물이다.
③ 남자는 자신의 개를 일주일에 두 번 목욕시킨다.
④ 개는 한국인들이 가장 많이 기르는 애완동물이다.
⑤ 남자는 개보다 고양이가 더 기르기 쉽다고 생각한다.

Take notes

11

대화를 듣고, 남자가 인터넷에서 옷을 사지 않는 이유를 고르시오.

① 값이 싸지 않아서
② 환불받기가 어려워서
③ 미리 입어 볼 수 없어서
④ 배송이 늦어서
⑤ 질이 떨어져서

12

대화를 듣고, 여자가 저녁에 먹기를 원하는 음식을 고르시오.

① 일본 음식
② 중국 음식
③ 한국 음식
④ 해산물 요리
⑤ 이탈리아 음식

13

대화를 듣고, 여자의 상황에 가장 관련 있는 속담을 고르시오.

① 일석이조
② 그림의 떡
③ 독 안에 든 쥐
④ 누워서 떡 먹기
⑤ 소귀에 경 읽기

14

다음을 듣고, 무엇에 관한 설명인지 고르시오.

① ticket
② receipt
③ check
④ stamp
⑤ cash

15

대화를 듣고, 알 수 없는 것을 고르시오.

① 남자는 공책을 사야 한다.
② 남자의 1학기는 3월에 시작한다.
③ 여자의 1학기는 9월에 시작한다.
④ 남자는 곧 1학기를 맞이할 것이다.
⑤ 남자는 교과서를 모두 가지고 있다.

Take notes

16

대화를 듣고, 여자가 한 마지막 말의 의도를 고르시오.

① 책망 ② 동의 ③ 감사 ④ 칭찬 ⑤ 제안

17

대화를 듣고, 여자가 남자에게 원하는 것을 고르시오.

① 숙제를 한 후에 쿠키를 먹어라.
② 쿠키를 먹고 나서 공부해라.
③ 이웃에게 쿠키를 주고 와라.
④ 쿠키 만드는 방법을 배워라.
⑤ 쿠키를 나눠 먹어라.

18

다음을 듣고, 두 사람의 대화가 어색한 것을 고르시오.

① ② ③ ④ ⑤

19-20 대화를 듣고, 여자의 마지막 말에 이어질 남자의 응답으로 가장 알맞은 것을 고르시오.

19

① That's a good idea.
② How can I get there?
③ No. It's just a short walk.
④ I'm a stranger here, too.
⑤ It's between the bank and the bakery.

20

① Take it easy.
② That's amazing.
③ I ran a full course.
④ That sounds terrible.
⑤ No, you were the winner.

1

M You _____ _____ _____ your brother, right? Where is he?

W He _____ _____ _____ with his friends.

M Is he wearing glasses or a cap?

W Neither. He is _____ _____ and a bit thin.

M I see. He is the one with short hair.

W That's right.

2

W What is _____ _____ _____ _____? We don't have much time. The movie starts in 20 minutes.

M I know, but I can't cut this coupon.

W Do we need that coupon? _____ _____?

M We cannot _____ _____ _____ without it.

W Oh, really? OK. I will go get something to cut it with.

3

W You seem so busy today.

M Yes. I don't _____ _____ _____ to talk to you.

W What makes you so busy?

M I have _____ _____ _____ tomorrow.

W So you're solving math problems?

M That's right.

W I think you should _____ _____ _____ first.

4

W I had a _____ _____ at your 15th birthday party.

M Good to hear that.

W Anyway, your mother is so _____ _____.

M She spends a lot of time _____ _____.

W How old is she?

M Well, she is 24 years older than me.

5

W This is _____ _____ _____ to see an opera, so I'm really excited.

M So am I.

W Do you know who the soprano is?

M Let's _____ _____ _____ at the pamphlet. This lady is the soprano, and the man _____ _____ her is the tenor.

W Now she _____ _____. Wow, she is wearing a wonderful dress.

6

M Where is Amanda?

W She's gone.

M Why? She said she _____ _____

__________ until three. It's only one o'clock.

W She said she had to __________ __________ __________.

M __________ __________ did she leave?

W She left 20 minutes ago.

7

W __________ __________, can I see that?

M You mean these earrings?

W Yes. They look beautiful. __________ __________ __________?

M They are 30 dollars.

W That's __________ __________. I will just take these hairpins.

8

W What are you __________ __________?

M My cell phone.

W What does it __________ __________?

M It's __________ __________ __________ and it's gray in color.

W I think Ann found one in the library, so why don't you call her?

M It __________ __________ __________ because I went there this morning.

W Good. Here is her number, and use my cell phone.

9

W These are two thin sticks that you __________ __________ eat food with in many countries in Asia. They originally __________ __________ China. It is very easy for Asian people to use them, __________ __________ __________ Westerners. Westerners usually use a fork. They __________ __________ __________ wood or metal.

10

M Do you have any pets, Lucy?

W Yes. I have __________ __________ __________ cats. They are so sweet.

M There aren't many people __________ __________ __________ in Korea.

W Really? Cats are the most popular pets in the States.

M I see. I think cats are easier to __________ __________ __________ than dogs. I have to give my dog a bath twice a week.

11

M Where did you get this shirt?

W I __________ __________ __________ the Internet. Do you like it?

M Yes. How much did you __________ __________ __________?

W I paid 20 dollars, but it was 30 dollars at the department store.

M I see.

W I think you should __________ __________ __________ through the Internet. They're much cheaper.

M I know, but I never buy clothes I can't __________ __________ __________.

Dictation

12

W Let's eat out tonight. I don't ______ ______.

M OK. What do you want to have?

W I want ______ ______ today.

M Like what, Chinese food?

W No, you know I don't like Chinese food. Um… I want some seafood.

M I know a famous place ______ ______ ______.

W Let's go there then.

13

W Look at the woman. She has a ______ ______ over her shoulder. I want to have one.

M We are just students, so we don't need an expensive bag like that.

W ______ ______, but most girls want to have one.

M ______ ______! It is too expensive for students to get one like that, and you don't even ______ ______ ______ to pay for this food.

14

W You need money to buy this, but some people get this ______ because they use coupons or points. This is ______ ______ printed paper that shows you have paid money to enter a cinema or many other places or to ______ ______ a bus, train, or airplane.

15

W What are you doing?

M I'm ______ ______ ______ the first semester.

W That's strange. Our first semester starts in September.

M Your country has ______ ______ ______. Ours starts in March.

W I see. What do you need, then?

M I need to buy some notebooks and ______ ______ ______. I have all the necessary textbooks.

16

W Did you turn this on?

M Yes, I did. ______ ______ ______?

W When I came to work this morning, it was still on.

M It was so hot, so I just ______ ______ ______.

W Yeah, I know it was hot yesterday, but it will cost a lot of money.

M That's OK. My boss will ______ ______ ______ not me.

W You shouldn't think that way.

17

M Mom, I'm home. What is ______ ______ ______?

W I've just baked some chocolate cookies. ______.

M These are really delicious. You are the best cook, Mom.

W Thanks. I'll put them in the cookie jar. Make sure to __________ __________ __________ your sister, OK?

M Yes, Mom.

18

① M Can I use your cell phone?

W I found it in the bathroom.

② M Can you tell me how to __________ __________ __________?

W Yes. First, turn it on.

③ M Do you want some more pizza?

W Yes, please. Thank you.

④ M __________ __________ __________ you.

W That's very kind of you.

⑤ M How was your trip to Japan?

W I __________ __________ __________, but the weather was bad.

19

W Excuse me. __________ __________ __________ __________ to the post office?

M Sorry?

W Where is the post office?

M It's __________ __________ the bank.

W Is it __________ __________ __________?

M No. It's just a short walk.

20

M Where did you __________ __________ __________?

W From the marathon race this morning.

M Was it a full course marathon?

W No, people under 18 aren't __________ __________ __________ a full course. I ran ten kilometers.

M You __________ __________ __________?

W Yes, I did.

M That's amazing.

13회 영어듣기모의고사

정답 및 해설 p.63

Take notes

1 대화를 듣고, 여자가 찾는 장소를 고르시오.

2 대화를 듣고, 현재의 날씨로 알맞은 것을 고르시오.

① rainy ② sunny ③ cloudy
④ foggy ⑤ windy

3 대화를 듣고, 두 사람이 대화하는 장소를 고르시오.

① 호텔 ② 식당 ③ 박물관
④ 사진관 ⑤ 놀이공원

4 대화를 듣고, 현재 시각을 고르시오.

① 4:10 ② 4:20 ③ 4:30 ④ 4:40 ⑤ 4:50

5 대화를 듣고, 남자가 좋아하는 영화 종류를 고르시오.

① Comedies ② SF movies
③ Action movies ④ Horror movies
⑤ Romantic movies

6 다음을 듣고, 남자가 추천하는 운동을 고르시오.

① 수영　② 걷기　③ 테니스
④ 달리기　⑤ 배드민턴

7 대화를 듣고, 여자의 습관으로 알맞은 것을 고르시오.

① biting nails　② biting lips
③ shaking legs　④ answering back
⑤ spitting on the street

8 대화를 듣고, 이어지는 질문에 가장 알맞은 답을 고르시오.

① 영어　② 한자　③ 역사　④ 국어　⑤ 수학

9 대화를 듣고, 남자가 잃어버린 가방을 고르시오.

① 
② 
③ 
④ 
⑤ 

10 대화를 듣고, 여자가 남자에게 부탁하는 것을 고르시오.

① 문을 열어 달라고
② 택시를 불러 달라고
③ 출장을 같이 가자고
④ 차를 운전해 달라고
⑤ 가방을 운반해 달라고

Take notes

11

대화를 듣고, 남자의 미국 방문 목적을 고르시오.

① 여행　② 유학　③ 쇼핑
④ 친척 방문　⑤ 어학연수

12

대화를 듣고, Sean의 직업으로 알맞은 것을 고르시오.

① 페인트 공　② 건축사　③ 정비사
④ 교사　⑤ 의사

13

대화를 듣고, 내용과 일치하지 않는 것을 고르시오.

① 장소는 Goodfood 식당이다.
② 6:30에 파티가 시작될 예정이다.
③ 행사 날짜는 13일로 변경되었다.
④ Patrick의 생일 파티에 관한 내용이다.
⑤ 중요한 회의가 있어 날짜를 변경한다.

14

대화를 듣고, 여자가 지불하게 될 금액을 고르시오.

① $30　② $40　③ $50
④ $80　⑤ $150

15

대화를 듣고, 두 사람의 관계로 가장 알맞은 것을 고르시오.

① 은행 – 손님　② 약사 – 손님
③ 호텔 직원 – 손님　④ 의사 – 환자
⑤ 세탁소 직원 – 손님

16

대화를 듣고, 여자가 바라는 이상형의 남자를 고르시오.

① 부유한 남자
② 잘 생긴 남자
③ 키가 큰 남자
④ 이해심 많은 남자
⑤ 공부 잘하는 남자

17

다음을 듣고, 두 사람의 대화가 어색한 것을 고르시오.

① ② ③ ④ ⑤

18

대화를 듣고, 여자가 한 마지막 말의 의도를 고르시오.

① 칭찬 ② 격려 ③ 책망 ④ 불평 ⑤ 제안

19

다음을 듣고, 마지막 질문에 가장 알맞은 답을 고르시오.

① I will buy two scarves.
② I'd like to have a refund.
③ Look! Here is a hole on it.
④ Could you give me a discount?
⑤ Can I exchange it for another color?

20

대화를 듣고, 여자의 마지막 말에 이어질 남자의 응답으로 가장 적절한 것을 고르시오.

① You are a great scientist.
② Don't worry about it too much.
③ You can do better next time.
④ Sorry, but I don't think I need it.
⑤ Thanks. It would be a great help.

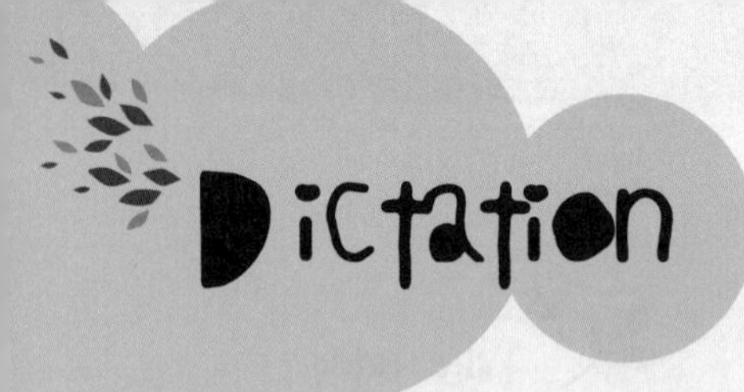

1

W Excuse me, I'm looking for Shelly's Beauty Salon. Do you know where it is?

M Yes. ______ ______ this way for two blocks, and then ______ ______ ______. It'll be the second building on your right.

W OK. Pass two blocks and turn left, and it's the second building ______ ______ ______.

M You got it.

2

W I think it's raining. I heard ______ ______ ______ ______.

M Did you? The weather forecast said it ______ ______ ______ all day.

W I sure did.

M OK. Let's look out the window. (pause) The sky is clear as crystal.

W ______ ______! I really heard rain.

3

M Hello. Please look at me.

W Okay.

M Please ______ ______ ______ a little bit to the left.

W Like this?

M That's it. Looking good. Now, I want to ______ ______ on your face.

W It's hard to do that.

M Then say, "Whiskey." Okay. I'll ______ ______ now.

4

M John hasn't ______ ______. He said he will be here soon.

W Does he know the show starts at five?

M I'm sure he does, but he said he ______ ______ ______ ______.

W That's his problem. ______ ______ traffic is terrible at this time of day.

M That's true. We only have 20 minutes left.

W Let's call him again.

5

M Why don't we see ______ ______ ______?

W No, I don't like love stories.

M Well, they're ______ ______. How about that one ______ ______?

W I saw that one last week with my sister.

M You like actions, don't you?

W Yes. I like mysteries, actions, and SFs.

M Okay. You ______ ______ ______, and I will buy some popcorn.

6

M This is the best exercise I've __________ __________, and I have lost 20 kilograms in three months. Running __________ __________ __________ in your knees, but you don't have to worry about it __________ __________ this exercise. You don't need to wear any special clothes. You can do it anywhere and anytime. This exercise is very simple but brings __________ __________ __________.

7

M Cathy, can you __________ __________ __________? It's bothering me.

W What do you want me to stop? I'm just sitting in the chair.

M You've __________ your legs for one hour.

W Oh, sorry! When I sit down, I begin moving my legs __________ __________. I've tried to stop this habit, but it is not easy.

M I used to have the bad habit of biting my lips, but I __________ __________ __________ __________ it. So try harder.

8

W Are you going to attend the after-school program?

M I don't want to, but my mother __________ __________ __________ __________ a Chinese characters class. How about you?

W I'm going to attend a __________ __________ with John and David.

M You know what? If we attend the after-school program, we'll __________ __________ __________ __________ every day.

Q What class is the man going to attend in his after-school program?

9

M Ashley, someone took my backpack.

W Where did you __________ __________ __________?

M I put it next to Cindy's backpack, but it's gone.

W What does it __________ __________?

M It has two small pockets near the bottom, and there is a big letter G __________ __________ __________.

W Let's ask the security guard over there.

10

M Are you going somewhere?

W Yes, I'm going __________ __________ __________ __________ to Chicago, so I need to put these suitcases in my car.

M You have lots of bags to take. How long are you __________ __________ __________ there for?

W I think it'll be more than a month. Can you __________ __________ __________ them?

M No problem.

11

M Do you have any plans for Thanksgiving?

W Not really. I ________ ________ my grandparents. How about you?

M I'm going to the States ________ ________.

W Are you ________ ________ ________?

M No, I'm going to visit a relative who I haven't seen for many years.

12

[Telephone rings.]

W Hello, this is Susan. How may I help you?

M Hi, it's Brian. Is Sean there?

W No, he is ________.

M Can you tell him to call me?

W Sure, but can you tell me ________ ________ ________ ________?

M The paint on the wall of my house ________ ________ ________, so I need him this weekend.

13

W Did you hear that Patrick's birthday party will not be held on the 13th?

M No, I didn't. ________ ________ ________?

W Patrick did. He said he ________ ________ ________ an important meeting on that day.

M I see. Then, when ________ ________ ________ ________?

W Two days later at Goodfood restaurant at 6:30.

14

W I've heard you are going to sell your bike. How much do you ________ ________ ________?

M 80 dollars.

W That's too much ________ ________ ________ ________.

M I paid 150 dollars when I bought it.

W Okay, I'll give you ________ ________ ________ you want.

M Ten more.

W Deal!

15

M Hello, may I help you?

W Hi, I have ________ ________ ________.

M Since when have you had a headache?

W Since yesterday.

M I'll give you some aspirin. And if ________ ________ ________, you should ________ ________ ________ ________.

W Okay. Thank you.

16

W Seth, what ________ ________ ________ do you like?

M Well, I don't know. I haven't thought much

about it. How about you? You like tall and good-looking men, don't you?

W __________ __________ __________.

M How about a guy with rich parents?

W Stop! I'm __________ __________ __________ of girl. I just like a guy who is very understanding.

17

① W Is she going to invite Ann to her party?
M Probably, not.

② W Is this your computer?
M No, my brother and I __________ __________ __________.

③ W I can never get up early in the morning.
M Why don't you __________ __________ __________ early?

④ W Why are you wearing this helmet?
M Because it __________ __________ __________.

⑤ W How have you been?
M I drove her car to get there.

18

W Wow, the house is so clean. __________ __________ it?

M Jess and I did.

W __________ __________? You don't even clean your room.

M Well, you've worked late these days, and you __________ __________ __________ last night. So Jess and I cleaned up, and we even did the laundry.

W Oh, __________ __________ __________ so sweet. Thank you.

19

W You are in the store to buy a gift for your mother. You __________ __________ to choose the right one for her and __________ __________ __________ a scarf. You ask the clerk __________ __________ it is, and she says it's 30 dollars. You really want to buy it, but you only have 28 dollars. In this situation, what would you say __________ __________ __________?

20

W Where are you going?

M I'm going to the library to look for some information on UFOs.

W You are writing a science report, right? I __________ __________ __________ __________.

M Then, can I read yours? I have no idea __________ __________ __________ it.

W Sure, I'll bring it to you tomorrow.

M Thanks. It would be __________ __________ __________.

14회 영어듣기모의고사

정답 및 해설 p.68

Take notes

1 다음을 듣고, 그림의 상황에 가장 알맞은 대화를 고르시오.

① ② ③ ④ ⑤

2 대화를 듣고, 남자가 한 마지막 말의 의도를 고르시오.

① 비난 ② 격려 ③ 동의 ④ 동정 ⑤ 거절

3 대화를 듣고, 두 사람이 대화하는 장소를 고르시오.

① hospital ② drugstore
③ hotel ④ airport
⑤ restaurant

4 대화를 듣고, 결혼식이 열리는 시각을 고르시오.

① 1:30 ② 1:40 ③ 2:00 ④ 2:20 ⑤ 3:00

5 대화를 듣고, Will이 오늘 여자를 만날 수 없는 이유를 고르시오.

① 엄마 심부름 때문에 ② 저녁 준비 때문에
③ 선약이 있기 때문에 ④ 보고서 준비 때문에
⑤ 운동을 해야 하기 때문에

6 다음을 듣고, 그림을 가장 적절하게 묘사한 것을 고르시오.

① 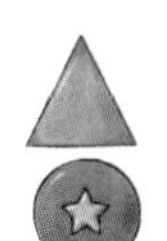
② 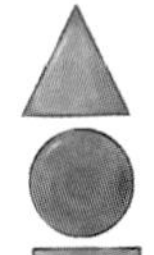
③ 
④ 
⑤ 

7 대화를 듣고, 남자가 수프에 넣을 재료를 고르시오.

① water ② salt ③ butter
④ sugar ⑤ pepper

8 대화를 듣고, 내용과 일치하지 않는 것을 고르시오.

① 남자는 미국에서 왔다.
② 남자는 지난주에 한국에 왔다.
③ 남자는 지금 한국에서 잘 지내고 있다.
④ 남자는 서울을 제2의 고향이라고 생각한다.
⑤ 남자는 처음 한국 생활을 할 때에는 힘들다고 느꼈다.

9 대화를 듣고, 남자의 심정으로 가장 알맞은 것을 고르시오.

① sad ② excited ③ scared
④ happy ⑤ bored

10 대화를 듣고, 남자에게 가장 필요한 것을 고르시오.

① 근면성 ② 자신감 ③ 배려심
④ 겸손함 ⑤ 정직함

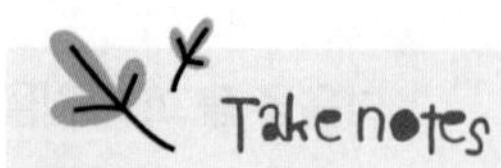

11 다음을 듣고, 무엇에 관한 안내 방송인지 고르시오.

① 분실물 안내
② 할인 판매 안내
③ 미술관 관람 안내
④ 행사 홍보 방송
⑤ 영화 시간 안내

12 대화를 듣고, 남자가 일주일 동안 일한 시간을 고르시오.

① 30시간
② 33시간
③ 36시간
④ 39시간
⑤ 42시간

13 대화를 듣고, 남자가 가고 싶어 하는 식당을 고르시오.

① 가까운 곳
② 맛있는 곳
③ 사람들이 많은 곳
④ 한적한 곳
⑤ 분위기 좋은 곳

14 대화를 듣고, 두 사람의 관계로 가장 알맞은 것을 고르시오.

① 동창 – 동창
② 점원 – 고객
③ 교사 – 학생
④ 의사 – 환자
⑤ 아빠 – 딸

15 다음을 듣고, 호랑이와 사자의 차이로 알맞지 않은 것을 고르시오.

Tigers	Lions
① bigger and heavier	② taller and faster
live alone	③ live in a group
④ like water	hate water
live in cold climates	⑤ live in wet climates

16 다음을 듣고, 두 사람의 대화가 어색한 것을 고르시오.

① ② ③ ④ ⑤

17 대화를 듣고, 여자의 성격으로 알맞은 것을 고르시오.

① 엄한 ② 친절한 ③ 게으른
④ 관대한 ⑤ 무책임한

18 대화를 듣고, 여자가 할 일로 알맞은 것을 고르시오.

① 약을 복용한다.
② 얼음 마사지를 한다.
③ 눈을 소금물로 씻는다.
④ 친구와 함께 안과에 간다.
⑤ 집에 가서 휴식을 취한다.

19-20 대화를 듣고, 여자의 마지막 말에 이어질 남자의 응답으로 가장 알맞은 것을 고르시오.

19

① That sounds really fun.
② I'm a good swimmer.
③ I enjoy going to the beach.
④ Same here, I will go with you.
⑤ You can learn how to swim easily.

20

① Sorry, but I don't need it.
② Then, why did you call me?
③ Thank you, but It's not my fault.
④ Thank you for giving me good advice.
⑤ Okay, I will bring the note next time.

1

① M Mom, I bought some flowers __________ __________ __________ __________.

W Oh, how sweet of you.

② M Well, you have two large cavities.

W Are you going to __________ __________ __________ __________?

③ M Could we have a table for five?

W Did you __________ __________ __________, sir?

④ M Your new hairstyle looks good on you.

W Thank you. I got a haircut yesterday.

⑤ M What will you do after school?

W I will go shopping with my sister.

2

M Where is he? Ryan is not a person __________ __________ __________.

W Sam, you didn't hear about Ryan, did you?

M No, __________ __________ __________ to him?

W His dad __________ __________ __________ __________ last night, and he is in the hospital now.

M What a pity!

3

W This is the front desk. May I help you?

M Yes. I'm Johnson from room number 210. __________ __________ __________ __________ near here?

W There are a couple, but they are closed. __________ __________ __________?

M Yes, my wife is coughing a lot.

W We __________ __________ __________ __________ here for our guests. I will have someone bring some up to you right away.

M Thanks.

4

M The bridegroom is here. He is handsome and tall.

W The bride is pretty, too. They are __________ __________ __________.

M Where are __________ __________, anyway?

W Downstairs at 2 o'clock.

M We still have to wait 20 minutes.

W That's right. Hey, look. I think they are going to __________ __________.

5

W Will, I will __________ __________ __________ tonight.

M Well, thanks, but I don't think I can.

W Why not?

M I have to go to the library and __________

__________ __________ about the Second World War.

W Is it __________ __________ your history report?

M Yes, I need to finish writing it by Friday.

6

W First, draw a circle, and next, draw a triangle __________ __________ __________. Third, draw a square below the circle. Last, __________ __________ __________ inside the circle.

7

M Taste this soup, and tell me __________ __________ __________.

W I'm afraid this soup tastes too salty.

M I don't have __________ __________ __________ it again. What should I do?

W Why don't you just __________ __________ __________?

M That's a brilliant idea.

8

M I've been here for almost two years already.

W Wow, __________ __________. It feels like I met you last week.

M Yeah, I feel that way, too.

W There are so many differences between America and Korea. I'm happy that you __________ __________ __________ in Korea.

M Life in Korea was tough when I first came. But Seoul has become __________ __________ __________ now.

9

W Kevin, can you hear that sound? I can __________ __________ __________ behind the door.

M Come on. It's three o'clock in the morning. It is just the wind blowing.

W Please go out, and see what it is.

M Let's just __________ __________ __________ __________.

W Oh, you are the man. Unless I know what it is, I won't __________ __________ __________ sleep again.

M But I'm afraid to see what it is, too.

10

W Lewis, how did you do on the test?

M I just __________ __________ __________.

W I'm sure you studied really hard.

M No, I __________ __________ __________ __________. The test was very easy. I don't understand why so many students spend a lot of time studying.

W I see. Then, why did you miss one question?

M I just __________ __________ __________. That's all.

11

W Today, our city ________ ________ ________ ________ everyone to our arm wrestling competition. If you think you are strong ________ ________ ________, come forward. It will start at 6 o'clock, and the winner will receive a computer. There will also be a match for left-handers, too. So ________ ________ enjoy our events. Thank you.

12

W I'm really tired and hungry. It was ________ ________ ________ ________.

M I think so. I've never worked so hard in my life. I even ________ ________ last night.

W I know. You worked overtime on Tuesday, too.

M That's right. I worked ________ ________ ________ than you did.

W Really? I worked for thirty hours this week.

13

M I'm ________ ________ ________.

W I know a nice Chinese restaurant.

M You mean the one ________ ________ ________?

W Yes. Have you been there?

M Yes, but I'm sick of Chinese food.

W Then, what do you want to have?

M I don't care, but I just want to go ________ ________ ________.

14

M Excuse me, do I know you?

W I ________ ________ ________. I just moved in.

M Gosh! Anne, you don't remember me?

W How do you know my name?

M I'm Matthew who ________ ________ ________ ________. We went to the same middle school.

W Oh, I remember now. I'm so ________ ________ ________ you again.

15

M How is a tiger ________ ________ a lion? First, a tiger is bigger and heavier, but a lion is taller and faster. Second, a tiger lives alone, but a lion ________ ________ ________ ________. Third, a tiger likes to spend time in the water, but a lion hates water. Finally, a tiger lives in cold climates, but a lion lives ________ ________ ________.

16

① **W** I studied hard, but I failed the test.
M Good for you. I knew you could do it.

② **W** Where did you get that?
M My mom got it for me ________ ________ ________.

③ W How long have you known her?

M Almost three years.

④ W Have you __________ __________ __________ __________?

M Yes, why?

⑤ W Our team lost the game.

M __________ __________!

17

M I can't find the money I __________ __________ __________ __________ last night. Do you know where it is?

W Oh, that money. Um....

M __________ __________, talk to me.

W I borrowed some money from Jake, and I paid him back with that money.

M How could you do that __________ __________ __________?

18

W My eyes are sore.

M Did you see an eye doctor?

W Sure, I did. I __________ __________ __________, too.

M My mother used to tell me to wash my eyes __________ __________ __________.

W Do you think that would work?

M You can try. You have __________ __________ __________.

W OK. Thank you.

19

W Do you have any plans for the summer?

M I'm going to learn __________ __________ __________ again.

W Can't you swim?

M I've tried to learn many times, but I __________ __________ __________ how. How about you?

W I'm going to visit my uncle who lives in New Zealand with my parents.

M That __________ __________ __________.

20

W Why are you late?

M I'm so sorry. I __________ __________ that I had an appointment.

W It's hard to believe. You usually don't forget appointments.

M I don't know why I forgot it.

W Why don't you __________ __________ __________ for yourself next time?

M Thank you for __________ __________ __________ __________.

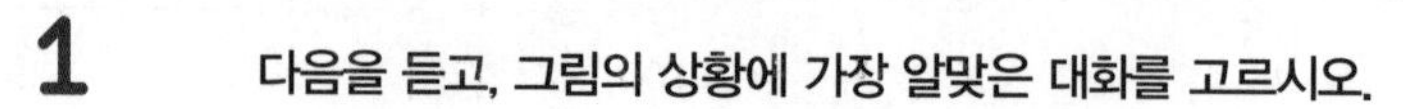

15회 영어듣기모의고사

정답 및 해설 p.73

Take notes

1 다음을 듣고, 그림의 상황에 가장 알맞은 대화를 고르시오.

① ② ③ ④ ⑤

2 대화를 듣고, 두 사람이 대화하는 장소를 고르시오.

① 비행기 안 ② 기차 안 ③ 연회
④ 결혼식 장 ⑤ 식당

3 대화를 듣고, 남자가 주말에 할 일을 고르시오.

① 숙제 ② 집 청소 ③ 친척 방문
④ 나무 심기 ⑤ 일기 예보 확인

4 대화를 듣고, 티켓의 가격을 고르시오.

① $10 ② $20 ③ $30 ④ $40 ⑤ $50

5 다음을 듣고, 여자의 고민으로 알맞은 것을 고르시오.

① 친구가 없어서 ② 수줍음을 너무 타서
③ 선생님이 무관심해서 ④ 성적이 오르지 않아서
⑤ 친구가 따돌림을 당해서

6 대화를 듣고, 여자가 자전거를 사게 될 곳을 고르시오.

① 백화점　　② 인터넷　　③ 할인점
④ 중고시장　　⑤ 자전거 전문점

7 대화를 듣고, 남자의 직업으로 알맞은 것을 고르시오.

①

②

③

④

⑤

8 대화를 듣고, 남자의 심정으로 가장 알맞은 것을 고르시오.

① 지루한　　② 기쁜　　③ 슬픈
④ 실망한　　⑤ 당황한

9 다음을 듣고, 무엇에 관한 설명인지 고르시오.

① 계단　　② 자동문　　③ 회전문
④ 엘리베이터　　⑤ 에스컬레이터

10 대화를 듣고, 남자가 야단을 맞은 이유를 고르시오.

① 수업 시간에 전화를 사용해서
② 점심시간에 학교 밖으로 나가서
③ 점심시간에 친구와 싸워서
④ 식당에서 줄을 서지 않아서
⑤ 수업 시간에 밥을 먹어서

Take notes

11

다음을 듣고, 비행기 표를 예약하려면 어떤 숫자를 눌러야 하는지 고르시오.

① one ② two ③ three
④ four ⑤ five

12

대화를 듣고, 여자가 남자에게 부탁하는 일이 아닌 것을 고르시오.

① 
②
③ 
④
⑤ 

13

대화를 듣고, 남자가 한 마지막 말의 의도를 고르시오.

① 거절 ② 칭찬 ③ 격려 ④ 축하 ⑤ 환영

14

대화를 듣고, 내용과 일치하지 않는 것을 고르시오.

① 남자는 뉴욕에서 대학을 다녔다.
② 여자는 뉴욕에 처음으로 가는 것이다.
③ 남자의 부모님은 아직도 뉴욕에서 살고 있다.
④ 남자는 햇빛이 강해서 창문 가리개를 닫아 달라고 부탁하고 있다.
⑤ 여자는 남자에게 뉴욕의 가볼 만한 곳을 알려달라고 요청하고 있다.

15

대화를 듣고, 남자가 집에 도착할 시각을 고르시오.

① 3:30 ② 4:00 ③ 4:30 ④ 5:30 ⑤ 6:00

16
대화를 듣고, 여자가 남자에게 부탁하는 것을 고르시오.

① 유리창을 깬 아이를 찾아 달라고
② 남자 아이를 소개해 달라고
③ 여자친구를 소개해 주려고
④ 같이 공부를 하려고
⑤ 점심을 사달라고

17
다음을 듣고, 남자의 말을 들을 수 있는 곳을 고르시오.

① 학교　② 공항　③ 상담소
④ 예식장　⑤ 지하철역

18
다음을 듣고, 두 사람의 대화가 어색한 것을 고르시오.

①　②　③　④　⑤

19-20 대화를 듣고, 여자의 마지막 말에 이어질 남자의 응답으로 알맞은 것을 고르시오.

19
① You made a right choice.
② I think it's too big.
③ I'll pay in cash.
④ I paid 60 dollars.
⑤ I didn't buy anything.

20
① Sounds great.
② It looks nice. I'll take it.
③ I have the same thing, too.
④ Can you show me how to use it?
⑤ I downloaded it off the Internet.

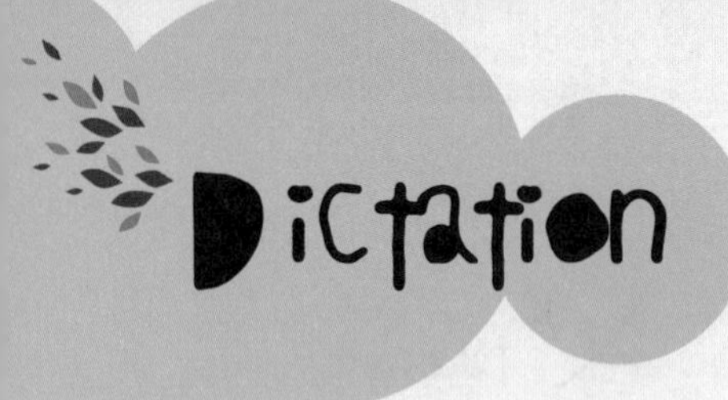

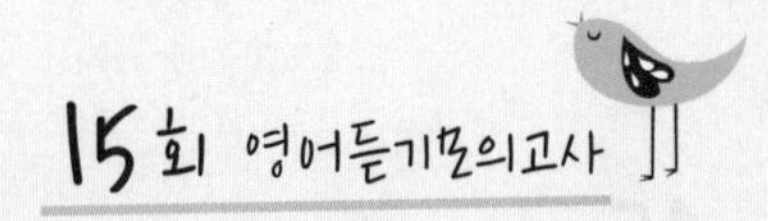

1

① M Thanks for __________ __________ __________ __________.

W Don't mention it.

② M Excuse me, you __________ __________.

W I can't thank you enough.

③ M Can you __________ __________ __________ now?

W Sure. Where are you?

④ M You shouldn't pick the flowers.

W I'm sorry. I will never do that again.

⑤ M Is this your bike?

W Yes. You can ride it __________ __________ __________.

2

W Sir, we are serving dinner now. Please __________ __________ your tray table.

M Okay.

W What would you like to have, beef or chicken?

M Chicken, please. By the way, can I use my laptop __________ __________ __________?

W Yes, sir. But you should __________ __________ __________ during take-offs and landings.

3

W What are you doing this weekend?

M I have to __________ __________ to help my father.

W With what?

M He bought some trees for the garden. He __________ __________ them. How about you?

W I'm __________ __________ with my parents.

4

W I have thirty dollars, so I need twenty dollars more to buy the ticket.

W I see. How are you going to __________ __________ __________?

M I'm not sure. I asked my mother for some money, but she __________ __________ __________.

W Why don't you borrow some from Jenny?

M I should __________ __________ __________ __________.

5

W I have a friend called Jasper. He often __________ __________, so many students in my class don't like him. They don't even want to talk to him. I don't think that's right, so I __________ __________ __________ with him and have lunch with him. My father teaches me to __________ __________ __________, but sometimes I feel it is not easy.

6

W I'm going to the department store to buy a bike.

M Why don't you buy one at __________ __________ __________? You can buy a bike at __________ __________ __________ __________ of a new one.

W Is that so? Where is the secondhand market?

M I know where it is, and if you want, I __________ __________ __________ with you.

W Thanks. Let's go.

7

M Excuse me, is this 3507 Charles Drive?

W Yes, it is.

M Did you __________ __________ __________?

W I sure did. Come on in.

M Sorry I'm late. I'm new to this town so I __________ __________.

W That's okay.

M Thank you. Can you __________ __________ __________ __________?

8

M Did you have a good weekend, Cindy?

W No, I studied for the test __________ __________.

M Do we __________ __________ __________ today?

W Yes. Did you forget, Peter?

M Oh, no! I __________ __________ __________ __________. I didn't study at all. I watched TV and played games all weekend.

9

W This is a vehicle that carries people and things between floors __________ __________ __________ __________. This is a type of small room that __________ __________ __________ __________. Inside the room, there are floor buttons. If you push __________ __________ __________ that you want to go, it will bring you to the floor.

10

W Matt, I need to talk to you now.

M Did I __________ __________ __________, Mrs. Margaret?

W Yes, you did. You __________ __________ __________ __________.

M What do you mean?

W I told you not to leave the school __________ __________, but you did.

11

M Thank you for calling Good Flying Airline. Please listen carefully and __________ __________ __________ __________. If you want Korean service, press one. If you want to know your __________ __________, press two. To book a ticket, press three. To __________ __________ __________ your booking, press four. For any other questions, press five. To listen to the menu again, press six.

12

W Kevin, I have to go out, so I want you to do some __________ __________. Turn off the computer, and clean it up __________ __________ __________.

M What else?

W Open all the windows, and clean up the rooms.

M Would __________ __________ __________?

W One more thing. __________ __________ the trash cans.

M Okay, Mom.

13

M Where are you going, Isabella?

W I'm going to buy a dress __________ __________ __________.

M What concert?

W You know I have a cello concert tomorrow. I sent you __________ __________ __________.

M Oh, I'm sorry. I forgot.

W You are coming, right?

M I'm afraid to say I can't __________ __________ __________.

14

M Excuse me, can you close __________ __________ __________? The sunlight is too strong.

W Of course. Sorry about that.

M Thank you. __________ __________ __________, I'm Jonathan.

W Hi, I'm Jennifer. Do you often travel to New York?

M Yes. I __________ __________ in New York, and my parents still live there.

W This is my first trip. So if you don't mind, can you tell me some good __________ __________?

M Why not?

15

W What time can you come home, Phillip? I need you __________ __________ __________ before 4.

M __________ __________, Mom.

W Then, what time can you get home?

M School finishes at four, and you know it takes thirty minutes to __________ __________ from school.

W Okay, come home __________ __________ __________ you finish school.

16

W Hi, John. Who was the boy that __________ __________ __________ you yesterday?

M He was Andrew.

W __________ __________ __________ to him?

M Yes, he and I went to the same elementary school.

W Can you __________ __________ __________ __________?

M Sure. Just buy me lunch.

17

M Today, a beautiful woman and a handsome man stand __________ __________ __________ us. They've decided to have their future together __________ __________ __________. I hope they love, understand, and support each other. As of today, each of them should do their role as husband and wife and __________ __________ __________ __________.

18

① W Why were you absent yesterday?
M I was __________ __________ __________.

② W Excuse me. Is __________ __________ __________?
M No. You can take it.

③ W What's wrong? You look sad.
M My dad praised me for my good score.

④ W Do you like Japanese food?
M Yes, it is __________ __________.

⑤ W How do you like my cookies?
M They're delicious.

19

W __________ __________ do you need?
M I need a size 10.
W Here they are.
M Thank you. They __________ __________.
W How would you like to pay for them?
M I'll __________ __________ __________.

20

W It's a really nice program.
M Do you __________ __________?
W Yes, it is easy to use, and it will __________ __________ __________ __________ time.
M I'm so glad I got this.
W Where did you get it, anyway?
M I __________ __________ __________ the Internet.

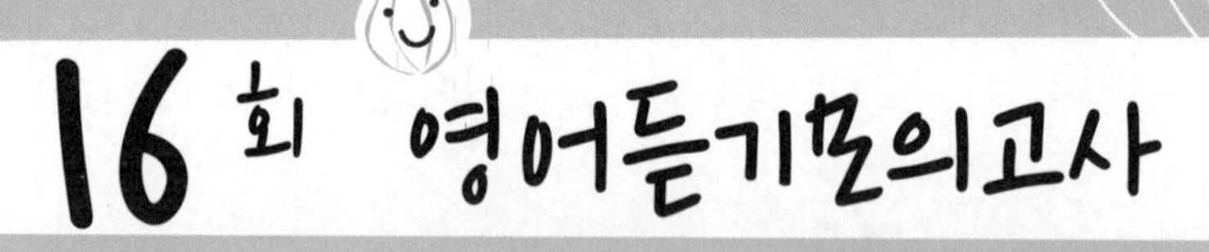

16회 영어듣기모의고사

정답 및 해설 p.78

Take notes

1 대화를 듣고, Susie를 고르시오.

2 대화를 듣고, 두 사람이 대화하는 장소를 고르시오.

① 시청　② 공항　③ 미술관
④ 버스 터미널　⑤ 지하철 역

3 대화를 듣고, 두 사람의 관계로 가장 알맞은 것을 고르시오.

① 점원 – 고객　② 주차 직원– 고객
③ 수영장 직원 – 고객　④ 백화점 직원 – 고객
⑤ 영화관 직원 – 고객

4 대화를 듣고, 남자가 내일 학교에 오지 못하는 이유를 고르시오.

① 머리가 아파서　② 사고를 당해서
③ 독감을 옮길까 봐　④ 이사를 가게 되어서
⑤ 엄마가 병원에 입원해서

5 대화를 듣고, 여자가 한 마지막 말의 의도를 고르시오.

① 격려　② 책망　③ 충고　④ 비판　⑤ 경고

6 대화를 듣고, 남자가 좋아하지 않는 스포츠를 고르시오.

① basketball ② baseball ③ soccer
④ volleyball ⑤ skiing

7 대화를 듣고, 여자가 살 T-shirt를 고르시오.

①

②

③

④

⑤

8 대화를 듣고, 현재의 날씨로 알맞은 것을 고르시오.

① sunny ② rainy ③ snowy
④ windy ⑤ foggy

9 대화를 듣고, 경기가 열리는 날짜를 고르시오.

① 12일 월요일 ② 13일 화요일
③ 14일 수요일 ④ 15일 목요일
⑤ 16일 금요일

10 대화를 듣고, 뉴욕의 현재 지하철 요금으로 알맞은 것을 고르시오.

① \$1 ② \$1.50 ③ \$2 ④ \$2.50 ⑤ \$3

Take notes

11

대화를 듣고, 두 사람이 가려는 장소를 고르시오.

① 아이스크림 가게
② 패스트푸드점
③ 도넛 가게
④ 편의점
⑤ 백화점

12

대화를 듣고, 남자의 심정으로 가장 알맞은 것을 고르시오.

① 흥미로운
② 짜증난
③ 안심한
④ 우울한
⑤ 즐거운

13

다음을 듣고, 한국의 식사 예절과 일치하지 않는 것을 고르시오.

① 밥그릇을 한 손에 들고 먹는다.
② 음식을 먹으면서 말을 하지 않는다.
③ 식사 중 탁자 위에 손을 올려놓지 않는다.
④ 어른들과 식사 시 먼저 자리를 뜨지 않는다.
⑤ 어른이 먼저 식사를 시작하면 식사를 시작한다.

14

대화를 듣고, 여자가 들려줄 속담으로 알맞은 것을 고르시오.

① Every dog has its day.
② Practice makes perfect.
③ A stitch in time saves nine.
④ The early bird catches the worm.
⑤ Don't put all your eggs in one basket.

15

대화를 듣고, 남자에게 필요한 것을 고르시오.

① 인내심
② 독립심
③ 근면성
④ 이해심
⑤ 성실성

16 다음을 듣고, 두 사람의 대화가 어색한 것을 고르시오.

① ② ③ ④ ⑤

17 대화를 듣고, 이어지는 질문에 가장 알맞은 답을 고르시오.

① soldier ② poet ③ reporter
④ magician ⑤ programmer

18 대화를 듣고, 여자가 남자에게 전화를 건 목적을 고르시오.

① 복사기를 구입하려고
② 복사기를 반품하려고
③ 복사기를 환불받으려고
④ 복사기 사용법을 알려 달라고
⑤ 복사기가 고장 나서 수리해 달라고

19-20 대화를 듣고, 남자의 마지막 말에 이어질 여자의 응답으로 알맞은 것을 고르시오.

19
① Yes, she lives alone.
② My father often visits her, too.
③ Yes, it's just a ten-minute walk.
④ My grandmother doesn't remember you.
⑤ I don't have to buy anything for her today.

20
① I'm not good at drawing pictures.
② Drawing a picture is my hobby.
③ I didn't draw pigeons, too.
④ Where did you get the bird?
⑤ It's terrific.

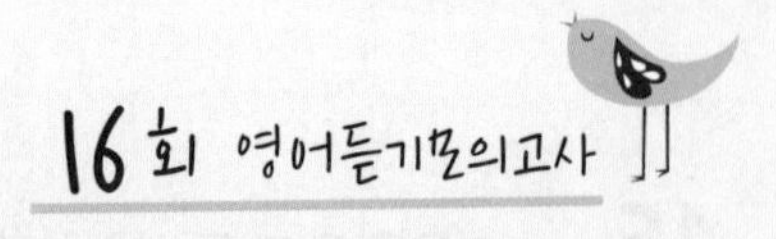

1

W All these people are my friends from elementary school.

M So which one is Susie? You're always __________ __________ __________. Is she the one standing by the window?

W No, that's Cathy. Susie is the one __________ __________ __________ __________.

M Oh, you mean the one __________ __________ __________ __________ and holding a cup?

W That's right.

2

W Excuse me, how can I get to City Hall?

M Sorry, I __________ __________ __________. Oh, there is a subway map over there.

W It says I should take the subway here and __________ __________ at Central Station, right?

M Yes, but you __________ __________ __________ to line number four there.

W Oh, I see. Thank you.

3

M Hi, ticket please.

W Here you go.

M Thank you. __________ __________ __________. It's three dollars.

W __________ __________ __________.

M You have been here for three hours, right?

W Yes, but I have a one-hour __________ __________ __________.

M Sorry, I didn't see that. It's two dollars, then.

W Thank you.

4

W I didn't see you at school yesterday. __________ __________?

M I couldn't come because I had the flu, and today I just __________ __________ to get something from my English teacher.

W I see. So are you leaving now?

M Yes. And I won't be at school tomorrow, either.

W Why not?

M Because other students __________ __________ __________ __________ from me.

5

M Mom, I'm home.

W You __________ __________. What happened?

M Ryan keeps bothering me __________ __________ __________.

W Does he?

M I told him to stop, but he doesn't.

W Just __________ __________ __________ him, I'll talk to him.

6

W What kind of sports do you like, Johnny?

M I __________ __________ __________ with a ball.

W I see. Do you like bowling then, too?

M __________ __________. What about you?

W I like swimming and __________ __________ __________.

M I see.

7

W Dad, will you buy me a shirt?

M Sure, just __________ __________ __________ you like.

W Thank you.

M Which one do you like?

W I like the ones with an animal design.

M Then, __________ __________ __________. It has a cute puppy on it.

W I don't like it. I like the one __________ __________ __________.

M Then, try it on.

8

W Look at you. You are __________ __________.

M I know. I didn't expect the weather to be like this.

W That's __________ __________ __________, too. It was really sunny this morning.

M I know. I didn't see anyone with an umbrella today.

W Me, either.

M I'm going to __________ __________ __________.

9

W I __________ __________ __________ the game. Is it held on the 21st?

M No, it is __________ __________ on the 15th.

W __________ __________ I didn't know about that?

M I got an e-mail from George.

W I see. Is it on a Tuesday?

M No, __________ __________ a Thursday.

10

W There are __________ __________ __________ of public transportation in New York.

M What is __________ __________ __________ one?

W It is, of course, the subway.

M In Seoul, too. __________ __________ __________?

W It used to be two dollars, but they raised it by 50% this year.

11

W There is __________ __________ __________ ice cream on a hot day.

M You're right. What's your __________ __________?

W I like strawberry. What about you?

M Well, I like the fruit flavors.

W Now that we are talking about ice cream, I suddenly __________ __________ __________ some.

M OK. I will buy you one.

12

W What's wrong with you?

M I cough a lot, and sometimes I have a __________ __________ __________. I think there is a big problem in my lungs.

W These days a lot of people come to see me __________ __________ __________ __________. It's just an allergy to spring flowers.

M Oh, is that true? I was so worried.

W Don't worry. Take medicine, and you will __________ __________ __________.

13

M In Korea, there are a few things that you shouldn't do __________ __________ __________. First, you shouldn't start eating until the oldest person at the table begins eating. Second, you shouldn't talk with __________ __________ __________. Third, you shouldn't put your hand and arm on the table. Last, you never __________ __________ __________ before the oldest person finishes his or her meal.

14

W Ross, why don't you __________ __________? It's ten.

M Mom, it's Sunday. Let me __________ __________ __________.

W You know what? Jenny got up early, had breakfast, and even __________ __________ __________ with Dad.

M Just ten more minutes, please.

W If you don't get up now, we'll __________ __________ without you.

15

W Michael, can I give you a piece of advice?

M Sure, what is it?

W I think you __________, but you always __________ __________ someone else.

M I don't get it.

W If you have a __________ __________, you ask for help. If you fix that habit, you will succeed in anything you do.

M Thank you. I will __________ __________ __________ it.

16

① M Would you __________ __________
__________ __________?

W That's okay. I had enough.

② M The big boy hit the small boy.

W __________ __________ __________.

③ M I'm so upset about the English test.

W __________ __________ __________.
You'll do better next time.

④ M How did she open the door?

W She found the key in her car.

⑤ M What time do you have?

W It's a __________ __________
__________.

17

W What do you want to be __________
__________ __________, Chandler?

M Me? I want to be a soldier.

W What do you want to do __________
__________ __________?

M I want to drive a tank. How about you?

W I couldn't make much money if I weren't famous, but I want to write poetry.

M I know you are __________ __________
__________.

Q What does the man want to be?

18

[Telephone rings.]

W Hello, this is Christine.

M Hi, Christine. What can I do for you?

W Our copy machine __________ __________
__________ __________.

M What's wrong?

W I have no idea. Can you __________
__________ here and take a look at it?

M Sure. I'll be there in ten minutes.

W Please, hurry up. There are a lot of
__________ __________ __________
__________ the machine.

19

M Where are you going?

W I'm going to visit my grandmother.

M I __________ __________ her at the grocery store last month.

W Yeah, she told me that she saw you there, too.

M Does she __________ __________
__________?

W Yes, it's just __________ __________
__________.

20

W Did you __________ __________?

M Yes, I did.

W What are you __________ __________
__________ in this picture?

M Peace.

W I see. __________ __________ you drew many pigeons.

M What do you think of my picture?

W It's terrific.

1회 실전모의고사

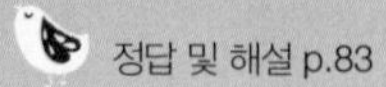
정답 및 해설 p.83

01 다음을 듣고, 그림을 가장 적절하게 묘사한 것을 고르시오.

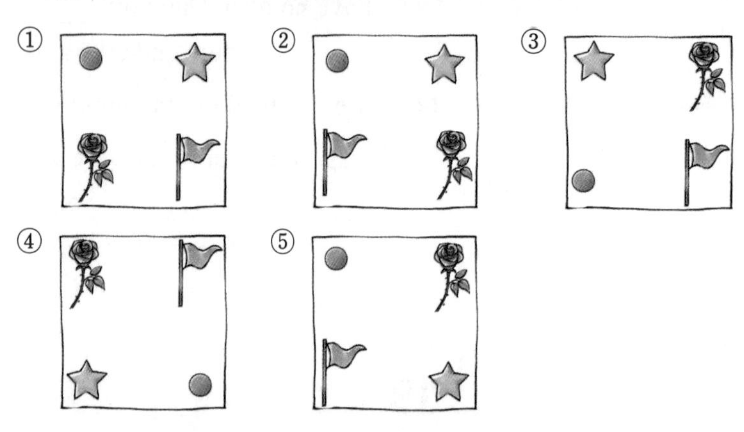

02 대화를 듣고, 남자가 이사할 날짜를 고르시오.

① 20일 수요일
② 21일 수요일
③ 22일 수요일
④ 23일 토요일
⑤ 24일 토요일

03 대화를 듣고, 남자가 가려고 하는 장소를 고르시오.

① 병원
② 약국
③ 지하철역
④ 세탁소
⑤ 옷가게

04 대화를 듣고, Scott이 태어난 국가를 고르시오.

① 미국
② 영국
③ 호주
④ 프랑스
⑤ 멕시코

05 대화를 듣고, 여자가 지불해야 하는 금액을 고르시오.

① $14 ② $15 ③ $16 ④ $18 ⑤ $20

06

대화를 듣고, 강에서 수영을 할 수 <u>없는</u> 이유를 고르시오.

① 깊어서
② 오염되어서
③ 물살이 빨라서
④ 시에서 금지해서
⑤ 자연보호 구역이라서

07

다음을 듣고, 무엇에 관한 설명인지 고르시오.

① 쥐
② 곰
③ 박쥐
④ 다람쥐
⑤ 두더지

08

대화를 듣고, 여자가 한 마지막 말의 의도를 고르시오.

① 충고 ② 제안 ③ 격려 ④ 책망 ⑤ 위로

09

대화를 듣고, 여자가 찾는 곳을 고르시오.

10

대화를 듣고, 내용과 가장 관련 있는 속담을 고르시오.

① Seeing is believing.
② Still waters run deep.
③ Two heads are better than one.
④ Too many cooks spoil the broth.
⑤ When in Rome, do as the Romans do.

11

대화를 듣고, 남자의 심정으로 가장 알맞은 것을 고르시오.

① 슬픈 ② 초조한 ③ 황당한
④ 반가운 ⑤ 안심한

12

다음을 듣고, 내용과 일치하지 않는 것을 고르시오.

① 나는 캐나다에서 일 년 동안 살았다.
② 나는 캐나다에서 많은 곳을 여행했다.
③ 나는 세계가 얼마나 넓은지 깨달았다.
④ 나는 캐나다에서 많은 사람을 만났다.
⑤ 나는 캐나다에서 영어 공부를 열심히 했다.

13

다음을 듣고, 표의 내용과 일치하는 것을 고르시오.

OPERA HOUSE	
Monday	Closed
Tuesday & Friday	From 10 a.m. to 8 p.m.
Wednesday & Thursday	From 10 a.m. to 7 p.m.
Saturday & Sunday	From 9 a.m. to 9 p.m.

① ② ③ ④ ⑤

14

대화를 듣고, 두 사람이 만날 시각을 고르시오.

① 5:40 ② 5:50 ③ 6:10 ④ 6:50 ⑤ 7:00

15

대화를 듣고, 이어지는 질문에 가장 알맞은 답을 고르시오.

① on foot ② by subway ③ by bus
④ by train ⑤ by car

16

대화를 듣고, 두 사람의 관계로 가장 알맞은 것을 고르시오.

① doctor – patient
② student – teacher
③ father – son
④ police – driver
⑤ photographer – customer

17

다음을 듣고, 두 사람의 대화가 어색한 것을 고르시오.

① ② ③ ④ ⑤

18

대화를 듣고, 다음 중 알 수 없는 것을 고르시오.

① 지난주에 박물관이 매우 붐볐다.
② Sam은 지난주에 박물관에 다녀왔다.
③ 전철이 박물관에 가는 가장 빠른 방법이다.
④ 여자는 다른 두 아이와 함께 박물관에 가려고 한다.
⑤ Jessica의 엄마가 여자를 박물관까지 데려다 줄 것이다.

19-20 대화를 듣고, 여자의 마지막 말에 이어질 남자의 응답으로 알맞은 것을 고르시오.

19

① That's a pity!
② I knew he would.
③ How wonderful!
④ I could go there alone.
⑤ What time was the party over?

20

① It's not mine, either.
② It's my pleasure.
③ Where did you find it?
④ I don't need any money.
⑤ I'm so happy to hear that.

2회 실전모의고사

정답 및 해설 p.88

01 다음을 듣고, 그림의 상황에 가장 알맞은 대화를 고르시오.

① ② ③ ④ ⑤

02 대화를 듣고, 여자의 직업으로 알맞은 것을 고르시오.

① clerk
② tour guide
③ waitress
④ history teacher
⑤ flight attendant

03 대화를 듣고, 남자가 집에 들어올 시각을 고르시오.

① 6:00 ② 6:30 ③ 7:00 ④ 7:30 ⑤ 8:00

04 대화를 듣고, 남자의 심정으로 가장 알맞은 것을 고르시오.

① 화난
② 슬픈
③ 고마운
④ 우울한
⑤ 즐거운

05 대화를 듣고, 남자가 문을 열지 못한 이유를 고르시오.

① 열쇠가 없어서
② 문이 고장 나서
③ 미닫이문이라서
④ 바깥쪽에서 누군가 당겨서
⑤ 양손에 짐을 들고 있어서

06

대화를 듣고, 두 사람이 대화하는 장소를 고르시오.

① 
② 
③ 
④ 
⑤ 

07

대화를 듣고, 남자의 고민을 고르시오.

① 성적이 부진해서
② 너무 할 일이 많아서
③ 여행 갈 돈이 없어서
④ 하는 일에 재능이 없어서
⑤ 친구와 사이가 좋지 않아서

08

다음을 듣고, 이 방송을 들을 수 있는 장소를 고르시오.

① 공항
② 배 안
③ 전철 안
④ 버스 안
⑤ 비행기 안

09

대화를 듣고, 내용과 일치하는 것을 고르시오.

① 비행기가 두 시간 연착될 것이다.
② 비행기의 원래 도착 시각은 5시였다.
③ 비행기 안에는 여자의 딸이 타고 있다.
④ 짙은 안개 날씨 때문에 연착이 되었다.
⑤ 남자는 큰 문제가 발생할 것으로 생각한다.

10

대화를 듣고, 여자의 성격을 고르시오.

① honest
② funny
③ curious
④ selfish
⑤ understanding

11

대화를 듣고, 두 사람이 사려는 거울을 고르시오.

①

②
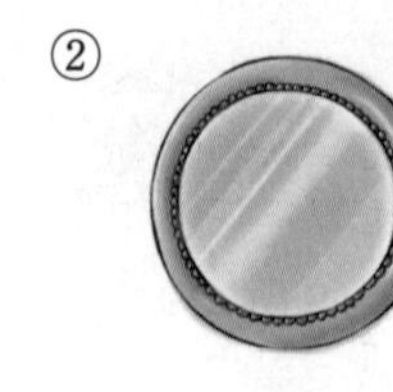
③

④

⑤

12

다음을 듣고, 버스 시간표의 내용과 일치하지 않는 것을 고르시오.

	Departure	Arrival
New York	7:00 a.m.	1:00 p.m.
New Jersey	8:00 a.m.	2:00 p.m.
Philadelphia	8:30 a.m.	7:00 p.m.
Washington D. C	9:00 a.m.	8:00 a.m.

① ② ③ ④ ⑤

13

대화를 듣고, 남자가 사려고 하는 신발 사이즈를 고르시오.

① 10 ② 10 1/2 ③ 11 ④ 11 1/2 ⑤ 12

14

대화를 듣고, 두 사람의 관계로 가장 알맞은 것을 고르시오.

① 작가 – 기자
② 고객 상담원 – 고객
③ 화가 – 모델
④ 진행자 – 게스트
⑤ 영화감독 – 영화배우

15

다음을 듣고, 두 사람의 대화가 어색한 것을 고르시오.

① ② ③ ④ ⑤

16

다음을 듣고, 무엇에 관한 설명인지 고르시오.

① a dairy ② a secret ③ a novel
④ a love letter ⑤ a school report

17

대화를 듣고, 여자가 남자에게 부탁하는 것을 고르시오.

① 운전을 배우려고 ② 돈을 빌리기 위해
③ 책을 빌리기 위해 ④ 은행에 데려다 달라고
⑤ 박물관에 같이 가자고

18

대화를 듣고, 내용과 가장 관련 있는 속담을 고르시오.

① No news good news.
② Better late than never.
③ Killing two birds with one stone.
④ A friend in need is a friend indeed.
⑤ Where there's a will, there's a way.

19-20 대화를 듣고, 남자의 마지막 말에 이어질 여자의 응답으로 알맞은 것을 고르시오.

19

① I miss him, too.
② He remembers you, too.
③ When is he arriving?
④ I'm going to the jewelry shop.
⑤ Please say hello to him for me.

20

① It's not a easy job to do.
② Sure, what can I do for you?
③ Sorry, I can't use them now.
④ That's fine with me. Go ahead.
⑤ That's OK. You can carry them all by yourself.

중학 영어듣기
한 방에 끝낸다

AFTER SCHOOL Listening

애프터스쿨
리스닝
level 2

정답 및 해설

NEXUS Edu

중학 영어듣기
한 방에 끝낸다

AFTER SCHOOL Listening

애프터스쿨 리스닝 level 2

정답 및 해설

NEXUS Edu

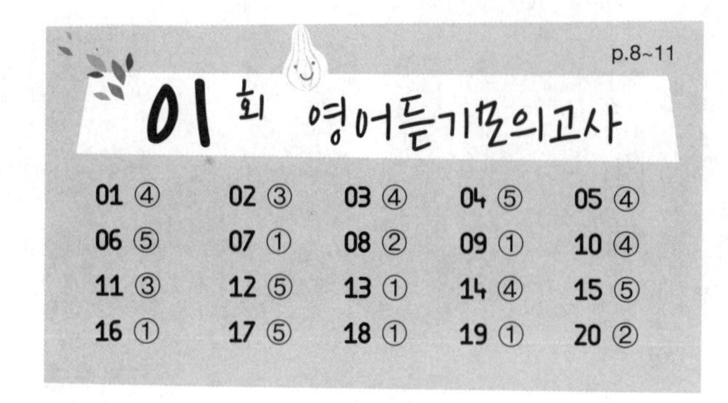

p.8~11

01회 영어듣기모의고사

01 ④	02 ③	03 ④	04 ⑤	05 ④
06 ⑤	07 ①	08 ②	09 ①	10 ④
11 ③	12 ⑤	13 ①	14 ④	15 ⑤
16 ①	17 ⑤	18 ①	19 ①	20 ②

01 ④

Script

W Excuse me, can you tell me how to get to the museum?

M Sure. It's right across from the bakery, next to the bank.

W I have a map here. Could you tell me again?

M Sure. Here is the bank. The museum is right beside the bank.

W Thank you.

해석

여 실례합니다. 제게 박물관에 가는 길 좀 알려 주시겠어요?

남 물론이죠. 박물관은 빵집 바로 건너편, 은행 옆에 있어요.

여 제게 지도가 있는데요. 다시 얘기해 주실래요?

남 네. 여기가 은행이고요. 박물관은 은행 바로 옆에 있어요.

여 감사합니다.

해설

It's right across from the bakery, next to the bank.라는 남자의 말을 통해 박물관은 빵집 맞은편, 은행 옆에 있음을 알 수 있다.

어휘

how to get 어떻게 가는지 / museum[mjuːzíːəm] 박물관 / right[rait] 바로 / across from ~의 맞은편에 (=opposite) / bakery[béikəri] 빵집, 제과점 / next to ~ 옆에 / beside[besàid] ~ 옆에

02 ③

Script

W You look so happy. What's going on with you?

M Dad will take my sister and me to Seaworld this Sunday.

W Wow! That's great.

M You know I like polar bears a lot. I will see them and enjoy the rides there as well.

W Good for you. Have fun!

해석

여 너 기분 정말 좋아 보여. 무슨 일이야?

남 아빠가 이번 주 일요일에 나와 여동생을 Seaworld에 데려가신다고 하셨어.

여 와! 좋겠다.

남 내가 북극곰을 정말 좋아하잖아. 거기서 북극곰도 보고, 놀이기구도 탈 거야.

여 좋겠다. 재미있게 놀다 와!

해설

남자는 이번 주말에 Seaworld에 가기 때문에 신이 나있다.

어휘

excited[iksáitid] 신이 난, 들뜬, 흥분한 / surprised[sərpráizd] 놀란, 놀라운 / bored[bɔːrd] 지루한 / polar bear 북극곰 / ride[raid] 탈 것, 놀이기구 / as well 게다가, ~도 / have fun 재미있게 놀다

03 ④

Script

W Stop! Don't run around here. It's very dangerous.

M Is it?

W Yes. It's very slippery. If you fall down, you will get hurt.

M I see. Can I go into the pool now?

W It's still break time. Wait five more minutes.

M Okay.

해석

여 멈춰! 여기서 뛰어다니지 마. 매우 위험해.

남 그래요?

여 그럼. 매우 미끄러워. 네가 넘어지면 다치게 될 거야.

남 알았어요. 지금 수영장에 들어가도 돼요?

여 아직 쉬는 시간이야. 5분 더 기다려야 해.

남 알았어요.

해설

Can I go into the pool now?라는 남자의 말과 slippery, break time 등과 같은 말을 통해 두 사람이 대화하는 장소가 수영장임을 알 수 있다.

어휘

dangerous[déindʒərəs] 위험한 / slippery[slípəri] 미끄러운 / fall down 넘어지다 / get hurt 다치다 / pool[puːl] 수영장 (= swimming pool) / still[stil] 여전히, 아직도 / break time 휴식 시간

04 ⑤

Script

W What time does the concert start?

M I think it starts in 30 minutes. Don't you have a ticket?

W Yes, I do.

M Why don't you read what is written on it? It says so.

W I see. (pause) It says it starts at three and it is three hours long.

M Yes, that's quite long.

해석

여 콘서트는 언제 시작하니?

남 내 생각에는 30분 후에 시작할 것 같아. 너 표 없니?

여 아니, 있어.

남 거기에 쓰여 있는 것을 읽어 보지 그러니? 그렇다고 쓰여 있어.

여 알았어. 3시에 시작하고 세 시간 길이라고 나와 있어.

남 응, 꽤 길다.

해설

콘서트는 3시에 시작하고, 세 시간 길이이므로 콘서트가 끝나는 시각은 6시이다.

어휘
concert[kɑ́nsə(:)rt] 콘서트, 음악회 / say[sei] ~이라고 쓰여 있다[나와 있다] / quite[kwait] 꽤, 상당히

05 ④

Script

M Here we are.

W Thank you, but would you just wait for a minute? My husband is going to be here soon, and we'll go to Hyde Park.

M No problem.

W Why don't you keep the meter running?

M OK. I will.

W By the way, how long have you driven a taxi?

M For nine years. I'm happy with my job.

해석

남 다 왔습니다.

여 고맙습니다. 그런데 여기서 잠깐 기다려 주시겠어요? 제 남편이 곧 여기 올 거고 저희는 Hyde Park로 가려고 하거든요.

남 알겠습니다.

여 미터기를 돌아가도록 내버려 두시겠어요?

남 네. 그러죠.

여 그런데 얼마나 오랫동안 택시를 운전하셨어요?

남 9년이요. 저는 제 직업에 만족합니다.

해설

how long have you driven a taxi?라는 여자의 말을 통해 남자의 직업이 택시기사임을 알 수 있다.

어휘
for a minute 잠깐 / husband[hʌ́zbənd] 남편 / meter[míːtər] 계량기, 미터 / run[rʌn] (기계가) 작동하다, 계속 움직이다 / by the way 그런데 (대화에서 화제를 바꿀 때 사용)

06 ⑤

Script

W What would you like to be in the future?

M I'm interested in science, so I'd like to be a scientist. How about you?

W I want to be an actress.

M You must be interested in movies, right?

W Yes. I usually see a movie twice a week.

M I guess you will be a great actress.

해석

여 너는 미래에 뭐가 되고 싶니?

남 나는 과학에 관심이 있어서 과학자가 되고 싶어. 너는?

여 나는 여배우가 되고 싶어.

남 너는 영화에 관심이 있겠구나, 그렇지?

여 응. 나는 보통 일주일에 두 번 정도 영화를 봐.

남 나는 네가 훌륭한 여배우가 될 거라고 생각해.

해설

I want to be an actress.라는 여자의 말을 통해 여자의 장래희망이 배우가 되는 것임을 알 수 있다.

어휘
would like to+동사원형 ~하고 싶다 / future[fjúːtʃər] 미래, 장래 / be interested in ~에 관심[흥미]이 있다 / scientist[sáiəntist] 과학자 / How about ~? ~는 어때? (상대방의 의향을 묻는 표현) / actress[ǽktris] 여배우 / twice[twais] 두 번 / guess[ges] 추측하다, ~라고 생각하다

07 ①

Script

M These are the seats on buses or subways. Young people don't usually sit there. These are for elderly people. Some young people sit there, but when an elderly person gets on, they get up and offer the seat to the person.

해석

남 이것들은 버스나 전철의 좌석입니다. 젊은이들이 보통 그곳에 앉지 않습니다. 이것들은 노인들을 위한 것입니다. 어떤 젊은이들은 그곳에 앉기도 하지만, 노인이 타면 일어나 그 자리를 노인에게 양보합니다.

해설

버스나 전철에 있고 노인들을 위한 좌석은 경로석이다.

어휘
seat[siːt] 좌석, 자리 / subway[sʌ́bwèi] 지하철 / young[jʌŋ] 젊은, 어린 / elderly[éldərli] 연세가 드신 / get on (~에) 타다 / get up 일어나다 / offer[ɔ́(:)fər] 권하다, 제공하다

08 ②

Script

M Did you do your homework?

W Yes, I have just finished it.

M Then, why don't you come over here and watch TV?

W What are you watching?

M I'm watching the news.

W My favorite drama is on now. Can I watch it?

M Why not?

해석

남 너 숙제 했니?

여 네, 방금 끝냈어요.

남 그러면, 여기 와서 TV를 보지 그러니?

여 지금 뭐 보고 계세요?

남 뉴스를 보고 있어.

여 지금 제가 좋아하는 드라마가 하고 있어요. 그거 봐도 돼요?

남 좋아.

해설

Why not?은 '좋아.', '왜 아니겠어?'라는 의미로 동의나 승낙을 나타내는 말이다.

어휘
do one's homework 숙제를 하다 / come over 오다 / favorite[féivərit]

매우 좋아하는 / drama[drɑ́:mə] (텔레비전, 극장 등에서 공연하는) 드라마[극] / be on (영화, TV 프로그램 등이) 방송[상영] 중이다 / Why not? (동의를 나타내어) 왜 아니겠어?, 좋아.

09 ①

Script

W I heard the game was more exciting than last year's. Did Jason win the game?

M No. Jason won the game last year, but not this time.

W How about Mike?

M He got second place. No one expected John to be the winner.

W He finally made it. I knew he would. He practiced hard every day.

해석

여 경기가 작년보다 더 흥미진진했다고 들었어. Jason이 경기에서 이겼니?

남 아니. 작년에 Jason이 우승했지만, 이번에는 아니야.

여 Mike니?

남 그는 2등을 했어. 아무도 John이 우승하리라고는 예상하지 못했어.

여 그가 마침내 해냈구나. 나는 그가 이길 거라는 걸 알고 있었어. 그는 매일 열심히 연습했거든.

해설

No one expected John to be the winner.라는 말을 통해 John이 경기에서 우승했다는 것을 알 수 있다.

어휘

exciting[iksáitiŋ] 신나는, 흥미진진한 / get second place 2등[준우승]을 하다 *cf.* get first place 1등[우승]을 하다 / expect[ikspékt] 예상하다, 기대하다 / winner[wínər] 우승자, 승자 / finally[fáinəli] 마침내, 결국 / practice[prǽktis] 연습하다

10 ④

Script

W ① Boarding is at eleven.

② Paul boards through gate thirty.

③ The seat number is 34H.

④ This flight leaves for Seoul.

⑤ GF12 is the airline and flight number.

해석

여 ① 탑승은 11시이다.

② Paul은 30번 탑승구를 통해 탑승한다.

③ 좌석 번호는 34H이다.

④ 이 비행기는 서울을 향하여 출발한다.

⑤ GF12는 항공사와 비행기 번호를 나타낸다.

해설

이 비행기는 서울에서 출발하는 도쿄행 비행기이다.

어휘

boarding[bɔ́:rdiŋ] 탑승, 승선 / boarding pass 탑승권 / flight[flait] 항공편, 편명 / date[deit] 날짜 / gate[geit] 대문, 문 (boarding gate 탑승구) / board[bɔ:rd] (비행기, 배, 기차 등에) 타다 / through[θru:] ~을 통해 / leave for ~을 향해 출발하다 / leave from ~에서 출발하다 / airline[ɛ́ərlàin] 항공사

11 ③

Script

M Where are you going?

W I'm going to the grocery store.

M For what?

W My mother told me to buy some vegetables like um… I wrote them down somewhere. I got it. Onions, carrots, potatoes, and spinach.

M You are a nice daughter.

해석

남 너 어디 가는 중이니?

여 나 식료품점에 가는 중이야.

남 왜?

여 엄마가 나에게 채소를 좀 사오라고 하셔서 음, 내가 어딘가에 써 놓았어. 찾았다. 양파, 당근, 감자, 그리고 시금치야.

남 넌 착한 딸이구나.

해설

여자가 식료품점에서 사야 하는 것은 양파, 당근, 감자, 시금치이다.

어휘

grocery store 슈퍼마켓, 식료품점 / For what? 왜?, 뭐 때문에? / vegetable[védʒətəbəl] 채소 / write down ~을 적다 / somewhere[sʌ́mhwὲər] 어딘가에 / onion[ʌ́njən] 양파 / carrot[kǽrət] 당근 / potato[pətéitou] 감자 / spinach[spínitʃ] 시금치 / daughter[dɔ́:tər] 딸

12 ⑤

Script

[Telephone rings.]

W Hello.

M Kathy, it's Richard.

W Hey, what's up?

M I have something to ask you. How come Susie never talks to me? She seems angry with me. Why?

W It's because you made fun of her in class.

M Really? I didn't know that.

해석

여 여보세요.

남 Kathy, 나 Richard야.

여 어, 웬일이니?

남 너에게 물어볼 게 있어. Susie가 왜 나와 얘기를 안 하니? 그 애가 나에게 화가 나 있는 것 같아. 왜?

여 그건 네가 수업 시간에 그 애를 놀렸기 때문이야.

남 정말이야? 나는 모르고 있었어.

해설

She seems angry with me. Why?라는 남자의 말을 통해 Susie가 왜 자신에게 화가 났는지 물어보려고 전화를 했음을 알 수 있다.

어휘
What's up? 무슨 일이야? / How come (주어+동사)? 왜~?, 어찌하여 ~? / seem[siːm] ~처럼 보이다 / make fun of ~을 놀리다 / in class 수업 중에

13 ①

Script

W How are you going to get to the flea market?

M I'm thinking of riding my bike.

W Isn't it too far from here? I think it will take at least an hour.

M Then, I will take the subway.

W But there is no subway going there.

M Then, I will just take the bus.

해석

여 너 벼룩시장에 어떻게 갈 거니?

남 자전거를 탈까 생각 중이야.

여 여기서 너무 멀지 않니? 내 생각에는 적어도 한 시간은 걸릴 것 같아.

남 그러면, 지하철 타고 갈래.

여 하지만, 거기 가는 지하철은 없어.

남 그러면, 그냥 버스를 타고 가야겠다.

해설

I will just take the bus.라는 남자의 마지막 말을 통해 남자가 이용하게 될 교통수단이 버스임을 알 수 있다.

어휘
flea market 벼룩시장 / ride a bike 자전거를 타다 / far[fɑːr] 멀리(에); 먼 / at least 적어도 / take the subway 지하철을 타다

14 ④

Script

W This is John's class. David was late for school today. Olivia is trying to open the window. Joshua is standing in front of the blackboard. He is as tall as our teacher. Jessica looks happy because our teacher praised her for good scores on the test. Jim looks sleepy.

해석

여 여기는 John의 교실입니다. David는 오늘 학교에 지각했습니다. Olivia는 창문을 열려고 하고 있습니다. Joshua는 칠판 앞에 서 있습니다. 그는 우리 선생님만큼 키가 큽니다. Jessica는 선생님이 그녀의 좋은 시험 성적을 칭찬했기 때문에 기분이 좋아 보입니다. Jim은 졸린 것 같습니다.

해설

Olivia는 창문을 닫으려고 하는 것이 아니라, 열려고 하고 있다.

어휘
late for school 학교에 지각한 / try to+동사원형 ~하려고 애쓰다 / stand[stænd] 서다 / in front of ~ 앞에 / blackboard[blǽkbɔ̀ːrd] 칠판 / as tall as ~ 만큼 키가 큰 / praise[preiz] 칭찬하다; 칭찬 / score[skɔːr] 점수, (성적의) 평점 / sleepy[slíːpi] 졸린, 졸음이 오는

15 ⑤

Script

W Let's go to the bookstore. I need to buy some books about India.

M OK. Why do you need books about India?

W Well, actually, I'm going to the bookstore to see some guy.

M Which guy?

W He works there as a part-timer, and he is really handsome.

해석

여 서점에 가자. 나 인도에 관한 책을 좀 사야 돼.

남 알았어. 왜 인도에 관한 책이 필요하니?

여 그게, 사실, 나 어떤 남자 애를 보러 그 서점에 가는 거야.

남 어떤 애?

여 거기서 시간제로 일하는 애인데 정말 잘생겼어.

해설

여자가 처음에는 인도에 관한 책을 하러 간다고 했지만, 나중에 어떤 남자를 보러 서점에 간다고 말하고 있다.

어휘
bookstore[búkstɔ̀ːr] 서점 / India[índiə] 인도 / actually[ǽktʃuəli] 사실 / some[sʌm] 〈단수명사와 함께〉 (분명히 알 수 없는 사람) 어떤 / part-timer[pɑ́ːrttáimər] 시간제 근무 직원 / handsome[hǽnsəm] 잘생긴, 미남의

16 ①

Script

W Ross, are you taller than your mother?

M Of course. I'm even taller than my father. But my elder brother is the tallest in my family.

W I think your sister is pretty tall for her age.

M That's right, but she is shorter than my mother.

W I see.

해석

여 Ross야, 너는 엄마보다 키가 크니?

남 당연하지. 난 우리 아빠보다도 키가 커. 하지만, 형이 우리 가족 중에 제일 키가 커.

여 너의 여동생도 나이에 비해서는 꽤 큰 것 같아.

남 맞아, 하지만 걔는 엄마보다 작아.

여 그렇구나.

해설

여동생, 엄마, 아빠, 나, 형의 순서로 키가 크다.

어휘
elder[éldər] 손위의, 연상의 / pretty[príti] 꽤, 대단히 / for one's age 나이에 비해서는

17 ⑤

Script

M Oh my god! Mom, it's already half past seven.

W You finally got up!

M Why didn't you wake me up?

W Don't you remember? I woke you up five different times already, but you didn't get up.

M If I'm late for school, it's all your fault.

해석

남 이런 세상에! 엄마, 벌써 일곱 시 반이잖아요.

여 네가 드디어 일어났구나!

남 왜 저를 깨우지 않으신 거예요?

여 기억 안 나니? 내가 너를 벌써 다섯 번이나 깨웠는데, 네가 일어나지 않은 거잖니.

남 내가 학교에 늦으면 다 엄마 탓이에요.

해설

① 누워서 떡 먹기.

② 옷이 날개다.

③ 겉을 보고 속을 판단하지 마라.

④ 선무당이 사람 잡는다.

남자는 자신이 잘못한 것을 오히려 엄마에게 화를 내고 있기 때문에 '방귀 뀐 놈이 성낸다(자기가 잘못하고 남에게 화를 낸다).'라는 속담, ⑤을 고른다.

어휘

already[ɔːlrédi] 벌써, 이미 / half[hæf] 반, 30분 / past[pæst] 지나서, 넘어서 / wake up ~을 깨우다, 일어나다 / remember[rimémbər] 기억하다 / different[dífərənt] 다른 / fault[fɔːlt] 잘못, 과오

18 ①

Script

① W Which club do you want to join?
M I had a really good time.

② W Why don't we take the bus here?
M Okay.

③ W Are you free this afternoon?
M I'm not sure. Why?

④ W What will you do after school?
M I'll go to the gym.

⑤ W Will you have some dessert?
M No, thanks. I'm full.

해석

① 여 너 어느 클럽에 가입하고 싶니?
남 정말 즐거운 시간을 보냈어.

② 여 우리 여기서 버스 탈래?
남 좋아.

③ 여 너 오늘 오후에 한가하니?
남 잘 모르겠어. 왜?

④ 여 방과 후에 뭐 할 거니?
남 체육관에 갈 거야.

⑤ 여 후식 좀 드시겠어요?
남 사양하겠습니다. 배가 불러서요.

해설

① 어떤 클럽에 가입할 것이지 묻는 질문에 알맞은 응답이 와야 한다.

어휘

club[klʌb] (특정 활동 · 스포츠를 위한) 클럽, 동호회 / join[dʒɔin] 가입하다, 참가하다 / free[friː] 한가한 / after school 방과 후 / gym[dʒim] 체육관 / dessert[dizə́ːrt] 후식 / full[fúl] 배가 부른

19 ①

Script

W Joey, can you lend me your digital camera?

M Dave borrowed it, and he hasn't returned it to me yet.

W Can you tell him that I need to borrow it?

M Sure. When do you need it by?

W As soon as possible.

해석

여 Joey야, 나에게 디지털 카메라 좀 빌려줄래?

남 Dave가 빌려갔는데 나에게 아직 안 돌려줬어.

여 그에게 내가 그것을 좀 빌려야 한다고 얘기해 줄래?

남 알았어. 언제까지 필요하니?

여 가능한 한 빨리.

해설

② 내일은 휴일이야.

③ 내일 그것을 가져올게.

④ 너의 충고 고마워.

⑤ Dave는 다음 주에 올 거야.

'언제까지 필요하니?'라는 시간을 묻는 질문이므로, 응답으로 시간이 나오는 것이 자연스럽다.

어휘

as soon as possible 가능한 한 빨리 / holiday[hálədèi] 휴일 / advice[ədváis] 충고, 조언 / lend[lend] 빌려주다 / borrow[bɔ́(ː)rou] 빌리다 / return[ritə́ːrn] 되돌려주다

20 ②

Script

W How are you doing?

M Not so good.

W You look down. What's wrong with you?

M Well, while I was writing a report on the computer, the power went out. I have to do it all over again because it wasn't saved.

W I'm sorry to hear that.

해석

여 어떻게 지내니?

남 별로 안 좋아.

여 너 기분이 안 좋아 보여. 무슨 일이니?

남 그게, 컴퓨터로 보고서를 쓰고 있는데 정전이 됐어. 그게 저장되지 않아

서 처음부터 완전히 다시 해야 해.

여 정말 안됐다.

해설

① 너 틀림없이 기쁘겠구나.

③ 그들은 에너지를 절약하려고 그렇게 했어.

④ 너는 그것을 어떻게 그렇게 빨리 끝냈니?

⑤ 너에게 다른 기회가 있을 거야.

숙제를 다시 해야 한다는 남자의 말에 남자를 위로하는 응답이 와야 한다.

어휘

save[seiv] 절약하다, 아끼다, 저장하다, 구하다 / energy[énərdʒi] 에너지 / chance[tʃæns] 기회, 행운 / down[daun] 의기소침한, 우울한 / power[páuər] 전력, 에너지 / go out (불 · 전기가) 나가다 / do all over again 처음부터 다시 하다

p.16~19

02회 영어듣기모의고사

01 ④	02 ①	03 ③	04 ⑤	05 ④
06 ⑤	07 ④	08 ①	09 ②	10 ⑤
11 ①	12 ③	13 ②	14 ①	15 ④
16 ②	17 ①	18 ⑤	19 ①	20 ①

01 ④

Script

W I came here with my uncle instead of my father.

M Where is he?

W He's over there. He is wearing a white shirt and has a mustache.

M Is he wearing glasses?

W No, he is next to the man wearing glasses.

해석

여 나는 여기 아빠 대신 삼촌과 함께 왔어.

남 그는 어디 계시니?

여 저기 계셔. 흰 셔츠를 입고 있고 콧수염이 있으셔.

남 안경을 쓰셨니?

여 아니, 안경 쓰신 분 옆에 계셔.

해설

여자의 삼촌은 흰 셔츠를 입고 콧수염이 있으며, 안경을 쓴 남자 옆에 있는 사람이다.

어휘

instead of ~ 대신에 / mustache[mʌ́stæʃ] 콧수염 *cf.* beard[biərd] 턱수염 / glasses[glǽsi:z] 안경

02 ①

Script

M Is it too early if we meet at seven?

W Yes, that's too early. I usually sleep late on Sundays.

M I usually get up at nine on weekends. But I think we should go to the amusement park early.

W What time does it open?

M Nine o'clock, but it takes an hour and a half to get there.

W OK. I will listen to you this time.

해석

남 우리 7시에 만나면 너무 이를까?

여 응, 너무 일러. 나는 보통 일요일에 늦잠을 자.

남 나도 주말에 보통 9시에 일어나. 하지만, 내일 놀이공원에 일찍 가야 할 것 같아.

여 놀이공원이 몇 시에 문을 여니?

남 9시야. 하지만, 거기 가는 데 한 시간 반이 걸려.

여 알았어. 이번에는 너의 말을 들을게.

해설

'아침 7시에 만나면 이를까?'라는 남자의 질문에 여자는 마지막에 남자의 말을 듣겠다고 말하고 있다.

어휘

sleep late 늦잠자다 / amusement[əmjú:zmənt] 재미, 오락, 놀이 / amusement park 놀이공원 / tomorrow[təmɔ́:rou] 내일

03 ③

Script

M How was your flight to London?

W It was fine.

M Your job must be tough. Because you work long hours standing in the airplane.

W Sometimes it is hard work, but I'm happy with my job.

M What makes you happy?

W I enjoy traveling to different countries and meeting lots of people.

해석

남 런던으로의 비행 어땠니?

여 좋았어.

남 틀림없이 네 일은 힘들 거야. 왜냐하면 너는 오랫동안 비행기에서 서서 일하잖아.

여 가끔 그게 힘든 일이긴 하지만, 나는 내 직업에 만족해.

남 뭐가 좋아?

여 난 다른 나라를 여행하고 많은 사람을 만나는 게 즐거워.

해설

비행기에서 오랫동안 서서 일하며 다른 나라를 여행하고 많은 사람을 만나는 직업은 승무원이다.

어휘

flight[flait] 비행, 비행기 여행 / fine[fain] 좋은, 만족할 만한 / tough[tʌf] 힘든, 고된 / sometimes[sʌ́mtàimz] 가끔, 이따금

04 ⑤

Script

M ① Cathy is going to see a movie.

② Mark is going to the baseball stadium.

③ Linda is going to the dance festival at six.

④ Cathy is going to meet someone at the box office at five.

⑤ Linda is going to meet someone at the main gate.

해석

남 ① Cathy는 영화를 볼 것이다.

② Mark는 야구장에 갈 것이다.

③ Linda는 6시에 댄스 축제에 갈 것이다.

④ Cathy는 5시에 매표소에서 누군가를 만날 것이다.

⑤ Linda는 정문에서 누군가를 만날 것이다.

해설

Linda는 6시에 정문이 아니라 Boston Hall에서 누군가를 만날 것이다.

어휘

festival[féstəvəl] 축제 / hall[hɔːl] 홀, 회관, 강당 / the movies 영화관 (=the cinema) / box office 매표소 / main gate 정문 / stadium[stéidiəm] 경기장

05 ④

Script

W Why did you come home so late, Bill?

M School finished late.

W Carrie came home early, and she even finished her homework. Did you stop by the Internet cafe again?

M Sorry, Mom. I was going to get home early, but....

W If you lie one more time, I will tell your father. You know what will happen next.

해석

여 너 왜 집에 늦게 들어왔니, Bill?

남 학교가 늦게 끝났어요.

여 Carrie는 집에 일찍 들어와서 숙제까지 다 했어. 또 피시방에 갔다 왔니?

남 죄송해요, 엄마. 집에 빨리 오려고 했는데…….

여 너 한 번만 더 거짓말하면 네 아빠한테 이를 거야. 그다음에 무슨 일이 일어나는지 너도 알지?

해설

엄마가 아들에게 다시 거짓말하면 아빠한테 이른다며 야단치고 있는 상황이다.

어휘

stop by 들르다 / Internet cafe 인터넷 카페, 피시방 / lie[lai] 거짓말을 하다

06 ⑤

Script

M I'd like to have a refund.

W Is something wrong?

M Actually, my mother bought this shirt for me, but I don't like the design.

W Then, why don't you look for something you like?

M I just did, but I didn't find anything.

해석

남 환불을 받고 싶어요.

여 무슨 문제가 있나요?

남 사실, 엄마가 저에게 이 셔츠를 사주셨는데 디자인이 맘에 안 들어서요.

여 그러시면, 마음에 드시는 걸 찾아보지 그러세요?

남 방금 찾아보았는데, 찾지 못하겠어요.

해설

셔츠의 디자인이 마음에 들지 않아 환불받고 싶어 하는 고객과 점원의 대화이다.

어휘

refund[ríːfʌnd/riːfʌ́nd] 환불; 환불하다 / have a refund 환불을 받다 / design[dizáin] 디자인

07 ④

Script

M I want to buy a regular computer with a big screen. How much do I need?

W A big screen costs 300 dollars, and a computer costs 500 dollars.

M That's a lot. How about a medium-sized screen?

W It's 200 dollars, and a small one is 150 dollars.

M Okay. I'll buy a computer with a medium-sized screen.

해석

남 대형 스크린과 일반 컴퓨터를 사고 싶어요. 돈이 얼마나 필요할까요?

여 대형 스크린은 300달러이고, 컴퓨터는 500달러입니다.

남 그렇게나 많이요. 중형 스크린은요?

여 그건 200달러이고, 소형은 150달러입니다.

남 알겠어요. 중형 스크린과 컴퓨터를 살게요.

해설

남자는 중형 스크린과 일반 컴퓨터를 살 것이다. 중형 스크린은 200달러이고 컴퓨터는 500달러이다.

어휘

regular[régjələr] 보통의, 평상시의, 일반적인 / screen[skriːn] 스크린, 화면 / cost[kɔːst] (값 · 비용이) ~들다[이다]; 값, 비용 / medium-sized 중형의, 보통형의

08 ①

Script

W You hear this in a place near a mountain or a big wall. When you yell out something, your voice goes forward and hits against a mountain or a big wall, and then comes back to you. This sounds very interesting and sometimes even makes you feel scared.

해석

여 당신은 이것을 산이나 큰 벽에 가까운 장소에서 들을 수 있습니다. 당

신이 뭔가를 외치면 당신의 목소리는 앞으로 나아가고, 산이나 큰 벽에 부딪혀서, 당신에게 되돌아갑니다. 이것은 매우 재미있게 들리지만, 때때로 무섭게 느껴지기도 합니다.

해설
무언가를 소리쳤을 때 그 소리가 물체에 부딪혀 그것을 다시 듣게 되는 것은 메아리이다.

어휘
echo[ékou] 메아리 / sound[saund] 소리 / gesture[dʒéstʃər] 동작 / near[niər] 가까운; 가까이에 / yell[jel] 고함치다, (큰 소리로) 외치다 / voice[vɔis] 목소리 / forward[fɔ́:rwərd] 앞에, 앞쪽으로 / against [əgénst] ~와 충돌하여, ~에 향하여 / scared[skɛərd] 무서워하는

09 ②

Script

M Are you looking for something?

W Do you sell diaries?

M Yes, there are many diaries here. How about this diary with hearts on it?

W No, I just want a black one.

M Okay, we have two types. You can buy one with or without a lock.

W I'll take the one with a lock.

해석

남 무엇을 찾고 계세요?

여 일기장 파나요?

남 네, 여기 일기장이 많이 있습니다. 하트가 그려진 이건 어떠세요?

여 아니요, 저는 그냥 검은색을 사고 싶어요.

남 알겠습니다. 두 가지 종류가 있습니다. 자물쇠가 있는 일기장과 자물쇠가 없는 일기장을 사실 수 있습니다.

여 자물쇠가 있는 것으로 살게요.

해설
여자는 자물쇠가 달린 검은색 일기장을 사려고 하고 있다.

어휘
diary[dáiəri] 일기장 / type[taip] 형태, 종류 / lock[lɑk] 자물쇠 / one ~, the other… 하나는 ~, 나머지 다른 하나는…

10 ⑤

Script

W John, can I give you a piece of advice?

M What is it?

W Why don't you be more careful? You made the same mistake again this morning.

M I tried not to, but....

W I know, but you should try harder.

해석

여 John, 내가 너에게 충고 하나 해도 되니?

남 뭔데?

여 좀 더 주의를 기울이지 그러니? 너 오늘 아침에도 똑같은 실수를 반복했잖아.

남 안 그러려고 했는데…….

여 알아, 하지만 더 열심히 노력해야 해.

해설
여자는 남자에게 똑같은 실수를 반복하고 있다며 좀 더 주위를 기울이라고 충고하고 있다.

어휘
a piece of advice 한마디 충고 / careful[kɛ́ərfəl] 주의 깊은, 조심성 있는 / make a mistake 실수를 하다 / again[əgén] 다시, 또

11 ①

Script

W I'm going camping this weekend.

M That sounds like fun.

W I usually have a violin lesson on Saturdays, but I canceled it to go camping. How about you?

M Well, on weekends I usually play tennis with my brothers.

W I see. But you're going to join me this weekend, right?

M Of course, just tell me what I have to bring.

해석

여 나 이번 주말에 캠핑 갈 거야.

남 재미있겠다.

여 나는 토요일에 보통 바이올린 레슨이 있는데 캠핑하러 가려고 그것을 취소했어. 너는 뭐 할 거니?

남 음, 주말에는 주로 형들과 테니스를 쳐.

여 그렇구나. 하지만, 이번 주말에는 나와 함께 갈 거지, 그렇지?

남 물론이지, 내가 뭘 가져가야 하는지 말만 해.

해설
자신과 함께 캠핑하러 갈 거냐는 여자의 질문에 남자는 Of course라고 응답하고 있기 때문에 남자가 주말에 여자와 함께 캠핑하러 갈 것임을 알 수 있다.

어휘
go camping 캠핑하러 가다 / lesson[lésn] 교습, 레슨 / cancel[kǽnsəl] 취소하다

12 ③

Script

M How many hours in a day do you play computer games?

W I don't play computer games. I think it's a waste of time.

M Really? I spend too much time playing computer games these days. I even went to bed at around one o'clock last night.

W Did you stay up until one playing computer games? Why don't you play less?

M I've tried, but it's not easy.

해석

남 너는 하루에 컴퓨터 게임을 몇 시간 동안 하니?

여 난 컴퓨터 게임 안 해. 시간 낭비라고 생각하거든.

남 정말? 나는 요즘 컴퓨터 게임을 하느라 너무 많은 시간을 보내. 심지어 어젯밤엔 1시쯤에 잤어.

여 컴퓨터 하느라고 1시까지 깨어 있었다고? 게임을 좀 덜 하는 게 어때?
남 그렇게 하려고 해 봤는데, 쉽지 않아.

해설

I spend too much time playing computer games.라는 남자의 말에서 남자의 고민이 게임 중독임을 알 수 있다.

어휘

waste[weist] 낭비; 낭비하다 / these days 요즘 / stay up 자지 않고 있다 / less[les] 보다 적게

13 ②

Script

M Where are you going?

W I'm going to the hospital near the park.

M Are you visiting someone?

W No, I work there doing simple jobs like holding patients and cleaning things.

M You mean you have a part-time job?

W No, it is volunteer work. I just go there twice a week.

해석

남 너 어디 가니?
여 공원 근처에 있는 병원에 가는 중이야.
남 누구를 방문하는 거니?
여 아니, 나는 거기에서 환자 부축하기, 청소하기 같은 단순한 일을 해.
남 아르바이트를 한다는 말이야?
여 아니, 자원 봉사야. 난 일주일에 두 번 그곳에 가.

해설

No, it is volunteer work.라는 여자의 말을 통해 병원에서 자원 봉사를 하고 있다는 것을 알 수 있다.

어휘

simple[símpəl] 단순한, 간단한 / hold[hould] (손, 팔 등으로) 받치고[들고] 있다 / patient[péiʃənt] 환자 / part-time job 시간제 일[아르바이트] / volunteer work 자원 봉사

14 ①

Script

W Attention Shoppers! We are having a year-end sale from December 26th to December 31st. Everything is on sale for 50% off. So don't miss out on this chance. We open at 8 in the morning and don't close until 10 p.m. We also have the largest parking lot in town.

해석

여 고객 여러분, 안내 말씀드리겠습니다! 저희는 12월 26일부터 12월 31일까지 연말 특별 세일을 합니다. 모든 것을 50% 할인합니다. 그러니 이번 기회를 놓치지 마십시오. 저희는 오전 8시에 개장하고 오후 10시까지 문을 닫지 않습니다. 저희는 또한 마을에서 가장 큰 주차장을 가지고 있습니다.

해설

아침 8시에 개장하고 오후 10까지 문을 닫지 않는다고 했으므로 영업시간은 12시간이 아니라 14시간이다.

어휘

attention[əténʃən] 주의 / shopper[ʃápər] 물건을 사는 사람, 고객 / year-end[jiərend] 연말; 연말의 / sale[sei] 세일, 판매 / be on sale 세일 중이다 / miss out on (기회를) 놓치다 / parking lot 주차장

15 ④

Script

M Did you bring everything?

W Sure. I brought some rice, a flashlight, a tent, and a small pillow.

M OK. I brought some fruits and vegetables.

W Did you bring your own tent?

M Sure. It's in the bag.

해석

남 너 모든 물건을 가져 왔니?
여 당연하지. 쌀, 손전등, 텐트 그리고 작은 베개를 가져 왔어.
남 그렇구나. 나는 과일하고 채소를 가져 왔어.
여 네가 쓸 텐트도 가져 왔니?
남 물론이야, 가방에 있어.

해설

I brought some rice, a flashlight, a tent, and a small pillow.라는 여자의 말을 통해 여자가 쌀, 손전등, 텐트, 작은 베개를 가져 왔다는 것을 알 수 있다.

어휘

rice[rais] 쌀 / flashlight[flǽʃlàit] 손전등 / tent[tent] 텐트 / pillow[pílou] 베개 / own[oun] 자기 소유의, 자기 자신의; 소유하다

16 ②

Script

① M How did you solve the problem?
W My big brother helped me.

② M Why don't we clean the park?
W Because it is very dirty.

③ M I won first prize in the contest.
W Wow. Congratulations!

④ M Will you carry this bag?
W Okay, I will.

⑤ M Where have you been all day?
W I went to Ryan's house.

해석

① 남 너 그 문제를 어떻게 풀었니?
여 큰 오빠가 도와줬어.
② 남 우리 공원을 청소하는 게 어떨까?
여 왜냐하면 공원이 정말 더럽기 때문이야.
③ 남 나 대회에서 1등 했어.
여 와, 축하해!
④ 남 이 가방 좀 들어줄래?
여 알았어.
⑤ 남 너 온종일 어디 갔다 왔니?

여 Ryan네 집에 갔다 왔어요.

해설

② Why don't we ~?는 '~게 어때?'라는 의미로 권유를 나타낸다.

어휘

solve[salv] 풀다, 해결하다 / problem[prábləm] 문제 / dirty[də́ːrti] 더러운, 불결한 / win first prize 일등상을 타다 / congratulation[kəngrӕtʃəléiʃən] 축하

17 ①

M My father always tells me not to waste anything. After he washes himself, he uses the water for flushing the toilet. He still wears the clothes he bought ten years ago. He wants me to gather bottles and paper for recycling. I really respect my father and try to follow his ways.

해석

남 우리 아버지는 항상 저에게 어떤 것도 낭비하지 말라고 말씀하십니다. 우리 아버지는 씻으신 다음 그 물을 변기 물을 내리는 데 사용하십니다. 그는 아직도 10년 전에 산 옷을 입습니다. 그는 재활용을 위해 제가 병이나 종이를 모으기를 원하십니다. 저는 정말 제 아버지를 존경하며 그의 방식을 따르려고 노력합니다.

해설

씻은 다음 그 물을 변기 물을 내리는 데 사용하기, 10년 전에 산 옷 입기, 병이나 종이 모으기는 절약에 해당하는 내용이다.

어휘

wash oneself 얼굴[몸]을 씻다 / flush[flʌʃ] (변기 등을) 씻어 내리다 / toilet[tɔ́ilit] 화장실, 변기 / gather[gǽðər] 모으다 / bottle[bátl] 병 / recycling[riːsáikəliŋ] 재활용 / respect[rispékt] 존경하다; 존경 / follow[fálou] 따르다

18 ⑤

Script

M How is your knee now?

W It's OK. I don't feel pain any more.

M That's good. Did you go see a doctor?

W No, I felt pain because I weighed too much, so I started walking a lot. Now it's gone.

M Wow, you have slimmed down.

W Yeah. I lost a lot of weight, maybe ten kilograms.

해석

남 지금은 무릎이 좀 어떠니?

여 괜찮아. 통증은 더 이상 없어.

남 잘됐어. 병원에 갔었니?

여 아니, 체중이 너무 많이 나가서 통증이 있었던 거라 많이 걷기 시작했어. 지금은 통증이 사라졌어.

남 와, 너 살 빠졌구나.

여 그래. 살이 많이 빠졌어, 아마 10킬로그램 정도.

해설

① 벽에도 귀가 있다. (낮말은 새가 듣고 밤말은 쥐가 듣는다.)

② 나쁜 소식은 빨리 퍼진다.

③ 부전자전.

④ 아니 땐 굴뚝에서 연기 날까.

걷기를 통해 무릎 통증도 사라지고 살도 빠졌으므로 한 가지 일을 해서 두 가지 이익을 본 경우이다. 따라서 일석이조라는 의미의 속담 ⑤을 고른다.

어휘

knee[niː] 무릎 / pain[pein] 아픔, 통증 / not ~ any more 더 이상 ~이 아닌 / go see a doctor 진찰을 받다, 병원에 가다 / weigh[wei] 무게가 ~이다[나가다] / slim down 날씬해지다 / lose weight 살이 빠지다, 체중이 줄다

19 ①

Script

M I did so poorly on the test. How about you?

W I did better than before, but still low.

M I see. I'm going to study math for one hour every day.

W Why?

M Because I'm especially bad at it.

W That's a good idea.

해석

남 나 시험을 엉망으로 봤어. 너는?

여 전보다는 잘 봤는데, 아직도 점수가 낮아.

남 그렇구나. 나는 매일 한 시간씩 수학공부를 하려고 해.

여 왜?

남 내가 특히 그 과목에 취약하기 때문이야.

여 그거 좋은 생각이야.

해설

② 미안한데, 나는 그렇게 할 수 없어.

③ 우리 엄마는 내 말에 동의하지 않으실 거야.

④ 알았어, 먼저 네 교과서를 가져와.

⑤ 그것에 대해서 우리 엄마에게 말하지 마.

매일 한 시간씩 수학을 공부하기로 했다는 남자의 계획을 격려하는 응답이 와야 한다.

어휘

agree[əgríː] 동의하다, 찬성하다 / textbook[tékstbùk] 교과서 / poorly[púərli] 부족하게, 서투르게 / low[lou] 낮은 / especially[ispéʃəli] 특히, 특별히

20 ①

Script

M How long will you stay here for?

W Two weeks.

M Okay. Is the boy behind you your son?

W Yes, he is.

M What's the reason for your trip?

W To visit my aunt.

해석

남 얼마 동안이나 여기에 머무르실 겁니까?

여 2주 동안이요.

남 알겠습니다. 당신 뒤에 있는 아이가 당신의 아들입니까?
여 네, 맞아요.
남 여행의 이유는 무엇입니까?
여 이모를 방문하려고요.

해설

② 제발, 제가 좀 바빠서요.
③ 여기 제 여권입니다.
④ 감사합니다. 즐거운 여행 되세요.
⑤ 제가 여기 제 아들을 잠깐 맡기겠습니다.
여행의 이유를 묻는 질문으로 그에 알맞은 응답이 와야 한다.

어휘

aunt[ænt] 이모, 고모 / be in a hurry 서두르다 / passport[pǽspɔ̀ːrt] 여권 / trip[trip] 여행 / leave[liːv] (~을 사람에게, 장소에) 맡기다, 위탁하다 / for a moment 잠깐 동안 / behind[biháind] ~ 뒤에 / reason[ríːzən] 이유

p.24~27

03회 영어듣기모의고사

01 ⑤	02 ③	03 ④	04 ②	05 ①
06 ④	07 ⑤	08 ②	09 ①	10 ③
11 ④	12 ③	13 ⑤	14 ①	15 ②
16 ③	17 ③	18 ②	19 ①	20 ⑤

01 ⑤

Script

W This is a picture my little daughter drew. It is a bit strange, but I decided to hang it on the wall. In the picture, there are two big stars, a small star between the two big stars, and a full moon a little above the small star.

해석

여 이것은 제 어린 딸이 그린 그림입니다. 그림이 조금 이상하긴 하지만 저는 그것을 벽에 걸기로 결심했습니다. 그림에는 두 개의 큰 별, 그 두 개의 큰 별 사이에 작은 별 하나, 그리고 그 작은 별 조금 위로 보름달이 있습니다.

해설

그림에는 두 개의 큰 별이 있고, 그 사이에 작은 별, 그 별 조금 위로 보름달이 그려져 있다.

어휘

picture[píktʃər] 그림, 사진 / draw[drɔː] 그리다 / strange[streindʒ] 이상한 / decide to+동사원형 ~하기로 결정하다 / hang[hæŋ] 걸다, 매달다 / wall[wɔːl] 벽 / between[bitwíːn] ~ 사이에 / full moon 보름달 / above[əbʌ́v] 위에

02 ③

Script

W It's time to leave.
M Already?
W Yes, it's 5 o'clock.
M Let's have something to eat. I'm hungry.
W I'm OK. You go ahead, but make it fast. We only have 20 minutes. If we miss this train, the next one isn't for another two hours.
M OK. I'll be back in 10 minutes.

해석

여 출발해야 할 시간이야.
남 벌써?
여 응, 다섯 시야.
남 뭘 좀 먹자. 나 배고파.
여 난 괜찮아. 너는 가서 먹고 와. 하지만, 빨리 먹어야 해. 20분밖에 안 남았어. 이 기차를 놓치면 다음 기차가 2시간 동안 없거든.
남 알았어. 10분 안에 돌아올게.

해설

현재 5시로 기차가 출발하려면 20분 남았다는 여자의 말을 통해 기차가 5시 20분에 출발할 것임을 유추할 수 있다.

어휘

go ahead 어서 ~하다 / miss[mis] 놓치다

03 ④

Script

M Do you remember what our teacher told us to bring tomorrow?
W I wrote it down here. Let me see. I need scissors, a ruler, and a compass.
M What about me?
W Um, you need some drawing paper and a brush.
M OK. I left some drawing paper in my locker at school, so I only need one thing.

해석

남 선생님이 내일 뭐 가지고 오라고 했는지 기억나?
여 여기 적어 놓았어. 보자. 나는 가위, 자, 그리고 컴퍼스가 필요해.
남 나는?
여 음, 너는 도화지하고 붓이 필요해.
남 알았어. 학교에 있는 내 사물함에 도화지를 두었으니까 한 가지만 있으면 되겠다.

해설

남자의 준비물은 도화지와 붓으로, 도화지는 학교 사물함에 있다고 했으므로 붓만 가져가면 된다.

어휘

scissors[sízərz] 가위 / ruler[rúːlər] 자 / compass[kʌ́mpəs] 컴퍼스 / drawing paper 도화지 / brush[brʌʃ] 붓 / locker[lɑ́kər] 사물함

04 ②

Script

W When do we get off?

M We have two more stops.

W Are you sure?

M Don't worry. I've been there before.

W You told me the same thing when we went to the museum, but we got lost.

M Believe me this time.

해석

여 우리는 언제 내리니?

남 두 정거장만 가면 돼.

여 확실하니?

남 걱정하지 마. 전에 거기 가 본 적 있어.

여 너 박물관에 갔을 때도 나에게 같은 말을 했지만, 우리 길을 잃었잖아.

남 이번에는 나를 믿어 봐.

해설

We have two more stops.라는 남자의 말에서 두 사람이 대화하는 장소가 버스 안임을 유추할 수 있다.

어휘

get off (차, 말, 버스 등에서) 내리다 / stop[stɑp] 정거장, 정류장; 멈추다 / get lost 길을 잃다

05 ①

Script

W What's your hobby, David?

M I like all kinds of sports, especially basketball and bowling.

W Now I see why you are so strong and healthy.

M Thank you. What about you?

W I like reading books, especially ones on history.

M I like reading, too, and I usually read books on nature and space.

해석

여 너는 취미가 뭐니, David?

남 나는 모든 운동, 특히 농구와 볼링을 좋아해.

여 네가 왜 그렇게 튼튼하고 건강한지 이제 알겠다.

남 고마워. 너는?

여 나는 책, 특히 역사에 관한 책을 읽는 것을 좋아해.

남 나도 책 읽는 것을 좋아하는데 주로 자연이나 우주에 관한 책을 읽어.

해설

여자는 책 특히, 역사에 관한 책을 좋아한다고 말하고 있다.

어휘

hobby[hɑ́bi] 취미 / kind[kaind] 종류 / bowling[bóuliŋ] 볼링 / strong[strɔ(:)ŋ] 튼튼한, 강한, 힘 센 / healthy[hélθi] 건강한 / history[hístəri] 역사 / nature[néitʃər] 자연 / space[speis] 우주

06 ④

Script

W The price tag says it's ten dollars, but can you give me a discount?

M I'm sorry, but I can't.

W But you always give me ten percent off.

M I know, but not on this. Instead, I will give you this for free. It's worth two dollars.

W Really? Thanks.

해석

여 가격표에는 10달러라고 쓰여 있는데, 깎아주세요.

남 죄송하지만, 안 됩니다.

여 하지만, 저에게 항상 10% 할인해 주시잖아요.

남 알고 있습니다. 하지만, 이건 안 됩니다. 대신 이것을 무료로 드리죠. 그건 2달러짜리에요.

여 정말이요? 고맙습니다.

해설

여자는 2달러짜리 물건을 무료로 받고, 사려는 물건의 할인은 받지 못했으므로 10달러를 모두 지불해야 한다.

어휘

price[prais] 가격 / tag[tæg] 꼬리표, 가격표 / give a discount 할인해주다 / instead[instéd] 대신에 / for free 무료로, 공짜로 / worth[wəːr] ~의 가치가 있는

07 ⑤

Script

W ① There is a vase on the table.

② A lamp is next to the vase.

③ There is a teddy bear on the bed.

④ The cat is sleeping under the chair.

⑤ A bookcase is between the table and the bed.

해석

여 ① 탁자 위에 꽃병이 있다.

② 전등은 꽃병 옆에 있다.

③ 침대 위에 곰인형이 있다.

④ 고양이가 의자 아래서 잠을 자고 있다.

⑤ 탁자와 침대 사이에 책꽂이가 있다.

해설

책꽂이는 탁자 뒤에 있기 때문에 ⑤은 A bookcase is behind the table.이 되어야 한다.

어휘

vase[veis] 꽃병 / lamp[læmp] 전등 / under[ʌ́ndər] ~의 아래 / bookcase[búkkèis] 책꽂이, 책장

08 ②

Script

W This is something that holds things together. If

something breaks, you can put it back together by using this. People usually use this for small things like a broken vase or a broken piece of plastic. Some people also use this to put something on the wall.

해석

여 이것은 물건을 붙여주는 것입니다. 어떤 것이 부러지면 여러분은 이것을 사용하여 그것을 다시 붙일 수 있습니다. 사람들은 주로 깨진 꽃병이나 부서진 플라스틱 조각과 같은 작은 것에 이것을 사용합니다. 어떤 사람들은 벽에 무언가를 붙일 때 이것을 사용하기도 합니다.

해설

깨진 꽃병이나 부서진 플라스틱 조각과 같은 것을 붙이는 것은 접착제이다.

어휘

nail[neil] 못 / glue[gluː] 접착제, 풀 / stapler[stéiplər] 스테이플러 / hammer[hǽmər] 망치 / hold together 결합하다, 단결하다, 뭉치다 / put together 조립하다, 합하다 / broken[bróukən] 깨진, 부러진 / piece[piːs] 조각, 단편 / plastic[plǽstik] 플라스틱 제품; 플라스틱의

09 ①

Script

W Hello, Jamie. This is Ashley from downstairs.

M Oh, hi, Ashley. What's up?

W I have a favor to ask you.

M Go ahead.

W I'm studying for a math test, so I'd like you to keep the noise down, please.

M Sorry for bothering you.

해석

여 안녕, Jamie. 나 아래층에 사는 Ashely야.

남 아, 안녕, Ashely. 무슨 일이니?

여 부탁할 게 한 가지 있어.

남 얘기해 봐.

여 수학 시험 때문에 공부하고 있는데 네가 좀 조용히 해줬으면 해.

남 신경 쓰이게 해서 미안해.

해설

I'm studying for a math test, so I'd like you to keep the noise down이라는 여자의 말에서 여자가 남자에게 조용히 해 달라고 부탁하고 있음을 알 수 있다.

어휘

downstairs[dáunstέərz] 아래층에서, 아래층으로 / favor[féivər] 부탁 / noise[nɔiz] 소음 / keep the noise down 조용히 하다 / bother[báðər] 신경 쓰이게 하다, 괴롭히다

10 ③

Script

W Hello, how can I help you?

M I'll have two cheeseburgers with french fries and a salad.

W What would you like to drink?

M A coke without ice and a vanilla milkshake, please.

W Anything else?

M That's all.

W For here or to go?

M Here, please.

해석

여 안녕하세요, 무엇을 도와드릴까요?

남 감자튀김 샐러드 하나, 그리고 치즈버거 두 개 주세요.

여 마실 건 무엇을 드릴까요?

남 얼음을 뺀 콜라 하나와 바닐라 밀크셰이크 하나요.

여 다른 건 없으신가요?

남 그게 전부입니다.

여 드시고 가실 건가요, 아니면 가지고 가실 건가요?

남 먹고 갈 겁니다.

해설

남자는 치즈버거 두 개, 감자튀김, 샐러드, 콜라, 그리고 바닐라 밀크셰이크를 주문했다.

어휘

cheeseburger[tʃíːzbə̀ːrgər] 치즈버거 / frech fries 프렌치프라이(감자튀김) / coke[kouk] 콜라 / vanilla[vənílə] 바닐라 / milkshake 밀크셰이크 / to go (식당에서) 가져가기 위한

11 ④

Script

M Wow! Look at you. Why did you dress up?

W I'm going to a concert with my family.

M That's great. Do you attend concerts often?

W Sometimes. Actually, I don't like to go to them, but my parents like classical music. So they tell me to come along.

M I see. If you can't avoid it, try to enjoy it.

해석

남 와! 너 좀 봐. 왜 옷을 차려입었니?

여 오늘 가족들과 연주회에 가.

남 좋겠다. 너는 연주회에 자주 가니?

여 가끔. 사실 난 연주회에 가는 것을 좋아하지 않는데 부모님께서 클래식 음악을 좋아하셔. 그래서 내가 같이 가야 한다고 하셔.

남 그렇구나. 피할 수 없으면 즐기려고 해 봐.

해설

So they tell me to come along.이라는 여자의 말에서 정답을 알 수 있다.

어휘

dress up (평소보다) 옷을 갖춰 입다 / attend[əténd] 참석하다 / come along 함께 가다 / avoid[əvɔ́id] 피하다

12 ③

Script

W People enjoy me in the summer, and I'm very popular. Actually, I'm the brother of a watermelon. I have two different colors. My outside is yellow, and my inside is white. I have lots of seeds. Some people just eat them, while others just throw them away. What am I?

해석

어 사람들은 여름에 저를 즐기며, 저는 매우 인기 있습니다. 사실, 저는 수박의 형제입니다. 나는 두 개의 다른 색을 가지고 있습니다. 제 바깥쪽은 노란색이고, 제 안쪽은 하얀색입니다. 저에게는 씨가 많은데 어떤 사람들은 그것을 먹고, 또 어떤 사람들은 그것을 그냥 버립니다. 저는 누구일까요?

해설

사람들이 여름에 즐겨 먹고 바깥은 노랗고 안은 하얀색이며, 씨가 많은 것을 고른다.

어휘

popular[pápjələr] 인기 있는 / watermelon[wɔ́:tərmèlən] 수박 / different[dífərənt] 다른 / outside[àutsáid] 밖 / inside[insáid] 안 / seed[si:d] 씨 / some ~, others... 어떤 사람들[것들]은 ~, 다른 일부는… / while[hwail] ~인데 반하여

13 ⑤

Script

W What are you going to do this summer, Daniel?

M I'm planning to do some volunteer work.

W What do you mean?

M Well, I'm going to help some people.

W Where?

M At a senior center in our neighborhood.

해석

여 이번 여름에 무엇을 할 거니, Daniel?

남 자원 봉사를 좀 하려고 계획 중이야.

여 무슨 말이니?

남 음, 사람들을 좀 도울 거라고.

여 어디서?

남 동네에 있는 노인센터에서.

해설

I'm planning to do some volunteer work.라는 남자의 말을 통해 남자가 여름방학에 자원 봉사를 하려고 한다는 것을 알 수 있다.

어휘

volunteer[vàləntíər] 자원의, 지원의; 자원 봉사자 / senior[sí:jər] 연장자, 노인 / neighborhood[néibərhùd] 이웃, 근처

14 ①

Script

W Did you do your homework?

M No, I didn't, but I will before I go to bed.

W How about cleaning your room?

M Should I clean my room?

W I told you this morning.

M I'm sorry. I forgot.

W Oh, you haven't made your bed yet, either.

해석

여 너 숙제 했니?

남 아, 안 했는데 자기 전에 할 거예요.

여 네 방 청소는?

남 제가 제 방 청소를 해야 해요?

여 오늘 아침에 내가 하라고 했잖니.

남 죄송해요. 잊었어요.

여 아, 너는 아직 네 이불도 개지 않았잖아.

해설

소년은 숙제와 청소도 하지 않았고, 이불도 개지 않았다.

어휘

make the bed (일어나서) 잠자리를 개다[정돈하다] / yet[jet] (부정문) 아직 ~ (않다), (의문문) 벌써, 이제 / either[í:ðər] (부정문) ~도 또한 (~아니다)

15 ②

Script

M I took my girlfriend to a nice Korean restaurant today. When we arrived, there were so many people. So we had to wait. A waitress called me, and we were guided to a room that didn't have chairs. As soon as I took off my shoes to enter the room, I found that my socks were not the same. One was black, and the other was red.

해석

남 나는 오늘 내 여자친구를 근사한 한국 식당에 데려갔다. 우리가 도착했을 때 사람들이 너무 많았다. 그래서 우리는 기다려야 했다. 여종업원이 나를 불렀고 우리는 의자가 없는 방으로 안내되었다. 내가 방으로 들어가려고 신발을 벗자, 나는 내 양말이 똑같지 않다는 것을 알게 되었다. 한 짝은 검은색, 다른 한 짝은 빨간색이었다.

해설

남자가 자신의 양말이 서로 다르다는 것을 발견하고 느낄만한 심정을 고른다.

어휘

take[teik] 데리고 가다 / girlfriend[gə:rlfrend] 여자친구 / waitress[wéitris] 여종업원 / guide[gaid] 안내하다 / as soon as ~하자마자 / take off 벗다 / enter[éntər] ~에 들어가다 / sock[sɑk] (주로 복수형) 양말 / one ~, the other... 하나는 ~, 나머지 하나는 …

16 ③

Script

W You seem to have gained so much weight.

M Yes, I put on about seven kilograms in a month.

W How is that possible?

M I have no idea. The doctor said I should lose weight.

W Why don't you go jogging every day? I think it's the best way.

M Is it? I'm swimming every morning these days.

Q What is the man doing to lose weight these days?

해석

여 너 살이 많이 찐 것 같아.

남 응, 한 달 만에 7킬로그램이나 쪘어.
여 어떻게 그게 가능하니?
남 모르겠어. 의사는 내가 체중을 줄여야 한대.
여 매일 조깅을 해보는 건 어때? 내 생각엔 그게 제일 좋은 방법이야.
남 그래? 나는 요즘 매일 아침 수영을 하고 있어.
질문 체중을 줄이기 위해 남자는 요즘 무엇을 하고 있는가?

해설

I'm swimming every morning these days.라는 남자의 마지막 말에서 남자는 살을 빼기 위해 수영을 하고 있다는 것을 알 수 있다.

어휘

gain[gein] 얻다, 증가하다 / gain weight 몸무게가 늘다, 살찌다 / put on weight 체중이 늘다, 살찌다 / possible[pάsəbəl] 가능한 / go jogging 조깅하러 가다

17 ③

Script

W You are late thirty minutes.
M I'm sorry. I didn't have the key to my house, so I had to wait until my mom came.
W You mean your mom is at home now?
M Yes, she is at home.
W Don't lie to me. Your mother is in my kitchen now.

해석

여 너 30분 늦었어.
남 미안해. 집 열쇠가 없어서 엄마가 오실 때까지 기다려야만 했어.
여 네 말은 지금 너희 엄마가 집에 계시다는 거야?
남 응, 집에 계셔.
여 거짓말하지 마. 너희 엄마가 지금 우리 집 부엌에 계시거든.

해설

소년은 늦은 것에 대한 핑계로 열쇠가 없어 엄마를 기다려야 했다고 말하고 있다.

18 ②

Script

① W Brian, can you give me a hand?
M Of course.
② W Carl, what do you see? Can you tell me?
M Yes, I will buy it.
③ W I bought a new camera.
M Show it to me.
④ W I read this book last night.
M How was it?
⑤ W Do you understand it now?
M Aha. I get it.

해석

① 여 Brian, 나를 좀 도와줄래?
남 물론이지.
② 여 Carl, 뭐가 보이니? 얘기해 줄래?
남 네, 그것을 살게요.
③ 여 나 새 카메라 샀어.
남 그거 나에게 보여줘.
④ 여 나는 어젯밤에 이 책을 읽었어.
남 어땠니?
⑤ 여 너 이제 이해되니?
남 아하! 알겠어.

해설

② 무엇이 보이는지 얘기해 달라는 여자의 요청에 그것을 사겠다는 남자의 응답은 알맞지 않다.

어휘

give ~ a hand ~을 도와주다 / understand[ʌ̀ndərstǽnd] 이해하다 / get[get] 이해하다, 알아듣다

19 ①

Script

M Will you have some cookies?
W Yes, thanks. Where did you get them?
M I made them myself. My mom taught me how to bake them.
W Really? What else can you make?
M Pancakes and donuts.
W That's great.

해석

남 쿠키 좀 먹을래?
여 응, 고마워. 그것들은 어디서 났니?
남 내가 직접 만들었어. 엄마가 쿠키를 굽는 방법을 가르쳐 주셨거든.
여 정말? 다른 거 뭘 만들 수 있니?
남 팬케이크하고 도넛.
여 대단하다.

해설

② 사양할래, 배가 부르거든.
③ 누워서 떡 먹기야.
④ 넌 요리를 해서는 안 돼.
⑤ 내가 너를 위해 그것들을 만들어 줄게.
다양한 음식을 만들 수 있다는 친구에게 해 줄 수 있는 말을 고른다.

어휘

bake[beik] 굽다 / pancake[pǽnkèik] 팬케이크 / donut[dóunʌ̀t] 도넛 (= doughnut)

20 ⑤

Script

M You are getting all of your old things together.
W Yes, I'm planning a yard sale.
M You mean a garage sale?
W Yes, it is the same thing.
M What is that for?

W I need money for a new phone.

해석

남 네가 가지고 있는 낡은 것들을 모두 모으고 있구나.

여 응, 나 마당 세일을 하려고 해.

남 차고 세일을 말하는 거지?

여 응, 같은 거야.

남 그것은 왜 하는 거니?

여 새 전화기를 사는 데 돈이 필요해.

해설

① 너도 나를 도와줄 수 있어.

② 그 소식을 듣게 돼서 기뻐.

③ 그것들은 내가 사용하기에 너무 새 것이야.

④ 내가 너에게 많은 것을 줄 수 있어.

차고 세일을 하는 이유를 묻는 남자의 질문에 알맞은 응답을 고른다.

어휘

get together 모으다[모이다] / yard[jɑːrd] 마당, 뜰 / yard sale 마당 판매 (개인 주택의 마당에서 사용하던 물건을 파는 것) / garage[gərɑ́ːʒ] 차고, 주차장 / garage sale (사람이 자기 집 차고에서 하는) 중고 물품 세일

p.32~35

04회 영어듣기모의고사

01 ②	02 ⑤	03 ⑤	04 ②	05 ③
06 ①	07 ①	08 ②	09 ②	10 ⑤
11 ④	12 ③	13 ⑤	14 ①	15 ②
16 ①	17 ⑤	18 ②	19 ①	20 ①

01 ②

Script

① M This shirt goes well with the pants.
W Can I try it on?

② M Will it hurt a lot?
W Don't look. You probably won't even feel it.

③ M Can I borrow a needle?
W No, you can't. I have to use it now.

④ M I'm so afraid of the dog.
W Don't worry. It won't bite you.

⑤ M Is it comfortable?
W Yes, you will feel wonderful, too.

해석

① 남 이 셔츠는 그 바지와 잘 어울립니다.
여 제가 그걸 입어 봐도 될까요?

② 남 많이 아플까요?
여 쳐다보지 마세요. 아마 아무 것도 못 느낄 거예요.

③ 남 제가 바늘을 좀 빌릴 수 있을까요?
여 안돼요. 지금 제가 써야 하거든요.

④ 남 나는 그 개가 정말 무서워.
여 걱정하지 마. 개가 너를 물지 않을 거야.

⑤ 남 그거 편하니?
여 응, 너도 기분이 좋을 거야.

해설

환자가 간호사에게 주사를 맞는 상황에 알맞은 대화를 고른다.

어휘

go well with ~와 잘 어울리다 / try on 입어보다 / probably[prɑ́bəbli] 아마도 / needle[níːdl] 바늘 / afraid[əfréid] 두려워하여, 무서워하여 / bite[bait] 물다 / comfortable[kʌ́mfərtəbəl] 편안한

02 ⑤

Script

W Hi, Mike. What's up?

M We had a soccer game yesterday, and we lost by three goals again.

W Oh, no. I thought you would win this time. What happened?

M I think I made too many mistakes.

W Maybe you weren't ready, but next time you can beat them.

해석

여 안녕, Mike. 잘 지내니?

남 어제 축구 시합이 있었는데 세 골 차이로 또 졌어.

여 아, 저런. 이번에는 너희가 이길 줄 알았는데. 어떻게 된 거야?

남 내가 실수를 너무 많이 한 것 같아.

여 아마 네가 오늘 준비가 안 되었나 봐. 하지만, 다음번에는 너희가 이길 수 있을 거야.

해설

next time you can beat them이라는 여자의 말을 통해 여자가 남자를 격려하고 있음을 알 수 있다.

어휘

goal[goul] 득점, 골 / make a mistake 실수를 하다 / maybe[méibiː] 아마도, 어쩌면 / beat[biːt] 패배시키다

03 ⑤

Script

W Have you ever been to the United States, Sammy?

M Yes, I have been there for two weeks.

W How about other countries?

M I have been to China, Spain, and Germany.

W Wow. You have been to many countries. I have only been to Italy.

해석

여 미국에 가 본 적이 있니, Sammy?

남 응, 2주 동안 거기에 있었어.

여 다른 나라는?

남 중국, 스페인, 그리고 독일에 갔었어.

여 우와. 많은 나라를 갔다 왔구나. 나는 이탈리아에만 갔다 왔는데.

해설

남자가 가본 나라는 미국, 중국, 스페인, 독일이며, 이탈리아는 여자가 다녀온 나라이다.

04 ②

Script

M I heard you are going to buy a new house next year. Do you have a house in mind?

W I like houses with many windows.

M You do? I like houses with a big garden.

W You like gardening, right?

M Yes, that's my hobby, but my wife doesn't like it.

해석

남 네가 내년에 새집을 살 거라고 들었어. 생각해 둔 집이라도 있니?

여 나는 창문이 많은 집이 좋아.

남 그래? 나는 큰 정원이 있는 집이 좋더라.

여 정원을 가꾸는 것을 좋아하는구나, 그렇지?

남 응, 그게 내 취미인데, 내 아내는 좋아하지 않아.

해설

I like houses with many windows.라는 여자의 말을 통해 여자는 창문이 많은 집을 좋아한다는 것을 알 수 있다.

어휘

have ~ in mind ~을 염두해 두다[생각하다] / garden[gáːrdn] 정원 / gardening[gáːrdniŋ] 정원 가꾸기 / wife[waif] 아내

05 ③

Script

W Harry, are you okay now?

M Not yet, but I'm getting much better.

W Sounds good. When will you leave the hospital?

M What day is it today?

W It's Saturday the 15th.

M I will be leaving the hospital the day after tomorrow.

해석

여 Harry, 지금은 괜찮니?

남 아직 안 좋은데 많이 나아지고 있어.

여 잘 됐어. 너 언제 퇴원할 거니?

남 오늘이 무슨 요일이니?

여 15일, 토요일이야.

남 나 모레 퇴원할거야.

해설

오늘이 15일이고 남자가 모레 퇴원한다고 말하고 있으므로 남자가 퇴원할 날짜는 17일이다.

어휘

get better 좋아지다 / leave the hospital 퇴원하다 / the day after tomorrow 모레

06 ①

Script

W Can I use your computer now?

M Sure. What happened to yours?

W My computer was very slow. So Robert took it apart to make it work faster.

M And?

W After that, it didn't work at all, so I took it to the repair shop.

M What did Robert say?

W He said it was my fault.

해석

여 내가 지금 네 컴퓨터 좀 사용해도 될까?

남 당연하지. 네 컴퓨터는 어떻게 됐니?

여 내 컴퓨터는 아주 느렸거든. 그래서 Robert가 그것을 더 빠르게 한다고 분해했어.

남 그런데?

여 그 이후로 아예 작동하지 않아. 그래서 내가 그것을 수리점에 맡겼어.

남 Robert가 뭐라고 얘기했니?

여 그는 그게 내 잘못이래.

해설

여자는 Robert가 자신의 컴퓨터를 고장 내고 오히려 여자의 잘못이라고 했다고 말하고 있다. 이때 여자가 느낄만한 감정을 고른다.

어휘

take apart (기계 등을) 분해하다 / work[wəːrk] 작동하다 / not ~ at all 전혀 ~ 아니다 / repair shop 수리점 / fault[fɔːlt] 잘못, 과실

07 ①

Script

M May I help you?

W Yes, I'd like to buy a desk lamp for my son.

M I see. How about this one?

W That looks fine. How much is it?

M It's 50 dollars.

W OK. I will take it.

해석

남 도와드릴까요?

여 네, 제 아들에게 줄 스탠드를 사고 싶어요.

남 알겠습니다. 이건 어떠세요?

여 좋은 것 같네요. 얼마죠?

남 50달러입니다.

여 알았어요. 그것으로 살게요.

해설

I'd like to buy a desk lamp라는 여자의 말을 통해 여자가 사려는 것이 스탠드임을 알 수 있다.

어휘

desk lamp 스탠드

08 ②

Script

W How much is this?

M It's 7 dollars and 25 cents.

W Is it a good price?

M Of course. We always offer the lowest price in town.

W Here is 10 dollars.

M Thank you.

W Wait a minute. I have a quarter.

M OK. Here is your change.

해석

여 이거 얼마에요?

남 그건 7달러 25센트입니다.

여 괜찮은 가격인가요?

남 물론이죠. 우리는 항상 마을에서 가장 저렴한 가격을 제시합니다.

여 여기 10달러 있습니다.

남 감사합니다.

여 잠깐만요. 저에게 25센트가 있네요.

남 알겠습니다. 여기 거스름돈입니다.

해설

물건 값은 7달러 25센트이고, 점원에게 10달러 25센트를 주었기 때문에 여자가 받을 거스름돈의 액수는 3달러이다.

어휘

cent[sent] 센트 / offer[ɔ́(:)fər] 제공하다, 주다 / lowest[lóuist] 가장 낮은, 최저의 / quarter[kwɔ́:rtər] 25센트 / change[tʃeindʒ] 거스름돈

09 ②

Script

W Tom, dinner's ready.

M Mom, can I skip dinner? I don't feel like eating.

W I made your favorite. Why don't you take a bite?

M Thanks, but I had a big lunch, and I'm still full now.

W OK. I will leave some for you.

해석

여 Tom, 저녁 준비 다 됐다.

남 엄마, 저 저녁 안 먹으면 안돼요? 먹고 싶지 않아요.

여 엄마가 네가 좋아하는 걸 만들었어. 한 입 먹어보지 그러니?

남 감사한데 점심을 거하게 먹어서 지금도 배가 불러요.

여 알았다. 내가 널 위해 좀 남겨 놓을게.

해설

I had a big lunch, and I'm still full now.라는 남자의 말을 통해 정답을 알 수 있다.

어휘

skip[skip] 건너뛰다, 생략하다 / feel like+-ing ~하고 싶다 / favorite[féivərit] 특히 좋아하는 것; 아주 좋아하는 / bite[bait] (한입의) 음식, 한입 거리 / take a bite 한입 먹다 *cf.* grab a bite 간단히 먹다

10 ⑤

Script

M You always sit with your legs crossed when talking to my parents. That is rude in Korea.

W Really? Why didn't you tell me before?

M I thought you knew.

W How could I know? I've been in Korea for only one month. You need to tell me Korean culture and etiquette.

해석

남 넌 항상 우리 부모님과 얘기할 때 다리를 꼬고 있더라. 그건 한국에서 무례한 행동이야.

여 정말? 왜 진작 나에게 말하지 않았어?

남 나는 네가 아는 줄 알았어.

여 내가 어떻게 알겠니? 내가 한국에 온 지 한 달밖에 안 됐어. 네가 나에게 한국 문화와 예절을 얘기해 줘야 해.

해설

여자가 예의에 어긋나는 행동한 이유는 한국 문화와 예절을 잘 모르기 때문이다. 따라서 여자의 문제는 한국 문화를 잘 모른다는 것이다.

어휘

cross[krɔ:s] (팔, 다리를) 꼬다 / rude[ru:d] 무례한, 버릇없는 / culture[kʌ́ltʃər] 문화 / etiquette[étikèt] 예의

11 ④

Script

M We make this hand gesture to wish for good luck or success. To make this gesture, you should cross your middle finger over your index finger. You can make this gesture to your friend who has a test, saying "Good luck on your test," or make it for yourself when you hope your wishes come true.

해석

남 우리는 행운이나 성공을 빌 때 이 손동작을 합니다. 이 동작을 하기 위해서는 당신의 가운뎃손가락을 집게손가락 위로 교차시켜야 합니다. 당신은 시험을 볼 친구에게 "시험에 행운을 빌어."라고 말하면서 이 동작을 할 수 있습니다. 또는 당신의 소원이 이루어지길 바랄 때 자신을 위해서도 할 수 있습니다.

해설

가운뎃손가락과 집게손가락을 사용한 손동작으로 행운이나 성공을 바라는 손동작은 ④이다.

어휘

gesture[dʒéstʃər] 동작, 몸짓 / wish[wiʃ] 바라다; 소망, 희망 / luck[lʌk] 운 / success[səksés] 성공 / cross[krɔ:s] 교차하다 / middle finger 가운뎃손가락 / index finger 집게손가락 / come true 실현되다, 사실로 되다

12 ③

Script

W The new Harry Potter movie is now showing. Ann and I are going to see it tonight. Will you join us?

M I don't think I can. I have to babysit my brother.

W Aren't your parents at home?

M They are going out for dinner tonight because it's their wedding anniversary.

W You're not going with them?

M Well, I can, but my little brother is too young.

해석

여 새 해리포터 영화가 지금 상영 중이래. Ann하고 나는 오늘 밤에 그걸 보러 갈 거야. 너도 갈래?

남 못 갈 것 같아. 내 동생을 돌봐야 하거든.

여 부모님이 집에 안 계시니?

남 오늘이 부모님의 결혼기념일이라 저녁식사를 하러 외출하실 거야.

여 너는 부모님이랑 같이 안 가니?

남 그게, 나는 갈 수 있는데, 남동생이 너무 어려.

해설

남자는 부모님이 저녁식사를 하러 외출하셔서 동생을 돌봐야 한다고 말하고 있다.

어휘

showing[ʃóuiŋ] 상영[상연] 중인 / tonight[tənáit] 오늘밤; 오늘 밤에 / babysit 아이를 보아주다 / go out for ~하러 외출하다 / wedding[wédiŋ] 결혼식 / anniversary[æ̀nəvə́:rsəri] 기념일

13 ⑤

Script

M Wow, there are many rides to try.

W Why don't we ride that one?

M Look at the screaming girls. It looks so scary. Let's just ride the merry-go-round instead.

W Come on! Look how many people are waiting in line. It must be exciting.

M Okay, okay!

W You won't regret this.

해석

남 와, 정말 타봐야 할 놀이기구가 많아.

여 우리 저거 보자.

남 저 소리지르는 소녀들 좀 봐. 정말 무서울 것 같아. 그냥 우리 회전목마나 타자.

여 제발! 얼마나 많은 사람이 줄을 서 있는 지 좀 봐. 틀림없이 재미있을 거야.

남 알았어, 알았다고!

여 너 후회하지 않을 거야.

해설

many rides to try, ride the merry-go-round라는 말을 통해 대화가 이루어지는 장소가 놀이공원임을 유추할 수 있다.

어휘

ride[raid] 타다; 타기, 놀이기구 / scream[skri:m] 소리지르다; 비명 / scary[skέəri] 무서운, 겁나는 / merry-go-round 회전목마 / wait in line 줄 서서 기다리다 / regret[rigrét] 후회하다; 후회

14 ①

Script

M You look so tired. What's wrong?

W I can't sleep well these days. I was up until three in the morning.

M Is something worrying you?

W No, not at all. I even quit drinking coffee.

M Why don't you exercise then? It will help you to relax and sleep better.

W Okay, I will try that.

해석

남 너 정말 피곤해 보여. 무슨 일 있니?

여 요즘 잠을 푹 잘 수가 없어. 새벽 3시까지 깨어 있었어.

남 뭐 걱정하는 거라도 있니?

여 아니, 전혀 없어. 나 심지어 커피도 끊었어.

남 그러면 운동을 하지 그러니? 그게 네가 긴장을 풀고 잠을 더 잘 잘 수 있도록 도와줄 거야.

여 알았어, 그렇게 해 볼게.

해설

Why don't you exercise then?이라는 말을 통해 남자가 여자에게 운동을 해보라고 권하고 있음을 알 수 있다.

어휘

be up 깨어있다 / worry[wə́:ri] 걱정시키다, 걱정하다 / quit[kwit] 끊다, 그만두다 / exercise[éksərsàiz] 운동하다 / relax[rilǽks] 긴장이 풀리다, 편하게 하다

15 ②

Script

M There are stories about numbers in some countries. For example, Koreans avoid using the number four because they believe it means death. In America, people think the number thirteen is bad luck. The Chinese like the number eight because they think the number brings lots of money.

해석

남 몇몇 나라에는 숫자에 대한 이야기가 있습니다. 예를 들면, 한국 사람들은 숫자 4가 죽음을 의미한다고 생각하기 때문에 그 숫자를 사용하는 것을 피합니다. 미국에서 사람들은 숫자 13이 불운하다고 생각합니다. 중국인들은 숫자 8이 많은 돈을 가져온다고 생각하기 때문에 그 숫자를 좋아합니다.

해설

한국, 미국, 중국에서 특정 수와 관련된 사람들의 믿음에 대해 이야기 하고 있다.

어휘

story[stɔ́:ri] 이야기 / country[kʌ́ntri] 나라, 국가 / example[igzǽmpəl] 예 / for example 예를 들면 / avoid[əvɔ́id] 피하다 / mean[mi:n] 의미하다 / death[deθ] 죽음

16 ①

Script

① **W** Mike, can you pass me the salt?
M No, thank you.

② **W** What are you interested in?
M I'm interested in basketball, but I'm not good at it.

③ **W** Thomas, how old is that TV?
M It's eight years old. It still works well.

④ **W** What are you planning?
M I'm preparing a concert.

⑤ **W** Long time no see! How have you been?
M Good, I've just been busy with work.

해석

① 여 Mike, 소금 좀 건네줄래?
남 고맙지만, 사양할래.

② 여 너는 무엇에 관심이 있니?
남 나는 농구에 관심 있는데, 잘하지는 못해.

③ 여 Thomas, 이 TV는 얼마나 오래되었니?
남 8년 됐어. 그거 아직도 잘 작동해.

④ 여 너 무엇을 계획하는 중이니?
남 나 음악회를 준비하고 있어.

⑤ 여 오래간만이야. 어떻게 지내니?
남 잘 지내. 그냥 일 때문에 좀 바쁠 뿐이야.

해설

① '소금을 건네줄래?'라는 부탁의 응답으로 사양을 뜻하는 No, thank you.는 안맞지 않다

어휘

pass[pæs] 건네주다, 전하다 / be good at ~을 잘하다 / prepare[pripέər] 준비하다 / Long time no see. 오랜만이야.

17 ⑤

Script

M Hi, my name is Jake. I'm very upset with one of my best friends, Kevin. He spoke ill of me to other classmates. He said I was selfish. I don't know why he said something like that. I guess it's because I didn't lend him money when he wanted to borrow some from me before.

해석

남 안녕하세요, 제 이름은 Jake예요. 저는 가장 친한 친구 중 한 명인 Kevin 때문에 정말 화가 나요. 그가 우리 반 친구들 앞에서 제 험담을 했어요. 그는 내가 이기적이라고 말했어요. 나는 그 애가 왜 그런 말을 했는지 잘 모르겠어요. 제 생각엔 전에 그가 나에게 돈을 빌리려고 했을 때 내가 빌려주지 않았기 때문인 것 같아요.

해설

Jake(나)가 Kevin에게 돈을 빌린 것이 아니라, Kevin이 Jake(나)에게 돈을 빌리려고 했다.

어휘

speak ill of 남을 나쁘게 말하다, 험담하다 / classmate[klǽsmèit] 반 친구, 급우 / selfish[sélfiʃ] 이기적인 / lend[lend] 빌려주다 / borrow[bɔ́(:)rou] 빌리다

18 ②

Script

W Why did you steal this ring?
M I told you I didn't steal it. I found it on the street.
W That's a good excuse. Where were you last night?
M I was at home watching TV.
W Oh, yeah? You said you found it on the street. But someone stole it from this lady's home last night. How about that?
M I don't know. I was at home.

해석

여 왜 이 반지를 훔치셨죠?
남 제가 그것을 훔치지 않았다고 말씀드렸잖아요. 길에서 주웠어요.
여 그것 참 그럴듯한 변명이군요. 어젯밤에 어디 있었죠?
남 집에서 TV를 보고 있었습니다.
여 어, 그래요? 당신이 그것을 길에서 주웠다고 말씀하셨죠. 그런데 어젯밤 누군가가 이 부인의 집에서 그것을 훔쳤어요. 그건 어떻게 된 걸까요?
남 전 몰라요. 전 집에 있었다고요.

해설

경찰이 반지 절도사건 용의자를 신문하는 상황이다.

어휘

steal[sti:l] 훔치다 / street[stri:t] 길, 거리 / excuse[ikskjú:z] 핑계, 변명

19 ①

Script

W There is a boy sitting next to you on a bus. You think his face is very familiar. You try hard to think when and where you met him, but you have no idea. You are so curious who the boy is. To ask if you know him, what would you say?

해석

여 버스에서 당신 옆 자리에 한 소년이 앉아 있습니다. 당신은 그 소년의 얼굴이 매우 낯이 익다고 생각합니다. 언제 어디서 그를 만났는지 생각하려고 노력합니다. 하지만, 생각이 나지 않습니다. 당신은 그 소년이 누구인지 정말 궁금합니다. 당신이 그를 알고 있는지 물어보려면 당신은 뭐라고 얘기하시겠어요?

해설

② 어디 가는 중이세요?
③ 우리 언제 내려야 하나요?
④ 여기가 어디인지 아세요?
⑤ 이 버스는 국립 박물관에 가나요?
전에 만난 적이 있는지를 묻는 질문을 고른다.

어휘

national[nǽʃənəl] 국가의, 국립의 / National Museum 국립 박물관 / familiar[fəmíljər] 낯익은, 친근한 / have no idea (전혀) 하나도 모른다 / curious[kjúəriəs] ~을 알고 싶어 하는

20 ①

Script

W Hey, Sam. You got a new MP3 player.

M Yes, my father bought me one last weekend.

W Why? Was it your birthday or something?

M Yes. It was last Saturday.

W Sorry. I forgot about your birthday.

M Never mind.

해석

여 Sam, 새로운 MP3 재생기를 가지고 있구나.

남 응, 아빠가 지난주에 사주셨어.

여 왜? 생일이나 뭐 그런 거였니?

남 응, 지난주 토요일이었어.

여 미안해. 너의 생일을 잊어버렸어.

남 신경 쓰지 않아도 돼.

해설

② 정말 좋겠다.

③ 그건 다음 주야.

④ 나는 너무 수줍어서 거기에 갈 수 없어.

⑤ 네 선물이 가장 마음에 들었어.

미안하다는 여자의 말에 가장 알맞은 응답을 고른다.

어휘

Never mind. 신경 쓰지 마. / shy[ʃai] 소심한, 수줍어하는

p.40~43

05회 영어듣기모의고사

01 ⑤	02 ②	03 ④	04 ③	05 ②
06 ④	07 ⑤	08 ③	09 ①	10 ④
11 ④	12 ④	13 ①	14 ①	15 ②
16 ④	17 ②	18 ①	19 ④	20 ③

01 ⑤

Script

M ① Stand on one leg.

② Raise your arms out to your sides.

③ Stand with your feet together.

④ Put your hands to your waist.

⑤ Raise your arms to the sky.

해석

남 ① 한 발로 서라.

② 손을 양 옆으로 들어라.

③ 두 발을 모아서 서라.

④ 양손을 허리에 얹어라.

⑤ 손을 하늘을 향해 들어라.

해설

⑤에 해당하는 설명은 Stand with your feet shoulder width apart.이다.

어휘

stand on 서다 / raise[reiz] 올리다, 들다 / arm[ɑːrm] 팔 / side[said] 옆, (사람 몸통의) 옆구리 / waist[weist] 허리

02 ②

Script

W Look at the water temperature. It's 41 degrees. I can't stay here any more.

M Come on. It's good for our bodies.

W I can't bear it any longer.

M OK. You go out and take a rest. I'll stay here for ten more minutes.

W Sounds good. Enjoy the hot spring as much as you want, but I'm getting out.

해석

여 물 온도를 봐. 41도야. 나는 더 이상 여기 못 있겠다.

남 왜 그래. 우리 몸에 좋아.

여 나 더 이상 못 참겠어.

남 알았어. 넌 나가서 쉬어. 나는 여기 10분 더 있을게.

여 좋아. 넌 네가 원하는 만큼 온천을 즐겨 하지만, 난 나갈 거야.

해설

water temperature, I can't bear it, hot spring과 같은 말에서 두 사람이 대화하는 장소가 온천이라는 것을 알 수 있다.

어휘

temperature[témpərətʃər] 온도, 기온 / degree[digríː] (온도계 등의) 도 / not ~ any more 더 이상[이제는] ~ 않다 / bear[bɛər] 참다, 견디다 / not ~ any longer 이젠 ~ 않다 / take a rest 휴식을 취하다 / hot spring 온천 / as much as ~만큼[정도]

03 ④

Script

W Today's payday. Can you tell me how much I am getting?

M Let me see. You started working here from Monday, right?

W That's correct.

M You have worked for five days and I promised to give you twenty dollars a day.

W Wow! I will get a lot of money.

해석

여 오늘은 돈 받는 날이네요. 제가 얼마를 받을 건지 얘기해 주실 수 있어요?

남 가만 있자. 네가 여기서 월요일부터 일하기 시작했지, 맞지?

여 맞아요.

남 네가 여기서 일한 지 5일이 됐고 내가 하루에 20달러를 주겠다고 약속했어.

여 와! 저 돈 많이 받겠네요.

해설

일을 시작한 지 5일이 되었고 하루에 20달러를 했으므로 여자가 받을 액수는 100달러이다.

어휘

payday[péidèi] 급여 지급일 / Let me see. (뭔가를 생각하거나, 기억하려고 할 때 사용하여) 글쎄, 가만 있자, 어디 보자 / correct[kərékt] 정확한, 올바른; 고치다, 수정하다 / promise[prámis] 약속하다; 약속

04 ③

Script

M This is the ability to keep doing or waiting for something. When we have to do something that we don't like, we need this. Without this, students can't stay at their desk for very long or easily give up on something that they are supposed to do.

해석

남 이것은 무엇을 계속 하거나, 기다리는 능력입니다. 우리가 하기 싫어하는 것을 해야 할 때 이것이 필요합니다. 이것 없이는 학생들이 오랫동안 책상에 앉아 있지 못하고, 그들이 해야 하는 것을 쉽게 포기합니다.

해설

계속해서 무엇을 하거나, 무언가를 기다리는 능력은 인내력이다.

어휘

ability[əbíləti] 능력, 재능 / keep+-ing 계속 ~하다 / give up on ~를 포기하다 / be supposed to+동사원형 ~하기로 되어 있다, ~할 의무가 있다

05 ②

Script

W If you had to choose only three things in your life, what would those three things be?

M That's a very difficult question. Um... family, health, and friends.

W What about money?

M You know money comes and goes. What about you?

W I think the most important thing is health. You know if we lose our health, we lose everything.

M That's why you exercise every day.

해석

여 너의 삶에서 세 가지를 고른다면 그 세 가지가 무엇이니?

남 그거 정말 어려운 질문인데. 음, 가족, 건강, 그리고 친구.

여 돈은?

남 돈은 있다가도 없고 없다가도 생기는 거잖아. 너는?

여 난 가장 중요한 것이 건강이라고 생각해. 건강을 잃으면 모든 것을 잃는 거라는 걸 너도 알잖아.

남 그래서 네가 매일 운동을 하는 거구나.

해설

I think the most important thing is health.라는 여자의 말에서 여자가 가장 중요하게 생각하는 것이 건강이라는 것을 알 수 있다.

어휘

choose[tʃuːz] 선택하다, 고르다 / come and go 오가다, 드나들다 / important[impɔ́ːrtənt] 중요한

06 ④

Script

W I'm here to see Mr. Johnson.

M He's right over there.

W Which one?

M The tall gentleman with wavy hair.

W Is he wearing a striped shirt?

M No, that is Mr. Hopkins. Mr. Johnson is wearing a black jacket.

W I see. Thank you.

해석

여 Johnson 씨를 만나러 왔습니다.

남 저기 계십니다.

여 어느 분이시죠?

남 곱슬머리이시고 키가 크신 신사분입니다.

여 줄무늬 셔츠를 입고 계신 분인가요?

남 아니오, 그는 Hopkins 씨입니다. Johnson 씨는 검은색 재킷을 입고 있습니다.

여 알겠습니다. 감사합니다.

해설

키가 크고 곱슬머리이며, 검은색 재킷을 입고 있는 사람이 Johnson 씨이다.

어휘

gentleman[dʒéntlmən] 신사 / wavy[wéivi] 웨이브가 있는 / striped[straipt] 줄무늬가 있는 / jacket[dʒǽkit] 재킷, 점퍼

07 ⑤

Script

W What's wrong? You don't look well.

M I have a terrible toothache. I think I have some cavities.

W That's too bad.

M I couldn't sleep at all last night.

W I can tell. Did you put some ice on your jaw?

M Yes, I did, but it didn't work.

해석

여 무슨 일이니? 몸이 안 좋아 보여.

남 이가 너무 아파. 충치가 있는 것 같아.

여 안됐다.

남 어젯밤에 한숨도 잘 수가 없었어.

여 그랬을 것 같아. 턱에 얼음을 좀 대봤어?

남 응, 그렇게 해봤는데 효과가 없었어.

해설

치통이 있기 때문에 남자가 가야 할 곳은 치과이다.

어휘
well[wel] 건강한 / look well 건강해 보인다 / terrible[térəbəl] 심한, 지독한 / toothache[tú:θèik] 치통 / cavity[kǽvəti] 충치 / I can tell. 알고 있어. *cf.* I can't tell. 알 수가 없지. / jaw[dʒɔ:] 턱

08 ③

Script

W Dad, what time are you going to be home tonight?

M Around eight. Why?

W I want to practice a song with my friends at home if you are okay with that.

M For what?

W We are having a contest at school next week.

M OK. I will let you bring your friends home.

해석

여 아빠, 오늘 밤에 몇 시에 집에 들어오세요?

남 8시쯤. 왜?

여 아빠가 괜찮으시면 집에서 친구들과 노래 연습을 하려고요.

남 뭐 하러?

여 다음 주에 학교에서 대회가 있어요.

남 알았다. 친구들을 집에 데려오는 걸 허락 하마.

해설

I will let you bring your friends home.이라는 남자의 말을 통해 딸에게 친구들을 집에 데려와도 된다고 허락하고 있음을 알 수 있다.

어휘
around[əràund] 대략, 쯤 / practice[prǽktis] 연습하다 / contest[kántest] 대회, 경기

09 ①

Script

W Mark, did you meet Rachel?

M Yes, I did. I met her the day before yesterday. We had a great time.

W What did you do?

M We went to the science museum.

W I see. Are you going to meet her again?

M Sure, we will meet tomorrow because tomorrow is Saturday.

해석

여 Mark, 너 Rachel 만났니?

남 응, 만났어. 그녀를 그저께 만났어. 우리 정말 즐거운 시간을 보냈지.

여 뭐 했어?

남 과학박물관에 갔어.

여 그랬구나. 그녀를 다시 만날 거니?

남 당연하지, 내일이 토요일이어서 내일 만나기로 했어.

해설

내일이 토요일이므로 오늘은 금요일이다. 남자는 Rachel을 그저께 만났다고 했으므로 남자가 여자를 처음 만난 요일은 수요일이다.

어휘
the day before yesterday 그저께 / have a great time 즐거운 시간을 보내다

10 ④

Script

W Did you do your math homework?

M Yes, I did. How about you?

W I did, but I wasn't quite sure of some of my answers. Can you take a look?

M Sure.

W If you find any wrong answers, please correct them.

M No problem.

해석

여 너 수학 숙제했니?

남 응, 했어. 너는?

여 나도 했는데 내가 쓴 답 중에 몇 개는 잘 모르겠어. 좀 봐 줄래?

남 물론이야.

여 네가 틀린 답을 찾으면 좀 고쳐 줘.

남 알았어.

해설

여자는 남자에게 자신이 한 수학 숙제를 보고 틀린 문제가 있으면 고쳐 달라고 부탁하고 있다.

어휘
be sure of ~을 확신하다 / quite[kwait] 확실히, 분명히 / take a look (at) (~을) 한 번 보다 / wrong[rɔ:ŋ] 틀린, 잘못된 / correct[kərékt] 고치다, 수정하다

11 ④

Script

M What time shall we meet tomorrow?

W What are you talking about?

M Don't you remember? We are going to go snowboarding tomorrow.

W I totally forgot about that. Um... I really want to go with you, but I have something important to do. Can we go another time?

M Oh, no. You can't go with me?

해석

남 우리 내일 몇 시에 만날까?

여 무슨 얘기하는 거니?

남 기억 안 나니? 우리 내일 스노보드 타러 가기로 했잖아.

여 나 완전히 잊고 있었어. 음, 정말로 너와 같이 가고 싶은데 중요한 할 일이 있어. 다음에 가면 안 될까?

남 오, 이런. 나랑 같이 갈 수 없다고?

해설

같이 가기로 하고 약속도 잊어버리고 중요한 일이 있어서 같이 못 가겠다는 여자의 말을 듣고 남자가 느낄만한 심정을 고른다.

어휘
pleased[pliːzd] 기쁜, 즐거운 / disappointed[dìsəpɔ́intid] 실망한, 낙담한 / satisfied[sǽtisfàid] 만족하는 / go snowboarding 스노보드를 타러 가다 / totally[tóutəli] 완전히, 모두

12 ④

Script

M ① Salad is five dollars or less.
② Lunch won't be served after 2:30.
③ This restaurant accepts credit cards.
④ This restaurant is open from Monday to Friday.
⑤ The restaurant won't serve dinner before 5:30 p.m.

해석

남 ① 샐러드는 5달러 이하이다.
② 점심은 2시 30분 이후에는 제공되지 않는다.
③ 이 식당에서 신용 카드를 사용할 수 있다.
④ 이 식당은 월요일부터 금요일까지 영업한다.
⑤ 식당은 5시 30분 이전에는 저녁을 제공하지 않는다.

해설

월요일부터 토요일까지 5시 30분부터 저녁 식사가 제공되므로 토요일에도 영업을 한다는 것을 알 수 있다.

어휘

salad[sǽləd] 샐러드 / serve[səːrv] 제공하다 / accept[æksèpt] 받다, 받아들이다 / credit card 신용카드 *cf.* debt card 직불[현금] 카드

13 ①

Script

① W I'm sorry for being late.
M Thanks for coming early.
② W Why don't you go for a swim with us?
M That would be great.
③ W Can I have a glass of cold water?
M Sure. I'll get one for you.
④ W Have you ever been to New York?
M No, but I'd like to go.
⑤ W Help yourself to the food.
M Thank you.

해석

① 여 늦어서 죄송해요.
남 일찍 와 주셔서 감사합니다.
② 여 우리와 같이 수영하러 갈래?
남 좋아.
③ 여 찬물 한 잔 마실 수 있을까요?
남 물론이죠. 제가 갖다 드릴게요.
④ 여 너 뉴욕에 가본 적 있니?
남 아니, 하지만 가보고 싶어.
⑤ 여 음식 마음껏 드세요.
남 감사합니다.

해설

① 늦어서 죄송하다는 여자의 말에 일찍 와주셔서 감사하다는 남자의 응답은 부자연스럽다.

어휘

go for a swim 수영하러 가다 / help oneself (to) 마음껏 먹다

14 ①

Script

W Chandler, I can't go to the concert tomorrow. There are no tickets left.
M What will you do then?
W I'm not sure. I might not go out at all. I'll probably stay home and watch movies.
M What film are you going to watch?
W I don't know. I'll probably pick up some horror movies. I like them.

해석

여 Chandler, 나 내일 콘서트에 못 가. 남아 있는 표가 없어.
남 그럼 뭐 할 거야?
여 잘 모르겠어. 아예 외출을 하지 않을지도 몰라. 집에서 영화나 보는 게 좋을 것 같아.
남 어떤 영화를 볼 거니?
여 모르겠어. 아마도 공포 영화를 빌릴 거야. 내가 공포 영화를 좋아하거든.

해설

여자의 마지막 말에서 여자가 공포 영화를 좋아한다는 것을 알 수 있다.

어휘

might[mait] ~일지도 모른다 / stay home 집에 있다 / had better ~하는 편이 낫다 / horror movie 공포 영화

15 ②

Script

W Hi, I'm Susie Collins. I just moved in.
M Hi, I'm John Baker. Please call me John.
W Have you lived here long?
M Yes, I have lived here for more than ten years. By the way, what do you do?
W I'm a police officer.

해석

여 안녕하세요. 저는 Susie Collins입니다. 방금 이사 왔어요.
남 안녕하세요. 저는 John Baker입니다. John이라고 불러 주세요.
여 여기서 오래 사셨나요?
남 네, 10년 이상 살았습니다. 그런데 어떤 일을 하시나요?
여 저는 경찰관이에요.

해설

이제 막 이사온 여자와 10년 이상 그곳에 살았다는 이웃이 인사하는 상황이다.

어휘

move in 이사 오다 / police officer 경찰관

16 ④

Script

W Hello, Mr. Brown. Jim said you wanted to see me.

M That's right. Because you are new here, I have a few things to ask you.

W Go ahead.

M First of all, what do your parents do?

W My father is a teacher just like you, and my mother is a scientist.

M Okay. You went to San Jones Middle School, right?

W Yes, I did.

Q What does the woman's father do?

해석

여 안녕하세요, Brown 선생님. Jim이 선생님께서 저를 만나고 싶어 하신다고 했어요.

남 맞단다. 네가 새로 전학을 와서 몇 가지 물어볼 게 있거든.

여 물어 보세요.

남 먼저, 부모님은 무엇을 하시니?

여 아버지는 선생님처럼 교사이시고, 어머니는 과학자세요.

남 알았단다. San Jones 중학교에 다녔지, 맞지?

여 네, 맞아요.

질문 여자의 아버지의 직업은 무엇인가?

해설

My father is a teacher just like you라는 여자의 말을 통해 여자의 아버지의 직업이 선생님이라는 것을 알 수 있다.

어휘

first of all 우선, 먼저

17 ②

Script

W Where are you going?

M I'm going to the subway station.

W Are you going somewhere?

M No. Actually, I left my bag in the subway.

W That's too bad. Do you want me to go with you?

M That's OK. Actually, the man working there has it now.

해석

여 너 어디 가는 중이니?

남 지하철역에 가고 있어.

여 어디 가려고?

남 아니. 사실, 지하철에 가방을 두고 왔어.

여 안됐다. 내가 같이 가줄까?

남 괜찮아. 사실, 거기에서 일하는 사람이 지금 그것을 가지고 있어.

해설

남자는 지하철에 가방을 두고 와서 가방을 찾으러 지하철역에 가고 있다고 말하고 있다.

어휘

somewhere[sʌ́mhwὲər] 어딘가로[에], 어디선가 / station[stéiʃən] 역

18 ①

Script

W Who won the race? You must have, right?

M Yes. How did you know?

W I thought you would. You set your goal high and try to reach it every day.

M Thank you.

W I've seen you run every morning while you deliver newspapers.

해석

여 누가 경주에서 이겼니? 너지, 맞지?

남 응. 어떻게 알았니?

여 나는 네가 이길 거라고 생각했어. 너는 목표를 높이 세우고 매일 그것을 달성하려고 노력하잖아.

남 고마워.

여 네가 신문 배달을 하면서 매일 달리는 것을 보았어.

해설

② 백지장도 맞들면 낫다.

③ 무소식이 희소식이다.

④ 안 보면 멀어진다.

⑤ 세월이 화살같이 흐른다. (세월은 유수와 같다.)

남자는 신문 배달을 꾸준히 하며 달리기 연습을 해서 결국 경주에서 이기게 되었으므로 '천천히 그리고 꾸준히 하는 것이 경기에서 이긴다.'라는 의미의 속담 ①을 고른다.

어휘

race[reis] 경주, 레이스 / goal[goul] 목표, 목적 / set one's goal 목표를 세우다 / reach[riːtʃ] 도달하다, 닿다 / deliver[dilívər] 배달하다

19 ④

Script

W This is great! Look at this poster.

M What does it say?

W The mask festival will be held from next Friday.

M That sounds very interesting. Where is that happening?

W In New Hyde Park.

해석

여 이거 굉장하다. 이 포스터 좀 봐.

남 뭐라고 써 있어?

여 가면 축제가 다음주 금요일부터 열린대.

남 재미있겠다. 어디서 하는데?

여 New Hyde Park에서.

해설

① 9시에 열어.

② 그들은 춤을 추고 있어.

③ 5월 5일부터 12일까지야.

⑤ 너는 지하철을 타면 돼.

남자는 축제가 어디서 열리는지 묻고 있으므로 응답으로 장소가 나오는 것이 자연스럽다.

어휘

poster[póustər] 포스터 / mask[mɑːsk] 가면, 마스크 / festival[féstəvəl] 축제 / hold[hould] (파티, 모임 등을) 열다, 개최하다

20 ③

Script

W Can you explain this to me again?

M Sure. Jacob said it took one and a half hours to get to New York, but Carl said it took him ninety minutes.

W So, were they the same distance from New York? How?

M Well, ninety minutes is the same as one and a half hours. Do you follow me?

W Now I'm with you.

해석

여 이것을 다시 설명 좀 해 줄래?

남 물론이지. Jacob이 뉴욕에 가는 데 한 시간 반이 걸리고, Carl은 90분 걸린다고 했잖아.

여 그래서 그들이 뉴욕에서 같은 거리만큼 떨어져 있는 거니? 어떻게?

남 그게, 90분은 1시간 반하고 같잖아. 이해되니?

여 이제 알겠어.

해설

① 나는 거기에 비행기로 갈 거야.

② 너 어디 가는 중이니?

④ 알았어. 내가 너를 따라갈게.

⑤ 그건 맞지 않다고 너에게 말했잖아.

Do you follow me?는 '이해되니?'라는 의미로 질문에 알맞은 응답을 고른다.

어휘

explain[ikspléin] 설명하다 / distance[dístəns] 거리 / follow[fálou] (내용을) 따라잡다, 이해하다 / be with ~ ~의 말을 알아 듣다[이해하다]

p.48~51

06회 영어듣기모의고사

01 ②	02 ③	03 ④	04 ①	05 ⑤
06 ④	07 ②	08 ④	09 ①	10 ②
11 ④	12 ②	13 ②	14 ⑤	15 ④
16 ②	17 ④	18 ④	19 ②	20 ④

01 ②

Script

① W Dinner's ready! Are you coming?
M I'm coming down, Mom.

② W I like spicy food a lot, but this is too much.
M Why don't you have some water?

③ W Did you see who ate my cake?
M No, I wasn't there.

④ W Hurry up! We will be late for the show.
M I'm almost ready!

⑤ W How many times do I have to tell you?
M Sorry, I won't play with my food again.

해석

① 여 저녁 준비 다 됐다! 오고 있니?
남 저 내려가요, 엄마.

② 여 나 매운 음식을 아주 좋아하는데, 이건 너무 심하다.
남 물 좀 마실래?

③ 여 내 케이크를 누가 먹었는지 봤니?
남 아니, 나는 거기에 없었어.

④ 여 서둘러! 우리는 쇼에 늦겠어.
남 준비 거의 끝났어!

⑤ 여 내가 몇 번이나 얘기해야 되니?
남 죄송해요. 다시는 음식을 가지고 장난치지 않을게요.

해설

여자가 음식을 먹고 매워하고 있는 상황에 알맞은 대화를 고른다.

어휘

spicy[spáisi] 매운, 향긋한 / hurry up 서두르다

02 ③

Script

W Good evening, this is the weather report for the weekend. Tomorrow will be cloudy with a very strong chance of snow, with a temperature down to zero degrees. On Sunday, it will be mostly sunny. The high will be around ten degrees, and the low will be about four degrees.

해석

여 안녕하세요, 주말의 일기 예보입니다. 내일은 눈이 올 확률이 아주 높으며 흐리고 기온은 영하로 떨어지겠습니다. 일요일은 대체로 화창하겠습니다. 최고 기온이 10도, 최저 기온은 4도가 되겠습니다.

해설

토요일은 눈이 내릴 확률이 높고 흐리지만, 일요일은 날씨가 화창하겠다고 예보하고 있다.

어휘

snowy[snóui] 눈이 내리는 / sunny[sʌ́ni] 화창한 / foggy[fɔ́(ː)gi] 안개가 낀 / rainy[réini] 비 오는 / cloudy[kláudi] 흐린, 구름이 많은 / chance[tʃæns] 가능성, 가망, 확률 / degree[digríː] (온도계 등의) 도 / mostly[móustli] 대부분은, 대개는 / high[hai] (기상) 그 날의 최고 기온 / low[lou] 최저치

03 ④

Script

W Jason, I will miss you.

M Me, too.

W Anyway, why don't you leave on Saturday? If you leave then, I will be able to see you off.

M I can't. There are no seats available.

W I see. That's why you are leaving one day earlier.

M That's right. I'm leaving on the 13th of July.

해석

여 Jason, 네가 보고 싶을 거야.

남 나도 그래.

여 그런데, 토요일에 떠나지 그러니? 만약 네가 그때 떠나면 내가 너를 배웅해 줄 수 있을 거야.

남 안 돼. 남아 있는 좌석이 없어.

여 그렇구나. 그게 네가 하루 일찍 떠나는 이유구나.

남 맞아. 나 7월 13일에 떠나.

해설

남자는 토요일에 좌석이 없기 때문에 하루 일찍 떠난다고 말하고 있다. 따라서 남자가 떠날 날짜는 7월 13일, 금요일이다.

어휘

see off 배웅하다 / available[əvéiləbəl] 이용할 수 있는

04 ①

Script

W How are we getting to the gallery, Seth?

M The best way is to take a cab, but it costs too much.

W You're right. Taking the bus is the second best was, but it takes too long.

M Taking the subway is fine, but we have to walk a lot.

W Why don't we just take a taxi and split the fare fifty-fifty?

M That's a good idea.

해석

여 우리는 미술관까지 어떻게 갈 거니, Seth?

남 가장 좋은 방법은 택시를 타는 것인데 돈이 너무 많이 들어.

여 네 말이 맞아. 버스 타는 것이 두 번째로 좋지만, 너무 오래 걸리잖아.

남 지하철을 타는 것도 괜찮지만, 많이 걸어야 해.

여 우리 그냥 택시를 타고 요금을 반반씩 나눠서 내는 건 어떨까?

남 그거 좋은 생각이야.

해설

Why don't we just take a taxi and split the fare fifty-fifty?라는 여자의 권유에 남자는 좋은 생각이라고 응답하고 있기 때문에 두 사람이 이용할 교통수단이 택시임을 알 수 있다.

어휘

gallery[gǽləri] 화랑, 미술관 / cost[kɔːst] 비용이 들다; 비용 / take a cab 택시를 타다 / second best 두 번째로 좋은, 차선의 / split[split] 나누다, 분할하다 / fare[fɛər] 요금 / fifty-fifty 반반의

05 ⑤

Script

[Telephone rings.]

M Hello.

W Dave, this is Kelly. I'm arriving in Seoul tonight at nine.

M Oh, do you want me to pick you up?

W No, you don't need to. I will just take a cab home.

M OK, then is there something you want me to do?

W Yes. Could you go into my room and turn the heater on?

M No problem.

해석

남 여보세요.

여 Dave, 나 Kelly야. 나 오늘 밤 9시에 서울에 도착해.

남 아, 내가 널 데리러 갈까?

여 아니, 그럴 필요 없어. 그냥 집까지 택시를 탈게.

남 알았어, 그러면 내게 뭐 부탁할 일이라도 있니?

여 응. 내 방에 가서 난방기 좀 켜 줄래?

남 알았어.

해설

Could you to go into my room and turn the heater on?이라는 여자의 말에서 정답을 알 수 있다.

어휘

tonight[tənáit] 오늘 밤; 오늘 밤에 / pick up ~을 (차에) 태우러 가다 / take a cab 택시를 타다 / turn on ~을 켜다 / heater[híːtər] 난방 장치

06 ④

Script

W What can I do for you?

M I'd like to send this letter to New York.

W Would you like to send it by airmail or surface mail?

M Airmail, please.

W Okay. Would you put it on the scale?

M Yes, here.

W That'll be three dollars.

해석

여 무엇을 도와드릴까요?

남 이 편지를 뉴욕으로 보내려고요.

여 항공 우편으로 보내시겠어요, 아니면 보통 우편으로 보내시겠어요?

남 항공 우편이요.

여 알겠습니다. 저울에 그 편지를 올려놓으시겠어요?

남 네, 여기요.

여 3달러입니다.

해설

I'd like to send this letter to New York.이라는 남자의 말을 통해 두 사람이 대화하는 장소가 우체국임을 알 수 있다.

어휘
airmail[ɛ́ərmèil] 항공 우편, 항공편 / surface[sə́ːrfis] 육상 수송 / surface mail 보통 우편, 선박 우편 / scale[skeil] 저울

07 ②

Script

M What do you want to be?

W I'm not sure. But I think teaching children is interesting. How about you?

M I'm very interested in the universe, so I want to study stars and planets.

W I see, but you are still taking piano lessons, and you are really good at it.

M Yes, but it's just a hobby.

해석

남 너는 무엇이 되고 싶니?

여 잘 모르겠어. 아이들을 가르치는 게 재미있을 것 같아. 넌?

남 나는 우주에 관심이 많아서 나중에 별과 행성들을 연구하고 싶어.

여 그렇구나. 하지만, 너는 아직도 피아노 레슨을 받고 있고, 너는 피아노를 잘 치잖아.

남 그래, 하지만 그건 그냥 취미일 뿐이야.

해설

남자는 우주에 관심이 많고 별과 행성을 연구하는 일을 하고 싶어한다.

어휘
universe[júːnəvə̀ːrs] 우주 / study[stʌ́di] 연구하다, 공부하다 / planet[plǽnət] 행성 / lesson[lésn] 교습, 레슨

08 ④

Script

M Susan, why don't you stop playing that music?

W Why? Does it bother you?

M I think listening to music is okay, but you keep playing the same music over and over.

W I'm sorry, but this music reminds me of my special friend, Sue.

M I understand that, but you're not the only person here.

해석

남 Susan, 그 음악을 좀 꺼줄래?

여 왜? 신경에 거슬리니?

남 음악을 듣는 건 좋은데 같은 음악을 반복해서 틀고 있잖아.

여 미안해, 그런데 이 음악이 내 각별한 친구, Sue를 생각나게 해.

남 이해는 하지만, 여기에 너 혼자 있는 게 아니잖아.

해설

this music reminds me of my special friend라는 여자의 말을 통해 친구 생각이 나서 계속해서 그 음악을 듣고 있음을 알 수 있다.

어휘
bother[bɑ́ðər] 괴롭히다, 귀찮게 하다, 성가시게 하다 / over and over 몇 번이고 되풀이해서 / remind ~ of... ~에게 …을 생각나게 하다, 상기시키다 / special[spéʃəl] 특별한

09 ①

Script

M Where did you go for your vacation last summer?

W I went to Hawaii, and I spent a lot of time on the beach.

M I see. Where else have you been?

W I've been to France, Sweden, and Greece. What about you?

M I went to Hong Kong and Japan last year.

W Really? How was your trip to Japan? I'd love to go there.

해석

남 너 지난 여름휴가로 어디 다녀왔니?

여 하와이에 다녀왔어. 해변에서 많은 시간을 보냈지.

남 그랬구나. 그 밖에 어떤 나라에 가봤니?

여 프랑스, 스웨덴 그리고 그리스에 가봤어. 너는?

남 나는 작년에 홍콩하고 일본에 다녀왔어.

여 정말? 일본 여행은 어땠니? 나 정말 거기 가고 싶어.

해설

작년에 일본에 갔다 왔다는 남자에게 여자는 일본 여행이 어땠는지 물으며 일본에 가고 싶다고 말하고 있다.

어휘
else[els] 그 밖의, 다른

10 ②

Script

M Excuse me, how much is a ticket?

W Do you want a children's ticket or an adult ticket?

M I want both. I'd like to buy one ticket for an adult and anther for a child.

W Okay. Ticket are 10 dollars for adults and 5 dollars for children.

M Thank you.

해석

남 실례합니다, 표가 얼마인가요?

여 어린이 표를 원하시나요, 아니면 성인 표를 원하시나요?

남 둘 다요. 어린이 표 한 장과 성인 표 한 장을 사고 싶어요.

여 알겠습니다. 성인은 10달러, 어린이는 5달러입니다.

남 감사합니다.

해설

남자는 어린이 표 한 장과 성인 표 한 장을 사려고 한다. 표 가격은 성인이 10달러, 어린이가 5달러로, 남자가 지불해야 할 입장료는 총 15달러이다.

어휘
adult[ədʌ́lt] 성인, 어른 / both[bouθ] 양쪽, 둘 다

11 ④

Script

W How did you do on the test?

M Not bad. I mean I did a little better than I did before. How about you?

W I messed up on the test. I thought I had enough time, but I was wrong. I couldn't answer at least six questions.

M That's too bad.

해석

여 너 시험 잘 봤니?

남 나쁘진 않아. 전보다 조금 잘 봤어. 너는?

여 난 시험을 망쳤어. 시간이 충분한 줄 알았는데 잘못 알고 있었어. 적어도 여섯 문제는 풀지 못했어.

남 정말 안됐다.

해설

여자는 시험 시간을 잘못 알고 여섯 문제를 풀지 못했다며 낙담해 하고 있다.

어휘

mess up 엉망으로 만들다, 망치다 / enough[inʌ́f] 충분한; 충분히 / answer[ǽnsər] (문제 등을) 풀다, 답하다; 대답 / at least 적어도

12 ②

Script

M What did you get for your birthday?

W I got a hair band from Paul and a key chain from Kelly.

M What else?

W I got a couple of CDs from Grace.

M And here is a diary for you.

W Oh, thank you.

해석

남 생일 선물로 무엇을 받았니?

여 Paul에게 머리띠와 Kelly에게 열쇠고리를 받았어.

남 다른 건?

여 Grace로부터 CD 두 장을 받았어.

남 그리고 여기 너에게 줄 일기장이 있어.

여 오, 고마워.

해설

여자는 생일 선물로 머리띠, 열쇠고리, CD 두 장을 받았으며 남자로부터 일기장을 받고 있다.

어휘

hair band 머리띠, 헤어밴드 / key chain 열쇠 고리 / a couple of 두 개[사람]의

13 ②

Script

W May I have your attention, please? Flight 101 to Paris is now ready for boarding at Gate 32. Passengers please proceed to Gate 32. Please have your boarding pass and passport ready. We will begin boarding with business class passengers.

해석

여 안내 말씀드리겠습니다. 파리 행 101 비행편이 32번 탑승구에서 지금 탑승 준비 중입니다. 승객께서는 32번 탑승구로 가주십시오. 항공권과 여권을 준비해 주십시오. 비즈니스석 승객 탑승을 시작하겠습니다.

해설

Flight 101 to Paris is now ready for boarding at Gate 32.를 통해 탑승 안내 방송임을 알 수 있다.

어휘

attention[əténʃən] 주의, 유의 / ready for 준비가 된 / board[bɔːrd] (기차, 비행기, 등) ~에 타다 / passenger[pǽsəndʒər] 승객, 여객 / proceed[prousíːd] 나아가다, 향하다 / business class (항공기의) 비즈니스 클래스

14 ⑤

Script

[Telephone rings.]

W Hello. Helen speaking.

M Hello. May I speak to Kelly, please?

W Sorry, she's not in the office. Can I take a message?

M This is Mark from the Service Center. Please tell her to call me.

W Sure. By the way, does she know your number?

M Yes, she has my number.

해석

여 여보세요. Helen입니다.

남 안녕하세요. Kelly 씨와 통화할 수 있을까요?

여 죄송하지만, 그녀는 사무실에 안 계세요. 메시지를 남기시겠어요?

남 저는 서비스 센터의 Mark입니다. 저에게 가능한 한 빨리 전화를 해달라고 전해 주십시오.

여 알겠습니다. 그런데 그녀가 당신의 전화번호를 알고 계시나요?

남 네, 제 번호를 알고 계십니다.

해설

Mark는 Kelly가 자신의 전화번호를 알고 있다며 전화번호를 남기지 않았다.

어휘

message[mésidʒ] 메시지 / service center 서비스 센터 / as soon as possible 가능한 한 빨리

15 ④

Script

W The movie starts in a minute. How long does it run?

M I think it runs for 120 minutes.

W It's almost five o'clock now. So it will be dinner by the time the movie ends.

M I'm a bit hungry already. Let's go for dinner as soon as the movie is over.

W Sounds good.

해석

여 영화가 곧 시작해. 영화가 얼마 동안이나 상영하니?

남 120분 동안 상영하는 것 같아.

여 지금이 거의 5시야. 그러니까 영화가 끝날쯤이면 저녁 시간이 되겠다.

남 나 벌써 배가 조금 고파. 영화가 끝나자마자 저녁 먹으러 가자.

여 좋아.

해설

지금이 5시이고 영화가 120분 길이이기 때문에 영화가 끝날 시각이 7시임을 알 수 있다.

어휘

in[in] (시간, 기한, 경과 등을 나타내) ~안에, ~후에, ~있으면 / run[rʌn] (언급된 시간에) 진행되다 / end[end] 끝나다 / be over 끝나다

16 ②

Script

M This day is a public holiday that always falls on August 15th. On this day in 1945, our country became independent from Japan. To celebrate our independence from Japanese rule, we hang our national flag in front of the house and have some parades.

해석

남 이날은 항상 8월 15일에 해당하는 국경일입니다. 1945년 이 날, 우리나라는 일본으로부터 독립했습니다. 일본의 통치로부터 독립한 것을 축하하기 위해 우리는 집 앞에 태극기를 걸고 거리행진을 합니다.

해설

일본으로부터 독립한 날로 8월 15일은 광복절이다

어휘

public[pʌ́blik] 공공의, 국가의 / public holiday 공휴일 / fall on (어떤 날이) ~에 해당되다 / August[ɔ́:gəst] 8월 / independent[ìndipéndənt] 독립한, 자치적인 / celebrate[séləbrèit] 축하하다, 기념하다 / independence[ìndipéndəns] 독립 / rule[ru:l] 지배, 통치, 규칙 / hang[hæŋ] 걸다 / national[nǽʃənəl] 국가의 / flag[flæg] 깃발 / national flag 국기 / parade[pəréid] 퍼레이드, 가두 행진

17 ④

Script

M Hey, Susan. The woman with the long curly hair is my sister.

W Really? She is pretty tall. Is she a college student?

M Yes, she is majoring in English.

W Then, she must be good at English.

M I think so. She often works as a tour guide on weekends.

해석

남 야, Susan. 저 긴 곱슬머리의 여자가 내 누나야.

여 정말이야? 키가 꽤 크다. 대학생이시니?

남 응, 영어를 전공해.

여 그러면, 영어 잘하겠다.

남 그럴 거야. 그녀는 종종 주말에 여행 안내원으로 일해.

해설

남자의 누나가 영어 선생님이 되고 싶어 한다는 말은 언급되지 않았다.

어휘

curly[kə́:rli] 곱슬머리의 / college student 대학생 / major[méidʒər] 전공하다 / tour guide 여행 안내원

18 ④

Script

① M What time can you make it?
　 W Maybe around 2 p.m.

② M What is your father like?
　 W He is funny, but sometimes very strict.

③ M Can I speak to Isabella?
　 W Speaking. Who's calling please?

④ M Can I get you something cold to drink?
　 W I'd better put on a jacket.

⑤ M How would you like your steak?
　 W Medium well done, please.

해석

① 남 너 언제 올 수 있니?
　 여 아마도 2시쯤.

② 남 너희 아버지는 어떤 분이시니?
　 여 재미있으신데, 가끔 매우 엄하셔.

③ 남 Isabella와 통화할 수 있을까요?
　 여 전데요. 누구세요?

④ 남 시원한 마실 것 좀 드릴까요?
　 여 재킷을 입는 것이 좋겠어.

⑤ 남 스테이크를 어떻게 구워 드릴까요?
　 여 중간에서 조금 더 익혀 주세요.

해설

④ 마실 것을 원하는지 상대방의 의향을 묻는 질문에 재킷을 입는 게 좋겠다는 여자의 응답은 알맞지 않다.

어휘

make it (어떤 곳에 간신히) 시간에 맞춰 가다 / funny[fʌ́ni] 재미있는 / strict[strikt] 엄격한, 엄한 / Speaking. (전화 받을 때) 접니다. / put on 입다, 쓰다, 걸치다 / steak[steik] 스테이크 / medium[mí:diəm] (음식, 고기를) 중간쯤 익힌 / well done (음식, 고기를) 완전히 익힌

19 ②

Script

W Hello! It's been a long time. Where have you been?

M I've been in London for three months.

W I see. Anyway, what would you like to have?

M What's today's special?

W It's New York steak.

해석

여 안녕하세요! 정말 오랜만이네요. 어디 계셨어요?

남 3개월 동안 런던에 다녀왔어요.

여 그렇군요. 어쨌든, 무엇을 드시겠어요?

남 오늘의 특별 메뉴는 뭐죠?
여 뉴욕 스테이크예요.

해설
① 그건 무료 식사입니다.
③ 제가 수프를 가져오겠습니다.
④ 제대로 고르셨습니다.
⑤ 네, 오늘은 매우 특별한 날이에요.

해설
'오늘의 특별 메뉴는 뭐죠?'라는 남자의 질문에 대한 응답으로 음식 메뉴가 오는 것이 자연스럽다.

어휘
free[fri:] 공짜의, 무료의 / meal[mi:l] 식사, 한 끼의 식사 / today's special 오늘의 특별 요리

20 ④

Script

M What a cute puppy!
W Thanks.
M Look at its small feet! I wish I had one. Where did you get it?
W My aunt gave it to me.
M I see. How old is he? How many months?
W Not even a month.

해석
남 강아지 정말 귀엽다!
여 고마워.
남 조그마한 발 좀 봐! 나도 한 마리 있었으면 좋겠다. 어디서 났니?
여 이모가 나에게 주셨어.
남 그렇구나. 나이가 어떻게 되니? 몇 개월이니?
여 한 달도 안 됐어.

해설
① Dooly라고 불러.
② 비싸지 않아.
③ 집에서 길러.
⑤ 동물 병원에 갔었어.
남자는 강아지의 나이를 묻고 있기 때문에 응답으로 나이가 오는 것이 자연스럽다.

어휘
cute[kju:t] 귀여운 / puppy[pʌ́pi] 강아지

p.56~59

07회 영어듣기모의고사

01 ③	02 ④	03 ①	04 ②	05 ①
06 ①	07 ③	08 ①	09 ③	10 ③
11 ①	12 ④	13 ⑤	14 ①	15 ②
16 ⑤	17 ①	18 ⑤	19 ①	20 ②

01 ③

Script

M ① No animals allowed.
② No left turn.
③ No passing allowed.
④ No swimming allowed.
⑤ Handicapped parking only.

해석
남 ① 동물 반입 금지
② 좌회전 금지
③ 통행금지
④ 수영 금지
⑤ 장애인 주차만 허용

해설
③은 '동물 조심(Animals Crossing)'이라는 의미를 나타내는 표지판이다.

어휘
allow[əláu] 허락하다, 허용하다 / left[left] 왼쪽 / turn[təːrn] 회전; 돌다, 회전하다 / handicapped[hǽndikæ̀pt] 신체[정신]적 장애가 있는 / park[pɑːrk] 주차하다; 주차

02 ④

Script

W Do you have all the ingredients?
M I think I have them all. Onions are here in the basket, and potatoes and carrots are in the refrigerator.
W I see, but I don't see any sesame oil here.
M It's in the cupboard, and I even bought some pepper yesterday.
W I don't think we need it today.

해석
여 요리에 필요한 모든 재료를 가지고 있니?
남 모두 있는 것 같아. 양파는 여기 바구니에 있고, 감자와 당근은 냉장고에 있어.
여 알았어. 하지만, 참기름이 안 보이는데.
남 그건 찬장에 있어. 그리고 어제 내가 심지어 후추도 샀단 말이야.
여 오늘은 그게 필요 없을 것 같은데.

해설
여자는 후추를 사왔다는 남자의 말에 후추가 필요 없을 것 같다고 말하고 있다.

어휘
ingredient[ingríːdiənt] 양념, 재료 / onion[ʌ́njən] 양파 / basket[bǽskit] 바구니 / potato[pətéitou] 감자 / carrot[kǽrət] 당근 / refrigerator[rifrìdʒəréitər] 냉장고 / sesame oil 참기름 / cupboard[kʌbərd] 찬장, 식기장 / pepper[pépər] 후추

03 ①

Script

W Do you know how old Sarah is? She doesn't look older than us, but she hangs out with high school students.

M I think she is three years older than us.

W You mean she is 17 years old?

M Yes. Our classmate, Carl is her brother, and he told me Sarah is three years older than him.

해석

여 너 Sarah가 몇 살인지 아니? 그녀가 우리보다 나이가 많아 보이지 않는데 고등학생이랑 어울려 다니더라.

남 내 생각에는 그녀가 우리보다 세 살 더 많을 거야.

여 네 말은 그녀가 열일곱 살이라는 거니?

남 응. 우리 반 친구, Carl이 그녀의 동생인데 그는 Sarah가 자신보다 세 살이 더 많다고 했어.

해설

Sarah는 열일곱 살이고 Carl은 Sarah보다 세 살이 더 어리다.

어휘

hang out with ~와 어울리다, 사귀다

04 ②

Script

W Hey, Adam. David said you are the best soccer player in the school.

M No, there are many better players like John and Peter. And Sam does much better than me.

W But you are the fastest player.

M That's true, but speed is not everything. Sam plays the best, and he scored three goals today.

W You're right. Anyway, I'm happy we won the game.

해석

여 야, Adam. David가 나에게 네가 학교에서 가장 훌륭한 축구 선수라고 했어.

남 아니야, John이나 Peter처럼 더 훌륭한 선수들이 많아. 그리고 Sam이 나보다 훨씬 축구를 잘해.

여 하지만, 네가 가장 빠른 선수잖아.

남 사실이긴 한데, 속도가 다는 아니잖아. Sam이 가장 잘해. 그리고 오늘도 그가 세 골이나 넣었잖아.

여 맞아. 어쨌든, 난 우리가 경기에서 이겨서 기뻐.

해설

Sam plays the best.라는 남자의 말에서 학교에서 Sam이 축구를 제일 잘한다는 것을 알 수 있다.

어휘

speed[spiːd] 속도 / score[skɔːr] (경기에서) 득점하다; 득점

05 ①

Script

W I know you read a lot of books. Do you have any favorite writers?

M No, I don't. I just like fantasy books.

W I've tried to read fantasy, but they were too long. So I gave up.

M You should read them. They are amazing books.

W Okay. By the way, I heard another Harry Potter book is coming out soon.

M I know. I'm dying to read it.

해석

여 네가 책을 많이 읽는다는 걸 알고 있어. 좋아하는 작가 있니?

남 아니, 없어. 나는 그냥 판타지 소설을 좋아할 뿐이야.

여 나도 판타지 소설을 읽어보려고 했는데 정말 길더라. 그래서 포기했어.

남 그 책들을 읽어보도록 해. 정말 재미있는 책이야.

여 알았어. 그런데 곧 해리포터 책이 한 권 더 나온다고 들었어.

남 나도 알아. 나 그 책이 정말 읽고 싶어.

해설

남자는 판타지 소설을 좋아하며 곧 출간될 해리포터를 정말 읽고 싶다고 말하고 있다.

어휘

favorite[féivərit] 아주 좋아하는 / writer[ráitər] 작가 / fantasy[fǽntəzi] 판타지 소설 / give up 포기하다 / come out (책이) 출간되다 / be dying to ~하고 싶어 죽다[못 견디다]

06 ①

Script

W Did you have a good weekend, Ian?

M Not really. My grandmother is in the hospital, so I visited her with my brother.

W Sorry to hear that. Is she sick or something?

M It was just a bad flu at first, but it has become worse. Now she is staying in the hospital.

W Cheer up! I'm sure she will feel better soon.

M Thank you. But I'm concerned about her health.

해석

여 너 좋은 주말 보냈니, Ian?

남 별로. 우리 할머니가 병원에 계셔서 동생이랑 병문안 다녀왔어.

여 안됐다. 할머니가 어디 아프시니?

남 처음에는 그냥 심한 독감이었는데 그게 심해지셨어. 지금 병원에 입원해 계셔.

여 힘내! 틀림없이 곧 나으실 거야.

남 고마워. 하지만, 그녀의 건강이 정말 걱정돼.

해설

I'm concerned about her health.라는 남자의 말에서 남자는 할머니의 건강을 염려하고 있음을 알 수 있다.

어휘

be in (the) hospital 입원하다 / flu[flu:] 독감 / feel better 기분이 좋아지다, 건강이 좋아지다 / Cheer up! 기운 내!, 힘내! / concerned[kənsə́:rnd] 걱정스러운, 염려하고 있는

07 ③

Script

W Ryan, did you turn off the lights and lock the door?

M I sure did.

W Okay, let's go. By the way, when are you coming home?

M School finishes at around four. I'll probably get home at about four thirty.

W Can you buy me some envelopes on the way home?

M No problem, Mom.

해석

여 Ryan, 불 끄고 문 잠갔지?

남 물론이죠.

여 알았어, 가자. 그런데 집에 몇 시에 들어오니?

남 4시쯤 학교가 끝나요. 아마 4시 반 정도에 집에 도착할 거예요.

여 집에 오는 길에 봉투 좀 사다 줄래?

남 그렇게 할게요, 엄마.

해설

Can you buy me some envelopes on the way home?라는 여자의 말을 통해 여자가 남자에게 봉투를 사오라고 부탁하고 있음을 알 수 있다.

어휘

turn off (전등, TV 등을) 끄다 / light[lait] 전등 / lock[lɑk] (자물쇠로) 잠그다; 자물쇠 / probably[prɑ́bəbli] 아마도 / envelope[énvəlòup] 봉투 / on the way home 집에 오는 도중에

08 ①

Script

W What seems to be the problem?

M My throat hurts, and I have a runny nose.

W I see. How long has it been like that?

M For two days.

W I think you caught a cold. Do you have a fever?

M Yes, I think so.

W OK. Let me check your temperature.

해석

여 뭐가 문제인가요?

남 목이 아프고 콧물이 나요.

여 그러시군요. 얼마 동안이나 그랬죠?

남 이틀 동안이요.

여 감기에 걸리신 거 같네요. 열이 있으신가요?

남 네, 그런 것 같아요.

여 알겠습니다. 제가 체온을 확인해보겠습니다.

해설

증상을 이야기하고 진단하는 상황으로 두 사람의 관계가 환자와 의사임을 알 수 있다.

어휘

throat[θrout] 목 / runny nose 콧물 / catch a cold 감기에 걸리다 / fever[fí:vər] 열 / have a fever 열이 있다 / check[tʃek] 확인하다 / temperature[témpərətʃər] 온도, 체온

09 ③

Script

M This musical instrument has wooden or metal bars. To play it, you hit them with special sticks. Some of them come with a different color on each bar. Many people think it is for children only, but you can see people playing it in an orchestra.

해석

여 이 악기는 나무 또는 금속 음판을 가지고 있습니다. 그것을 연주하기 위해 당신은 특별한 막대로 그 음판을 칩니다. 그것 중 어떤 것들은 각 음판 마다 다른 색을 가지고 있습니다. 많은 사람은 그것을 단지 아이들을 위한 것으로 생각하지만, 오케스트라에서 그것을 연주하는 사람을 볼 수 있습니다.

해설

막대기를 가지고 음판을 치는 악기는 실로폰이다.

어휘

musical[mjú:zikəl] 음악의, 음악용의 / instrument[ínstrəmənt] 악기, 기구 / wooden[wúdn] 나무로 된 / metal[métl] 금속의 / bar[bɑ:r] 바, 막대기, 빗장 / hit[hit] 치다 / stick[stik] 막대기 / come with ~이 딸려 있다 / orchestra[ɔ́:rkəstrə] 오케스트라

10 ③

Script

M I'm getting nervous.

W Don't worry. You'll do fine.

M There are so many cameras in the studio. I don't know which camera to look at.

W Just look in front of you. Try to relax and calm down.

M OK.

W When the director raises his thumb, we will start.

해석

남 점점 긴장이 돼요.

여 걱정하지 마세요. 잘하실 겁니다.

남 스튜디오 안에 카메라가 너무 많네요. 어떤 카메라를 봐야 할지 모르겠어요.

여 그냥 앞을 보세요. 긴장을 풀고 침착하세요.

남 알겠습니다.

여 감독이 엄지손가락을 올리면 시작하겠습니다.

해설

스튜디오에 카메라가 많고 떨린다는 남자의 말에서 두 사람이 대화하는 장소가 방송국임을 알 수 있다.

어휘
nervous[nə́:rvəs] 긴장한, 불안해하는 / studio[stjú:diòu] (방송국의) 스튜디오 / front[frʌnt] (위치상으로) 앞쪽 / relax[rilǽks] 긴장을 풀다 / calm down 진정하다 / director[diréktər] 감독 / raise[reiz] 올리다 / thumb[θʌm] 엄지손가락

11 ①

Script

M There was a big fire in a small store on Jackson Street. When the fire broke out, there were more than ten customers and three clerks inside. The store was on the third floor, and the people inside were frightened. But 119 rescuers got there in time and saved all of them.

해석

남 Jackson가에 있는 작은 가게에서 큰 화재가 발생했습니다. 화재가 발생했을 때 안에는 10명 이상의 고객과 3명의 직원이 있었습니다. 그 가게는 3층에 있었고 안에 있는 사람들은 겁에 질려 있었습니다. 그러나 119구조대가 제시간에 도착했고, 그들 모두를 구조했습니다.

해설

화재가 난 가게는 13층이 아니라 3층이다.

어휘
break out 발생하다 / customer[kʌ́stəmər] 손님, 고객 / clerk[klə:rk] 직원, 점원 / inside[insáid] ~의 안에 / frightened[fráitned] 겁먹은, 무서워하는 / rescuer[réskju:ər] 구조자 / save[seiv] 구하다

12 ④

Script

W Are you having a garage sale?

M Yes, I am. Are there any things that interest you?

W Let me see. How much is that bike?

M It's thirty dollars. It still rides well.

W I see. How about that radio?

M It's five dollars more than the bike. If it's not working, I will give you a refund.

해석

여 너는 지금 차고 세일을 하고 있니?

남 응, 그래. 네 관심을 끄는 물건이 있니?

여 좀 볼까. 저 자전거는 얼마니?

남 그건 30달러야. 아직 잘 나가.

여 그렇구나. 저 라디오는?

남 자전거보다 5달러 더 비싸. 작동하지 않으면 너에게 돈을 돌려줄게.

해설

자전거의 가격이 30달러이고 라디오가 자전거보다 5달러 더 비싸므로 라디오의 가격은 35달러이다.

어휘
interest[íntərist] 관심[주의]를 끌다, 관심을 갖게 하다; 관심, 흥미 / refund[rí:fʌnd/ri:fʌ́nd] 환불; 환불하다 / give a refund 환불해주다

13 ⑤

Script

W Good morning. It's Monday, August 14th. This is today's world weather report. London will be foggy, and New York will see heavy rainfall. Sydney will be cloudy and cold, but Beijing will be hot and humid. Finally, it will be sunny in Seoul.

해석

여 안녕하세요. 8월 14일 월요일입니다. 오늘의 세계 일기 예보입니다. 런던은 안개가 끼고, 뉴욕은 폭우가 내리겠습니다. 시드니는 흐리고 춥겠으나 베이징은 무덥고 습하겠습니다. 마지막으로 서울은 맑겠습니다.

해설

런던은 안개가 끼고, 뉴욕은 폭우가 내릴 것이며, 시드니는 흐리고 춥고, 베이징은 덥고 습하다고 예보하고 있다.

어휘
foggy[fɔ́(:)gi] 안개가 낀 / rainfall[réinfɔ̀:l] 강우 / humid[hjú:mid] 습한 / finally[fáinəli] 마지막으로, 결국

14 ①

Script

M Is this your bag?

W Yes, it is.

M I thought yours was pink, not red.

W I bought a pink one yesterday.

M But they are the same style.

W I know, but the colors are different. And I also have another color, too.

M You should stop wasting money on useless stuff.

해석

남 이것이 네 가방이니?

여 응, 맞아.

남 나는 네 가방이 빨간색이 아니고, 분홍색인 줄 알았는데.

여 어제 분홍색으로 하나 샀어.

남 하지만, 같은 모양이잖아.

여 알아, 하지만 색이 다르잖아. 그리고 나에게 다른 색이 하나 더 있어.

남 너는 그런 쓸모없는 것에 돈을 낭비하지 말아야 해.

해설

같은 모양의 가방을 세 개나 가지고 있다는 여자에게 남자는 쓸모없는 것에 돈을 낭비하지 말아야 한다고 충고하고 있다.

어휘
useless[jú:slis] 쓸모없는 / stuff[stʌf] 물건

15 ②

Script

M I'm very upset that Mom didn't wake me up.

W So you were late for school. Come on, you're not a child any more.

M But she promised that she would.

W Don't you have an alarm clock?

M No, I don't. Mom always wakes me up. Why do I need one?

해석

남 엄마가 나를 깨워 주시지 않아서 정말 화가 나.

여 그래서 네가 학교에 늦었구나. 제발, 너는 더 이상 아이가 아니잖아.

남 하지만 엄마가 깨워주겠다고 약속했단 말이야.

여 너 자명종 시계 없니?

남 응, 없어. 엄마가 항상 나를 깨워줘. 왜 내게 그것이 필요하겠니?

해설

남자는 엄마가 깨워주지 않아 늦잠을 잤다고 말하고 있다.

어휘

upset[ʌpsét] 화난, 초조한 / wake up 일어나다, ~를 깨워주다, 정신이 들게 하다 / alarm clock 자명종 시계

16 ⑤

Script

M ① Susan is taking a nap.

② Jacob is reading a comic book.

③ Ross and Rachel are exchanging notes.

④ Anne sitting in the back seat is listening to music.

⑤ Christine is listening carefully to the teacher.

해석

남 ① Susan은 낮잠을 자고 있다.

② Jacob은 만화책을 읽고 있다.

③ Ross와 Rachel은 쪽지를 주고받고 있다.

④ 뒷좌석에 앉아 있는 Anne은 노래를 듣고 있다.

⑤ Christine은 선생님의 말씀을 주의 깊게 듣고 있다.

해설

수업 시간에는 선생님의 말씀에 주의를 기울여야 한다.

어휘

take a nap 낮잠을 자다 / comic book 만화책 / exchange[ikstʃéindʒ] 교환하다 / note[nout] 쪽지, 메모 / listen carefully 주의 깊게 듣다

17 ①

Script

W I have so many things to do, but not enough time. I should finish my report, do some volunteer work, and go to the library.

M Take it easy. Sometimes I feel the same way. What is the most important thing to do?

W Well, the report has to be done by tomorrow, so it is the most important thing!

M Then, do it first.

해석

여 해야 할 일은 정말 많은데 시간이 충분하지 않아. 보고서를 끝내야 하고, 봉사 활동도 해야 하고, 책을 반납하러 도서관에도 가야 해.

남 진정해. 가끔 나도 똑같이 느낄 때가 있어. 가장 중요한 일이 무엇이니?

여 글쎄, 보고서를 내일까지 끝내야 하니까, 그것이 가장 중요한 일이야.

남 그러면, 그것을 먼저 해.

해설

남자는 여자에게 가장 중요한 일을 먼저 하라고 충고하고 있다.

어휘

Take it easy. 진정해.

18 ⑤

Script

① M I think it's true.
W Why do you think so?

② M She lost the game.
W That's too bad.

③ M He's much better now.
W I'm glad to hear that.

④ M Can you go shopping with me?
W I'd love to, but I can't.

⑤ M Will you come to my house?
W Sure, I have an appointment.

해석

① 남 난 그게 사실인 것 같아.
여 왜 그렇게 생각하니?

② 남 그녀가 경기에 졌어.
여 정말 안됐다.

③ 남 그는 지금 훨씬 나아졌어.
여 그 얘길 들으니 기뻐.

④ 남 나와 쇼핑하러 갈래?
여 정말 가고 싶은데, 안 돼.

⑤ 남 우리 집에 올 수 있니?
여 물론이야. 나 약속이 있어.

해설

⑤ 자신의 집에 오라는 남자의 질문에 갈 수 있다고 응답하고 갈 수 없는 이유를 말하고 있다.

어휘

glad[glæd] 기쁜, 즐거운 / appointment[əpɔ́intmənt] 약속

19 ①

Script

W What are you doing?

M I'm searching for the weather forecast for this weekend.

W For what?

M Mike, Grace, and I are planning to go hiking up Mount Forest this weekend.

W Count me in, too.

해석

여 너 뭐 하고 있니?

남 이번 주말의 일기 예보를 검색하고 있어.

여 왜?

남 Mike, Grace, 그리고 나는 이번 주말에 Forest 산으로 하이킹하러 갈 계획이야.

여 나도 끼워 줘.

해설

② 너는 돈을 낭비하고 있어.

③ 알았어. 나는 내일부터 시작할 수 있어.

④ 나 지난주에 소풍 갔다 왔어.

⑤ 나 너에게 보여줄 것이 있어.

하이킹하러 갈 거라는 남자의 말에 나도 끼워 달라는 말이 가장 알맞다.

어휘

count ~ in ~을 포함시키다[끼우다] / go on a picnic 소풍 가다 / search[səːrtʃ] 찾다, 검색하다 / forecast[fɔ́ːrkæ̀st] 예측, (일기의) 예보 / go hiking 하이킹하러 가다

20 ②

Script

W Happy birthday to you, Alex! Here is a little gift for you. I hope you will like it.

M Thank you. Can I open it now?

W Sure, go ahead.

M Wow! It's a baseball cap. I really like it. Thanks a million.

W It's my pleasure.

해석

여 생일 축하해, Alex! 여기 너에게 줄 작은 선물이 있어. 네 마음에 들었으면 좋겠어.

남 고마워. 지금 열어 봐도 될까?

여 물론이지, 어서 열어 봐.

남 와! 야구 모자구나. 정말로 마음에 들어. 정말 고마워.

여 천만에.

해설

① 마음껏 먹어!

③ 내 걱정은 하지 마.

④ 응, 그건 정말 비싸.

⑤ 어떤 음식은 정말 맛있어.

고맙다는 남자의 말에 이어질 알맞은 응답을 고른다.

어휘

help oneself 마음껏 먹다 / It's my pleasure. 천만에요. / delicious[dilíʃəs] 맛있는 / gift[gift] 선물 / go ahead 어서 ~하시오 / Thanks a million. 정말 감사합니다.

p.64~67

08회 영어듣기모의고사

01 ②	02 ①	03 ③	04 ③	05 ⑤
06 ②	07 ③	08 ④	09 ①	10 ③
11 ⑤	12 ④	13 ⑤	14 ③	15 ④
16 ②	17 ①	18 ①	19 ⑤	20 ③

01 ②

Script

W Someone just took my bag away. I was too scared to cry for help. He is wearing a striped shirt and blue jeans. And he has short hair with a mustache. Please find him.

해석

여 누군가 제 가방을 방금 빼앗아 갔어요. 저는 너무 무서워서 도움을 요청할 수 없었어요. 그는 줄무늬 셔츠에 청바지를 입고 있어요. 그리고 콧수염이 있고 머리가 짧아요. 제발, 그를 찾아주세요.

해설

여자의 가방을 빼앗아 간 남자는 줄무늬 셔츠에 청바지를 입고 있으며 머리가 짧고 콧수염이 있다.

어휘

too ~ to+동사원형 너무 ~해서 …할 수 없다 / cry for help 도와[구해]달라고 외치다 / striped[straipt] 줄무늬가 있는 / mustache[mʌ́stæʃ] 콧수염

02 ①

Script

W Did you pack everything?

M Um... I have my toothbrush, socks, and underwear. I just need to pack a towel. How about you?

W I haven't even started yet.

M Let me help you then.

해석

여 너 짐 다 쌌니?

남 음, 칫솔, 양말, 속옷은 넣었어. 수건만 있으면 돼. 너는?

여 난 아직 시작도 못 했어.

남 그러면 내가 도와줄게.

해설

I just need to pack a towel.라는 남자의 말에서 수건이 필요하다는 것을 알 수 있다.

어휘

pack[pæk] 짐을 싸다; 짐, 꾸러미 / toothbrush[túːθbrʌ̀ʃ] 칫솔 / underwear[ʌ́ndərwɛ̀ər] 속옷 / towel[táuəl] 수건

03 ③

Script

M What do you want to be in the future?

W I want to be a doctor, but my parents want me to be a professor.

M You can be both when you become a doctor.

W That's a good idea. How about you?

M I want to invent something for handicapped people.

W Sounds wonderful!

해석

남 너는 미래에 무엇이 되고 싶니?

여 나는 의사가 되고 싶은데, 부모님은 내가 교수가 되기를 원하셔.

남 네가 의사가 되면 둘 다 할 수 있잖아.

여 그거 좋은 생각이다. 너는?

남 나는 장애인들을 위해 무언가를 발명하고 싶어.

여 멋지다!

해설

I want to invent something for handicapped people.라는 남자의 말에서 남자가 발명가가 되고 싶어 한다는 것을 알 수 있다.

어휘

future[fjúːtʃər] 미래 / in the future 미래에 / professor[prəfésər] 교수 / both[bouθ] 둘 다, 양쪽 모두 / invent[invént] 발명하다 / handicapped[hǽndikæ̀pt] 신체적[정신적] 장애가 있는

04 ③

Script

M He has two sharp teeth and usually wears a long black coat. He appears at night and sucks human blood. People believe that he hates sunlight and silver and he could die from them. There have been a lot of books and movies about him.

해석

남 그는 두 개의 날카로운 이를 가지고 있고 주로 긴 검은 코트를 입습니다. 그는 밤에 나타나며 사람들의 피를 빨아 먹습니다. 사람들은 그가 햇빛과 은을 싫어하고 그것 때문에 죽을 수도 있다고 믿습니다. 그에 대한 영화와 책들이 많이 있습니다.

해설

두 개의 날카로운 이를 가지고 있으며, 검은 코트를 주로 입고, 햇빛과 은을 싫어한다는 말에서 드라큘라임을 알 수 있다.

어휘

sharp[ʃɑːrp] 날카로운 / tooth[tuːθ] 이, 치아 (pl. teeth) / appear[əpíər] 나타나다, 등장하다 / suck[sʌk] 빨아먹다[마시다] / human[hjúːmən] 사람, 인간; 인간의 / blood[blʌd] 피, 혈액 / hate[heit] 싫어하다 / sunlight[sʌ́nlàit] 햇빛 / silver[sílvər] 은 / die from ~ 때문에 죽다

05 ⑤

Script

M Good morning, madam.

W Good morning. I'm checking out.

M OK. Can I have your key?

W Sure. Here you are.

M Thank you. Let me see. You stayed for three nights, right?

W That's right. I believe it's thirty dollars per night.

M That's correct.

해석

남 안녕하세요, 부인?

여 안녕하세요. 체크아웃 하려고요.

남 알겠습니다. 열쇠를 주시겠어요?

여 물론이죠. 여기 있습니다.

남 감사합니다. 어디 보자. 3일 밤을 묵으셨네요, 그렇죠?

여 맞습니다. 하룻밤에 30달러라고 알고 있어요.

남 맞습니다.

해설

하루 숙박 요금이 30달러이고 3일 동안 묵었기 때문에 여자가 지불해야 하는 숙박 요금은 90달러이다.

어휘

check out (계산을 치르고) 호텔에서 나오다 / per[pəːr] 당, 각 / correct[kərékt] 올바른, 정확한

06 ②

Script

M I didn't take the test today. Our teacher got sick and couldn't come to class.

W So are you taking it tomorrow?

M No.

W Why not?

M We have class twice a week on Tuesday and Thursday. Tomorrow is Friday, so we don't have class until next week.

W I see.

해석

남 나 오늘 시험 보지 않았어. 선생님이 아프셔서 수업에 오지 못하셨거든.

여 그러면 내일 그 시험을 볼 거니?

남 아니.

여 왜?

남 우리는 수업이 일주일에 두 번, 화요일과 목요일에 있어. 내일은 금요일이어서 다음 주까지 수업이 없어.

여 그렇구나.

해설

내일이 금요일이고 수업이 화요일과 목요일에 있기 때문에 남자는 다음 주 화요일에 시험을 볼 것이다.

어휘

take a test 시험을 보다 / until[əntíl] ~까지, ~할 때까지

07 ③

Script

W Sean, I'm very upset with Jacob.

M Did he do something wrong?

W I told Jacob not to tell Bella about our plan, but he did.

M Oh, no. We are in trouble.

W We have to come up with a good excuse for her.

해석

여 Sean, 나 Jacob 때문에 무척 화가 나.

남 그가 뭘 잘못했니?

여 내가 Jacob에게 우리의 계획에 대해서 Bella에게 말하지 말라고 했는데 했어.

남 아, 안돼. 우리 이제 큰일 났다.

여 우리는 그녀에게 할 그럴싸한 변명을 생각해내야 해.

해설

I told Jacob not to tell Bella about our plan, but he did.를 통해 여자가 화난 이유를 알 수 있다.

어휘

be in trouble 어려움에 처하다 / come up with 떠올리다, 마련하다 / excuse[ikskjúːz] 핑계, 변명

08 ④

Script

M I'm back, Melissa. Did anyone call for me while I was out?

W Yes, there was, Mr. Brown. Someone named Jennifer called. She wants you to call her back at work. Her number is 555-1234.

M Did she say what it was about?

W She said she has something to tell you about the design.

M Thank you. I'd better call her right now.

해석

남 Melissa, 저 돌아왔어요. 제가 나간 사이에 저에게 전화한 사람이 있나요?

여 네, 있어요, Brown 씨. Jennifer라는 사람이 전화했어요. 당신이 회사로 전화를 해주길 원하고 있어요. 그녀의 번호가 555-1234이에요.

남 그녀가 무슨 일 때문에 그런지 얘기했나요?

여 디자인에 관해서 얘기를 할 것이 있다고 했어요.

남 고마워요. 그녀에게 지금 바로 전화를 해보는 게 좋을 것 같군요.

해설

She wants you to call her back at work.라는 여자의 말을 통해 Jennifer가 집이 아니라 회사로 전화해 달라고 부탁했음을 알 수 있다.

어휘

name[neim] 이름; 이름을 붙이다, ~라고 부르다 / call back 다시 전화를 하다

09 ①

Script

M Eeek, it is a grasshopper. Do you keep it in your house?

W Yes, I'm very interested in insects.

M It is hard to imagine that a girl likes insects. Even some boys like me don't like them.

W I know. Some people hate insects. But if you look at them closely, you'll find them to be amazing.

해석

남 윽, 그거 메뚜기잖아. 집에서 그걸 키우니?

여 응, 나는 곤충에 관심이 많아.

남 여자애가 곤충을 좋아한다는 걸 상상하기 어려워. 심지어 나 같은 몇몇 남자 아이들도 곤충을 싫어하는데.

여 알아. 어떤 사람들은 곤충을 싫어하지. 하지만, 곤충들을 가까이에서 보면 그것들이 대단하다는 것을 알 수 있을 거야.

해설

I'm very interested in insects.라는 여자의 말을 통해 여자가 곤충에 관심이 있다는 것을 알 수 있다.

어휘

grasshopper[grǽshɑ̀pər] 메뚜기 / insect[ínsekt] 곤충 / imagine[imǽdʒin] 상상하다 / closely[klóusli] 가까이

10 ③

Script

M What is taking you so long? I need to use the computer, too.

W I'm sorry, but will you wait for a minute?

M What are you doing? Are you writing a report?

W No, I'm writing an email to my elementary school teacher.

M What for?

W I want to invite him to our school concert. He is the one who taught me how to play the violin.

해석

남 너 뭐가 그렇게 오래 걸리니? 나도 컴퓨터를 써야 한단 말이야.

여 미안한데, 조금 기다려 줄래?

남 뭐 하고 있는 중이니? 보고서 쓰고 있니?

여 아니, 초등학교 때 선생님에게 이메일을 쓰고 있어.

남 왜?

여 선생님을 학교 음악회에 초대하고 싶어. 그 선생님이 나에게 바이올린 가르쳐 주신 분이거든.

해설

I want to invite him to our school concert.라는 여자의 말을 통해 이메일을 쓰는 목적이 초대임을 알 수 있다.

어휘

elementary school 초등학교 / invite[inváit] 초대하다 / how to play 어떻게 연주하는지

11 ⑤

Script

W Does your mother have a job?

M Yes, she is a nurse. How about your mom?

W She is a reporter, and she is always busy. Even after work, she cleans the house, cooks, and does the laundry.

M Does your father help your mom?

W No, he is busy watching TV and reading newspapers. That's not fair.

M You can say that again.

해석

여 너희 어머니는 일을 하시니?

남 응, 우리 엄마는 간호사야. 너희 어머니는?

여 기자인데, 항상 바쁘셔. 일이 끝나고 나서도 집 청소하고, 요리하고, 빨래를 하셔.

남 너의 아빠는 엄마를 좀 도와주시니?

여 아니, 아빠는 TV 보고, 신문 읽으시느라 바쁘셔. 불공평하지.

남 내 말이 그 말이야.

해설

You can say that again.은 '바로 그거야.', '내 말이 그 말이야.'라는 뜻으로 동의를 나타내는 표현이다.

어휘

nurse[nəːrs] 간호사 / reporter[ripɔ́ːrtər] 기자 / do the laundry 세탁하다 / busy+-ing ~하느라 바쁘다 / fair[fɛər] 공평한

12 ④

Script

W What time are we going to the library?

M Eight in the morning.

W How do you want to get there?

M Let's take the subway.

W There are too many people on the subway around that time. How about using our own two feet?

M Sounds good.

해석

여 우리 몇 시에 도서관에 갈 거야?

남 아침 8시에.

여 거기 어떻게 갈까?

남 지하철을 타자.

여 그 시간에는 지하철에 사람이 너무 많아. 우리 두 발을 사용하는 건 어떨까?

남 좋아.

해설

How about using our two feet?라는 여자의 말에 남자가 동의하고 있기 때문에 두 사람이 도서관까지 걸어갈 거라는 것을 알 수 있다.

어휘

own[oun] 자기 자신의, 자기 소유의

13 ⑤

Script

M I have a son, Jake. He never listens to anyone. When someone tells him something, he thinks of something else. Later, he says nobody told him about it. For example, one week ago I said we would visit his grandparents on the coming Saturday, but he didn't listen. And yesterday he asked me to go fishing on that day.

해석

남 나에게 Jake라는 아들이 한 명 있습니다. 그 아이는 다른 사람의 말을 절대 듣지 않아요. 다른 사람들이 그에게 무언가를 얘기할 때 그는 다른 생각을 합니다. 나중에, 그는 누구도 그것을 얘기해 주지 않았다고 합니다. 예를 들면, 일주일 전에 다가오는 토요일에 조부모님 댁에 갈 거라고 제가 얘길 했는데도 듣지 않았죠. 그러고 어제 그날 낚시를 가자는 거예요.

해설

남자는 자신의 아들, Jake가 다른 사람이 말할 때는 듣지 않는다는 말하고 있다.

어휘

grandparent[grǽndpὲərənt] 조부모 / coming[kʌ́miŋ] 다가오는, 다음에 / go fishing 낚시하러 가다

14 ③

Script

W I can't believe that you didn't join the basketball club. You are definitely tall and fast enough. Don't they need any more players?

M No, that's not it. Actually, I still have pain in my shoulder.

W Still?

M Yes, I thought I was OK, but when I stretched my arm, it hurt.

W That's too bad.

Q Why couldn't the man join the basketball club?

해석

여 네가 농구 클럽에 가입하지 않았다니 믿어지지 않아. 분명히 너는 충분히 키가 크고 빠르잖아. 더 이상 선수가 필요 없대?

남 아니, 그게 아니야. 사실, 아직도 내 어깨에 통증이 있어.

여 아직도?

남 그래, 나는 괜찮은 줄 알았는데, 내가 팔을 뻗었을 때 아팠어.

여 정말 안됐다.

질문 남자는 왜 농구 클럽에 가입할 수 없었습니까?

해설

I still have pain in my shoulder.에서 남자는 어깨 통증 때문에 클럽에 가입할 수 없었다는 것을 알 수 있다.

어휘

definitely[défənitli] 분명히, 확실히 / still[stil] 아직도, 여전히 / shoulder[ʃóuldər] 어깨 / stretch[stretʃ] 뻗다, 펴다

15 ④

Script

M Jessica, who is the woman with the blond hair? She is talking to Jimmy now.

W She is Amanda, Jimmy's twin sister.

M I didn't know he had such a pretty sister. Can you tell me more about her?

W She is 28 years old, and she is a nurse at Saint Jones Hospital. She and I went to the same high school.

해석

남 Jessica, 저 금발 머리 여자는 누구니? 지금 Jimmy와 얘기하고 있어.

여 그녀는 Jimmy의 쌍둥이 여동생, Amanda야.

남 그에게 저렇게 예쁜 여동생이 있다는 걸 몰랐어. 그녀에 대해서 더 얘기해 줘.

여 그녀는 28살이고, Saint Jones 병원의 간호사야. 그녀와 나는 같은 고등학교에 다녔어.

해설

① 그녀의 머리는 금발이다.

② 그녀는 Jimmy의 여동생이다.

③ 그녀는 스물여덟 살이다.

⑤ 그녀와 Jessica는 같은 고등학교에 다녔다.

she is a nurse at Saint Jones Hospital.라는 여자의 말을 통해 Amanda의 직업이 간호사임을 알 수 있다.

어휘

blond[blɔnd] 금발의 / twin[twin] 쌍둥이 중의 하나, 쌍둥이; 쌍둥이의

16 ②

Script

M We are going to hike 100 kilometers over a three-day period. Here are a few rules for hiking. Please drink a lot of water while hiking. Helping each other and not getting hurt are two of the most important things on our trip. So help other students. If anything happens, please let your teacher know at once.

해석

남 우리는 3일의 기간 동안 100킬로미터를 하이킹하려고 합니다. 하이킹하는 동안 몇 가지 규칙이 있습니다. 하이킹하는 동안 많은 양의 물을 마십시오. 서로 돕고 다치지 않는 것이 우리 일정 중에서 가장 중요한 두 가지 사항입니다. 따라서 다른 학생들을 도와주십시오. 만약 일이 발생하면 여러분의 선생님에게 즉시 알리십시오.

해설

개인 소지품에 대한 언급은 없다.

어휘

hike[haik] 하이킹하다 / kilometer[kilámitər] 킬로미터 / period[píəriəd] 기간 / rule[ruːl] 규칙, 원칙 / get hurt 다치다 / trip[trip] 여행, 이동 / at once 즉시

17 ①

Script

① **W** Where are you going for summer vacation?
M My vacation starts from next week.

② **W** Have you ever heard of a koala?
M Yes, it lives in Australia.

③ **W** Would you give my puppy a bath?
M Sure, where is the puppy?

④ **W** Let's keep this a secret.
M Okay. I won't tell anybody.

⑤ **W** Are you ready to order?
M I'd like a tuna sandwich.

해석

① 여 너는 여름휴가로 어디에 갈 거니?
남 내 휴가는 다음 주부터 시작해.

② 여 너는 코알라에 대해 들어 본 적 있니?
남 응, 그건 호주에 살아.

③ 여 내 강아지 목욕 좀 시켜줄래?
남 알았어. 강아지는 어디에 있니?

④ 여 이거 비밀로 하자.
남 알았어. 아무에게도 말하지 않을게.

⑤ 여 주문할 준비 되셨습니까?
남 참치 샌드위치로 주세요.

해설

① 여자가 휴가를 어디로 갈 것인지를 묻고 있기 때문에 응답으로 장소가 와야 자연스럽다.

어휘

vacation[veikéiʃən] 휴가, 방학 / koala[kouáːlə] 코알라 / Australia[ɔːstréiljə] 호주 / give a bath 목욕시키다 / puppy[pʌ́pi] 강아지 / secret[síːkrit] 비밀 / order[ɔ́ːrdər] 주문하다; 주문 / tuna[tjúːnə] 참치 / sandwich[sǽndwitʃ] 샌드위치

18 ①

Script

W When are we going out for dinner?

M As soon as your brother comes back.

W Are we going to the same restaurant that we went to last time, Dad?

M No. We are going to a Japanese restaurant this time.

W Sounds good.

M Here he comes. Let's go.

해석

여 우리 언제 저녁 먹으러 나가요?

남 네 오빠가 오자마자.

여 우리 지난번에 갔던 식당과 같은 식당 가나요, 아빠?

남 아니. 이번에는 일본 식당에 가려고 해.

여 좋아요.

남 저기 네 오빠가 오는구나. 가자꾸나.

해설
여자가 남자에게 외식하러 언제, 어디로 갈 것인지 대해 묻고 있다.

어휘
go out for dinner 저녁 먹으러 나가다 / as soon as ~하자마자 / come back 돌아오다

19 ⑤

Script

W It's raining outside.

M Is it? Oh, no.

W You're going on a picnic to Disneyland, right?

M Yes. If it keeps raining, we are not going.

W Don't worry. I'm sure it will stop.

M But I'm afraid it won't stop.

해석

여 밖에 비가 오네.

남 그래? 아, 안 돼.

여 너 디즈니랜드로 소풍 갈 거지, 맞지?

남 응. 비가 계속 오면 가지 않을 거야.

여 걱정하지 마. 분명히 비가 그칠 거야.

남 하지만, 비가 멈추지 않을 것 같아 걱정돼.

해설
① 아마도 다음에.
② 갈 준비됐니?
③ 너는 정말 즐거운 시간을 보냈어.
④ 나는 거기 세 번 가 봤어.
비가 틀림없이 그칠 거라는 여자의 말에 알맞은 응답을 고른다.

어휘
outside[àutsáid] 밖에, 밖으로 / go on a picnic 소풍 가다 / keep+-ing 계속 ~하다

20 ③

Script

M Where is John?

W He is sleeping in his bed.

M What made him so tired?

W Well, he spent all day helping the elderly.

M Was it part of his school activities?

W No, it wasn't. He said he just wanted to do it.

M We should give him a big hand.

해석

남 John은 어디 있나요?

여 침대에서 자고 있어요.

남 그는 뭐가 그렇게 피곤한 거예요?

여 그게, 온종일 노인들을 도왔어요.

남 그게 학교 활동의 일부였어요?

여 아니, 그게 아니에요. 그가 얘기하는데 자신이 그냥 그것을 하고 싶었대요.

남 그에게 박수를 쳐줘야겠어요.

해설
① 그가 곧 감기에 걸릴지도 몰라요.
② 그는 피아노를 매우 잘 치지는 않아요.
④ 내가 다시는 그렇게 하지 말라고 그에게 말할게요.
⑤ 그는 운동하는 데 시간을 덜 보내야 해요.
착한 일을 한 John에게 칭찬을 해주자는 말을 고른다.

어휘
give a big hand 큰 박수를 보내다 / elderly[éldərli] 연세가 드신 / the elderly 노인 / activity[æktívəti] 활동

09회 영어듣기모의고사

p.72~75

01 ③	02 ①	03 ①	04 ⑤	05 ④
06 ④	07 ①	08 ⑤	09 ①	10 ②
11 ⑤	12 ②	13 ①	14 ⑤	15 ②
16 ②	17 ②	18 ①	19 ⑤	20 ②

01 ③

Script

M Jenny, let's go to the beach.

W I'm afraid we can't. Did you hear the weather forecast?

M No, I didn't.

W Look at the dark clouds in the sky. It may rain soon.

M Do you want me to check the weather?

W I think that's no use. Let's go next time.

해석

남 Jenny, 해변에 가자.

여 우리 못 갈 것 같아. 너 일기 예보 들었어?

남 아니, 못 들었어.

여 하늘에 먹구름을 봐. 곧 비가 올지도 몰라.

남 내가 일기 예보를 확인할까?

여 소용없을 것 같아. 다음에 가자.

해설
하늘에 먹구름을 보라며 곧 비가 올지도 모른다는 여자의 말을 통해 날씨가 흐리다는 것을 알 수 있다.

어휘
dark[dɑːrk] 어두운, 짙은, 검은 / cloud[klaud] 구름 / check[tʃek] 확인하다 / use[juːs] 사용, 쓰임; 사용하다, 쓰다 / be no use 소용없다, 쓸모없다

02 ①

Script

M Excuse me. I'm looking for a book titled *Oliver Twist*.

W You mean the book written by Charles Dickens?

M Yes, that's right.

W Okay, let me do a search for you. (pause) I'm afraid that the book has already been checked out.

M Then, when would I be able to check out the book?

W It says it will be returned by next Monday.

해석

남 실례합니다. '올리버 트위스트'라는 책을 찾고 있는데요.

여 찰스 디킨스가 쓴 책 말씀하시는 건가요?

남 네, 맞아요.

여 알겠습니다. 제가 검색을 해보겠습니다. 죄송한데 그 책은 이미 대출 중입니다.

남 그러면, 언제 제가 그 책을 대출할 수 있을까요?

여 다음 주 월요일까지는 반납될 거라고 쓰여 있네요.

해설

남자가 빌리려고 책의 대출 상태를 여자와 확인하고 있는 상황으로 대화가 이루어지는 곳이 도서관임을 알 수 있다.

어휘

title[táitl] 표제를 붙이다; 제목 / search[səːrtʃ] 조사, 검색; 검색하다, 찾다 / do a search 찾다, 검색하다 / check out (도서관 등에서) 대출하다

03 ①

Script

W Carl, I talked to your mother on the phone yesterday.

M Did my mother call you?

W Yes, because you are a new student, she is worried about you. Do you have any problems with school life?

M No, not at all.

W Great. Have you made some friends?

M Yes, I have a few friends. They are very friendly.

해석

여 Carl, 어제 너희 어머니와 통화를 했단다.

남 저희 어머니가 전화하셨나요?

여 그래, 네가 새로 전학 온 학생이어서 걱정을 하고 계셔. 학교생활에 문제가 있니?

남 아니오, 전혀 없어요.

여 잘 됐구나. 친구는 좀 사귀었니?

남 네, 친구가 몇 명 있어요. 그들은 매우 친절해요.

해설

선생님이 새로 전학 온 학생에게 학교생활에 대해 물어보는 상황이다.

어휘

talk on the phone 전화로 이야기하다 / make a friend 친구를 사귀다 / friendly[fréndli] 친절한, 다정한

04 ⑤

Script

W James, the museum opens at ten o'clock, doesn't it?

M Yes, how are we going to get there?

W If we take the bus, it takes thirty minutes, but if we take the subway, it takes twenty minutes.

M I see. Let's just take the bus.

W Sounds good to me.

M The bus leaves at nine twenty, so let's meet at nine fifteen at the bus stop.

W OK. See you then.

해석

여 James, 박물관이 10시에 문을 열지, 그렇지 않니?

남 응, 우리 거기 어떻게 갈까?

여 버스를 타면 30분 걸리고 지하철을 타면 20분 걸려.

남 그렇구나. 우리 그냥 버스를 타자.

여 좋아.

남 버스가 9시 20분에 출발하니까 버스 정거장에서 9시 15분에 만나자.

여 알았어. 그때 보자.

해설

두 사람은 박물관까지 버스를 타고 갈 예정으로 박물관까지 30분이 걸리며 버스는 9시 20분에 출발한다고 했다. 따라서 박물관에 도착할 시간은 9시 50분이다.

어휘

bus stop 버스 정거장

05 ④

Script

M I have two tickets to a concert, and I'll give them to you at half price.

W Sorry, but I don't want them.

M Why? You like the singer. You don't have the time?

W No, I just don't want them.

M Give me a reason why. Are they still too expensive?

W No, I just don't want to go alone.

해석

남 나에게 콘서트 표가 두 장 있는데 내가 너에게 그것을 절반 가격에 줄게.

여 미안한데, 난 필요 없어.

남 왜? 너 그 가수 좋아하잖아. 시간이 없니?

여 아니, 그냥 필요 없어.

남 이유를 말해 봐. 아직도 많이 비싸니?

여 아니, 그냥 혼자 가기 싫단 말이야.

해설

I just don't want to go alone.라는 여자의 말을 통해 같이 갈 사람이 없다는 것을 알 수 있다.

어휘

have the time 시간이 있다 / give a reason 이유를 대다 / expensive[ikspénsiv] 값이 비싼 / alone[əlóun] 혼자, 홀로

06 ④

Script

W I came here with my father. Do you want to meet him?

M Of course. Where is he?

W He is over there next to the man wearing glasses.

M He is going bald, right?

W That's not him. My father is not going bald. He has short hair.

M Okay. I know which one.

해석

여 저는 여기에 저희 아빠와 같이 왔어요. 만나 보시겠어요?

남 당연하지. 어디 계시니?

여 그는 저기 안경을 쓴 사람 옆에 계세요.

남 대머리가 되어 가고 있으시지, 그렇지?

여 그분이 아니에요. 저희 아버지는 머리가 벗겨지지 않으셨어요. 그는 머리가 짧아요.

남 그렇구나. 누구인지 알겠다.

해설

안경 낀 남자 옆에 있는 머리가 짧은 남자가 여자의 아빠이다.

어휘

bald[bɔːld] 머리가 벗겨진, 대머리의

07 ①

Script

W Daniel, here is your notebook.

M Thanks. I actually needed it today.

W Where have you been? I was looking for you.

M I was playing soccer with my classmates.

W I see. You are covered in dirt from head to toe.

M I know. That's why I'm going home now.

W OK. See you later.

해석

여 Daniel, 여기 네 공책이 있어.

남 고마워. 사실 나 오늘 그게 필요했거든.

여 너 어디 있었니? 너를 찾아다녔어.

남 반 친구들과 축구를 하고 있었어.

여 그렇구나. 너 머리끝에서 발끝까지 먼지를 뒤집어썼구나.

남 알아. 그게 지금 내가 집에 가는 이유야.

여 그래. 나중에 보자.

해설

'온몸에 먼지를 뒤집어썼구나.'라는 여자의 말에 남자는 That's why I'm going home now.라고 응답하고 있기 때문에 남자가 집에 가서 할 일이 샤워임을 알 수 있다.

어휘

notebook[nóutbùk] 공책, 노트 / be covered in ~로 덮여 있다 / dirt[dəːrt] 먼지 / from head to toe 머리끝에서 발끝까지

08 ⑤

Script

W What's wrong? You look depressed.

M I really studied hard, but I didn't get a good grade. My mom will be angry at me.

W Was it worse than the last test?

M No, it is better but not by much.

W Hey, John. Try to look on the bright side of things.

해석

여 무슨 일 있니? 너 우울해 보여.

남 나 정말 열심히 공부했는데 좋은 성적을 받지 못했어. 엄마가 내게 화를 내실 거야.

여 지난번 성적보다 안 좋으니?

남 아니, 좋아지기는 했는데 많이는 아냐.

여 이 봐, John. 좋은 면을 보려고 노력해봐.

해설

시험 성적이 안 좋아 우울해하는 남자에게 여자는 좋은 면을 보려고 노력해 보라고 위로를 하고 있다.

어휘

depressed[diprést] (기분이) 우울한 / get a good grade 좋은 성적을 얻다[받다] / worse[wəːrs] 더 나쁜 (bad-worse-worst) / by much 대단히, 훨씬, 크게 / look on the bright side 긍정적으로 생각하다

09 ①

Script

M Look at that wall. Oliver has drawn many things on it.

W It looks terrible.

M What do you want to do about it?

W I think we should change the wallpaper.

M Since we have guests this weekend, we'd better do it now.

W I'll go and get some. What color do you want?

해석

남 벽 좀 봐요. Oliver가 벽에 많은 것을 그렸네요.

여 보기가 안 좋아요.

남 그걸 어떻게 했으면 좋겠어요?

여 제 생각엔 벽지를 바꿔야 할 것 같아요.

남 이번 주말에 손님이 오실 거니까 지금 하는 게 좋겠어요.

여 제가 가서 벽지를 좀 사 올게요. 어떤 색깔이 좋으세요?

해설

벽에 낙서가 되어 있어 벽지를 바꾸자는 여자의 말을 통해 여자가 사려는 물건이 벽지임을 알 수 있다.

어휘

had better ~하는 편이 낫다 / wallpaper[wɔ́ːlpèipər] 벽지 / since[sins] ~ 때문에 / guest[gest] 손님

10 ②

Script

W ① A writer is as popular as a businessman.
② A singer is more popular than an artist.
③ A teacher is the most popular job.
④ Eight students would like to be a singer.
⑤ Fifteen students wish to be a programmer.

해석

여 ① 작가는 사업가만큼 인기가 있다.
② 가수는 화가보다 인기가 더 많다.
③ 선생님이 가장 인기 있는 직업이다.
④ 8명의 학생이 가수가 되기를 원한다.
⑤ 15명의 학생이 프로그래머가 되고 싶어 한다.

해설

② 화가가 되기를 원하는 학생의 수는 13명이고, 가수가 되기를 원하는 학생의 수는 8명으로 화가가 가수보다 더 인기 있다.

어휘

survey[səːrvéi] 조사; 조사하다 / programmer[próugræmər] 프로그래머 / singer[síŋər] 가수 / businessman[bíznismæ̀n] 사업가 / artist[άːrtist] 예술가, 화가 / lawyer[lɔ́ːjər] 변호사 / others 기타 / law[lɔː] 법 / as 형용사/부사 as ~만큼 …한/하게

11 ⑤

Script

W I had a busy weekend.
M What made you so busy, Lisa?
W I went hiking with my family on Saturday.
M What about Sunday?
W I had a piano lesson in the morning. After that, I cleaned my room and made a cake with my mom. It's for my grandmother's birthday.
M Wow, you did lots of things.

해석

여 나 바쁜 주말을 보냈어.
남 뭐가 그렇게 바빴니, Lisa?
여 토요일엔 가족과 함께 하이킹하러 갔었어.
남 일요일은?
여 아침에는 피아노 레슨이 있었어. 그 다음엔 방 청소를 하고 엄마랑 케이크를 만들었어. 그건 할머니의 생신을 위한 거였어.
남 와, 너 정말 많은 것을 했구나.

해설

Lisa는 할머니의 생신을 위해 케이크를 만들었다고 했지 할머니의 생신 파티를 했다고는 하지 않았다.

어휘

lesson[lésn] 수업, 교훈 / grandmother[grǽndmʌ̀ðər] 할머니

12 ②

Script

W I'd like to copy this book from page 10 to 19.
M How many pages will that be?
W 10 pages.
M It's 20 cents per page.
W Okay. Please make it fast.

해석

여 저는 이 책 10부터 19페이지까지 복사하고 싶습니다.
남 몇 페이지나 되나요?
여 열 페이지입니다.
남 알겠습니다. 한 장당 20센트입니다.
여 알겠습니다. 빨리해주십시오.

해설

복사할 페이지는 열 장이고 복사 비용은 한 페이지당 20센트이므로 여자가 지불해야 하는 금액은 2달러이다.

어휘

copy[kάpi] 복사하다 / page[peidʒ] 페이지 / per[pəːr] 각각, 당 / cent[sent] 센트

13 ①

Script

M Mom, I need to go out early tomorrow.
W For what?
M I need to practice basketball.
W I see. Do you want me to prepare breakfast for you?
M No, that's OK.
W How about some money? You can buy something to eat.
M I have some. I just need you to give me a ride.

해석

남 엄마, 저는 내일 일찍 나가야 해요.
여 왜?
남 농구연습 해야 해요.
여 알았다. 너를 위해 아침 식사를 준비해 줄까?
남 아니요, 괜찮아요.
여 돈은 어때? 먹을 것을 사먹을 수 있잖아.
남 저에게 돈이 좀 있어요. 그냥 저를 데려다 주시면 돼요.

해설

I just need you to give me a ride.라는 남자의 말에서 정답을 알 수 있다.

어휘

give a ride 태어주다, 태우다

14 ⑤

Script

M Mom, there are five boxes under the Christmas tree.

Which one is mine? Is it the striped box?

W No, it's not. That one is for your elder sister.

M How about the checkered one?

W That one is for Dad.

M Now I know which one is mine. It has a ribbon on it, right?

W You got it.

해석

남 엄마, 크리스마스트리 밑에 다섯 개의 상자가 있어요. 어떤 것이 제거에요? 줄무늬 상자예요?

여 아니야. 그건 네 누나 거야.

남 그럼, 체크무늬 상자예요?

여 그건 아빠 거야.

남 어떤 것인지 이제 알겠어요. 리본이 있는 상자죠, 맞죠?

여 맞았어.

해설

줄무늬 상자는 누나, 체크무늬 상자는 아빠 것이고 남자의 선물 상자는 리본이 달린 것이다.

어휘

striped[straipt] 줄무늬가 있는 / elder 손위의, 연상의 / checkered[tʃékərd] 체크무늬의 / ribbon[ríbən] 리본

15 ②

Script

W Do you like your new life in the country?

M Yes, I think it's one of the best places in the world.

W What makes you think that?

M Because there's no pollution. And people are so nice here.

W I agree. What else?

M We can grow our own plants more easily, and it's very quiet.

해석

여 너 시골에서의 새로운 생활이 마음에 드니?

남 응, 나는 이곳이 세상에서 가장 좋은 장소 중 하나인 것 같아.

여 왜 그렇게 생각하니?

남 왜냐하면 공해도 없지. 그리고 여기 사람들도 매우 친절해.

여 맞아. 다른 건?

남 우리는 식물도 더 쉽게 기를 수 있고, 그리고 정말 조용해.

해설

남자는 시골에 사는 장점으로 공해가 없는 것, 친절한 사람들, 식물을 쉽게 기를 수 있는 것, 조용함을 언급했다.

어휘

country[kʌ́ntri] 시골 / pollution[pəlúːʃən] 오염, 공해 / agree[əgríː] 동의하다 / own[oun] 자기 자신의, 자기 소유의; 소유하다 / plant[plænt] 식물, 초목 / easily[íːzəli] 쉽게 / quiet[kwáiət] 조용한

16 ②

Script

① W Do you like cats?

M No, I have an allergy to cats.

② W What size do you want?

M I want the black one.

③ W How did you know that?

M My sister told me about it.

④ W Have you seen any movies lately?

M Yes. I saw a horror movie yesterday.

⑤ W What do you think of this picture?

M Wow, it's beautiful. Where did you take it?

해석

① 여 너 고양이 좋아하니?

남 아니, 나는 고양이 알레르기가 있어.

② 여 어떤 사이즈를 입으세요?

남 저는 검은색이 마음에 들어요.

③ 여 너 그걸 어떻게 알았니?

남 내 여동생이 그것에 대해 나에게 말해줬어.

④ 여 너 최근에 영화 본 적 있니?

남 응. 어제 공포 영화를 한 편 보았어.

⑤ 여 이 사진에 대해 어떻게 생각해?

남 와, 아름다워. 너 그거 어디서 찍었니?

해설

② 사이즈를 묻는 여자의 질문에 검은색을 원한다는 남자의 응답은 알맞지 않다.

어휘

allergy[ǽlərdʒi] 알레르기 / have an allergy to ~에 (대해) 알레르기가 있다 / lately[léitli] 최근에

17 ②

Script

W There are a lot of foreigners in our town.

M That's true. In fact, many of them do 3D jobs for us.

W What do you mean by 3D?

M 3D means dirty, difficult, and dangerous. And most Koreans don't want to do 3D jobs.

W I see. That's a big problem.

해석

여 우리 마을에 외국인이 많아.

남 맞아. 사실, 그들 중 많은 사람들이 우리 대신 3D 직종에서 근무해.

여 3D가 무슨 뜻이니?

남 3D는 더럽고, 힘들고, 위험하다는 뜻이야. 그리고 대부분의 한국 사람들이 3D 직종을 하기 싫어하지.

여 그렇구나. 그건 큰 문제다.

해설

3D 직종이 대도시에 많다는 언급은 없다.

어휘
foreigner[fɔ́(:)rənər] 외국인 / in fact 사실 / difficult[dífikʌ̀lt] 어려운 / dangerous[déindʒərəs] 위험한

18 ①

Script

W This is an imaginary animal that is common in stories and legends. It has wings and a long tail, and it can breathe fire. Koreans believe if they see it in a dream, it will bring them good luck.

해석

여 이것은 이야기나 전설 속에 흔히 등장하는 상상의 동물입니다. 그것은 날개와 긴 꼬리를 가지고 있으며 불을 내뿜을 수 있습니다. 한국 사람들은 꿈속에서 그것을 보면 그것이 그들에게 행운을 가져다 줄 거라고 믿습니다.

해설
이야기나 전설 속에 등장하며 불을 내뿜는 상상의 동물은 용이다.

어휘
imaginary[imǽdʒənèri] 상상의, 공상의 / common[kɑ́mən] 흔한 / legend[lédʒənd] 전설 / wing[wiŋ] 날개 / tail[teil] 꼬리 / dream[driːm] 꿈; 꿈꾸다

19 ⑤

Script

M It's time to go already.

W Oh, is it? Time flies by so quickly.

M That's right. Time flies so fast when we are having fun.

W I wish I had more time to talk to you.

M I hope we will meet again soon.

해석

남 벌써 가야 할 시간이네요.

여 오, 그래요? 시간이 정말 빨리 가네요.

남 맞아요. 즐거운 시간을 보내고 있으면 시간이 더 빨리 흐르죠.

여 당신과 얘기할 시간이 좀 더 있었으면 좋을 텐데요.

남 곧 다시 뵙길 바랄게요.

해설
① 당신과 함께 갈게요.
② 그러고 싶지만, 안 돼요.
③ 전 그것이 옳지 않은 것 같아요.
④ 저에게 전화해 주셔서 감사합니다.
좋은 시간을 보내고 헤어지기 아쉬워하는 상황으로 '당신과 얘기할 시간이 좀 더 있었으면 좋을 텐데요.'라는 여자의 말에 가장 적절한 응답을 고른다.

어휘
time flies 시간이 빨리 간다 / quickly[kwíkli] 빨리, 서둘러 / have fun 재미있게 놀다

20 ②

Script

W How was the test, Ethan?

M It was very difficult, and I think I missed five questions.

W That's too bad. Anyway, I haven't seen Jenny all day. Have you?

M No, in fact, she didn't come to school.

W Do you know why she was absent?

M No one knows.

해석

여 오늘 수학 시험 어땠어, Ethan?

남 너무 어려워서 다섯 문제는 틀린 것 같아.

여 정말 안됐다. 그건 그렇고, 나는 오늘 온종일 Jenny를 못 봤어. 너는?

남 못 봤어. 사실, 그애 오늘 학교에 안 왔어.

여 그녀가 결석한 이유를 아니?

남 아무도 몰라.

해설
① 좋은 것 같아.
③ 그건 좋은 생각이 아니야.
④ 학교에서 그녀를 보았어.
⑤ 그녀는 지금 우리 선생님과 같이 있어.
결석한 이유를 묻는 질문으로 이에 알맞은 응답이 와야 한다.

어휘
No one knows. 아무도 모른다. / question[kwéstʃən] 문제 / be absent 결석하다

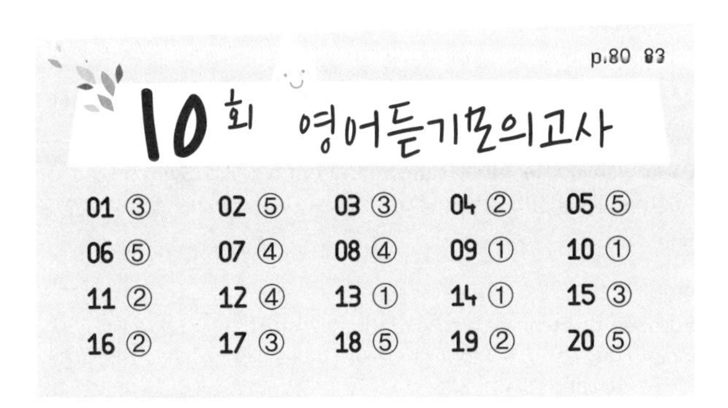

01 ③

Script

W There are many signs around here. Do you know what they mean?

M I think the one behind you says not to bring any food, and the one next to you is for handicapped only.

W Wow, you are good. How about these?

M It means you cannot park here, and that one says animals are not allowed.

W That's correct.

해석

여 여기에 많은 표지판이 있어. 너는 그것들이 무슨 의미인지 아니?

남 네 뒤에 있는 것은 음식을 가져오지 말라는 것이고, 네 옆에 있는 것은 장애인만을 위한 것이라는 것 같아.

여 와, 너 잘한다. 이것들은?

남 그것은 여기에 주차하지 말라는 뜻이고, 저것은 애완동물은 반입하지 말라는 거야.

여 맞아.

해설

대화에서 언급된 표지판은 음식물 반입 금지, 장애인을 위한 공간, 주차 금지, 동물 반입 금지이다.

어휘

sign[sain] 표지판 / allow[əláu] 허용하다, 허락하다

02 ⑤

Script

W Where are you planning to visit this time?

M Well, I've been to Germany and France, so I think I will visit some other European country like Switzerland or Austria.

W You're a lucky man. You travel so much because you are a tour guide.

M Actually, it's a tiring and boring job.

해석

여 이번에는 어디를 방문할 계획이니?

남 글쎄, 독일과 프랑스를 가 봤으니까, 스위스나 오스트리아 같은 다른 유럽 국가를 방문할 생각이야.

여 너는 운이 좋은 사람이야. 너는 관광 안내원이라서 여행을 많이 할 수 있잖아.

남 사실, 그건 너무 피곤하고 지루한 직업이야.

해설

I will visit some other European country like Switzerland or Austria.라는 남자의 말에서 남자는 스위스나 오스트리아를 방문할 것임을 알 수 있다.

어휘

European[jùərəpíːən] 유럽의 / country[kʌ́ntri] 국가, 나라 / lucky[lʌ́ki] 운이 좋은 / tour guide 여행 가이드 / tiring[táiə] 고된, 피곤하게 하는 / boring[bɔ́ːriŋ] 지루한

03 ③

Script

W Don't look down.

M Is it really safe?

W How many times have I told you?

M I know, but I'm a little scared.

W Don't worry. I've never heard of any accidents.

M OK. Let me try.

W I'm sure you can do it.

해석

여 내려다보지 마.

남 정말 안전한 거야?

여 몇 번이나 내가 너에게 말했니?

남 알아, 하지만, 나 좀 무서워.

여 걱정하지 마. 나는 사고에 대해 들어 본 적이 없어.

남 알았어. 해 볼게.

여 네가 할 수 있을 거라고 난 확신해.

해설

여자는 '네가 할 수 있을 거라고 난 확신해.'라는 말로 남자를 격려하고 있다.

어휘

safe[seif] 안전한 / accident[ǽksidənt] 사고 / be sure ~을 확신하다

04 ②

Script

W What a mess! When did you clean the house?

M About two weeks ago. I've been so busy.

W Do you want me to help you?

M Why not? I'll take care of the garden after doing the laundry. Will you do the dishes?

W Okay. Is there anything else that I can help you with?

M No, I think I can do the rest of the chores myself.

해석

여 정말 엉망이다! 너 언제 집 청소했니?

남 2주 전일 거야. 정말 바빴거든.

여 내가 좀 도와줄까?

남 좋아. 난 빨래를 한 다음 정원을 손볼게. 넌 설거지를 해 줄래?

여 알았어. 내가 뭐 더 도와줄 거 없어?

남 아니, 나머지 집안일은 내가 직접 할 수 있을 것 같아.

해설

빨래와 정원 손보기는 남자가, 설거지는 여자가 할 것이다.

어휘

mess[mes] 혼란, 엉망, 지저분함 / take care of ~을 돌보다, 처리하다 / do the dishes 설거지하다 / else[els] 그 밖의 / chore[tʃɔːr] 가사

05 ⑤

Script

M What time is Linda arriving at the airport?

W She said she took a flight at 2 o'clock.

M How long does it usually take?

W About 2 hours.

M I see. Let's have a snack while we wait.

W Sounds good.

해석

남 Linda가 몇 시에 공항에 도착하니?

여 그녀가 2시에 비행기를 탔다고 했어.

남 보통 몇 시간이 걸리니?

여 2시간 정도.

남 알았어. 우리 기다리는 동안에 간식이나 먹자.

여 좋아.

해설
Linda는 2시에 비행기를 탔고, 2시간이 걸린다는 여자의 말로 Linda의 도착 시각이 4시임을 알 수 있다.

어휘
arrive[əráiv] 도착하다 / airport[έərpɔ̀:rt] 공항 / probably[prάbəbli] 아마도 / snack[snæk] 간식 / while[hwail] ~하는 동안

06 ⑤

Script

① W How often do you go for a walk?
M Three times a week.

② W Is this your book?
M Yes, where did you find it?

③ W Mark, don't talk to your classmate.
M But I don't know what the homework is.

④ W Please check your answer sheet.
M I forgot to write my name on it.

⑤ W Shh... will you be quiet, please?
M Oh, I'm sorry.

해석

① 여 너는 산책을 얼마나 자주 하니?
남 일주일에 세 번.

② 여 이것이 너의 책이니?
남 응, 그거 어디서 찾았니?

③ 여 Mark, 네 반 친구와 말하지 마라.
남 하지만, 숙제가 뭔지 잘 모르겠어요.

④ 여 답안지를 확인해주세요.
남 이름을 쓰는 걸 잊었어.

⑤ 여 쉿, 좀 조용히 해줄래?
남 아, 죄송해요.

해설
시끄러워서 조용히 해 달라는 상황에 알맞은 대화를 고른다.

어휘
go for a walk 산책하다 / sheet[ʃi:t] (종이) 한 장 / answer sheet 답지 / quiet[kwáiət] 조용한, 시끄럽지 않은

07 ④

Script

M Excuse me. It really bothers me.

W What do you mean?

M Because you keep talking on the phone, I can't concentrate on the movie. Please don't use your cell phone.

W I'm sorry, but it's a really important call.

M Then, you need to go out to the lobby.

W Then, I will miss some parts of the movie.

해석

남 실례합니다. 그게 정말 신경 쓰여요.

여 무슨 말씀이시죠?

남 계속 전화 통화를 하셔서 제가 영화에 집중할 수가 없잖아요. 휴대 전화를 사용하지 마세요.

여 미안합니다. 하지만, 정말 중요한 전화예요.

남 그러면, 로비로 나가셔야죠.

여 그러면, 제가 영화의 일부분을 놓치게 되잖아요.

해설
여자는 극장 안에서 전화 통화를 해서 다른 사람들에게 피해를 주고 있다.

어휘
concentrate[kάnsəntrèit] 집중하다 / call[kɔ:l] 통화; 전화하다 / lobby[lάbi] (호텔, 극장 등의) 로비

08 ④

Script

W This is a kind of food that can be prepared and served quickly. You can enjoy this at popular restaurant chains that serve this. And you can buy this even at convenience stores these days. This has high calories. If you eat this for a long time, you could experience health problems.

해석

여 이것은 빨리 만들어져 제공되는 음식의 한 종류입니다. 당신은 이것을 파는 인기 있는 식당 체인점에서 이것을 즐길 수 있습니다. 그리고 요즘은 편의점에서도 이것을 살 수 있습니다. 이것은 열량이 높습니다. 당신이 오랫동안 이것을 먹는다면 건강상의 문제를 경험할 수도 있습니다.

해설
빨리 만들어져서 팔리고, 열량이 높은 음식은 패스트푸드이다.

어휘
prepare[pripέər] 준비하다 / serve[sə:rv] 제공하다 / chain[tʃein] 체인점 / convenience store 편의점 / calorie[kǽləri] 칼로리, 열량 / experience[ikspíəriəns] 경험하다; 경험

09 ①

Script

M Mom, have you seen my cell phone?

W Yes, I have. It's in my drawer.

M Why did you put it in there?

W Because your teacher called and said that you often use it during class. So I will keep it in my drawer for two weeks.

M I'm sorry, Mom.

해석

남 엄마, 제 휴대 전화 보셨어요?

여 그래, 내 서랍 안에 있다.

남 왜 거기에 넣어 놓으셨어요?

여 왜냐하면 너희 선생님이 전화하셔서 네가 수업시간에 자주 전화를 사용한다고 말씀하셨어. 그래서 내가 그것을 2주 동안 내 서랍에 보관하려고 한다.

남 죄송해요, 엄마.

해설

아들이 수업 시간에 휴대 전화를 너무 많이 사용했다는 말을 듣고 엄마가 느낄만한 심정을 고른다.

어휘

pleased[pli:zd] 기쁜, 만족스러운 / proud[praud] 자랑스러운 / cell phone 휴대 전화 / during class 수업시간에 / drawer[drɔ́:ər] 서랍

10 ①

Script

M Hold it, Jenny! What are you doing?

W What are you talking about?

M Don't you recycle? How can you just throw the bottles away?

W Don't get so upset. I was only trying to....

M If we recycle, we can save energy and reduce pollution.

W Okay, I'll put these bottles into the recycling box.

해석

남 잠깐만, Jenny! 너 뭐 하는 거니?

여 무슨 말을 하는 거니?

남 재활용 안 하니? 어떻게 병을 그냥 버릴 수 있니?

여 너무 화내지 마. 나는 단지…….

남 재활용하면 우리는 에너지를 절약하고 공해를 줄일 수가 있어.

여 알았어, 이 병들을 재활용 상자에 넣을게.

해설

If we recycle, we can save energy and reduce pollution.라는 남자의 말을 통해 남자가 여자에게 충고하는 것이 재활용임을 알 수 있다.

어휘

hold it (명령문으로 쓰여) 기다려 / recycle[ri:sáikəl] 재활용하다 / throw away 던지다 / reduce[ridjú:s] 줄이다 / recycling box 재활용 상자

11 ②

Script

W Do you still have the money that Mom gave you?

M No, I spent it all on games.

W You mean you already spent 100 dollars?

M Yes, I did. How about you? Do you still have your 100 dollars?

W I wish, but I spent 20 dollars on clothes and 10 dollars on food.

해석

여 너 엄마가 주신 100달러 아직 가지고 있니?

남 아니, 게임 하는 데 다 썼어.

여 백 달러를 벌써 다 썼단 말이니?

남 응, 맞아. 누나는? 누나는 아직도 백 달러를 가지고 있어?

여 그러면 좋겠지만, 20달러는 옷 사고 10달러는 음식에 썼어.

해설

여자는 100달러 중 20달러는 옷을 사는 데, 10달러는 음식에 사용했기 때문에 남은 돈은 70달러이다.

어휘

wish[wiʃ] 바라다, 원하다; 소원, 희망 / clothes[klouðz] 옷, 의류

12 ④

Script

M Sorry for being late.

W I've waited for about an hour. Didn't you take the subway?

M Yes, I did, but I had to go back home.

W How come?

M I left my wallet on the desk.

W I'll forgive you this time. Never be late again.

해석

남 늦어서 미안해.

여 나 너를 한 시간이나 기다렸어. 너 전철 안 탔니?

남 탔어. 그런데 집에 다시 가야만 했어.

여 왜?

남 지갑을 책상 위에 두고 왔었거든.

여 이번은 용서해 줄게. 다신 늦지 마.

해설

남자는 지갑을 집에 두고 와서 집에 갔다가 다시 나왔다고 말하고 있다.

어휘

How come(주어+동사)? 왜?, 어찌하여? / go back 되돌아가다 / wallet[wálit] 지갑 / forgive[fərgív] 용서하다

13 ①

Script

W Excuse me, I brought my car for an engine check yesterday. When can I get my car back?

M May I have your name, please?

W Jenny Parker.

M I think it will be ready tomorrow.

W Thank you. And could you check the oil, too?

M No problem.

해석

여 실례하지만, 엔진을 점검하려고 어제 차를 맡겼는데요. 언제 제 차를 찾을 수 있을까요?

남 성함이 어떻게 되시죠?

여 Jenny Parker입니다.

남 내일 준비될 거예요.

여 감사합니다. 그리고 오일도 좀 확인해 주시겠어요?

남 물론입니다.

해설

an engine check, check the oil이라는 말에서 남자의 직업이 정비사임을 알 수 있다.

어휘

engine[éndʒən] 엔진 / check[tʃek] 확인, 점검; 확인하다, 점검하다 / get back 찾다

14 ①

Script

M Are we having vegetables for dinner again? I'm tired of eating these kinds of dishes every day.

W I was going to buy some fish, but I couldn't. It wasn't fresh. And vegetables are good for your health.

M I know, but I don't think I have to eat them every day.

W All right. I will prepare some meat tomorrow.

해석

남 우리 저녁으로 또 채소를 먹어요? 이런 음식을 매일 먹는 게 지겨워요.

여 생선을 사려고 했는데 살 수가 없었어. 싱싱하지 않았거든. 그리고 채소는 건강에 좋잖니.

남 알지만, 제가 매일 채소를 먹을 필요는 없다고 생각해요.

여 알았다. 내일은 고기를 준비 하마.

해설

I will prepare some meat tomorrow라는 여자의 말로 여자가 내일 고기를 준비할 것임을 알 수 있다.

어휘

tired of ~ 지겨운, 싫증난 / dish[diʃ] 요리, 먹을 것, 접시 / fresh[freʃ] 신선한, 싱싱한 / meat[miːt] (식용으로 하는 짐승, 조류의) 고기

15 ③

Script

[Telephone rings.]

W Hello, can I speak to Dylan?

M Speaking.

W This is Kelly. I have a question. We had English class together this afternoon, right?

M Yes. Why?

W I fell asleep during the class, and I don't know where we ended up.

M I see. Let me get the book, and I will let you know.

해석

여 여보세요, Dylan과 통화할 수 있을까요?

남 전데요.

여 나 Kelly야. 질문이 있어. 우리 오후에 영어 수업을 같이 들었지, 그렇지?

남 응. 왜?

여 내가 수업 시간에 잠을 자서 어디서 끝났는지 모르겠어.

남 알았어. 책을 가져와서 너에게 알려 줄게.

해설

I don't know where we ended up이라는 여자의 말을 통해 수업 진도가 얼마만큼 나갔는지 물어보려고 전화를 했다는 것을 알 수 있다.

어휘

fall asleep 잠들다 / end up 끝나다, 결국 ~이 되다

16 ②

Script

W This is a six-letter-word. The second letter in the word is "d", and the last is "e". Can you guess it? Okay. I can give you one more clue. The letter "c" is the second to last letter. I guess that is enough.

해석

여 이것은 여섯 개의 철자로 된 단어입니다. 이 단어의 두 번째 글자는 'd'이고 마지막 글자는 'e'입니다. 아시겠어요? 그럼, 힌트를 하나 더 드리겠습니다. 글자 'c'가 끝에서 두 번째 글자입니다. 이 정도면 충분하죠.

해설

6개의 글자로 된 단어로 두 번째에 d, 마지막에 e, 끝에서 두 번째 글자가 c인 단어를 고른다.

어휘

divide[diváid] 나누다 / choice[tʃɔis] 선택 / honest[ɑ́nist] 정직한 / letter[létər] 글자, 문자 / second[sékənd] 두 번째의 / word[wəːrd] 단어 / last[læst] 마지막 / clue[kluː] 단서 / second to last 끝에서 두 번째

17 ③

Script

W Look! The man in this picture looks alive.

M Yes, it's amazing. It took ten years for the painter to complete it.

W Wow, that's incredible.

M Look at this crown. It is covered with diamonds.

W It says King Edward used to wear it.

M There are lots of things to see. We need at least two hours to look around.

해석

여 봐! 그림 속에 있는 남자가 살아 있는 것 같아.

남 응, 굉장해. 화가가 그걸 완성하는 데 5년이나 걸렸대.

여 와, 믿을 수가 없어.

남 이 왕관 좀 봐. 다이아몬드로 뒤덮여 있네.

여 Edward 왕이 썼던 것이라고 쓰여 있어.

남 볼 게 정말 많다. 둘러보려면 적어도 두 시간은 필요하겠어.

해설

그림과 왕관을 볼 수 있을 만한 곳을 고른다.

어휘

playground[pléigràund] 운동장 / police station 경찰서 / painter[péintər] 화가 / complete[kəmplíːt] 완성하다, 마치다 / incredible[inkrédəbəl] 믿을 수 없는, 놀라운 / crown[kraun] 왕관 / be covered with ~로 뒤덮여 있다 / diamond[dáiəmənd] 다이아몬드 / at least 적어도 / look around 둘러보다

18 ⑤

Script

① M What's the matter?
W I don't feel well today.

② M Will she come here?

W She said she would.

③ M I bought this necklace for you.

W Oh, how sweet of you.

④ M I'm fifteen years old.

W David is your age.

⑤ M Writing the same thing every day is boring.

W Right. It really makes me happy.

해석

① 남 무슨 일 있니?

여 나 오늘 몸이 좀 안 좋아.

② 남 그녀가 여기 올까?

여 그녀가 온다고 얘기했어.

③ 남 제가 당신에게 주려고 이 목걸이를 샀어요.

여 오, 정말 친절도 하셔라.

④ 남 난 열다섯 살이야.

여 David가 네 나이야.

⑤ 남 똑같은 것을 매일 쓰는 건 지루해.

여 맞아. 정말로 나를 행복하게 해.

해설

⑤ '똑같은 것을 매일 쓰는 건 지루해.'라는 남자의 말에 동의하고, 남자의 말과 상반된 내용을 말하고 있다.

어휘

feel well 건강 상태가 좋다 / necklace[néklis] 목걸이 / sweet[swiːt] 상냥한, 친절한

19 ②

Script

M Your friend, Abigail is going to take a big test today. You know she has studied very hard to prepare for it. You're sure that she will pass the test. You want to wish her good luck. In this situation, what would you say to her?

해석

남 당신의 친구, Abigail은 오늘 큰 시험을 볼 예정입니다. 당신은 그녀가 그 시험을 준비하려고 공부를 매우 열심히 했다는 것을 알고 있습니다. 당신은 그녀가 그 시험에 합격할 거라고 확신합니다. 당신은 그녀에게 행운을 빌어주고 싶습니다. 이 상황에서 당신은 그녀에게 뭐라고 얘기하시겠습니까?

해설

① 나에게 행운을 빌어줘.

③ 시험이 정말 어려울 거래.

④ 시험 준비느라 공부 많이 했니?

⑤ 나는 네가 그 시험에 통과할 거라는 것을 알고 있었어.

시험을 볼 친구에서 해줄 수 있는 격려의 말은 '네가 시험을 잘 보길 빌게.'라는 의미의 ②가 가장 적절하다.

어휘

take a test 시험을 보다 / pass[pæs] 통과하다

20 ⑤

Script

W Mike, I heard that you finished your school project.

M Yes, I did.

W How could you do that in such a short period of time?

M I did it little by little every day.

해석

여 Mike, 네가 학교 연구 프로젝트를 끝마쳤다고 들었어.

남 응, 맞아.

여 어떻게 그렇게 짧은 시간에 그것을 끝낼 수 있었니?

남 매일 그것을 조금씩 했어.

해설

① 아니, 내가 그걸 하지 않았어.

② 나는 많은 도움이 필요해.

③ 네 도움 없이도 나는 그것을 끝낼 수 있어.

④ 그 프로젝트에 대해서 아는 것이 하나도 없어.

여자는 남자에게 어떻게 학교 프로젝트를 일찍 끝냈는지 묻고 있다.

어휘

by oneself 혼자, 스스로 / know nothing 전혀 모른다 / little by little 조금씩, 차츰 / project[prədʒékt] 과제, 연구 프로젝트 / short[ʃɔːrt] 짧은 / period[píəriəd] 기간

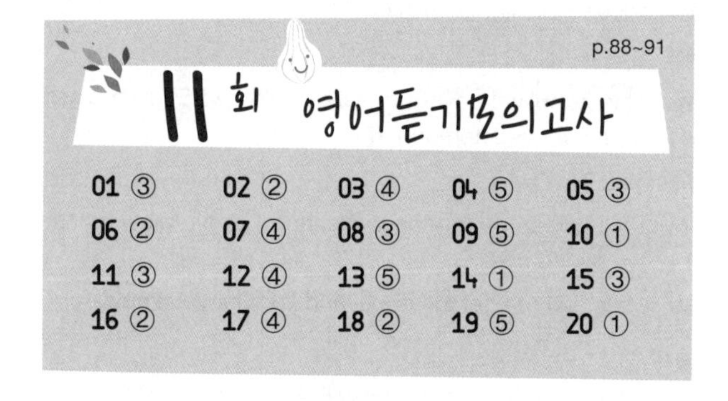

p.88~91

11회 영어듣기모의고사

01 ③	02 ②	03 ④	04 ⑤	05 ③
06 ②	07 ④	08 ③	09 ⑤	10 ①
11 ③	12 ④	13 ⑤	14 ①	15 ③
16 ②	17 ④	18 ②	19 ⑤	20 ①

01 ③

Script

W Patrick, I brought some gifts for you and your brothers.

M What are they?

W They're buckles for your belt. You can choose any one you like.

M I want the one with the star. No, I mean the one with the eagle.

W OK. I think you made a good choice.

해석

여 Patrick, 너와 네 형들에게 줄 선물을 가져 왔어.

남 뭐에요?

여 벨트에 들어가는 버클이야. 마음에 드는 거 아무거나 골라봐.

남 저는 별이 있는 것이 좋아요. 아니, 독수리가 있는 걸로 할래요.

여 알았어. 내 생각에는 네가 잘 고른 것 같구나.

해설

No, I mean the one with the eagle.이라는 말을 통해 남자가 결국 독수리가 있는 버클을 골랐다는 것을 알 수 있다.

어휘

buckle[bʌ́kəl] 버클, 혁대쇠 / belt[belt] 허리띠, 벨트 / choose[tʃu:z] 고르다, 선택하다 / eagle[í:gəl] 독수리 / make a choice 선택하다

02 ②

Script

M Excuse me, but there's no money left on your card.

W I thought there was.

M You need to pay in cash instead.

W But I don't have any money right now.

M Then, you have to get off.

W Oh, no. Can you just give me a free ride, please? I will pay you back next time.

M Okay, I will give you a free ride just this once.

해석

남 실례합니다만, 카드에 잔액이 없습니다.

여 있는 줄 알았어요.

남 대신에 현금으로 내셔야겠네요.

여 그런데 지금 당장 저에게 돈이 없는데요.

남 그러면, 내리셔야죠.

여 오, 안 돼요. 저 공짜로 태워주실 수 있나요? 다음에 갚을게요.

남 알겠습니다. 이번 한 번만 공짜로 태워 드리겠습니다.

해설

교통카드에 돈이 없어서 운전사 아저씨가 공짜로 버스를 태워준 상황으로 여자가 느꼈을 심정을 고른다.

어휘

cash[kæʃ] 현금 / pay in cash 현금으로 지불하다 / get off (버스, 열차 등에서) 내리다 / give a free ride 공짜로 태워주다 / pay back 갚다

03 ④

Script

W How about this brown shirt, Mark?

M I don't like it, Mom. I like that red one.

W Mark, brown is a popular color this fall.

M But red suits me.

W Let's do it this way. Today I'll buy you what you want. But next time, you will take my advice, okay?

M Okay.

해석

여 이 갈색 셔츠는 어떠니, Mark?

남 마음에 안 들어요, 엄마. 저는 저 빨간색이 좋아요.

여 Mark, 갈색이 올가을에 인기 있는 색이야.

남 하지만, 저에게 빨간색이 어울려요.

여 이렇게 하자. 오늘은 네가 원하는 것을 사지만, 다음에는 엄마의 충고를 들어야 한다, 알았지?

남 네.

해설

여자는 아들이 갈색 셔츠를 사길 원했지만, Today I'll buy you what you want.라는 여자의 말을 통해 결국 남자가 사게 될 셔츠가 빨간색임을 알 수 있다.

어휘

fall[fɔ:l] 가을 (=autumn) / suit[su:t] 맞다, 어울리다; 양복, 한 벌 / take advice 충고를 받아들이다

04 ⑤

Script

M ① Do not run or speak loudly.

② Do not take up more than one seat.

③ Wait for people to get off before you get on.

④ Put your cell phone on vibration mode.

⑤ Spread your legs as wide as you can while sitting.

해석

남 ① 뛰어다니거나 시끄럽게 이야기하지 마라.

② 한 좌석 이상을 차지하지 마라.

③ 타기 전에 내리는 사람을 기다려라.

④ 휴대 전화를 진동 모드로 놓아라.

⑤ 앉아 있을 때는 가능한 한 다리를 넓게 벌려라.

해설

지하철에 앉아 있을 때는 가능한 한 다리를 좁게 하고 앉아야 한다.

어휘

loudly[láudli] 큰 소리로, 소란스럽게 / take up 차지하다 / get on 타다 / vibration[vaibréiʃən] 진동, 떨림 / mode[moud] 양식, 방식 / vibration mode 진동 모드 / spread[spred] 펼치다, (팔, 다리 등을) 벌리다 / wide[waid] 넓은; 활짝

05 ③

Script

W Excuse me, does Mrs. Smith live here?

M Yes, she is my wife.

W There is no Mrs. Smith in this address book.

M We have just moved in.

W I see. Here is some mail for her. Could you sign here, please?

M No problem.

해석

여 실례합니다, Smith 부인이 여기 사시나요?

남 네, 제 아내입니다.

여 그렇군요, 이 주소록에는 Smith 부인이 없네요.

남 저희가 방금 이사 왔거든요.

여 그렇군요. 여기 그녀 앞으로 온 우편물이 있습니다. 여기 서명해주시겠

어요?

남 물론이죠.

해설

address book, mail, sign 등의 단어를 통해 여자의 직업이 우편배달부임을 알 수 있다.

어휘

address[ədrés] 주소 / address book 주소록, 주소명부 / mail[meil] 우편, 우편물 / sign[sain] 서명하다; 서명

06 ②

Script

[Telephone rings.]

M Good morning, this is room service, how may I help you?

W Good morning, this is room 707. Could you send up some breakfast to my room?

M Sure. What would you like?

W I'd like to have two fried eggs, toast, and some fresh orange juice.

M Is there anything else you would like?

W No, that's all.

해석

남 안녕하십니까, 룸서비스입니다. 무엇을 도와드릴까요?

여 안녕하세요. 707호인데요. 제 방으로 아침을 좀 갖다 주시겠어요?

남 물론이죠. 무엇을 드시겠습니까?

여 달걀 프라이 두 개, 토스트, 그리고 신선한 오렌지 주스로 할게요.

남 더 필요하신 거 없으신가요?

여 네, 그게 전부에요.

해설

호텔 투숙객이 룸서비스로 아침을 주문하는 상황이다.

어휘

room service 룸서비스 (호텔에서 객실로 음식을 날라다 주는 것) / fried egg 달걀 프라이 / toast[toust] 토스트, 구운 빵

07 ④

Script

M May I help you?

W Yes, I'd like to buy an umbrella.

M We have a few here, and the prices are all the same.

W I want to buy a medium-sized one.

M How about the black one?

W No, I'll just take the white one with black polka dots.

해석

남 도와드릴까요?

여 네, 우산을 하나 사려고요.

남 여기에 몇 개 있는데 가격은 모두 같아요.

여 저는 중간 크기를 사고 싶어요.

남 검은색은 어떠세요?

여 아니오, 그냥 검은 물방울무늬가 있는 흰색 우산으로 살게요.

해설

여자는 검은 물방울무늬가 있는 중간 크기의 흰색 우산을 사려고 한다.

어휘

polka dot 물방울무늬

08 ③

Script

W Let's go. The concert starts at two o'clock.

M But Brian hasn't come here yet.

W I know, but we are going to be late.

M Let me call Brian again.

W It's no use. The concert starts in ten minutes.

M Okay, let's do it this way. We leave his ticket at the box office with his name on it.

해석

여 가자. 콘서트가 2시에 시작해.

남 하지만, Brian이 아직 여기 오지 않았어.

여 알고 있지만, 우리 늦을 거야.

남 내가 Brian에게 다시 전화해 볼게.

여 소용없어. 콘서트가 10분 후에 시작해.

남 좋아, 이렇게 하자. Brian의 표에 그의 이름을 쓰고 매표소에 맡기자.

해설

콘서트 시작 시각이 2시이고 콘서트가 시작하려면 10분이 남았기 때문에 현재 시각이 1시 50분이다.

어휘

It is no use. 소용없다. / at least 적어도 / box office 매표소

09 ⑤

Script

W ① If you have 5 dollars, you can have a hamburger with a coke.

② If you have 7 dollars, you can have a cheeseburger with a salad.

③ If you have 4 dollars, you can have a chicken burger with a coffee.

④ If you have 6 dollars, you can have a cheeseburger with a milkshake.

⑤ If you have 5 dollars, you can have a hamburger with a salad.

해석

여 ① 당신에게 5달러가 있으면 콜라와 햄버거를 먹을 수 있다.
② 당신에게 7달러가 있으면 샐러드와 치즈버거를 먹을 수 있다.
③ 당신에게 4달러가 있으면 커피와 치킨버거를 먹을 수 있다.
④ 당신에게 6달러가 있으면 밀크셰이크와 치즈버거를 먹을 수 있다.
⑤ 당신에게 5달러가 있으면 당신은 샐러드와 햄버거를 먹을 수 있다.

해설

샐러드와 햄버거를 먹으려면 6달러 30센트가 필요하다.

10 ①

Script

M I missed the movie because you didn't show up!

W What are you talking about? We were supposed to meet at 3:30, weren't we?

M That's right. I arrived on time, but you weren't there.

W Are you kidding me? I was there until 3:50. You're the one who didn't show up and didn't answer my calls.

M Did you call me?

W Yes, I called you three times. You are to blame not me.

해석

남 네가 나오지 않아서 영화를 못 봤잖아!

여 무슨 얘길 하는 거니? 우리 3시 30분에 만나기로 했었잖아, 아니니?

남 맞아. 내가 제시간에 도착했는데, 넌 없던데.

여 장난하니? 나 거기 3시 50분까지 있었어. 나타나지도 않았고, 내 전화까지 안 받은 건 너잖아.

남 나에게 전화했었니?

여 그래, 너에게 세 번이나 전화했어. 비난을 받아야 할 사람은 내가 아니고 너야.

해설

You are to blame not me.라는 말을 통해 여자의 의도를 알 수 있다.

어휘

show up 나타나다 / be supposed to+동사원형 ~하기로 되어 있다, ~할 의무가 있다 / on time 시간을 어기지 않고, 정각에 / blame[bleim] (남을) 나무라다, 비난하다, ~의 탓으로 돌리다

11 ③

Script

[Telephone rings.]

W Hello, Happy Life Dentist, how may I help you?

M Hi, my name is John Ford. I have an appointment at ten.

W John, Ford. Um, yes. That's right. Go ahead.

M I just called to confirm my appointment.

W Okay, we'll see you then.

해석

여 안녕하십니까, Happy Life 치과입니다. 무엇을 도와드릴까요?

남 안녕하세요, 제 이름은 John Ford입니다. 제가 10시에 예약을 했는데요.

여 John Ford 씨. 음, 네, 맞습니다. 말씀하세요.

남 저는 예약을 확인하려고 전화를 했습니다.

여 알겠습니다. 그러면 그때 뵙겠습니다.

해설

I just called to confirm my appointment.를 통해 남자가 예약을 확인하기 위해 전화를 걸었다는 것을 알 수 있다.

어휘

dentist[déntist] 치과의사, 치과 / appointment[əpɔ́intmənt] 약속, 예약 / have an appointment 약속이 있다, 예약을 해두다 / confirm[kənfə́ːrm] 확인하다, 확실하게 하다

12 ④

Script

M Here is what you ordered.

W Thank you. How much is it?

M It's 50 dollars.

W I'm a gold member here, so I can get ten percent off, right?

M Sure. May I see your membership card?

W Here it is.

해석

남 여기 주문한 거 나왔습니다.

여 고맙습니다. 얼마인가요?

남 50달러입니다.

여 나는 여기 골드 회원이라 10% 할인받을 수 있죠, 그렇죠?

남 물론입니다. 회원카드를 볼 수 있을까요?

여 여기 있습니다.

해설

음식 값은 50달러이고 여자는 골드 회원으로 10퍼센트를 할인받을 수 있기 때문에 여자가 지불해야 할 금액은 45달러이다.

어휘

member[mémbər] 회원, 일원 / membership card 회원 카드

13 ⑤

Script

W My brother, Joseph is really good at math, and he has won many prizes from math contests. Joseph really hates reading books, but he is very interested in science. He also likes putting things together and taking things apart, so he often breaks things such as watches or bikes.

해석

여 내 남동생 Joseph는 수학을 정말 잘하고 대회에서 상도 많이 받았습니다. Joseph는 책을 읽는 것을 정말 싫어하지만, 과학에는 관심이 아주 많습니다. 그는 또한 무언가를 조립하고 분해하는 것을 좋아해서 시계나 자전거 같은 것들을 종종 고장 냅니다.

해설

여자는 자신의 남동생이 시계나 자전거를 자주 망가뜨린다고 말하고 있다.

어휘
prize[praiz] 상, 상품 / put together 조립하다, 모으다 / take apart 분해하다 / break[breik] 고장 내다, 망가뜨리다 / such as ~와 같은

14 ①

Script

M Melissa, I think I have a problem.

M What is it?

W I often speak carelessly, and it hurts other people's feelings.

W I think sometimes you talk so rudely. I'm your close friend, so I understand you, but others can't.

M How can I change my bad habit?

W Try to think before you speak.

해석

남 Melissa, 나에게 한 가지 문제가 있는 것 같아.

여 그게 뭔데?

남 내가 종종 말을 함부로 해서 다른 사람의 기분을 상하게 해.

여 내 생각에도 네가 가끔 너무 무례하게 말을 하는 것 같아. 나는 네 친한 친구여서 너를 이해하지만, 다른 사람들은 이해하지 못할 거야.

남 어떻게 하면 이 나쁜 습관을 고칠 수 있을까?

여 말을 하기 전에 생각하도록 해 봐.

해설

남자는 자주 함부로 말을 해 다른 사람의 기분을 상하게 한다며 여자에게 자신의 고민을 털어놓고 있다.

어휘

carelessly[kέərlisli] 부주의하게, 경솔하게 / rudely 버릇[예의]없이 / close[klouz] 친한, 가까운 / habit[hǽbit] 습관

15 ③

Script

W May I ask what you do for a living?

M Sure, I'm an English teacher.

W You are?

M Yes. It's hard to believe, isn't it? I've heard that a lot. Many people think I'm a coach or a policeman or something.

W Is that true?

M Yes, but I don't care.

해석

여 직업이 무엇인지 여쭤봐도 될까요?

남 물론이죠, 저는 영어 선생님입니다.

여 그러세요?

남 네. 믿기에 어렵죠, 그죠? 그런 말 자주 들어요. 많은 사람들은 제가 코치나 경찰 또는 뭐 그런 것 같다고 생각해요.

여 정말이에요?

남 네, 하지만 전 신경 쓰지 않아요.

해설

① 노력이 없으면 얻는 것도 없다.

② 백지장도 맞들면 낫다.

④ 사공이 많으면 배가 산으로 간다.

⑤ 한 가지에 모든 것을 걸지 마라.

여자는 남자의 겉모습만을 보고는 남자의 직업이 선생님인 것을 알고 놀라고 있다. 따라서 '겉만 보고 판단하지 마라.'라는 의미의 ③이 적절하다.

어휘

do for a living 생계를 위해 일하다 / coach[koutʃ] (스포츠 팀의) 코치 / policeman[pəlíːsmən] 경찰관 / care[kεər] 상관하다, 관심을 가지다

16 ②

Script

M This is clear, salty liquid that comes from our skin when we are hot, or when we exercise. When our body gets hotter than 37 degrees, our body cools itself by making this. But some people get this when they are nervous, scared, or ill.

해석

남 이것은 우리가 덥거나, 운동을 할 때 우리의 피부로부터 나오는 투명하고 짠 액체입니다. 우리의 몸이 37도보다 더워지면 우리의 몸은 이것을 만들어서 온도를 낮춥니다. 하지만, 어떤 사람들은 긴장하거나, 무섭거나 아플 때 이것이 나옵니다.

해설

덥거나 운동을 할 때 우리의 피부에서 나오는 투명하고 짠 액체는 땀이다.

어휘

clear[kliər] 맑은, 투명한 / salty[sɔ́ːlti] 짠 / liquid[líkwid] 액체 / come from ~에서 나오다 / cool[kuːl] 차갑게 하다, 식히다 / nervous[nə́ːrvəs] 초조한 / scared[skεərd] 무서운 / ill[il] 아픈

17 ④

Script

① W What did you do last weekend?
M I went to the beach with my family.

② W Did you watch TV yesterday?
M No, I didn't. I had no time to watch TV.

③ W How was the movie?
M It was long and boring.

④ W I got full marks on my math exam.
M Sorry to hear that.

⑤ W A young boy swam across the Han River.
M Really? That's amazing.

해석

① 여 너는 지난 주말에 뭐 했니?
남 나는 가족들과 해변에 갔었어.

② 여 어제 TV 봤니?
남 아니, 안 봤어. TV 볼 시간이 없었어.

③ 여 영화는 어땠어?
남 길고 지루했어.

④ 여 나 수학 시험에서 만점을 맞았어.
남 그것 참 안됐다.

⑤ 여 어린 소년이 한강을 수영해서 건넜대.
남 정말이야? 그거 굉장하다.

해설
④ 만점을 맞았다는 여자의 말에 축하한다는 응답이 와야 한다.

어휘
get full marks 만점을 받다 / exam[igzǽm] 시험 / swim across 수영해서 ~를 건너다

18 ②

Script

W Hey, Jonathan. I didn't see you at the race. What happened?

M I couldn't run.

W Did your mother stop you from running?

M No, she didn't. I hurt myself by dropping a cup on my foot.

W That's too bad.

해석
여 Jonathan, 경주에서 너 못 봤는데. 무슨 일이야?
남 달릴 수가 없었어.
여 엄마가 네가 뛰지 못하게 말렸니?
남 아니, 그렇지 않아. 발에 컵을 떨어뜨려서 다쳤어.
여 정말 안됐구나.

해설
남자는 발에 컵을 떨어뜨려 발을 다쳐 마라톤에 참가하지 못했다.

어휘
stop ~ from+-ing ~에게 …를 하지 못하게 하다 / hurt oneself 다치다 / drop[drɑp] 떨어뜨리다

19 ⑤

Script

[Telephone rings.]

W Hello.

M Hello, this is Will. I dropped some dry cleaning off yesterday. When will it be ready?

W Who are you calling?

M Isn't this Jim's Laundry? Is Jim there?

W No, it's not. And there is no one here by that name. What number are you calling?

M Uh... I dialed 777-4567.

W I think you've got the wrong number.

해석
여 여보세요.
남 여보세요, Will이라고 하는데요. 어제 드라이클리닝을 맡겼는데 언제쯤 준비 될까요?
여 누구한테 전화하셨어요?
남 Jim 씨네 세탁소 아닌가요? Jim 씨 있나요?
여 아니오, 아닙니다. 그리고 여기 그런 이름을 가진 사람이 없는데요. 몇 번으로 전화를 거셨나요?
남 어, 777-4567번으로 전화를 걸었습니다.
여 전화를 잘못하신 것 같군요.

해설
① 전데요.
② 메시지를 남겨드릴까요?
③ 지금 그는 없습니다.
④ 2시간이면 준비됩니다.
There is no one here by that name.라는 말을 통해 남자가 전화를 잘못했다는 것을 알 수 있다.

어휘
wrong number 잘못 걸린 전화; 틀린 전화 번호 / have the wrong number 전화를 잘못 걸다 / drop off 맡기다 / dry cleaning 드라이클리닝 / laundry[lɑ́:ndri] 세탁소, 빨래, 세탁물 / dial[dáiəl] 전화의 다이얼을 돌리다

20 ①

Script

W Hey, Brian. Do you have a digital camera?

M Sure, my parents bought one for me for my birthday.

W I envy you. I bought one with money I had saved for three months.

M How did you save the money?

W I got a part-time job.

해석
여 Brian, 너 디지털 카메라 있니?
남 물론이야, 부모님께서 내 생일 선물로 사주셨어.
여 나는 네가 부러워. 난 내가 석 달 동안 모은 돈으로 하나 샀어.
남 너 어떻게 그 돈을 모았니?
여 아르바이트를 구했어.

해설
② 길에서 그것을 주웠어.
③ 나는 내 디지털 카메라를 팔았어.
④ 아버지가 나에게 그것을 보여주셨어.
⑤ 누나가 돈을 좀 빌렸어.
돈을 어떻게 모았는지에 관한 응답이 와야 한다.

어휘
get a part-time job 아르바이트[시간제 일]을 구하다 / envy[énvi] 부러워하다 / save[seiv] 저축하다, 아끼다

12회 영어듣기모의고사

p.96~99

01 ⑤	02 ②	03 ④	04 ④	05 ②
06 ②	07 ⑤	08 ③	09 ⑤	10 ④
11 ③	12 ④	13 ②	14 ①	15 ⑤
16 ①	17 ⑤	18 ①	19 ③	20 ②

01 ⑤

Script

M You came here with your brother, right? Where is he?

W He is over there with his friends.

M Is he wearing glasses or a cap?

W Neither. He is average height and a bit thin.

M I see. He is the one with short hair.

W That's right.

해석

남 너 여기 남동생이랑 같이 왔지, 그렇지? 동생은 어디에 있니?

여 그는 자기 친구들과 함께 저기 있어.

남 안경이나 모자를 썼니?

여 둘 다 아냐. 그는 평균 키에 약간 말랐어.

남 알겠다. 머리가 짧은 아이구나.

여 맞아.

해설

여자의 동생은 평균 키에 약간 말랐으며, 안경과 모자를 쓰지 않았고 머리가 짧다.

어휘

cap[kæp] 모자 / average[ǽvəridʒ] 평균의, 보통의; 평균 / height[hait] 키, 신장, 높이 / thin[θin] 마른, 날씬한

02 ②

Script

W What is taking you so long? We don't have much time. The movie starts in 20 minutes.

M I know, but I can't cut this coupon.

W Do we need that coupon? What for?

M We cannot get a discount without it.

W Oh, really? OK. I will go get something to cut it with.

해석

여 뭐가 그렇게 오래 걸리니? 우리 시간이 별로 없어. 영화가 20분 후에 시작한단 말이야.

남 알아, 하지만 이 쿠폰을 자를 수 없어.

여 그 쿠폰이 필요하니? 뭐 때문에?

남 이 쿠폰이 없으면 할인을 받을 수 없어.

여 아, 그러니? 알았어. 그것을 자를 수 있는 것을 가서 가져올게.

해설

I will go get something to cut it with.라는 남자의 말을 통해 여자가 쿠폰을 자를 수 있는 무언가를 가져올 거라는 걸 알 수 있다.

어휘

coupon[kjúːpɑn] 쿠폰, 우대권, 할인권 / get a discount 할인을 받다

03 ④

Script

W You seem so busy today.

M Yes. I don't even have time to talk to you.

W What makes you so busy?

M I have a math exam tomorrow.

W So you're solving math problems?

M That's right.

W I think you should review the textbook first.

해석

여 너 오늘 정말 바쁜 것 같아.

남 응. 너와 얘기를 나눌 시간조차 없어.

여 뭐가 그렇게 바쁘니?

남 내일 수학 시험이 있거든.

여 그래서 수학 문제를 푸는 중이구나?

남 맞아.

여 나는 네가 교과서를 먼저 복습해야 한다고 생각해.

해설

I think you should review the textbook first.라는 여자의 말을 통해 정답을 알 수 있다.

어휘

seem[siːm] ~인 것 같다, ~인 듯하다 / solve[sɑlv] 풀다, 해결하다 / problem[prábləm] 문제 / review[rivjúː] 복습하다; 복습 / textbook[tékstbùk] 교과서

04 ④

Script

W I had a really good time at your 15th birthday party.

M Good to hear that.

W Anyway, your mother is so young and pretty.

M She spends a lot of time on her looks.

W How old is she?

M Well, she is 24 years older than me.

해석

여 나는 너의 열다섯 번째 생일 파티에서 정말 즐거운 시간을 보냈어.

남 그랬다니 기뻐.

여 그건 그렇고, 너의 엄마는 정말 젊고 예쁘시더라.

남 엄마는 외모에 가꾸는 데 많은 시간을 보내셔.

여 연세가 어떻게 되시는데?

남 글쎄, 나보다 스물네 살이 더 많아.

해설

15번째 생일 파티를 했기 때문에 남자는 15세이며 엄마의 나이가 자신보다 스물네 살이 많다고 했기 때문에 엄마의 나이는 39세이다.

어휘

pretty[príti] 예쁜, 매력적인 / spend[spend] (시간을) 보내다, (돈을) 쓰다 / look[luk] 외모, 매력

05 ②

Script

W This is my first time to see an opera, so I'm really excited.

M So am I.

W Do you know who the soprano is?

M Let's take a look at the pamphlet. This lady is the soprano, and the man next to her is the tenor.

W Now she is coming. Wow, she is wearing a wonderful dress.

해석

여 오페라를 처음 보는 거라 정말로 흥분돼.

남 나도 그래.

여 너 소프라노가 누군지 아니?

남 팸플릿을 한 번 보자. 이 여자가 소프라노고 그녀 옆에 있는 남자가 테너야.

여 지금 그녀가 나와. 와, 정말 아름다운 드레스를 입고 있어.

해설

This is my first time to see an opera라는 여자의 말에서 두 사람의 대화하는 장소가 음악회임을 알 수 있다.

어휘

opera[ápərə] 오페라 / soprano[səprá:nou] 소프라노 / take a look at ~을 보다 / pamphlet[pǽmflit] 팸플릿, 소책자 / lady[léidi] 귀부인, 숙녀, 여성 / tenor[ténər] 테너

06 ②

Script

M Where is Amanda?

W She's gone.

M Why? She said she would be here until three. It's only one o'clock.

W She said she had to stop by somewhere.

M What time did she leave?

W She left 20 minutes ago.

해석

남 Amanda는 어디 있니?

여 갔어.

남 왜? 그녀가 3시까지 여기 있을 것이라고 했는데. 아직 1시밖에 안 됐잖아.

여 그녀가 어디 들를 곳이 있다고 했어.

남 몇 시에 떠났니?

여 20분 전에 떠났어.

해설

현재 시각이 1시로 여자가 Amanda는 20분 전에 떠났다고 했기 때문에 Amanda가 떠난 시각이 12시 40분이다.

어휘

stop by 들르다 / somewhere[sʌ́mhwɛ̀ər] 어딘가에

07 ⑤

Script

W Excuse me, can I see that?

M You mean these earrings?

W Yes. They look beautiful. Aren't they expensive?

M They are 30 dollars.

W That's too much. I will just take these hairpins.

해석

여 실례합니다. 저것을 볼 수 있을까요?

남 이 귀고리를 말하는 건가요?

여 네. 예쁘네요. 저거 비싼가요?

남 30달러입니다.

여 너무 비싸네요. 저는 그냥 이 머리핀을 살게요.

해설

여자는 귀고리를 사고 싶었지만, 너무 비싸 머리핀을 사려고 한다.

어휘

earring[íərìŋ] 귀고리 / hairpin[hɛ́ərpìn] 머리핀

08 ③

Script

W What are you looking for?

M My cell phone.

W What does it look like?

M It's the latest model and it's gray in color.

W I think Ann found one in the library, so why don't you call her?

M It must be mine because I went there this morning.

W Good. Here is her number, and use my cell phone.

해석

여 너 무엇을 찾고 있니?

남 내 휴대 전화.

여 어떻게 생겼는데?

남 최신형 모델이고 색깔은 회색이야.

여 Ann이 도서관에서 하나 주은 것 같던데, 그녀에게 전화를 해보지 그러니?

남 내가 오늘 아침에 갔었기 때문에 그게 분명히 내 휴대 전화일 거야.

여 잘됐네. 여기 그녀의 번호가 있고 내 휴대 전화를 써.

해설

잃어버린 휴대 전화를 찾다가 누군가가 그것을 가지고 있다는 얘길 듣고 느낄만한 심정을 고른다.

어휘

latest[léitist] 최근의, 최신의 / model[mádl] 모델 / gray[grei] 회색

09 ⑤

Script

W These are two thin sticks that you use to eat food with in many countries in Asia. They originally came from China. It is very easy for Asian people to use them, but not for Westerners. Westerners usually use a fork. They are made of wood or metal.

해석

여 이것들은 아시아의 많은 나라에서 음식을 먹을 때 사용하는 두 개의 얇은 막대기입니다. 그것들은 원래 중국에서 유래하였습니다. 아시아 사람들이 그것들을 사용하기는 쉽지만, 서양인들에게는 그렇지 않습니다. 서양인들은 주로 포크를 사용합니다. 이것들은 나무나 금속으로 만들어집니다.

해설

아시아에서 음식을 먹을 때 사용하는 두 개의 얇은 막대는 젓가락이다.

어휘

stick[stik] 막대기 / Asia[éiʒə] 아시아 / originally[ərídʒənəli] 원래는 / Asian[éiʒən] 아시아의; 아시아인 / Westerner[wéstərnər] 서양인 / fork[fɔːrk] 포크 / wood[wud] 나무 / metal[métl] 금속

10 ④

Script

M Do you have any pets, Lucy?

W Yes. I have a couple of cats. They are so sweet.

M There aren't many people who raise cats in Korea.

W Really? Cats are the most popular pets in the States.

M I see. I think cats are easier to take care of than dogs. I have to give my dog a bath twice a week.

해석

남 너 애완동물 있니, Lucy?

여 응. 나에게 고양이 두 마리가 있어. 고양이들은 너무 사랑스러워.

남 한국에서는 고양이를 기르는 사람들이 많지 않아.

여 정말이니? 고양이는 미국에서는 가장 인기가 있는 애완동물이야.

남 그렇구나. 내 생각엔 강아지보다 고양이 돌보기가 더 쉬운 것 같아. 나는 내 개를 일주일에 두 번 목욕을 시켜야 해.

해설

개가 한국인들이 가장 많이 기르는 애완동물이라는 언급은 없다.

어휘

pet[pet] 애완동물 / raise[reiz] 기르다, (식물을) 재배하다 / take care of ~을 돌보다 / give a bath 목욕시키다

11 ③

Script

M Where did you get this shirt?

W I got it off the Internet. Do you like it?

M Yes. How much did you pay for it?

W I paid 20 dollars, but it was 30 dollars at the department store.

M I see.

W I think you should start buying clothes through the Internet. They're much cheaper.

M I know, but I never buy clothes I can't try on first.

해석

남 이 셔츠는 어디서 났니?

여 인터넷에서 샀어. 마음에 드니?

남 응. 얼마 주고 샀니?

여 20달러를 줬는데 백화점에서는 30달러였어.

남 그렇구나.

여 나는 네가 인터넷을 통해서 옷을 사기 시작해야 한다고 생각해. 훨씬 싸거든.

남 알아, 하지만 나는 내가 먼저 입어 볼 수 없는 옷을 절대 사지 않아.

해설

I never buy clothes I can't try on first.라는 남자의 마지막 말을 통해 정답을 알 수 있다.

어휘

cheap[tʃiːp] 값이 싼, 저렴한 / try on 입어보다

12 ④

Script

W Let's eat out tonight. I don't feel like cooking.

M OK. What do you want to have?

W I want something different today.

M Like what, Chinese food?

W No, you know I don't like Chinese food. Um... I want some seafood.

M I know a famous place that serves seafood.

W Let's go there then.

해석

여 오늘 외식하자. 오늘은 요리하기 싫어.

남 알았어. 뭐 먹고 싶니?

여 오늘은 좀 다른 것을 먹고 싶어.

남 어떤 거, 중국 음식?

여 아니, 내가 중국 음식을 좋아하지 않는 거 너 알잖아. 음, 해산물이 먹고 싶어.

남 내가 해산물을 하는 유명한 곳을 알고 있어.

여 그러면 거기로 가자.

해설

I want some seafood.라는 말을 통해 여자가 해산물을 먹고 싶어 한다는 것을 알 수 있다.

어휘

eat out 외식하다 / feel like+-ing ~하고 싶다 / seafood[siːfuːd] 해산물

13 ②

Script

W Look at the woman. She has a brand-name bag over

her shoulder. I want to have one.

M We are just students, so we don't need an expensive bag like that.

W That's true, but most girls want to have one.

M Get real! It is too expensive for students to get one like that, and you don't even have enough money to pay for this food.

해석

여 저 여자 좀 봐. 어깨에 명품 가방을 메고 있어. 나도 하나 있었으면 좋겠다.

남 우린 단지 학생이기 때문에 저런 비싼 가방은 필요 없어.

여 그게 사실이긴 하지만, 대부분 소녀들은 그런 걸 갖고 싶어해.

남 정신 차려! 저런 가방을 학생이 사기에는 너무 비싸고 넌 이 음식값을 낼 돈조차 없잖아.

해설

보기에는 근사하나 학생 신분에는 어울리지도 않고, 갖고 싶어도 돈이 없어서 살 수 없기 때문에 그림의 떡이다.

어휘

brand-name (유명) 상표가 붙은, 유명한 / Get real! 정신 차려라!, 꿈 깨라!

14 ①

Script

W You need money to buy this, but some people get this for free because they use coupons or points. This is a piece of printed paper that shows you have paid money to enter a cinema or many other places or to travel on a bus, train, or airplane.

해석

여 당신은 이것을 사기 위해 돈이 필요하지만, 어떤 사람들은 쿠폰이나 포인트를 사용하여 이것을 공짜로 받습니다. 이것은 인쇄된 한 장의 종이로 영화관이나 다른 많은 장소에 들어가거나, 버스, 기차, 또는 비행기로 여행하는 데 당신이 돈을 지불을 했다는 것을 보여줍니다.

해설

영화관이나 다른 장소에 들어가거나 비행기 등 대중교통을 이용하기 위해 돈을 지불했다는 것을 보여주는 것은 표이다.

어휘

for free 공짜로, 무료로 / point[pɔint] 점수, 포인트 / printed[príntid] 인쇄된 / cinema[sínəmə] 영화관, 영화 / place[pleis] 장소 / travel on ~로 여행하다

15 ⑤

Script

W What are you doing?

M I'm busy preparing for the first semester.

W That's strange. Our first semester starts in September.

M Your country has a different system. Ours starts in March.

W I see. What do you need, then?

M I need to buy some notebooks and make sure if I have all the necessary textbooks.

해석

여 지금 뭐하니?

남 나는 첫 학기 준비하느라 바빠.

여 이상하네. 우리는 첫 학기가 9월에 시작해.

남 너희 나라는 다른 체계를 가지고 있어. 우리는 3월에 시작해.

여 그렇구나. 그럼, 너는 뭐가 필요하니?

남 공책도 사야하고 내게 필요한 교과서가 모두 있는지 확인해야 해.

해설

남자는 공책을 사야하고 필요한 모든 교과서를 가지고 있는지 확인해야 한다고 했지, 모든 교과서를 전부 가지고 있다고는 하지 않았다.

어휘

be busy+-ing ~하느라 바쁘다 / semester[siméstər] 학기 / strange[streindʒ] 이상한 / system[sístəm] 체계, 시스템 / notebook[nóutbùk] 공책 / necessary[nésəsèri] 필요한, 필수의 / textbook[tékstbùk] 교과서

16 ①

Script

W Did you turn this on?

M Yes, I did. Is something wrong?

W When I came to work this morning, it was still on.

M It was so hot, so I just left it running.

W Yeah, I know it was hot yesterday, but it will cost a lot of money.

M That's OK. My boss will pay for it not me.

W You shouldn't think that way.

해석

여 당신이 이것을 켰나요?

남 네, 그래요. 뭐가 잘못되었나요?

여 제가 아침에 출근했을 때 그게 아직도 켜져 있었어요.

남 너무 더워서 제가 그냥 켜 놓았어요.

여 네, 어제가 더웠다는 건 알지만, 비용이 많이 들잖아요.

남 괜찮아요. 제가 아니라, 우리 사장님이 내실 거예요.

여 그런 식으로 생각하면 안 되죠.

해설

여자는 냉방 비용을 사장님이 낼 것이니 밤에 냉방기를 켜두어도 상관없다는 남자의 태도를 책망하고 있다.

어휘

turn on 켜다 / cost[kɔːst] 비용; 비용이 들다 / boss[bɔ(ː)s] 사장, 고용주, 우두머리 / pay for 지불하다

17 ⑤

Script

M Mom, I'm home. What is this sweet smell?

W I've just baked some chocolate cookies. Try some.

W These are really delicious. You are the best cook, Mom.

M Thanks. I'll put them in the cookie jar. Make sure to share them with your sister, OK?

W Yes, Mom.

해석

남 엄마, 저 집에 왔어요. 이 달콤한 냄새는 뭐예요?

여 막 초콜릿 쿠키를 구웠단다. 좀 먹어보렴!

남 정말 맛있어요. 엄마는 최고의 요리사예요.

여 고마워. 쿠키들을 쿠키 단지에 넣어둘게. 여동생과 나누어 먹어야 한다, 알겠니?

남 네, 엄마.

해설

Make sure to share them with you sister라는 여자의 말을 통해 정답을 알 수 있다.

어휘

sweet[swi:t] 달콤한 / smell[smel] 냄새; 냄새가 나다 / delicious[dilíʃəs] 맛있는 / cook[kuk] 요리사; 요리하다 / jar[dʒɑːr] 단지, 항아리 / make sure to+동사원형 반드시 ~하다 / share[ʃɛər] 나누다, 공유하다

18 ①

Script

① M Can I use your cell phone?
W I found it in the bathroom.

② M Can you tell me how to use this machine?
W Yes. First, turn it on.

③ M Do you want some more pizza?
W Yes, please. Thank you.

④ M Let me help you.
W That's very kind of you.

⑤ M How was your trip to Japan?
W I enjoyed the trip, but the weather was bad.

해석

① 남 네 휴대 전화를 사용해도 될까?
여 나는 그걸 화장실에서 찾았어.

② 남 이 기계를 어떻게 사용하는지 나에게 얘기해 줘.
여 응. 먼저, 기계를 켜.

③ 남 피자를 좀 더 먹을래?
여 응, 고마워.

④ 남 제가 좀 도와드리겠습니다.
여 당신은 매우 친절하시군요.

⑤ 남 일본 여행은 어땠어?
여 여행은 즐거웠는데 날씨가 안 좋았어.

해설

① 휴대 전화를 사용해도 되는지를 묻는 문장으로 거절이나 허락을 의미하는 응답이 와야 한다.

어휘

cell phone 휴대 전화 / how to use 어떻게 사용하는지 / machine[məʃíːn] 기계

19 ③

Script

W Excuse me. How can I get to the post office?

M Sorry?

W Where is the post office?

M It's next to the bank.

W Is it far from here?

M No. It's just a short walk.

해석

여 실례합니다만, 어떻게 우체국에 갈 수 있을까요?

남 뭐라고요?

여 우체국이 어디 있습니까?

남 은행 옆에 있습니다.

여 여기서 먼 가요?

남 아니요. 조금만 걸으시면 돼요.

해설

① 좋은 생각이에요.
② 어떻게 내가 거기에 갈 수 있나요?
④ 저도 여기가 초행입니다.
⑤ 은행과 빵집 사이에 있습니다.

여자는 우체국이 거리가 얼마나 되는지를 묻고 있으므로 응답으로 거리가 나오는 것이 자연스럽다.

20 ②

Script

M Where did you get that medal?

W From the marathon race this morning.

M Was it a full course marathon?

W No, people under 18 aren't allowed to run a full course. I ran ten kilometers.

M You won the race?

W Yes, I did.

M That's amazing.

해석

남 너 그 메달 어디서 났니?

여 오늘 아침 마라톤 경주에서.

남 풀코스 마라톤 경주였니?

여 아니, 18세 이하는 풀코스 마라톤을 뛰는 게 허용되지 않아. 나는 10킬로미터를 뛰었어.

남 네가 우승했니?

여 응, 내가 우승했어.

남 굉장하구나.

해설

① 진정해.
③ 나는 풀코스를 뛰었어.
④ 끔찍해.

⑤ 아니야, 네가 우승했잖아.

우승했다는 여자의 말에 축하나 놀람을 나타내는 응답이 와야 자연스럽다.

어휘

winner[wínər] 승자, 우승자 / medal[médl] 메달 / marathon[mǽrəθàn] 마라톤 / full course marathon 풀코스 마라톤 (49.192Km를 뛰는 마라톤) / kilometer[kilámətər] 킬로미터

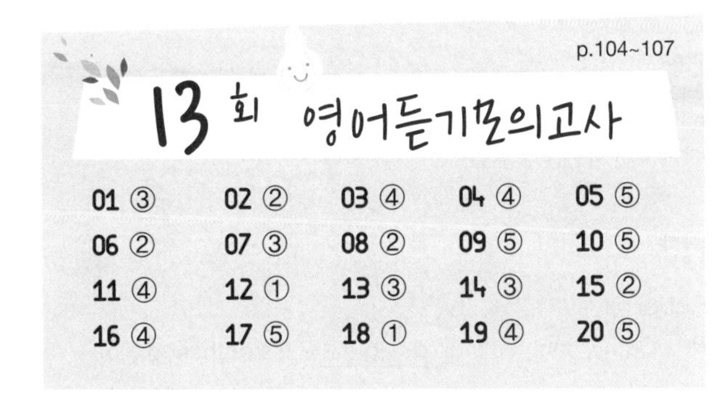

01 ③

Script

W Excuse me, I'm looking for Shelly's Beauty Salon. Do you know where it is?

M Yes. Go straight this way for two blocks, and then make a left. It'll be the second building on your right.

W OK. Pass two blocks and turn left and it's the second building on my right.

M You got it.

해석

여 실례합니다만, 저는 Shelly 미용실을 찾고 있어요. 그곳이 어디 있는지 아세요?

남 네. 이 길을 따라 두 블록을 지나서 왼쪽으로 도세요. 미용실은 오른쪽 두 번째 건물이에요.

여 알겠습니다. 두 블록을 지나서 왼쪽으로 돌아 오른쪽 두 번째 건물이요.

남 맞습니다.

해설

Shelly 미용실은 두 블록을 지나서 왼쪽으로 돌아, 오른쪽 두 번째 건물이다.

어휘

beauty[bjúːti] 아름다움, 미 / salon[səlán] (미용실 · 의상실 같은) 상점 / beauty salon 미용실 / go straight 직진하다 / pass[pæs] 지나가다, 통과하다 / make a left 좌회전하다, 왼쪽으로 돌다

02 ②

Script

W I think it's raining. I heard what sounds like rain.

M Did you? The weather forecast said it would be fine all day.

W I sure did.

M OK. Let's look out the window. (pause) The sky is clear as crystal.

W How strange! I really heard rain.

해석

여 지금 비가 오는 것 같아. 비가 오는 것 같은 소리를 들었어.

남 그래? 일기 예보에서 온종일 날씨가 좋을 거라고 했는데.

여 정말 들었어.

남 알았어. 창밖을 보자. 하늘이 수정처럼 맑아.

여 정말 이상해! 나 정말로 빗소리를 들었어.

해설

The sky is clear as crystal.라는 남자의 말에서 날씨가 맑음을 알 수 있다.

어휘

fine[fain] 맑은, 비가 안 오는 / clear[kliər] 맑은, 화창한 / crystal[krístl] 크리스털

03 ④

Script

M Hello. Please look at me.

W Okay.

M Please turn your face a little bit to the left.

W Like this?

M That's it. Looking good. Now, I want to see a smile on your face.

W It's hard to do that.

M Then say, "Whiskey." Okay. I'll take a picture now.

해석

남 저기요. 저를 보세요.

여 알았어요.

남 얼굴을 왼쪽으로 약간 돌리세요.

여 이렇게요?

남 바로 그겁니다. 좋습니다. 이제 얼굴에 미소를 띠세요.

여 그렇게 하기 어려워요.

남 그러면 '위스키.'라고 말하세요. 좋아요. 지금 사진을 찍겠습니다.

해설

얼굴을 왼쪽으로 약간 돌리라는 말과 얼굴에 미소를 띠라는 말 등으로 사진관에서 사진을 찍는 상황임을 알 수 있다.

어휘

turn[təːrn] 돌리다 / smile[smail] 미소 / take a picture 사진을 찍다

04 ④

Script

M John hasn't arrived yet. He said he will be here soon.

W Does he know the show starts at five?

M I'm sure he does, but he said he got caught in traffic.

W That's his problem. Everyone knows traffic is terrible at this time of day.

M That's true. We only have 20 minutes left.

W Let's call him again.

해석

남 John이 아직 오지 않았어. 곧 여기에 도착할 거라고 했어.

여 그가 쇼가 5시에 시작하는 걸 알고 있니?

남 분명히 알고 있을 거야. 하지만, 그가 교통 체증으로 꼼짝도 못하고 있대.

여 그게 그 애의 문제야. 모든 사람이 이 시간에 교통 체증이 심하다는 걸 알잖아.

남 그건 사실이야. 20분밖에 안 남았어.

여 그에게 다시 전화해보자.

해설

쇼는 5시에 시작하며, 지금이 쇼 시작 20분 전이므로 현재 시각이 4시 40분임을 알 수 있다.

어휘

get caught in[up] ~에 휘말리다 / traffic[trǽfik] 교통(량) / get caught in traffic 교통 체증에 막히다, 차가 막히다 / terrible[térəbəl] 심한, 지독한

05 ⑤

Script

M Why don't we see the romantic movie?

W No, I don't like love stories.

M Well, they're my favorite. How about that one over there?

W I saw that one last week with my sister.

M You like actions, don't you?

W Yes. I like mysteries, actions, and SFs.

M Okay. You choose the movie, and I will buy some popcorn.

해석

남 우리 저 로맨스 영화를 보는 게 어떨까?

여 아니, 난 사랑 이야기를 좋아하지 않아.

남 이런, 그게 내가 가장 좋아하는 건데. 저기 저건 어때?

여 저건 지난주에 언니랑 같이 봤어.

남 너는 액션을 좋아하는구나, 그렇지 않니?

여 응. 나는 미스터리, 액션, 그리고 공상과학 영화를 좋아해.

남 좋아. 네가 영화를 골라. 내가 가서 팝콘을 사올게.

해설

남자가 좋아하는 영화 장르는 로맨스, 여자가 좋아하는 영화 장르는 미스터리, 액션, 공상과학이다.

어휘

romance[roumǽns] 로맨스 / favorite[féivərit] 좋아하는 사람, 특히 좋아하는 것; 매우 좋아하는 / mystery[místəri] 미스터리, 추리 / action[ǽkʃən] 액션 / science fiction 공상과학 / popcorn[pápkɔ̀ːrn] 팝콘

06 ②

Script

M This is the best exercise I've ever done, and I have lost 20 kilograms in three months. Running may cause pain in your knees, but you don't have to worry about it while doing this exercise. You don't need to wear any special clothes. You can do it anywhere and anytime. This exercise is very simple but brings the best result.

해석

남 이것은 제가 해 본 최고의 운동이고 저는 3개월 동안 20킬로그램을 감량했습니다. 달리기는 무릎에 통증을 야기할 수 있지만, 이 운동을 하는 동안에는 그것에 대해서 걱정할 필요가 없습니다. 특별한 옷을 입지 않으셔도 됩니다. 언제 어디서나 이것을 할 수 있습니다. 이 운동은 매우 간단하지만, 최고의 결과를 가져옵니다.

해설

특별한 옷을 입을 필요도 없고 달리기처럼 무릎 통증을 야기하지도 않으며, 언제, 어디서나 할 수 있다는 설명에 해당하는 운동을 고른다.

어휘

exercise[éksərsàiz] 운동; 운동하다 / cause[kɔːz] 일으키다 / anywhere[énihwὲər] 어디서나 / anytime[énitàim] 언제든지 / simple[símpəl] 단순한, 간단한 / result[rizʌ́lt] 결과

07 ③

Script

M Cathy, can you stop doing that? It's bothering me.

W What do you want me to stop? I'm just sitting in the chair.

M You've been moving your legs for one hour.

W Oh, sorry! When I sit down, I begin moving my legs without thinking. I've tried to stop this habit, but it is not easy.

M I used to have the bad habit of biting my lips, but I was able to break it. So try harder.

해석

남 Cathy야, 그거 좀 그만 하면 안 되니? 신경 쓰이잖아.

여 뭘 멈추라는 거니? 난 그냥 의자에 앉아 있는데.

남 너 한 시간 동안 다리를 움직이고 있잖아.

여 아, 미안해! 내가 앉아 있을 때 무의식적으로 내 다리를 움직이기 시작하게 돼. 이 습관을 고치려고 노력하는데 그게 쉽지 않아.

남 나도 입술을 깨무는 나쁜 버릇이 있었는데 그것을 고쳤어. 그러니까 더 노력해 봐.

해설

여자의 버릇은 앉아 있을 때 다리는 움직이는 것이다.

어휘

bite[bait] 씹다, 깨물다 / nail[neil] 손톱, 발톱 / lip[lip] 입술 / shake[ʃeik] 흔들다 / answer back 말대꾸하다 / spit[spit] 침 뱉다 / without thinking 무의식적으로, 생각지도 않고 / break a habit 습관을 고치다

08 ②

Script

W Are you going to attend the after-school program?

M I don't want to, but my mother told me to attend a Chinese characters class. How about you?

W I'm going to attend a history class with John and David.

M You know what? If we attend the after-school program, we'll finish school at six every day.

Q What class is the man going to attend in his after-school program?

해석

여 너는 방과 후 프로그램에 참여할 거니?

남 나는 하기 싫은데, 엄마가 나보고 한자 수업을 받으래. 너는?

여 나는 John하고 David와 함께 역사 과목 들을 거야.

남 있잖아. 우리가 방과 후 수업에 참여하면 매일 6시에 학교가 끝나.

질문 남자는 방과 후 수업으로 어떤 과목을 수강할 것인가?

해설

my mother told me to attend a Chinese characters class.라는 남자의 말을 통해 남자가 한자 수업을 받을 거라는 것을 알 수 있다.

어휘

attend[əténd] 참석하다, 참여하다 / after-school 방과 후의 / program[próugræm] 프로그램, 계획, 교과 과정(표) / subject[sʌ́bdʒikt] 과목 / character[kǽriktər] 문자, 기호 / Chinese character 한자

09 ⑤

Script

M Ashley, someone took my backpack.

W Where did you last see it?

M I put it next to Cindy's backpack, but it's gone.

W What does it look like?

M It has two small pockets near the bottom, and there is a big letter G between the pockets.

W Let's ask the security guard over there.

해석

남 Ashley, 누가 내 가방을 가져갔어.

여 어디서 그것을 마지막으로 보았니?

남 그걸 Cindy 가방 옆에 놓았는데 사라졌어.

여 가방이 어떤 모양이니?

남 가방 바닥 가까이에 두 개의 작은 주머니가 있고, 주머니 사이에 대문자 G가 있어.

여 저기 있는 경비원에게 물어보자.

해설

남자의 가방은 아래쪽에 두 개의 작은 주머니가 있고 그 사이에 대문자로 G라는 글자가 새겨져 있다.

어휘

backpack[bǽkpæ̀k] (등에 짊어지는) 가방 / pocket[pɑ́kit] 호주머니, 포켓 / bottom[bɑ́təm] 맨 아래, 바닥 / big letter 대문자 / security[sikjúəriti] 안전, 치안 / guard[gɑːrd] 보호자, 경호원 / security guard 경비원

10 ⑤

Script

M Are you going somewhere?

W Yes, I'm going on a business trip to Chicago, so I need to put these suitcases in my car.

M You have lots of bags to take. How long are you going to stay there for?

W I think it'll be more than a month. Can you help me carry them?

M No problem.

해석

남 너 어디 가는 중이니?

여 응, 시카고로 출장 가고 있어. 그래서 이 여행 가방들을 내 차에 넣어야 해.

남 갖고 갈 가방이 정말 많구나. 거기서 얼마나 머무를 거니?

여 한 달 이상이 될 것 같아. 그것들을 옮기는 걸 좀 도와줄래?

남 물론이지.

해설

Can you help me carry them?이라는 여자의 말로 여자가 남자에게 가방을 옮기는 것을 도와달라고 부탁하고 있음을 알 수 있다.

어휘

go on a business trip 출장을 가다 / suitcase[súːtkèis] 여행 가방

11 ④

Script

M Do you have any plans for Thanksgiving?

W Not really. I may visit my grandparents. How about you?

M I'm going to the States during the break.

W Are you taking a tour?

M No, I'm going to visit a relative who I haven't seen for many years.

해석

남 너 이번 추수 감사절 계획 있니?

여 특별한 건 없어. 난 조부모님을 방문할 것 같아. 너는?

남 난 휴일에 미국에 갈 거야.

여 여행하는 거야?

남 아니, 오랫동안 못 뵙던 친척을 방문할 거야.

해설

I'm going to visit a relative who I haven't seen for many years.라는 남자의 말로 친척을 방문할 것이라는 것을 알 수 있다.

어휘

Thanksgiving[θæ̀ŋksgíviŋ] 추수 감사절 / grandparent[grǽndpɛ̀ərənt] 조부모 / during[djúəriŋ] ~ 동안 / break[breik] 짧은 방학, 휴가, 휴식 시간 / take a tour 여행하다, 구경하다

12 ①

Script

[Telephone rings.]

W Hello, this is Susan. How may I help you?

M Hi, it's Brian. Is Sean there?

W No, he is out of town.

M Can you tell him to call me?

W Sure, but can you tell me what this is about?

M The paint on the wall of my house has come off, so I need him this weekend.

해석

여 안녕하세요. 저는 Susan입니다. 무엇을 도와드릴까요?

남 여보세요. Brian인데요. Sean 있나요?

여 아니요. 출타 중이에요.

남 저에게 전화 좀 해달라고 전해 주실래요?

여 그러죠. 그런데 무슨 일인지 말씀해 주시겠어요?

남 저희 집의 벽 페인트가 벗겨지고 있어요. 그래서 이번 주말에 그가 필요해요.

해설

The paint on the wall of my house has come off, so I need him this weekend.라는 남자의 말로 Sean의 직업이 페인트공이라는 것을 알 수 있다.

어휘

be out of town (출장 등으로) 도시를 떠나 있다 / paint[peint] 페인트; 페인트칠하다 / come off (~에서) 떨어지다 / be back 돌아오다

13 ③

Script

W Did you hear that Patrick's birthday party will not be held on the 13th?

M No, I didn't. Who said that?

W Patrick did. He said he has to attend an important meeting on that day.

M I see. Then, when will it be held?

W Two days later at Goodfood restaurant at 6:30.

해석

여 너 Patrick의 생일 파티가 13일에 열리지 않을 거라는 소식 들었니?

남 아니, 못 들었어. 누가 그 얘길 했니?

여 Patrick이 그랬어. 그는 그날 중요한 회의가 참석해야 한대.

남 그렇구나. 그러면 언제 생일 파티가 열리니?

여 이틀 후 Goodfood 식당에서 6시 반이야.

해설

생일 파티는 13일이 아니라 이틀 후인, 15일 6시 반에 Goodfood 식당에서 열릴 예정이다.

어휘

meeting[míːtiŋ] 회의

14 ③

Script

W I've heard you are going to sell your bike. How much do you want for it?

M 80 dollars.

W That's too much for a used bike.

M I paid 150 dollars when I bought it.

W Okay, I'll give you half the price you want.

M Ten more.

W Deal!

해석

여 네가 자전거를 팔 거라고 들었어. 얼마를 받기를 원하니?

남 80달러.

여 중고 자전거에 비해 너무 비싸.

남 내가 살 때는 150달러를 줬어.

여 좋아. 네가 원하는 가격의 절반을 줄게.

남 10달러 더 줘.

여 좋아!

해설

남자가 원하는 가격(80달러)의 반을 주겠다는 여자의 말에 10달러를 더 달라고 남자가 말하고 있으므로 자전거의 가격은 50달러이다.

어휘

sell[sel] 팔다 / used[juːst] 중고의

15 ②

Script

M Hello, may I help you?

W Hi, I have a terrible headache.

M Since when have you had a headache?

W Since yesterday.

M I'll give you some aspirin. And if it gets worse, you should go see a doctor.

W Okay. Thank you.

해석

남 안녕하세요. 도와드릴까요?

여 안녕하세요. 두통이 너무 심해서요.

남 언제부터 두통이 있었나요?

여 어제부터요.

남 제가 아스피린을 드리겠습니다. 그리고 더 심해지면 병원에 가보셔야 합니다.

여 알겠습니다. 감사합니다.

해설

두통이 있다는 여자에게 아스피린을 주겠다는 남자의 말을 통해 두 사람의 관계가 약사와 손님임을 알 수 있다. if it gets worse, you should go see a doctor라는 말로 남자의 직업이 의사는 될 수 없다.

어휘

headache[hédèik] 두통 / medicine[médəsən] 약 / aspirin[ǽspərin] 아스피린 / get worse 악화되다

16 ④

Script

W Seth, what type of girl do you like?

M Well, I don't know. I haven't thought much about it. How about you? You like tall and good-looking men, don't you?

W Not at all.

M How about a guy with rich parents?

W Stop! I'm not that kind of girl. I just like a guy who is very understanding.

해석

여 Seth, 너는 어떤 여자를 좋아하니?

남 글쎄, 잘 모르겠어. 나는 그거에 대해 깊이 생각해 본 적이 없어. 너는? 너는 키 크고 잘생긴 남자를 좋아하지, 그렇지 않니?

여 전혀 아니거든.

남 돈 많은 부모가 있는 남자는?

여 그만해! 나는 그런 소녀가 아니야. 나는 그냥 이해심이 많은 남자가 좋아.

해설

I just like a guy who is very understanding라는 여자의 말을 통해 여자가 좋아하는 남자는 이해심이 많은 남자라는 것을 알 수 있다.

어휘

good-looking[gúdlúkiŋ] 잘생긴, 보기 좋은 / rich[ritʃ] 부유한, 돈 많은 / understanding[ʌ̀ndərstǽndiŋ] 이해력이 있는

17 ⑤

Script

① W Is she going to invite Ann to her party?
M Probably, not.

② W Is this your computer?
M No, my brother and I share the computer.

③ W I can never get up early in the morning.
M Why don't you go to bed early?

④ W Why are you wearing this helmet?
M Because it protects my head.

⑤ W How have you been?
M I drove her car to get there.

해석

① 여 그녀가 Ann을 자신의 생일 파티에 초대할까?
남 아마도, 아닐걸.

② 여 이것이 네 컴퓨터니?
남 아니, 우리 형과 내가 같이 사용해.

③ 여 난 아침 일찍 절대 못 일어나겠어.
남 일찍 자는 게 어때?

④ 여 너는 왜 이 헬멧을 쓰고 있니?
남 왜냐하면 그것이 내 머리를 보호해 주니까.

⑤ 여 잘 지냈니?
남 나는 거기에 가려고 그녀의 차를 운전했어.

해설

⑤ How have you been?은 안부를 묻는 질문으로 그에 알맞은 응답이 와야 한다.

어휘

share[ʃɛər] 나누다, 함께 쓰다 / get up 일어나다 / helmet[hélmit] 헬멧 / protect[prətékt] 보호하다

18 ①

Script

W Wow, the house is so clean. Who cleaned it?

M Jess and I did.

W How come? You don't even clean your room.

M Well, you've worked late these days, and you looked so tired last night. So Jess and I cleaned up, and we even did the laundry.

W Oh, you two are so sweet. Thank you.

해석

여 와, 집이 정말 깨끗하구나. 누가 청소했니?

남 Jess와 제가 했어요.

여 웬일이니? 너는 네 방도 청소를 안 하잖니.

남 그게, 엄마가 요즘 늦게까지 일하시고, 어젯밤에 정말 피곤해 보이셨거든요. 그래서 Jess와 제가 청소를 했어요. 그리고 우리가 빨래도 했어요.

여 오, 정말 착하기도 해라. 고맙구나.

해설

피곤한 엄마를 위해 청소했다는 얘기를 듣고 엄마가 아이들을 칭찬하는 상황이다.

어휘

work late 늦게까지 일하다 / do the laundry 빨래를 하다

19 ④

Script

W You are in the store to buy a gift for your mother. You look around to choose the right one for her and decide to buy a scarf. You ask the clerk how much it is, and she says it's 30 dollars. You really want to buy it, but you only have 28 dollars. In this situation, what would you say to the clerk?

해석

여 당신은 어머니께 드릴 선물을 사려고 상점에 있습니다. 당신은 어머니께 드릴 적당한 것을 고르기 위해 돌아보고는 스카프를 사기로 결정합니다. 점원에게 가격이 얼마인지 묻자, 점원이 30달러라고 얘기합니다. 당신은 그것을 정말로 사고 싶지만, 당신에게는 28달러밖에 없습니다. 이런 상황에서 당신은 점원에게 뭐라고 얘기하시겠습니까?

해설

① 스카프 두 개를 살게요.

② 환불받고 싶어요.

③ 보세요! 여기 구멍이 나 있어요.

⑤ 다른 색깔로 교환할 수 있을까요?

스카프를 사고 싶은데 가지고 있는 돈이 모자란 상황으로 '할인을 해주시겠어요?'라는 의미의 ④이 가장 적절하다.

어휘

scarf[skɑːrf] 스카프, 목도리 / hole[houl] 구멍 / discount[dískaunt] 할인; 할인하다 / give a discount 할인해 주다 / exchange[ikstʃéindʒ] 교환하다, 주고받다 / look around 둘러보다

20 ⑤

Script

W Where are you going?

M I'm going to the library to look for some information on UFOs.

W You are writing a science report, right? I did that last semester.

M Then, can I read yours? I have no idea how to start it.

W Sure, I'll bring it to you tomorrow.

M Thanks. It would be a great help.

해석

여 너 어디 가니?

남 UFO에 대한 자료를 찾으러 도서관에 가고 있어.

여 너 과학 보고서 쓰는 중이지, 맞지? 지난 학기 때 나도 그거 했거든.

남 그러면, 내가 네 보고서를 읽어봐도 될까? 어떻게 시작해야 할지 모르겠어.

여 물론이야, 내일 그것을 너에게 갖다줄게.

남 고마워. 그게 큰 도움이 될 거야.

해설

① 너는 정말 훌륭한 과학자야.

② 그거에 대해 너무 걱정하지 마.

③ 다음번에 더 잘할 수 있을 거야.

④ 미안해, 하지만 나는 네가 그것이 필요하다고 생각하지 않아.

보고서를 읽어보고 싶다는 남자의 부탁에 내일 갖다 주겠다는 여자의 말에 이어질 남자의 응답으로 알맞은 것을 고른다.

어휘

look for 찾다 / information[ìnfərméiʃən] 정보, 자료 / UFO 미확인 비행물체(비행접시 등)

p.112~115

14회 영어듣기모의고사

01 ①	02 ④	03 ③	04 ②	05 ④
06 ①	07 ①	08 ②	09 ③	10 ④
11 ④	12 ③	13 ④	14 ①	15 ⑤
16 ①	17 ⑤	18 ③	19 ①	20 ④

01 ①

Script

① M Mom, I bought some flowers on the way home.
W Oh, how sweet of you.

② M Well, you have two large cavities.
W Are you going to pull the teeth out?

③ M Could we have a table for five?
W Did you make a reservation, sir?

④ M Your new hairstyle looks good on you.
W Thank you. I got a haircut yesterday.

⑤ M What will you do after school?
W I will go shopping with my sister.

해석

① 남 엄마, 제가 집에 오는 길에 꽃을 좀 사왔어요.
여 오, 정말 착하기도 하지.

② 남 음, 충치가 두 개 있습니다.
여 그 이를 뽑으실 건가요?

③ 남 다섯 명이 앉을 테이블 있을까요?
여 예약을 하셨나요, 손님?

④ 남 새 머리 모양이 너에게 잘 어울려.
여 고마워. 어제 머리 잘랐어.

⑤ 남 방과 후에 뭐 할 거니?
여 언니랑 쇼핑하러 갈 거야.

해설

아들이 엄마에게 꽃을 주는 상황에 알맞은 대화를 고른다.

어휘

on the way home 집에 오는 길에 / cavity[kǽvəti] 충치 / tooth[tuːθ] 이, 치아 (pl. teeth) / pull out 빼다 / reservation[rèzərvéiʃən] 예약 / make a reservation 예약하다 / hairstyle[hέərstàil] 머리 모양, 헤어스타일 / haircut[hέərkʌ̀t] 머리 깎기 / get a haircut 머리를 자르다

02 ④

Script

M Where is he? Ryan is not a person to be late.

W Sam, you didn't hear about Ryan, did you?

M No, did something happen to him?

W His dad had a car accident last night, and he is in the hospital now.

M What a pity!

해석

남 그는 어디 있니? Ryan이 늦을 사람은 아닌데.

여 Sam, 너 Ryan에 대한 소식 못 들었구나, 그렇지?

남 응, 그에게 무슨 일이 있니?

여 어젯밤에 그의 아빠가 교통사고가 나셔서 지금 병원에 계셔.

남 불쌍해라!

해설

What a pity!는 동정을 나타내는 표현이다.

어휘

accident[ǽksidənt] 사고 / pity[píti] 연민의 정, 동정 / What a pity! 가엾어라!, 불쌍해라!

03 ③

Script

W This is the front desk. May I help you?

M Yes. I'm Johnson from room number 210. Is there a drugstore near here?

W There are a couple, but they are closed. Is someone sick?

M Yes, my wife is coughing a lot.

W We keep some cold medicine here for our guests. I will have someone bring some up to you right away.

M Thanks.

해석

여 프런트 데스크입니다. 무엇을 도와드릴까요?

남 네. 전 210호에 Johnson인데요. 이 근처에 약국이 있나요?

여 네, 두 곳이 있는데 문을 닫았어요. 누가 아픈가요?

남 네, 제 아내가 기침을 심하게 해요.

여 저희는 고객을 위해 감기약을 상비해 두고 있습니다. 누군가를 시켜서 고객님께 가져다드리도록 하겠습니다.

남 감사합니다.

해설

프런트 데스크와 방에 투숙하고 있는 손님 사이의 대화로 대화가 이루어지는 장소가 호텔임을 알 수 있다.

어휘

front desk (호텔 등의) 접수처, 프런트 / drugstore[drʌ́gstɔ̀ːr] 약국 / cough[kɔ(ː)f] 기침하다 / cold[kould] 감기 / medicine[médəsən] 약 / guest[gest] 손님, 숙박객 / right away 즉시, 바로

04 ②

Script

M The bridegroom is here. He is handsome and tall.

W The bride is pretty, too. They are a perfect couple.

M Where are we having lunch, anyway?

W Downstairs at 2 o'clock.

M We still have to wait 20 minutes.

W That's right. Hey, look. I think they are going to start the wedding

해석

남 신랑이 나왔어. 키도 크고 잘생겼어.

여 신부도 예뻐. 완벽한 커플이야.

남 그런데, 우리 점심은 어디서 먹니?

여 2시에 아래층에서.

남 아직도 20분을 기다려야 해.

여 맞아. 야, 봐. 지금 결혼식을 시작하려는 것 같아.

해설

2시가 되려면 20분이 남았다는 남자의 말로 현재 시각이 1시 40분이며, 이제 막 예식을 시작하려고 한다고 했기 때문에 결혼식이 열리는 시각이 1시 40분임을 알 수 있다.

어휘

bridegroom[bráidgrù(ː)m] 신랑 / handsome[hǽnsəm] 잘 생긴 / bride[braid] 신부 / perfect[pə́ːrfikt] 완벽한 / couple[kʌ́pəl] 한 쌍, 커플 / downstairs[daunstɛ́ərz] 아래층의

05 ④

Script

W Will, I will buy you dinner tonight.

M Well, thanks, but I don't think I can.

W Why not?

M I have to go to the library and get some information about the Second World War.

W Is it because of your history report?

M Yes, I need to finish writing it by Friday.

해석

여 Will, 내가 오늘 너에게 저녁을 살게.

남 글쎄, 고맙긴 하지만 난 안 될 것 같아.

여 왜?

남 도서관에 가서 2차 세계 대전에 대한 자료를 찾아야 해.

여 역사 보고서 때문이니?

남 응, 금요일까지 그것을 써야 해.

해설

보고서를 쓰는 데 필요한 자료를 찾기 위해 남자는 도서관에 가야 한다고 말하고 있다.

어휘

information[ìnfərméiʃən] 정보 / because of ~ 때문에

06 ①

Script

W First, draw a circle, and next, draw a triangle above the circle. Third, draw a square below the circle. Last, put a star inside the circle.

해석

여 첫째, 원을 하나 그리고 다음에 원 위에 삼각형을 하나 그리세요. 셋째, 원 아래에 사각형을 하나 그리세요. 마지막으로, 원 안에 별을 하나 그리세요.

해설

원 위에 삼각형, 원 아래에는 사각형이 있고, 원 안에 별이 있는 그림을 고른다.

어휘

circle[sə́ːrkl] 원 / triangle[tráiæ̀ŋgəl] 삼각형 / above[əbʌ́v] ~의 위에 / third[θəːrd] 세번째로 / square[skwɛər] 사각형 / below[bilóu] ~의 아래 / last[læst] 마지막으로 / inside[insáid] 안에

07 ①

Script

M Taste this soup, and tell me what it needs.

W I'm afraid this soup tastes too salty.

M I don't have time to make it again. What should I do?

W Why don't you just add some water?

M That's a brilliant idea.

해석

남 이 수프의 간을 보고 무엇이 필요한지 얘기해 줘.

여 이 수프는 너무 짠 것 같아.

남 다시 만들 시간이 없어. 내가 어떻게 하면 좋을까?

여 그냥 물을 더 넣는 게 어때?

남 그거 좋은 생각이야.

해설

Why don't you just add some water?라는 여자의 말을 통해 남자가 수프에 물을 넣을 것임을 알 수 있다.

어휘
taste[teist] 맛을 보다, 시식하다 / salty[sɔ́ːlti] 짠 / add[æd] 더하다 / brilliant[bríljənt] 훌륭한, 빛나는

08 ②

Script

M I've been here for almost two years already.

W Wow, time flies. It feels like I met you last week.

M Yeah, I feel that way, too.

W There are so many differences between America and Korea. I'm happy that you are doing great in Korea.

M Life in Korea was tough when I first came. But Seoul has become my second home now.

해석

남 나 여기 온 지 벌써 거의 2년이 다 됐어.

여 와, 시간 빠르다. 지난주에 너를 만난 것 같아.

남 맞아. 나도 그렇게 느껴.

여 미국과 한국 사이에는 다른 점이 많잖아. 나는 네가 한국에서 잘 지내는 것 같아서 기뻐.

남 처음 여기에 왔을 땐 한국 생활이 힘들었어. 하지만, 이제 서울은 내 제 2의 고향이 되었어.

해설

I've been here for almost two years라는 남자의 말로 남자가 한국에 온 지 2년이 되었다는 것을 알 수 있다.

어휘

time flies 시간이 쏜살같다 / difference[dífərəns] 다름, 차이 / tough[tʌf] 힘든, 고된

09 ③

Script

W Kevin, can you hear that sound? I can hear something moving behind the door.

M Come on. It's three o'clock in the morning. It is just the wind blowing.

W Please go out, and see what it is.

M Let's just go back to sleep.

W Oh, you are the man. Unless I know what it is, I won't be able to sleep again.

M But I'm afraid to see what it is, too.

해석

여 Kevin, 저 소리 들려요? 문 뒤에서 뭔가 움직이는 소리가 들려요.

남 제발, 새벽 세 시야. 그건 그냥 바람이 부는 소리일 뿐이라고.

여 나가서 그게 무엇인지 봐 주세요.

남 그냥 다시 잠이나 자자.

여 오, 당신은 남자잖아요. 그게 무언지 모르면 다시 잠을 잘 수가 없어요.

남 하지만, 나도 그것이 무엇인지 확인하는 게 무서워.

해설

남자는 밖에서 무슨 소리가 들린다는 여자의 말에 처음에는 귀찮은 듯이 얘기하다가 결국 I'm afraid to see what it is, too.라고 말하고 있다.

어휘

blow[blou] 바람이 불다 / unless[ənlés] ~하지 않으면 / be able to+동사원형 ~할 수 있다

10 ④

Script

W Lewis, how did you do on the test?

M I just missed one question.

W I'm sure you studied really hard.

M No, I didn't study at all. The test was very easy. I don't understand why so many students spend a lot of time studying.

W I see. Then, why did you miss one question?

M I just made a mistake. That's all.

해석

여 Lewis, 시험 어떻게 봤니?

남 한 문제밖에 안 틀렸어.

여 너 정말 열심히 공부했나 보구나.

남 아니, 나는 공부를 하나도 안 했어. 시험이 정말 쉬웠거든. 나는 왜 많은 학생이 공부하는 데 많은 시간을 보내는지 이해가 안 돼.

여 그렇구나. 그러면, 너 한 문제는 왜 틀린 거니?

남 난 실수를 했을 뿐이야. 그게 다야.

해설

남자는 시험이 정말 쉬웠고 단지 실수를 해서 한 문제를 틀렸을 뿐이며, 많은 학생이 왜 시험공부를 하면서 많은 시간을 보내는지 모르겠다고 말하고 있다.

어휘

miss[mis] 놓치다 / spend+-ing ~하는 데 …시간을 보내다

11 ④

Script

W Today, our city would like to invite everyone to our arm wrestling competition. If you think you are strong enough to challenge, come forward. It will start at 6 o'clock, and the winner will receive a computer. There will also be a match for left-handers, too. So feel free to enjoy our events. Thank you.

해석

여 오늘, 우리 시는 모든 분들을 저희 팔씨름 대회에 초대하고 싶습니다. 도전할 정도로 힘이 세다고 생각되시면 지원하세요. 경기는 여섯 시에 시작하며 우승자는 컴퓨터를 받게 됩니다. 왼손잡이들을 위한 경기도 있습니다. 그러니 주저하지 마시고 우리의 행사에 참가하세요. 감사합니다.

해설

our city would like to invite everyone to our arm wrestling competition이라는 말을 통해 행사 홍보 방송임을 알 수 있다.

어휘

arm wrestling 팔씨름 / competition[kɑ̀mpətíʃən] 대회, 시합, 경쟁 / challenge[tʃǽlindʒ] 도전하다 / forward[fɔ́ːrwərd] 앞으로 / come forward 나서다, 지원하다 / match[mætʃ] 경기 / left-hander 왼손잡이 / feel free to+동사원형 거리낌 없이 ~하다

12 ③

Script

W I'm really tired and hungry. It was such a long week.

M I think so. I've never worked so hard in my life. I even worked overtime last night.

W I know. You worked overtime on Tuesday, too.

M That's right. I worked six more hours than you did.

W Really? I worked for thirty hours this week.

해석

여 나 정말 피곤하고 배고파. 정말로 긴 한 주였어.

남 나도 그렇게 생각해. 살면서 열심히 일을 해 본 적 없거든. 나 심지어 어젯밤에는 초과 근무를 했어.

여 알고 있어. 너는 화요일에도 초과 근무를 했잖아.

남 맞아. 난 네가 일한 것보다 여섯 시간 더 일했어.

여 그래? 나는 이번 주에 30시간 동안 일을 했어.

해설

여자는 이번 주에 30시간을 일했고 남자는 여자보다 6시간을 더 일했다고 말하고 있으므로 남자가 일한 총 시간은 36시간이다.

어휘

overtime[óuvərtàim] 시간 외 근무, 규정 외 노동 시간

13 ④

Script

M I'm starving to death.

W I know a nice Chinese restaurant.

M You mean the one on the corner?

W Yes. Have you been there?

M Yes, but I'm sick of Chinese food.

W Then, what do you want to have?

M I don't care, but I just want to go somewhere not crowded.

해석

남 배가 고파서 죽을 것 같아.

여 괜찮은 중국 음식점을 하나 알고 있어.

남 모퉁이에 있는 거 말이니?

여 응. 너 거기 가봤니?

남 응, 그런데 나는 중국 음식이 싫증이 나.

여 그러면, 뭘 먹고 싶니?

남 상관없어. 단지 붐비지 않는 곳에 갔으면 좋겠어.

해설

I just want to go somewhere not crowded.라는 말을 통해 남자는 한적한 곳에 가고 싶어한다는 것을 알 수 있다.

어휘

starve[stɑːrv] 굶주리다 / starve to death 굶어 죽다 / corner[kɔ́ːrnər] 구석, 모퉁이 / be sick of ~ 지치다, 지겹다 / crowded[kráudid] 혼잡한

14 ①

Script

M Excuse me, do I know you?

W I don't think so. I just moved in.

M Gosh! Anne, you don't remember me?

W How do you know my name?

M I'm Matthew who used to live next-door. We went to the same middle school.

W Oh, I remember now. I'm so glad to see you again.

해석

남 실례합니다. 저를 아세요?

여 아닌 것 같은데요. 저 막 이사 왔거든요.

남 어머! Anne, 나 기억 안 나니?

여 제 이름을 어떻게 아시죠?

남 나 옆집에 살던 Matthew야. 우리 같은 중학교 다녔잖아.

여 아, 이제 기억난다. 너를 다시 만나게 돼서 정말 기뻐.

해설

같은 중학교에 다녔던 Anne과 Matthew가 다시 만난 상황으로 두 사람의 관계가 동창임을 알 수 있다.

어휘

next-door 이웃에, 이웃으로

15 ⑤

Script

M How is a tiger different from a lion? First, a tiger is bigger and heavier, but a lion is taller and faster. Second, a tiger lives alone, but a lion lives in a group. Third, a tiger likes to spend time in the water, but a lion hates water. Finally, a tiger lives in cold climates, but a lion lives in dry climates.

해석

여 호랑이가 사자는 뭐가 다를까요? 첫째, 호랑이는 사자보다 더 크고 무거우나, 사자는 키가 더 크고 빠릅니다. 둘째, 호랑이는 혼자 살지만, 사자는 무리를 지어 삽니다. 셋째, 호랑이는 물에서 시간을 보내는 것을 좋아하지만, 사자는 물을 싫어합니다. 마지막으로, 호랑이는 추운 기후에 살지만, 사자는 건조한 기후에 삽니다.

해설

호랑이는 추운 기후에, 사자는 건조한 기후에 산다.

어휘

be different from ~와 다르다 / live alone 혼자 살다 / group[gruːp] 그룹, 무리 / in a group 무리 지어 / climate[kláimit] 기후 / dry[drai] 건조한

16 ①

Script

① **W** I studied hard, but I failed the test.

M Good for you. I knew you could do it.

② **W** Where did you get that?

M My mom got it for me for my birthday.

③ W How long have you known her?

M Almost three years.

④ W Have you finished with the newspaper?

M Yes, why?

⑤ W Our team lost the game.

M Cheer up!

해석

① 여 나는 열심히 공부했는데 시험에 떨어졌어.

남 잘됐어. 나는 네가 그것을 해낼 줄 알았어.

② 여 너 그거 어디서 났니?

남 엄마가 내 생일 선물로 사주셨어.

③ 여 너는 그녀를 알고 지낸 지 얼마나 되었니?

남 거의 3년 됐어.

④ 여 너 신문 다 읽었니?

남 응, 왜?

⑤ 여 우리 팀이 경기에서 졌어.

남 힘내!

해설

① 공부를 열심히 했지만, 시험에 떨어졌다는 여자를 위로하는 응답이 와야 한다.

어휘

fail[feil] 낙방하다, 낙제하다 / cheer up 기운 내다

17 ⑤

Script

M I can't find the money I put on the table last night. Do you know where it is?

W Oh, that money. Um....

M Come on, talk to me.

W I borrowed some money from Jake, and I paid him back with that money.

M How could you do that without asking me?

해석

남 내가 어젯밤에 테이블 위에 올려놓은 돈이 보이지 않아. 너 그게 어디 있는지 아니?

여 아, 그 돈. 음…….

남 제발, 얘기 좀 해 봐.

여 내가 Jake에게 돈을 빌렸는데 그 돈으로 그에게 돈을 갚았어.

남 어떻게 나한테 물어보지도 않고 그럴 수가 있니?

해설

여자는 돈의 주인에게 물어보지도 않고 함부로 돈을 사용했기 때문에 여자의 성격이 무책임하다는 것을 알 수 있다.

어휘

pay back 갚다

18 ③

Script

W My eyes are sore.

M Did you see an eye doctor?

W Sure, I did. I took some medicine, too.

M My mother used to tell me to wash my eyes with salt water.

W Do you think that would work?

M You can try. You have nothing to lose.

W OK. Thank you.

해석

여 눈이 쓰려.

남 안과에 가 봤니?

여 응, 갔다 왔어. 약도 먹었어.

남 우리 어머니는 소금으로 눈을 씻으라고 내게 말씀하시고는 했는데.

여 그게 효과가 있을까?

남 해 봐. 손해 볼 것은 없잖아.

여 알았어. 고마워.

해설

My mother used to tell me to wash my eyes with salt water.라는 남자의 말로 여자가 할 일이 소금물로 눈을 씻는 것임을 알 수 있다.

어휘

sore[sɔːr] 아픈, 염증을 일으킨 / take medicine 약을 복용하다 / used to+동사원형 ~하곤 했다 / salt[sɔːlt] 소금

19 ①

Script

W Do you have any plans for the summer?

M I'm going to learn how to swim again.

W Can't you swim?

M I've tried to learn many times, but I still don't know how. How about you?

W I'm going to visit my uncle who lives in New Zealand with my parents.

M That sounds really fun.

해석

여 여름에 무슨 계획 있니?

남 난 다시 수영을 배울까해.

여 너 수영 못하니?

남 여러 번 배우려고 했는데, 아직도 수영할 줄 몰라. 너는?

여 난 부모님과 뉴질랜드에 계신 삼촌을 방문할 거야.

남 정말 재미있겠다.

해설

② 난 수영을 잘해.

③ 나는 해변에 가는 것을 즐겨.

④ 나도 마찬가지야. 너와 함께 갈게.

⑤ 너는 쉽게 수영을 배울 수 있을 거야.

여름 방학 때 뉴질랜드에 있는 삼촌을 방문할 거라는 여자의 말에 알맞은 응답으로 알맞은 것을 고른다.

어휘
Same here. 나도 마찬가지야.

20 ④

Script

W Why are you late?

M I'm so sorry. I totally forgot that I had an appointment.

W It's hard to believe. You usually don't forget appointments.

M I don't know why I forgot it.

W Why don't you make a note for yourself next time?

M Thank you for giving me good advice.

해석

여 너 왜 늦었니?

남 정말 미안해. 약속이 있다는 걸 까맣게 잊고 있었어.

여 믿을 수 없어. 넌 대개 약속을 잊지 않잖아.

남 나도 왜 내가 약속을 잊었는지 모르겠어.

여 다음에는 메모해 두는 게 어때?

남 좋은 충고해 줘서 고마워.

해설

① 미안한데, 난 그거 필요 없어.

② 그러면, 왜 나에게 전화했니?

③ 고맙지만, 그건 내 잘못이 아니야.

⑤ 알았어. 다음에 노트를 가지고 올게.

메모하는 게 어떻겠냐며 충고하는 여자의 말에 알맞은 응답을 고른다.

어휘
forget[fərgét] 잊다 / appointment[əpɔ́intmənt] 약속 / make a note 메모하다

15회 영어듣기모의고사

p.120~123

01 ②	02 ①	03 ④	04 ⑤	05 ⑤
06 ④	07 ②	08 ⑤	09 ④	10 ②
11 ③	12 ②	13 ①	14 ①	15 ③
16 ②	17 ④	18 ③	19 ③	20 ⑤

01 ②

Script

① M Thanks for giving me a ride.
W Don't mention it.

② M Excuse me, you dropped this.
W I can't thank you enough.

③ M Can you pick me up now?
W Sure. Where are you?

④ M You shouldn't pick the flowers.
W I'm sorry. I will never do that again.

⑤ M Is this your bike?
W Yes. You can ride it if you want.

해석

① 남 태워 주셔서 감사합니다.
여 천만에요.

② 남 실례합니다만, 이것을 떨어뜨리셨네요.
여 뭐라고 감사의 말씀을 드려야 할지 모르겠네요.

③ 남 지금 저를 데리러 오실 수 있나요?
여 그럼. 어디에 있는데?

④ 남 꽃을 꺾으면 안 돼.
여 죄송해요. 다시는 그러지 않을게요.

⑤ 남 이게 네 자전거니?
여 그래. 네가 원하면 타도 돼.

해설
땅에 떨어진 여자의 열쇠를 남자가 주어주는 상황에 알맞은 대화를 고른다.

어휘
give a ride 태워 주다 / Don't mention it. 천만에요. / pick ~ up ~을 (차에) 태우러 가다

02 ①

Script

W Sir, we are serving dinner now. Please put down your tray table.

M Okay.

W What would you like to have, beef or chicken?

M Chicken, please. By the way, can I use my laptop during the flight?

W Yes, sir. But you should turn it off during take-offs and landings.

해석

여 손님, 지금 저녁 식사를 나눠 드리고 있습니다. 좌석 테이블을 내려주세요.

남 알겠습니다.

여 쇠고기와 치킨 중 어떤 것을 드시겠습니까?

남 치킨으로 하겠습니다. 그런데 비행 중에 노트북 컴퓨터를 써도 되나요?

여 네, 손님. 하지만, 이착륙 시에는 전원을 꺼주셔야 합니다.

해설
저녁 식사를 나눠 주는 승무원에게 남자가 비행 중에 노트북 컴퓨터를 사용해도 되는지를 묻고 있는 상황으로 대화가 이루어지는 장소가 비행기 안임을 알 수 있다.

어휘
serve[səːrv] (음식을) 제공하다, 봉사하다 / tray[trei] 쟁반 / tray table (쟁반을 얹는) 접게 만들어진 테이블 / laptop[lǽptɑ̀p] 노트북 컴퓨터 / flight[flait] 비행, 비행기 / turn off 끄다 / take-off 이륙 / landing[lǽndiŋ] 착륙

03 ④

Script

W What are you doing this weekend?

M I have to stay home to help my father.

W With what?

M He bought some trees for the garden. He needs help planting them. How about you?

W I'm visiting my aunt with my parents.

해석

여 너 이번 주말에 뭐 할 거니?

남 나 아버지를 도와드려야 해서 집에 있을 거야.

여 뭘 도와드릴 건데?

남 아버지가 정원에 심을 나무를 사셨거든. 나무들을 심는 데 도움을 필요로 하셔. 너는?

여 난 부모님과 이모 댁을 방문할 거야.

해설

He needs help planting them.이라는 남자의 말을 통해 남자가 아빠를 도와 정원에 나무를 심을 것이라는 거을 알 수 있다.

어휘

plant[plænt] 심다; 식물

04 ⑤

Script

W I have thirty dollars, so I need twenty dollars more to buy the ticket.

W I see. How are you going to get the money?

M I'm not sure. I asked my mother for some money, but she didn't say anything.

W Why don't you borrow some from Jenny?

M I should give her a call.

해석

남 나에게 30달러가 있으니까 그 표를 사려면 20달러가 더 필요해.

여 그렇구나. 그 돈을 어떻게 구할 거니?

남 잘 모르겠어. 엄마에게 부탁 드렸는데 아무 말씀도 안 하셔.

여 Jenny에게 빌리지 그러니?

남 그녀에게 전화를 한 번 해봐야겠어.

해설

남자에게 지금 30달러가 있고 그 표를 사기 위해서는 20달러가 더 필요하다고 말하고 있으므로 표의 가격이 50달러임을 알 수 있다.

어휘

give ~ a call ~에게 전화를 하다

05 ⑤

Script

W I have a friend called Jasper. He often acts strangely, so many students in my class don't like him. They don't even want to talk to him. I don't think that's right, so I try to chat with him and have lunch with him. My father teaches me to help the weak, but sometimes I feel it is not easy.

해석

여 저에게는 Jasper라는 친구가 있습니다. 그는 종종 이상하게 행동해서 우리 반의 많은 학생이 그를 싫어합니다. 그들은 그와 얘기조차 하는 것을 좋아하지 않습니다. 나는 그것이 옳다고 생각하지 않기 때문에 그와 잡담도 하고 점심도 같이 먹으려고 합니다. 제 아버지는 약자들을 도와주라고 말씀하지만, 가끔 나는 그게 쉽지 않다는 것을 느낍니다.

해설

여자는 따돌림을 당하는 친구를 도와주려고 하지만, 가끔 그것이 쉽지 않다고 말하고 있다.

어휘

act[ækt] 행동하다 / strangely[stréindʒli] 이상하게 / right[rait] 옳은 / chat[tʃæt] 이야기를 나누다 / weak[wiːk] 약한 / the weak 약한 사람

06 ④

Script

W I'm going to the department store to buy a bike.

M Why don't you buy one at the secondhand market? You can buy a bike at almost half the price of a new one.

W Is that so? Where is the secondhand market?

M I know where it is, and if you want, I can go there with you.

W Thanks. Let's go.

해석

여 나 자전거 사러 백화점에 가려고 해.

남 중고 시장에서 사지 그러니? 새 자전거의 거의 반 가격에 자전거를 살 수 있어.

여 그래? 중고 시장이 어디에 있니?

남 그게 어디 있는지 알아. 네가 원하면 내가 거기 같이 가줄게.

여 고마워. 가자.

해설

자전거를 중고 시장에서 사면 훨씬 싸다는 남자의 말을 듣고 여자는 남자와 함께 중고 시장에 가려고 하고 있다.

어휘

department store 백화점 / secondhand[sékəndhǽnd] 중고 / market[máːrkit] 시장

07 ②

Script

M Excuse me, is this 3507 Charles Drive?

W Yes, it is.

M Did you order a chair?

W I sure did. Come on in.

M Sorry I'm late. I'm new to this town so I got lost.

W That's okay.

M Thank you. Can you show me the receipt?

해석

남 실례합니다. 여기가 Charles 드라이브 3507번지인가요?

여 네, 맞습니다.

남 의자 주문하셨죠?

여 네. 들어오세요.

남 늦어서 죄송합니다. 제가 이 마을은 처음이라 길을 잃었어요.

여 괜찮습니다.

남 감사합니다. 영수증을 좀 보여 주시겠어요?

해설

의자를 주문한 여자와 그 의사를 배달하는 택배 회사 직원 간의 대화이다.

어휘

receipt[risíːt] 영수증

08 ⑤

Script

M Did you have a good weekend, Cindy?

W No, I studied for the test all weekend.

M Do we have a test today?

W Yes. Did you forget, Peter?

M Oh, no! I forgot all about it. I didn't study at all. I watched TV and played games all weekend.

해석

남 좋은 주말 보냈니, Cindy?

여 아니, 나는 주말 내내 시험공부만 했어.

남 우리 오늘 시험 있니?

여 응. 너 잊어버렸니, Peter?

남 아, 안 돼! 나 까맣게 잊고 있었어. 나 공부 하나도 안 했는데. 주말 내내 TV 보고 컴퓨터 게임만 했어.

해설

시험이 있는 것을 모르고 주말 내내 TV보고 게임을 한 남자가 시험이 있다는 얘길 듣고 느낄만한 심정을 고른다.

09 ④

Script

M This is a vehicle that carries people and things between floors in a high building. This is a type of small room that moves up and down. Inside the room, there are floor buttons. If you push the floor button that you want to go, it will bring you to the floor.

해석

남 이것은 높은 빌딩에서 사람과 물건을 층 사이로 나르는 운반 기구입니다. 이것은 위, 아래로 움직이는 작은 방 같은 것입니다. 방 안에는 층 버튼이 있습니다. 당신이 가고자 하는 층 버튼을 누르면 그것이 그 층으로 당신을 데려다 줍니다.

해설

상하로 움직이면서 높은 빌딩 안에서 물건이나 사람을 나르는 것은 엘리베이터이다.

어휘

vehicle[víːikəl] 탈것 / floor[flɔːr] 층 / building[bíldiŋ] 건물 / a type of ~의 한 형태 / move up and down 아래위로 움직이다 / button[bʌ́tn] 단추, 버튼

10 ②

Script

W Matt, I need to talk to you now.

M Did I do something wrong, Mrs. Margaret?

W Yes, you did. You never follow the rules.

M What do you mean?

W I told you not to leave the school during lunchtime, but you did.

해석

여 Matt, 지금 너와 할 얘기가 있어.

남 제가 뭐 잘못한 것이라도 있나요, Margaret 선생님?

여 응, 그래. 너는 절대 규칙을 따르지 않는구나.

남 무슨 말씀이세요?

여 내가 너에게 점심시간에 학교를 나가지 말라고 했지만, 넌 그랬잖니.

해설

여자는 남자가 점심시간에 학교 밖에 나갔기 때문에 남자를 야단치고 있다.

어휘

follow[fálou] 따르다 / rule[ruːl] 규칙 / lunchtime[lʌtʃtaim] 점심시간

11 ③

Script

M Thank you for calling Good Flying Airline. Please listen carefully and enter the correct number. If you want Korean service, press one. If you want to know your flight schedule, press two. To book a ticket, press three. To make sure of your booking, press four. For any other questions, press five. To listen to the menu again, press six.

해석

남 Good Flying 항공사로 전화해 주셔서 감사합니다. 주의 깊게 들으시고 정확한 번호를 입력해 주십시오. 한국어 서비스를 원하시면 1번을 누르십시오. 비행기 운항 일정을 알고 싶으시면 2번을 누르십시오. 표를 예약하시려면 3번을 누르십시오. 예약 확인하시려면 4번을 누르십시오. 다른 질문에 대해서는 5번을 눌러 주십시오. 메뉴를 다시 들으시려면 6번을 누르십시오.

해설

To book a ticket, press three.라는 말을 통해 비행기 표를 예약하려면 3번을 눌러야 한다는 것을 알 수 있다.

어휘

carefully[kέərfəli] 주의 깊게 / enter[éntər] 입력하다, 들어가다 / correct[kərékt] 정확한, 올바른 / press[pres] 누르다 / schedule[skédʒu(ː)l] 일정, 스케줄 / book[buk] 예약하다 / make sure of ~을 확인하다 / booking[búkiŋ] 예약

12 ②

Script

W Kevin, I have to go out, so I want you to do some house chores. Turn off the computer, and clean it up with a cloth.

M What else?

W Open all the windows, and clean up the rooms.

M Would that be all?

W One more thing. Empty all the trash cans.

M Okay, Mom.

해석

여 Kevin, 내가 외출을 해야 해서 네가 집안일을 좀 해줬으면 한단다. 컴퓨터를 끄고 걸레로 닦아라.

남 그 밖에는요?

여 창문을 모두 열고 방을 청소하거라.

남 그게 다예요?

여 한 가지 더. 쓰레기통 비우도록 해라.

남 알겠어요, 엄마.

해설

엄마가 부탁한 집안일은 컴퓨터 걸레로 닦기, 창문 열고 방 청소하기, 쓰레기통 비우기이다.

어휘

go out 외출하다 / cloth[klɔ(:)θ] 걸레, 직물 / chore[tʃɔːr] 자질구레한 일 / empty[émpti] 비리다 / trash can 쓰레기통

13 ①

Script

M Where are you going, Isabella?

W I'm going to buy a dress for the concert.

M What concert?

W You know I have a cello concert tomorrow. I sent you an invitation card.

M Oh, I'm sorry. I forgot.

W You are coming, right?

M I'm afraid to say I can't accept your invitation.

해석

남 너 어디 가니, Isabella?

여 콘서트 때문에 드레스를 사러 가는 중이야.

남 무슨 콘서트?

여 내가 내일 첼로 콘서트 하는 거 너도 알잖아. 내가 너에게 초대 카드를 보냈는데.

남 오, 미안해. 잊고 있었어.

여 너 오는 거지, 맞지?

남 네 초대를 받을 수 없다고 얘기하게 돼서 미안해.

해설

I can't accept your invitation.이라는 남자의 말을 통해 여자의 초대를 거절하고 있다는 것을 알 수 있다.

어휘

cello[tʃélou] 첼로 / invitation[ìnvətéiʃən] 초대 / accept[æksèpt] 받아들이다, 수락하다

14 ①

Script

M Excuse me, can you close the window shade? The sunlight is too strong.

W Of course. Sorry about that.

M Thank you. By the way, I'm Jonathan.

W Hi, I'm Jennifer. Do you often travel to New York?

M Yes. I grew up in New York, and my parents still live there.

W This is my first trip. So if you don't mind, can you tell me some good places to visit?

M Why not?

해석

남 실례지만, 창문 가리개를 닫아 주시겠어요? 햇빛이 너무 강하네요.

여 당연하죠. 죄송해요.

남 감사해요. 그런 그렇고, 저는 Jonathan이에요.

여 안녕하세요. 전 Jennifer에요. 뉴욕에 자주 가시나요?

남 네. 저는 뉴욕에서 자랐고 제 부모님들이 아직 거기 사세요.

여 이번이 제 첫 여행이어서요. 그래서 괜찮으시면 갈만한 좋은 곳 좀 알려주시겠어요?

남 물론이죠.

해설

남자는 뉴욕에서 자랐다고 했지, 뉴욕에서 대학을 다녔다고는 하지 않았다.

어휘

shade[ʃeid] 그늘, 차양, 해가리개 / sunlight[sʌ́nlàit] 햇빛 / grow up 자라다, 성장하다 / mind[maind] 꺼리다

15 ③

Script

W What time can you come home, Phillip? I need you to be here before 4.

M That's impossible, Mom.

W Then, what time can you get home?

M School finishes at four, and you know it takes thirty minutes to get home from school.

W Okay, come home as soon as you finish school.

해석

여 몇 시에 집에 올 수 있니, Phillip? 나는 네가 4시 전에 여기 왔으면 하는데.

남 그건 불가능해요, 엄마.

여 그러면, 몇 시에 집에 올 수 있니?

남 학교가 4시에 끝나고 학교에서 집에 도착하는 데 30분 걸린다는 거 엄마도 아시잖아요.

여 알았단다. 학교가 끝나자마자 집에 오도록 해라.

해설

학교가 끝나면 4시이고 집에 오는 데 30분이 걸리기 때문에 집에 도착할 시각은 4시 30분이다.

어휘

impossible[impάsəbəl] 불가능한

16 ②

Script

W Hi, John Who was the boy that played tennis with you yesterday?

M He was Andrew.

W Are you close to him?

M Yes, he and I went to the same elementary school.

W Can you introduce him to me?

M Sure. Just buy me lunch.

해석

여 안녕, John. 너와 함께 어제 테니스 친 소년은 누구니?

남 그 애는 Andrew야.

여 그 애와 친하니?

남 응, 그는 나와 같은 초등학교에 다녔어.

여 그를 나에게 소개해 줄 수 있니?

남 물론이지. 내게 점심만 사.

해설

Can you introduce him to me?라는 여자의 말로 남자에게 Andrew를 소개해 달라고 부탁하고 있음을 알 수 있다.

어휘

elementary school 초등학교 / introduce[ìntrədjúːs] 소개하다

17 ④

Script

M Today, a beautiful woman and a handsome man stand in front of us. They've decided to have their future together from now on. I hope they love, understand, and support each other. As of today, each of them should do their role as husband and wife and live happily ever after.

해석

남 오늘, 우리 앞에 선남선녀가 서 있습니다. 그들은 지금부터 그들의 미래를 함께하기로 결심했습니다. 저는 그들이 사랑하고 이해하며 서로 지지해 주기를 바랍니다. 오늘로써, 그들은 각각 남편과 아내로서 역할을 해야 하고 앞으로 행복하게 살아야 합니다.

해설

each of them should do their role as husband and wife and live happily ever after.라는 말을 통해 남자의 말을 들을 수 있는 곳이 예식장이라는 것을 알 수 있다.

어휘

from now on 앞으로는 / support[səpɔ́ːrt] 지지하다, 후원하다 / role[roul] 역할 / happily[hǽpili] 행복하게 / live happily ever after 이후로 행복하게 살다

18 ③

Script

① **W** Why were you absent yesterday?

M I was sick in bed.

② **W** Excuse me. Is this seat taken?

M No. You can take it.

③ **W** What's wrong? You look sad.

M My teacher praised me for my score.

④ **W** Do you like Japanese food?

M Yes, it is my favorite.

⑤ **W** How do you like my cookies?

M They're delicious.

해석

① 여 너는 어제 왜 결석했니?

남 아파서 누워 있었어.

② 여 실례합니다. 이 자리 주인 있나요?

남 아니오. 거기에 앉으셔도 됩니다.

③ 여 무슨 일이니? 슬퍼 보이는구나.

남 우리 선생님께서 내 성적을 칭찬해 주셨어.

④ 여 너는 일본 음식을 좋아하니?

남 응, 내가 가장 좋아하는 음식이야.

⑤ 여 내 쿠키 어때?

남 맛있어.

해설

③ 슬퍼 보인다는 여자의 말에 선생님께 칭찬을 받았다는 남자의 응답은 부자연스럽다.

어휘

be sick in bed 아파서 누워 있다 / praise[preiz] 칭찬하다 / favorite[féivərit] 아주 좋아하는 것

19 ③

Script

W What size do you need?

M I need a size 10.

W Here they are.

M Thank you. They look wonderful.

W How would you like to pay for them?

M I'll pay in cash.

해석

여 어떤 크기가 필요하죠?

남 10 사이즈요.

여 여기 있습니다.

남 감사합니다. 멋있는데요.

여 어떻게 지불하시겠습니까?

남 현금으로 하겠습니다.

해설

① 잘 고르셨어요.

② 너무 큰 것 같아요.
④ 제가 60달러를 지불했잖아요.
⑤ 저는 아무것도 사지 않았어요.
어떻게 지불하겠냐는 질문에 가장 알맞은 응답을 고른다.

어휘
make a choice 선택하다, 고르다 / pay in cash 현금으로 지불하다 / wonderful[wʌ́ndərfəl] 멋진 / pay for 지불하다 /

20 ⑤

Script

W It's a really nice program.

M Do you think so?

W Yes, it is easy to use, and it will save a lot of time.

M I'm so glad I got this.

W Where did you get it, anyway?

M I downloaded it off the Internet.

해석

여 그거 정말로 좋은 프로그램이야.

남 그렇게 생각하니?

여 응, 사용하기도 쉽고, 많은 시간을 절약할 수 있어.

남 이 프로그램을 구해서 정말 기분이 좋아.

여 그런데, 어디서 그것을 구했니?

남 그것을 인터넷에서 다운로드 받았어.

해설
① 재미있을 것 같아.
② 그거 좋아 보인다. 나 그거 살래.
③ 나한테도 똑같은 게 있어.
④ 그거 어떻게 쓰는지 알려 줄래?
어디서 그것을 구했냐는 질문에 가장 알맞은 응답을 고른다.

어휘
for free 무료로, 공짜로 / download[dáunlòud] 다운로드하다[내려받다]

16회 영어듣기모의고사

p.128~131

01 ③	02 ⑤	03 ②	04 ③	05 ③
06 ⑤	07 ②	08 ②	09 ④	10 ⑤
11 ①	12 ③	13 ①	14 ④	15 ②
16 ①	17 ①	18 ⑤	19 ③	20 ⑤

01 ③

Script

W All these people are my friends from elementary school.

M So which one is Susie? You're always talking about her. Is she the one standing by the window?

W No, that's Cathy. Susie is the one sitting on the couch.

M Oh, you mean the one wearing a striped sweater and holding a cup?

W That's right.

해석

여 이 사람들은 모두 내 초등학교 친구들이야.

남 그러면, 누가 Susie니? 너 항상 그 애에 대해 말하잖아. 창문 옆에 있는 아이니?

여 아니, 그 애는 Cathy야. Susie는 소파에 앉아 있는 아이야.

남 아, 줄무늬 스웨터에 입고 있고 컵을 들고 있는 아이 말이니?

여 맞아.

해설
Susie는 줄무늬 스웨터를 입고 있으며 컵을 들고 소파에 앉아 있는 소녀이다.

어휘
by[bai] ~ 옆에 / couch[kautʃ] 긴 의자

02 ⑤

Script

W Excuse me, how can I get to City Hall?

M Sorry, I have no idea. Oh, there is a subway map over there.

W It says I should take the subway here and get off at Central Station, right?

M Yes, but you have to transfer to line number four there.

W Oh, I see. Thank you.

해석

여 실례지만, 시청까지 가는 방법을 알려 주시겠어요?

남 죄송한데, 저도 잘 모르겠어요. 아, 저기 지하철 노선도가 있네요.

여 제가 여기서 지하철을 타서 Central Station에서 내려야 된다고 쓰여 있는데, 맞죠?

남 네, 하지만 거기서 4호선으로 갈아타셔야 해요.

여 아, 알겠습니다. 감사합니다.

해설
여자가 길을 묻고 지하철 노선도를 보면서 어떻게 가야 하는지 대화하는 상황이다.

어휘
map[mæp] 지도 / subway map 지하철 노선도 / transfer[trænsfə́ːr] 갈아타다, 옮기다, 이동하다

03 ②

Script

M Hi, ticket please.

W Here you go.

M Thank you. Let me see. It's three dollars.

W That's too much.

M You have been here for three hours, right?

W Yes, but I have a one-hour free parking ticket.

M Sorry, I didn't see that. It's two dollars, then.

W Thank you.

해석

남 안녕하세요. 티켓 좀 보여주세요.

여 여기 있습니다.

남 감사합니다. 가만 있자. 3달러입니다.

여 너무 비싸네요.

남 여기 3시간 있으셨죠, 맞죠?

여 네, 하지만 1시간 무료 주차권이 있습니다.

남 미안합니다만, 그것을 보지 못했습니다. 그러면 2달러입니다.

여 감사합니다.

해설

주차 요금을 지불하는 상황으로 주차 직원과 고객과의 대화임을 알 수 있다.

어휘

free[fri:] 무료의, 공짜의 / parking[pá:rkiŋ] 주차

04 ③

Script

W I didn't see you at school yesterday. What happened?

M I couldn't come because I had the flu, and today I just stopped by to get something from my English teacher.

W I see. So are you leaving now?

M Yes. And I won't be at school tomorrow, either.

W Why not?

M Because other students might catch the flu from me.

해석

여 너 어제 학교에서 못 봤는데, 무슨 일 있었니?

남 내가 독감에 걸려서 나올 수가 없었어. 오늘도 영어 선생님께 뭘 좀 받으려고 들린 거야.

여 그렇구나. 그래서 지금 가는 거야?

남 응. 그리고 내일도 학교에 있을 수 없어.

여 왜?

남 왜냐하면 다른 학생들이 나에게 독감이 전염될 수 있기 때문이야.

해설

Other students might catch the flu from me.라는 남자의 말을 통해 내일 남자가 학교에 오지 않는 이유가 독감을 옮길 수도 있기 때문임을 알 수 있다.

어휘

flu[flu:] 독감 / stop by 들르다 / rest[rest] 휴식

05 ③

Script

M Mom, I'm home.

W You look down. What happened?

M Ryan keeps bothering me for no reason.

W Does he?

M I told him to stop, but he doesn't.

W Just stay away from him, I'll talk to him.

해석

남 엄마, 저 집에 들어 왔어요.

여 너 기분이 안 좋아 보여. 무슨 일 있니?

남 이유 없이 Ryan이 저를 계속 괴롭혀요.

여 그래?

남 제가 하지 말라고 했는데도 멈추지 않아요.

여 그냥 그 애를 멀리하거라. 내가 그와 얘기해 볼 테니.

해설

Just stay away from him, I'll talk to him.라는 말을 통해 괴롭히는 Ryan을 멀리하라고 충고하고 있음을 알 수 있다.

어휘

stay away from ~을 가까이하지 않다, ~에서 떨어져 있다

06 ⑤

Script

W What kind of sports do you like, Johnny?

M I like any kind with a ball.

W I see. Do you like bowling then, too?

M Of course. What about you?

W I like swimming and riding a bike.

M I see.

해석

여 너는 어떤 운동을 좋아하니, Johnny?

남 난 공을 가지고 하는 것이면 어떤 운동이든 좋아.

여 그렇구나. 그러면 너는 볼링도 좋아하니?

남 당연하지. 너는?

여 나는 수영하고 자전거 타는 것을 좋아해.

남 알았어.

해설

I like any kind with a ball.라는 남자의 말을 통해 남자가 공으로 하는 스포츠를 좋아한다는 것을 알 수 있다. 스키는 공으로 하는 운동이 아니다.

07 ②

Script

W Dad, will you buy me a shirt?

M Sure. just pick anything out you like.

W Thank you.

M Which one do you like?

W I like the ones with an animal design.

M Then, try this on. It has a cute puppy on it.

W I don't like it. I like the one with the kitten.

M Then, try it on.

해석

여 아빠, 저 셔츠 하나 사주세요.

남 좋아. 마음에 드는 것을 고르렴.

여 감사해요.

남 어떤 게 네 마음에 드니?

여 동물이 있는 디자인의 셔츠가 좋아요.

남 그러면, 이걸 입어 보거라. 셔츠에 귀여운 강아지가 그려져 있구나.

여 마음에 안 들어요. 새끼 고양이가 있는 게 마음에 들어요.

남 그러면, 그것을 입어 보거라.

해설

I like the one with the kitten.이라는 여자의 말을 통해 새끼 고양이가 그려진 셔츠를 살 것이라는 것을 알 수 있다.

어휘

cute[kjuːt] 귀여운 / kitten[kítn] 새끼 고양이

08 ②

Script

W Look at you. You are all wet.

M I know. I didn't expect the weather to be like this.

W That's what I thought, too. It was really sunny this morning.

M I know. I didn't see anyone with an umbrella today.

W Me, either.

M I'm going to take a shower.

해석

여 너 좀 봐. 너 완전히 젖었어.

남 알고 있어. 날씨가 이럴 거라곤 예상하지 못했는데.

여 나도 그렇게 생각했어. 오늘 아침에는 정말 화창했는데.

남 알아. 우산을 가지고 다니는 사람을 보지 못했거든.

여 나도 못 봤어.

남 나 샤워해야겠어.

해설

옷이 다 젖었다는 말을 통해 밖에 비가 오고 있음을 알 수 있다.

어휘

wet[wet] 젖은 / expect[ikspékt] 예상하다, 기대하다 / sunny[sʌ́ni] 화창한 / umbrella[ʌmbrélə] 우산 / take a shower 샤워하다

09 ④

Script

W I can't wait for the game. Is it held on the 21st?

M No, it is being held on the 15th.

W How come I didn't know about that?

M I got an e-mail from George.

W I see. Is it on a Tuesday?

M No, it's on a Thursday.

해석

여 경기가 너무 기대가 돼. 경기는 21일에 열리는 거지?

남 아니, 15일에 열려.

여 내가 왜 그것을 모르고 있었지?

남 George로부터 이메일을 받았어.

여 그렇구나. 그날이 화요일이니?

남 아니, 목요일이야.

해설

경기가 21일이 아니라 15일, 목요일에 열릴 거라고 남자는 말하고 있다.

10 ⑤

Script

W There are three different means of public transportation in New York.

M What is the most popular one?

W It is, of course, the subway.

M In Seoul, too. What's the fare?

W It used to be two dollars, but they raised it by 50% this year.

해석

여 뉴욕에는 세 개의 다른 대중교통 수단이 있어.

남 가장 인기 있는 것이 무엇이니?

여 당연히 지하철이지.

남 서울도 그래. 요금은 얼마니?

여 2달러였는데 올해에 50%를 올렸어.

해설

지하철 요금이 2달러였지만, 올해 2달러의 50%를 올렸다고 말하고 있으므로 현재 지하철 요금은 3달러임을 알 수 있다.

어휘

means[miːnz] 수단, 방법 / public[pʌ́blik] 공공의 / transportation[trӕnspərtéiʃən] 운송, 수송 / public transportation 공공 교통 기관 / fare[fɛər] 요금 / raise[reiz] 올리다

11 ①

Script

W There is nothing better than ice cream on a hot day.

M You're right. What's your favorite flavor?

W I like strawberry. What about you?

M Well, I like the fruit flavors.

W Now that we are talking about ice cream, I suddenly feel like having some.

M OK. I will buy you one.

해석

여 더운 날에는 아이스크림만 한 게 없지.

남 네 말이 맞아. 너는 무슨 맛을 좋아하니?

여 나는 딸기 맛을 좋아해. 너는?

남 글쎄, 나는 과일 맛은 다 좋아.

여 아이스크림에 대해 이야기하고 있으니까 갑자기 먹고 싶어진다.

남 알았어. 내가 하나 사줄게.

해설

Now that we are talking about ice cream, I suddenly feel like having some.라는 말에서 두 사람이 아이스크림 가게에 갈 것이라는 것을 알 수 있다.

어휘

flavor[fléivər] 맛 / strawberry 딸기 / suddenly[sʌ́dnli] 갑자기

12 ③

Script

W What's wrong with you?

M I cough a lot, and sometimes I have a hard time breathing. I think there is a big problem in my lungs.

W These days a lot of people come to see me with the same reason. It's just an allergy to spring flowers.

M Oh, is that true? I was so worried.

W Don't worry. Take medicine, and you will feel better soon.

해석

여 어디가 아프신가요?

남 기침을 많이 하고 가끔 숨을 쉬는 게 힘들어요. 제 폐에 큰 문제가 있는 것 같아요.

여 요즘 많은 분들이 똑같은 이유로 저를 찾아옵니다. 그냥 봄꽃 알레르기일 뿐이에요.

남 아, 그런가요? 걱정을 많이 했거든요.

여 걱정하지 마세요. 약을 드시면 곧 괜찮아지실 겁니다.

해설

건강에 큰 문제가 있는 것은 아닌지 걱정하는 남자에게 의사가 그냥 알레르기일 뿐이며, 걱정하지 않아도 된다고 말하고 있다.

어휘

chest[tʃest] 가슴 / breathe[bri:ð] 숨쉬다 / lung[lʌŋ] 폐 / allergy[ǽlərdʒi] 알레르기 / medicine[médəsən] 약

13 ①

Script

M In Korea, there are a few things that you shouldn't do when you dine. First, you shouldn't start eating until the oldest person at the table begins eating. Second, you shouldn't talk with your mouth full. Third, you shouldn't put your hand and arm on the table. Last, you never leave the dining table before the oldest person finishes his or her meal.

해석

남 한국에서는 식사할 때 해서는 안 되는 몇 가지가 있습니다. 첫째, 가장 나이 든 사람이 식사하기 전에는 식사를 시작하면 안 됩니다. 두 번째, 입에 음식을 가득 넣고 말을 하면 안 됩니다. 세 번째, 식사하는 동안 손과 팔을 테이블 위에 올려서는 안 됩니다. 마지막으로, 가장 나이 든 사람이 식사를 마칠 때까지 자리를 떠나서는 안 됩니다.

해설

한 손으로 밥그릇을 들고 먹는 것은 언급되어 있지 않으며, 한국의 식사예절에도 어긋난다.

어휘

dine[dain] 식사하다 / meal[mi:l] 식사, 식사 시간 / have a meal 식사를 하다 / dining table 식탁

14 ④

Script

W Ross, why don't you get up? It's ten.

M Mom, it's Sunday. Let me sleep some more.

W You know what? Jenny got up early, had breakfast, and even went for a walk with Dad.

M Just ten more minutes, please.

W If you don't get up now, we'll go shopping without you.

해석

여 Ross, 좀 일어나지 그러니? 열 시야.

남 엄마, 일요일이에요. 저 잠 좀 더 자게 해 주세요.

여 너 이거 아니? Jenny는 일찍 일어나서 아침도 먹고, 아빠와 산책도 다녀왔다.

남 10분만 더 잘게요.

여 네가 지금 안 일어나면 우리는 너 빼고 쇼핑하러 갈 거다.

해설

① 쥐구멍에도 볕 들 날이 있다.

② 연습이 완벽을 만든다.

③ 제 때의 한 바늘이 뒤에 아홉 바늘을 던다.

⑤ 한 가지 일에 몽땅 걸지 마라.

아침에 일찍 일어난 Jenny는 많은 일을 했고, 늦잠을 자는 Ross에게 엄마가 일어나지 않으면 쇼핑을 데려가지 않겠다고 말하고 있으므로 '일찍 일어나는 새가 벌레를 잡는다.'라는 의미의 ④을 고른다.

어휘

go for a walk 산책 가다 / go shopping 쇼핑하러 가다

15 ②

Script

W Michael, can I give you a piece of advice?

M Sure, what is it?

W I think you work hard, but you always depend on someone else.

M I don't get it.

W If you have a slight difficulty, you ask for help. If you fix that habit, you will succeed in anything you do.

M Thank you. I will try to fix it.

해석

여 Michael, 내가 너에게 충고 하나 해도 될까?

남 당연하지, 그게 뭔데?

여 나는 네가 열심히 일한다고 생각해. 하지만, 너는 항상 다른 사람에게 의존하잖아.

남 무슨 말인지 잘 모르겠어.

여 너는 조금만 어려움이 있으면 도움을 청하잖아. 그 습관만 고치면 너는 무엇을 하든지 성공할 거야.

남 고마워. 고치도록 해 볼게.

해설

항상 다른 사람에게 의존하는 것이 남자의 문제라고 여자는 말하고 있다.

어휘

depend on ~에 의지[의존]하다 / slight[slait] 약간의, 적은 / difficulty[dífikʌ̀lti] 어려움, 곤란 / ask for help 도움을 청하다 / fix[fiks] 고치다, 수정하다 / habit[hǽbit] 습관, 버릇 / succeed[səksíːd] 성공하다

16 ①

Script

① M Would you do me a favor?
W That's okay. I had enough.

② M The big boy hit the small boy.
W That's not fair.

③ M I'm so upset about the English test.
W Take it easy. You'll do better next time.

④ M How did she open the door?
W She found the key in her car.

⑤ M What time do you have?
W It's a quarter to nine.

해석

① 남 내 부탁 좀 들어줄래?
여 괜찮아. 충분히 먹었어.

② 남 큰 아이가 작은 아이를 때렸어.
여 그건 공평하지 않잖아.

③ 남 영어 시험 때문에 화가 나.
여 진정해. 다음에 잘 볼 수 있을 거야.

④ 남 그녀가 어떻게 문을 열었니?
여 자신의 차 안에서 열쇠를 찾았어.

⑤ 남 지금 몇 시니?
여 8시 45분이야.

해설

① 자신의 부탁을 들어 달라고 요청하는 남자의 말에 승낙이나 거절의 응답이 와야 한다.

어휘

fair[fɛər] 공평한 / quarter[kwɔ́ːrtər] 4분의 1; 15분; 25센트

17 ①

Script

W What do you want to be in the future, Chandler?

M Me? I want to be a soldier.

W What do you want to do as a soldier?

M I want to drive a tank. How about you?

W It couldn't make much money if I weren't famous, but I want to write poetry.

M I know you are good at writing.

Q What does the man want to be?

해석

여 너는 미래에 무엇이 되고 싶니, Chandler?

남 나? 군인이 되고 싶어.

여 군인이 돼서 뭘 하고 싶은데?

남 탱크를 운전하고 싶어. 너는?

여 유명해지지 않으면 돈을 많이 벌지 못하겠지만, 나는 시를 쓰고 싶어.

남 네가 글을 잘 쓴다는 것은 알고 있었어.

질문 남자는 무엇이 되길 원하는가?

해설

I want to be a soldier.라는 남자의 말에서 남자의 장래희망이 군인이라는 것을 알 수 있다.

어휘

poet[póuit] 시인 / magician[mədʒíʃən] 마술사, 마법사 / soldier 군인 / tank[tæŋk] 탱크 / famous[féiməs] 유명한 / poetry[póuitri] 시

18 ⑤

Script

[Telephone rings.]

W Hello, this is Christine.

M Hi, Christine. What can I do for you?

W Our copy machine doesn't work at all.

M What's wrong?

W I have no idea. Can you come down here and take a look at it?

M Sure. I'll be there in ten minutes.

W Please, hurry up. There are a lot of people waiting to use the machine.

해석

여 안녕하세요, Christine인데요.

남 안녕하세요, Christine 씨. 무엇을 도와드릴까요?

여 저희 복사기가 작동이 잘 안 돼요.

남 뭐가 잘못되었나요?

여 잘 모르겠어요. 내려오셔서 좀 봐주세요?

남 그러죠. 10분 안에 내려가겠습니다.

여 서둘러 주세요. 그 기계를 사용하려고 많은 사람이 기다리고 있어요.

해설

복사기가 고장 나서 남자에게 와서 봐 달라고 부탁하는 상황이다.

어휘

take a look at ~을 보다 / hurry up 서두르다 / copy machine 복사기

19 ③

Script

M Where are you going?

W I'm going to visit my grandmother.

M I remember seeing her at the grocery store last month.

W Yeah, she told me that she saw you there, too.

M Does she live near here?

W Yes, it's just a ten-minute walk.

해석

남 너 어디 가니?

여 할머니 댁에 가고 있어.

남 지난달에 슈퍼에서 네 할머니를 본 것이 기억나.

여 그래, 할머니도 너를 거기서 봤다고 말씀하셨어.

남 이 근처 사시니?

여 응, 걸어서 10분 거리야.

해설

① 맞아, 혼자 사셔.

② 우리 아버지도 할머니 댁에 자주 가셔.

④ 우리 할머니는 너를 기억하지 못하셔.

⑤ 오늘은 내가 그녀에게 사 드릴 게 없어.

이 근처에 사냐는 남자의 질문에 응답으로 거리나 시간이 오는 것이 자연스럽다.

20 ⑤

Script

W Did you draw this?

M Yes, I did.

W What are you trying to say in this picture?

M Peace.

W I see. That's why you drew many pigeons.

M What do you think of my picture?

W It's terrific.

해석

여 네가 이것을 그렸니?

남 응, 그래.

여 이 그림에서 무엇을 보여 주려고 했니?

남 평화.

여 그렇구나. 그래서 네가 비둘기를 많이 그렸구나.

남 내 그림에 대해서는 어떻게 생각하니?

여 훌륭해.

해설

① 나는 그림을 잘 못 그려.

② 그림 그리기가 내 취미야.

③ 나도 비둘기를 그리지 않았어.

④ 그 새 어디서 났니?

남자는 자신의 그림에 대해 어떻게 생각하는지 의견을 묻고 있기 때문에 그에 알맞은 응답을 고른다.

어휘

pigeon[pídʒən] 비둘기 / terrific[tərifik] 훌륭한, 아주 멋진 / peace[piːs] 평화

1회 실전모의고사

p.136~139

01 ①	02 ④	03 ④	04 ②	05 ⑤
06 ①	07 ③	08 ④	09 ②	10 ④
11 ③	12 ⑤	13 ⑤	14 ③	15 ①
16 ④	17 ②	18 ③	19 ①	20 ②

01 ①

Script

M I'd like you to draw a picture on this blank piece of paper. It's difficult to draw, so listen carefully. First, draw a rose on the bottom left. Second, draw a star on the top right. Third, draw a small circle on the top left. Last, draw a flag on the bottom right.

해석

남 저는 여러분이 이 빈 종이에 그림을 하나 그리길 원해요. 그리기 어려우니 주의 깊게 들으세요. 먼저, 왼쪽 아래에 장미꽃을 하나 그리세요. 두 번째, 오른쪽 위에 별을 하나 그리세요. 세 번째, 왼쪽 위에 작은 원을 그리세요. 마지막으로, 오른쪽 아래 깃발을 하나 그리세요.

해설

왼쪽 아래에는 장미가, 오른쪽 아래에는 깃발이, 왼쪽 꼭대기에는 작은 원이, 오른쪽 꼭대기에는 별이 있는 그림을 고른다.

어휘

blank[blæŋk] 공백의, 백지의, 빈 / bottom[bátəm] 밑바닥, 아래쪽 / top[tɑp] 꼭대기, 윗면 / circle[sə́ːrkl] 원 / flag[flæg] 깃발

02 ④

Script

W Ben, I'm sorry that I can't see you often.

M Don't worry. I'll visit you often. By the way, will you see me off?

W When are you leaving?

M It was supposed to be last Wednesday, the 20th, but we couldn't get a truck that day. So we decided to move out this Saturday.

W I see.

해석

여 Ben, 너를 자주 못 보게 되어 아쉬워.

남 걱정하지 마. 내가 너를 자주 방문할게. 그건 그렇고, 나 배웅해 줄 거지?

여 너 언제 떠나니?

남 20일, 지난 수요일이었는데 그날 트럭을 빌리지 못했어. 그래서 이번 주 토요일에 이사 가기로 했어.

여 그렇구나.

해설

20일, 수요일에 이사 가려고 했지만, 토요일에 이사를 가기로 했다는 말로 23일, 토요일을 고른다.

어휘

see off 배웅하다 / be supposed to+동사원형 ~하기로 되어 있다, ~할 의무가 있다 / move out 이사 가다

03 ④

Script

M Honey, where is my black jacket?

W Oh, I dropped it off at the cleaner's, and I forgot to pick it up.

M I said I needed to wear it for the meeting today.

W There is a gray jacket in the closet. Can't you just wear that? I'll get the black one tonight.

M Don't worry. I'll stop by the cleaner's and pick it up on the way to work.

해석

남 여보, 내 검은색 재킷 어디 있어요?

여 아, 세탁소 맡기고 찾아오는 걸 잊고 있었어요.

남 내가 오늘 회의 때 입어야 한다고 얘기했었는데요.

여 옷장에 회색 재킷이 있는데, 그냥 그것을 입으시면 안 돼요? 검은색은 오늘 밤에 제가 찾아올게요.

남 걱정하지 마세요. 회사 가는 길에 세탁소에 들러서 내가 찾을게요.

해설

I'll stop by the cleaner's and pick it up on the way to work.라는 남자의 말에서 남자는 회사에 가기 전에 세탁소에 들러 검은색 재킷을 찾아 갈 것임을 알 수 있다.

어휘

drop off 맡기다 / cleaner's 세탁소 / pick up 찾다 / closet[klάzit] 옷장 / on the way to work 출근하는 길에

04 ②

Script

W Do you know who Scott Kim is?

M Yes, he is my classmate.

W Where is he from? He looks like he's from Asia.

M His parents are Korean, but he wasn't born in Korea.

W I see. Was he born in America?

M No, he was born and raised in the United Kingdom.

W That's why his accent is a little different.

해석

여 너는 Scott Kim이 누구인지 아니?

남 응, 그는 같은 반 친구야.

여 그 애는 어디서 왔니? 그는 아시아 출신 같아 보이는데.

남 부모님이 한국인이지만, 한국에서 태어나지는 않았어.

여 그렇구나. 그애는 미국에서 태어났니?

남 아니, 그는 영국에서 태어나고 자랐어.

여 그래서 그애 발음이 약간 달랐구나.

해설

he was born and raised in the United Kingdom이라는 남자의 말로 Scott이 태어난 국가가 영국임을 알 수 있다.

어휘

Asia[éiʒə] 아시아 / be born 태어나다 / raise[reiz] (아이를) 기르다 / the United Kingdom[kíŋdəm] 영국 / accent[ǽksent] 억양

05 ⑤

Script

W Can you tell me how much this is?

M It's 20 dollars, but if you have a membership card, you can get 20 percent off.

W How do I get one?

M There is a booth at the corner. You can register there. Are you new here?

W Yes, I am.

M Then, you can't get one. Sorry, but you can get one from your second visit.

해석

여 이게 얼마인지 말씀해 주실래요?

남 20달러입니다. 하지만, 회원카드가 있으시면 20% 할인을 받으실 수 있습니다.

여 어떻게 그것을 발급받을 수 있나요?

남 구석에 창구가 하나 있습니다. 거기서 신청하실 수 있어요. 여기 처음이신가요?

여 네.

남 그러면, 발급받으실 수 없습니다. 죄송합니다. 두 번째 방문부터 받을 수 있어요.

해설

이번이 여자의 첫 방문이기 때문에 회원 카드를 발급받을 수 없어 할인을 받을 수가 없다.

어휘

membership card 회원 카드 / booth[bu:θ] 창구 / register[rédʒistər] 등록하다 / visit[vízit] 방문; 방문하다

06 ①

Script

W Look at this river. It looks so clean and beautiful.

M There are so many tourists coming to this city to see the river.

W I see. I want to swim in it tomorrow.

M You can't. It's too deep for you.

W Is it?

M Yes, it's probably 5 meters deep or deeper.

해석

여 이 강을 봐. 정말 깨끗하고 아름다워.

남 이 강을 보려고 많은 관광객들이 와.

여 그렇구나. 내일 여기서 수영하고 싶은데.

남 안 돼. 네가 수영하기엔 너무 깊어.

여 그래?

남 응, 아마도 5미터 혹은 더 깊을걸.

해설

It's too deep for you.라는 남자의 말에서 정답을 알 수 있다.

어휘

tourist[túərist] 관광객 / deep[diːp] 깊은

07 ③

Script

W This is a small animal like a mouse with wings that flies around at night. It lives in a cave. Some people think that this animal feeds on human blood, but that's not true. This animal doesn't even attack humans.

해석

여 이것은 밤에 날아다니는 날개를 가진 쥐와 같은 작은 동물입니다. 그것은 동굴 안에 거주합니다. 어떤 사람들은 이 동물이 인간의 피를 먹고 산다고 생각하지만, 그것은 사실이 아닙니다. 이 동물은 심지어 인간을 공격하지도 않습니다.

해설

동굴 안에 살고, 밤에 날아다니는 동물은 박쥐이다.

어휘

mouse[maus] 쥐 / wing[wiŋ] 날개 / at night 밤에 / cave[keiv] 동굴 / feed on ~을 먹이로 하다 / human[hjúːmən] 인간의, 사람의 / blood[blʌd] 피 / attack[ətǽk] 공격하다

08 ④

Script

W I don't believe this. This is the third time you have done this.

M Sorry.

W I think I told you at least 5 times not to touch the red button.

M I kept remembering that before I went there.

W Then, what?

M I don't know. When I use the machine, I just forget what to do and what not to do.

W You're too careless.

해석

여 도대체 믿을 수가 없군. 너 이렇게 하는 게 이번이 벌써 세 번째야.

남 미안해.

여 내가 너에게 빨간 버튼을 누르지 말라고 적어도 다섯 번은 말한 것 같은데.

남 거기에 가기 전까지 계속 기억을 하는데.

여 그런데, 뭐?

남 잘 모르겠어. 내가 기계를 사용하려고 하면 무엇을 해야 하고, 무엇을 하지 말아야 하는지 잊어버리게 돼.

여 넌 너무 부주의해.

해설

여자는 같은 실수를 반복하고 있는 남자를 꾸짖고 있다.

어휘

touch[tʌtʃ] 손대다, 만지다 / button[bʌ́tn] 단추, 버튼 / machine[məʃíːn] 기계 / careless[kɛ́ərlis] 부주의한

09 ②

Script

W Excuse me. Could you show me the way to the police station?

M Sure. Go straight for two blocks. Then turn right, and walk half a block. It's going to be on your right.

W Okay. Go straight for two blocks, turn right and go half a block. It's on my right.

M Yes, that's right.

W Thank you.

해석

여 실례합니다. 경찰서에 가는 길 좀 알려 주실래요?

남 물론이죠. 두 블록을 직진하세요. 그 다음 오른쪽으로 돌고 반 블록을 가세요. 경찰서가 오른쪽에 있을 거예요.

여 알겠어요. 두 블록을 가서 오른쪽으로 돌고 반 블록을 걸어가는 거죠. 내 오른쪽에 있는 거죠.

남 네, 맞습니다.

여 감사합니다.

해설

두 블록을 가서 오른쪽으로 돌고 나서 반 블록을 간 다음 오른쪽에 있는 건물이 경찰서이다.

어휘

police station 경찰서 / go straight 직진하다 / turn right 오른쪽으로 돌다

10 ④

Script

W What do you want to be in the future?

M I want to be a teacher, but my mother wants me to be a doctor.

W I see. What about your father?

M He wants me to be a scientist.

W Your father has the same idea as my father.

M Yesterday my uncle visited us, and he told me that I should be a businessman.

W You must be confused.

해석

여 너는 미래에 뭐가 되고 싶니?

남 난 선생님이 되고 싶은데 어머니는 내가 의사가 되기를 원하셔.

여 그렇구나. 너의 아버지는?

남 아버지는 내가 과학자가 되길 바라셔.

여 네 아버지는 우리 아버지와 같은 생각을 하고 계시는구나.

남 어제는 삼촌이 오셔서 내게 사업가가 되어야 한다고 말씀하셨어.

여 너 혼란스럽겠다.

해설

① 백문의 불여일견이다.

② 깊은 물이 고요히 흐른다.

③ 백지장도 맞들면 낫다.

⑤ 로마에 가면 로마법을 따르라.

남자의 부모님과 삼촌은 남자가 각기 다른 직업을 갖기를 원하기 때문에 남자가 혼란스러워하고 있다. 따라서 의견이 너무 많으면 일을 그르칠 수도 있다는 의미의 ④을 고른다.

어휘
idea[aidíːə] 생각, 사고, 아이디어 / businessman[bíznismæ̀n] 사업가 / confused[kənfjúːzd] 혼란스러운, 어찌할 바를 모르는

11 ③

Script

W I know you don't have a girlfriend. So what type of girl do you like?

M I like a girl who is comfortable to talk to.

W And?

M A girl who is not too tall and not too short.

W OK. I know a girl who exactly fits your description.

M Who is she?

W You are looking at her now.

해석

여 네가 여자친구가 없다는 걸 알고 있어. 그래서 그러는데 넌 어떤 타입의 여자를 좋아하니?

남 난 대화하기 편한 사람이 좋아.

여 그리고?

남 너무 키가 크지도 작지도 않은 소녀.

여 그렇구나. 네 설명에 정확히 맞는 여자아이를 알고 있어.

남 그게 누군데?

여 네가 지금 바라보고 있잖아.

해설
남자가 좋아하는 타입의 여자가 자신이라고 얘기하는 여자의 얘기를 듣고 남자가 어떤 기분이 들지 고른다.

어휘
comfortable[kʌ́mfərtəbəl] 편한 / exactly[igzǽktli] 정확하게 / fit[fit] 맞다, 적합하다, 어울리다 / description[diskrípʃən] 묘사, 설명

12 ⑤

Script

M I lived in Canada for one year, and it changed my life. Before I went to Canada, I was a very shy boy. But while I was in Canada, I traveled a lot and met many people. I realized how big our world actually is. Now I feel comfortable meeting new people and talking to them.

해석

남 저는 1년 동안 캐나다에 살았고, 그것이 제 인생을 바꿨습니다. 캐나다에 가기 전에는 저는 아주 소심한 소년이었습니다. 하지만 제가 캐나다에 있는 동안 여행을 많이 했고, 많은 사람들을 만났습니다. 저는 세계가 실제로 얼마나 넓은지 깨닫게 되었습니다. 지금 저는 새로운 사람들을 만나고 그들과 이야기를 나누는 것에 편안함을 느낍니다.

해설
소년이 캐나다에서 영어 공부를 했다는 언급은 없다.

어휘
realize[ríːəlàiz] 깨닫다

13 ⑤

Script

W ① The opera house opens every weekday at 10 a.m.
② On the weekends, the opera house is open for 13 hours.
③ On Tuesday and Friday, the opera house closes at 7 p.m.
④ The closing hours of the opera house are always the same.
⑤ The opera house is closed on Monday.

해석

여 ① 오페라 하우스는 평일에는 항상 10시에 문을 연다.
② 주말에 오페라 하우스는 13시간 동안 문을 연다.
③ 화요일과 금요일은 오페라 하우스는 7시에 문을 닫는다.
④ 오페라 하우스의 폐점 시간은 항상 같다.
⑤ 오페라 하우스는 월요일에 문을 닫는다.

해설
① 오페라 하우스는 월요일에는 문을 닫기 때문에 평일에 항상 10시에 문을 여는 것은 아니다. ② 주말에 오페라 하우스는 아침 9시부터 저녁 9시까지 12시간 동안 문을 연다. ③ 화요일과 금요일은 7시에 문을 닫는다. ④ 오페라 하우스의 폐점 시간은 요일에 따라 8시, 7시, 9시로 다르다.

어휘
open[óupən] 열다; 열려 있는 / close[klouz] 닫다 / closing time 폐점 시간 / closed[klouzd] 닫힌

14 ③

Script

M I'm not sure what time I can make it. Is it OK to call you when I'm ready?

W I still have to find out what time we can meet because I'm supposed to see my mother at 6 in front of the mall.

M Where will we meet?

W At the same place. I just need to give her her cellular phone. That's it.

M Then, let's meet there at ten past six.

W Okay.

해석

남 언제 시간을 낼 수 있을지 잘 모르겠어. 내가 준비되면 너에게 전화해도 되니?

여 내가 6시에 쇼핑몰 앞에서 엄마를 만나야 해서 몇 시에 만날 건지 알아야 해.

남 어디서 만날까?

여 같은 장소에서. 엄마에게 엄마 휴대 전화를 전해 주기만 하면 되거든.

남 그러면, 거기서 6시 10분에 만나자.

여 알았어.

해설

let's meet there at ten past six라는 남자의 말을 통해 두 사람이 만날 시각이 6시 10분임을 알 수 있다.

어휘

make it (어떤 곳에 간신히) 시간 맞춰 가다 / cellular phone 휴대 전화 / past[pæst] (시간이) 지나서, 넘어서

15 ①

Script

M You are driving an expensive car.

W It's not mine. It's my father's.

M I envy you. Do you often drive that car?

W Not really. I had to take my mother to the airport. What about you? Do you have your own car?

M No, I used to have one. I moved closer to my company, and I sold it.

W Then, how do you go to work?

M I walk to work every morning.

W Good for you.

Q How does the man go to work?

해석

남 너는 비싼 차를 모는구나.

여 내 것 아니야. 아버지거야.

남 부럽다. 너 저 차를 자주 운전하니?

여 그렇지는 않아. 어머니를 공항에 모셔다 드려야 했어. 너는? 너는 차 있니?

남 아니, 하나 있었는데. 회사와 더 가까이 이사해서 팔아버렸어.

여 그러면, 어떻게 출근하니?

남 매일 아침 걸어서 출근해.

여 잘 됐다.

질문 남자는 어떻게 출근하는가?

해설

남자는 회사 근처로 이사해 매일 아침 회사까지 걸어 다닌다고 말하고 있다.

어휘

envy[énvi] 부러워하다; 부러움 / airport[έərpɔ̀ːrt] 공항

16 ④

Script

W What did I do wrong?

M You ran a red light.

W No, I didn't.

M We don't have to argue about this. I can show you the picture.

W Really?

M Yes, the camera takes a picture of the car that passes through the red signal.

W Oh, no. Here is my driver's license.

해석

여 제가 무엇을 잘못했나요?

남 빨간불을 그냥 지나치셨어요.

여 아니, 안 그랬어요.

남 우리는 이것에 대해 논쟁할 필요가 없습니다. 제가 당신에게 사진을 보여 줄 수 있습니다.

여 정말로요?

남 네, 저 카메라가 빨간불에 통과한 차의 사진을 찍습니다.

여 오, 이런. 여기 운전면허증 있습니다.

해설

신호를 위반한 운전자에게 경찰관이 운전면허증을 보여 달라고 요청하는 상황이다.

어휘

argue[άːrgjuː] 논쟁하다 / signal[sígnl] 신호 / driver's license 운전면허증

17 ②

Script

① W Do I know you?
M Yes, we've met before.

② W Will you help me with the dishes?
M I'll have a ham sandwich.

③ W Jenny moved out last week.
M I will miss her a lot.

④ W Do you have some change?
M Yes, I have some coins.

⑤ W Are there any available tickets?
M No, they're all sold out.

해석

① 여 제가 당신을 아나요?
남 네, 우리는 전에 만난 적이 있어요.

② 여 내가 설거지하는 걸 좀 도와줄래?
남 햄 샌드위치로 할게요.

③ 여 Jenny는 지난주에 이사 갔어.
남 그녀가 많이 보고 싶을 거야.

④ 여 너 잔돈 있니?
남 응, 동전이 몇 개 있어.

⑤ 여 남아 있는 표 있습니까?
남 아니오, 모두 팔렸습니다.

해설

② 설거지를 도와달라는 요청에 배가 부르니 그만 먹겠다는 응답은 부자연스럽다.

어휘

change[tʃeindʒ] 잔돈 / coin[kɔin] 동전 / available[əvéiləbəl] 이용 가능한 / be sold out 매진되다

18 ③

Script

W Sam, did you go to the museum last week?

M Yes, I did. There were so many people that I couldn't even see the whole exhibit. How about you?

W I'm going today with Mike and Jessica.

M I see. You'd better take the subway, then.

W Well, Jessica's mother is going to give us a ride.

해석

여 Sam, 너는 지난주에 박물관 갔었니?

남 응. 너무 사람들이 많아서 나는 전시물을 모두 볼 수 없었어. 너는?

여 난 오늘 Mike, Jessica와 함께 갈 거야.

남 그렇구나. 그러면, 전철을 타는 편이 좋을 거야.

여 그게, Jessica의 엄마가 우리를 데려다 주실 거야.

해설

박물관이 붐벼서 일찍 가야 한다는 언급은 없다.

어휘

whole[houl] 전체의, 전부의 / exhibit[igzíbit] 전시, 전시품 / had better ~하는 것이 더 낫다 / give a ride 태워 주다

19 ①

Script

M Did you have a good time at the party?

W Yes, there were a lot of people.

M How about Jason? Was he there?

W He said he would come, but he couldn't make it.

M Why?

W His brother got injured in an accident.

M That's a pity!

해석

남 파티에서 좋은 시간 보냈니?

여 응, 사람들이 많았어.

남 Jason은? 그 애도 왔니?

여 그는 온다고 했는데 오지 못했어.

남 왜?

여 그의 형이 사고로 부상 입었대.

남 안됐다!

해설

② 그가 그럴 줄 알았다니까.

③ 정말 멋져!

④ 나는 거기 혼자 갈 수 있었어.

⑤ 언제 파티가 끝났니?

안 좋은 일이 발생한 것에 대한 위로나 동정의 표현이 와야 한다.

어휘

get injured 다치다

20 ②

Script

M You got your wallet from your sister, Angela?

W Yes, how did you know?

M Well, I'm the one who found it on the street.

W Are you? Then, why didn't you tell me?

M It is not a big deal. I'm just glad to see you smiling again.

W Thanks a lot.

M It's my pleasure.

해석

남 너 네 동생 Angela한테 지갑 받았지?

여 응, 어떻게 알았어?

남 그게, 그것을 길에서 주운 사람은 나야.

여 너라고? 그러면, 왜 나에게 말을 안 했니?

남 뭐 큰일도 아닌데 뭐. 나는 네가 웃는 모습을 다시 보게 되서 기뻐.

여 정말 고마워.

남 천만에.

해설

① 그것은 내 것도 아니야.

③ 어디서 그것을 찾았니?

④ 나는 돈이 필요 없어.

⑤ 그 소식을 들으니 기분이 좋아.

고맙다는 여자의 말에 알맞은 응답을 고른다.

어휘

wallet[wálit] 지갑 / deal[di:l] 거래, 장사, 인물, 사건 / a big deal 중대 사건, 중요 인물

2회 실전모의고사

p.140~143

01 ⑤	02 ②	03 ⑤	04 ③	05 ③
06 ①	07 ④	08 ②	09 ④	10 ①
11 ⑤	12 ⑤	13 ②	14 ④	15 ③
16 ①	17 ④	18 ③	19 ⑤	20 ②

01 ⑤

Script

① **M** The floor is wet, so watch your step.

W Thank you.

② **M** What should I do?

W You'd better ask your parents for help.

③ **M** I can't climb all these stairs.

W Why? Does your knee hurt?

④ M Be careful.

W Don't worry. I can ride a bike well.

⑤ M Bend your knees more, and look straight ahead.

W Hold my hand please. I'm scared.

해석

① 남 바닥이 젖었으니까 걸을 때 조심해.

여 고마워.

② 남 내가 어떻게 해야 할까?

여 부모님께 도움을 요청하는 것이 좋겠어.

③ 남 나 계단을 모두 오를 수 없어.

여 왜? 무릎이 아프니?

④ 남 조심해.

여 걱정하지 마. 나 자전거 잘 타.

⑤ 남 무릎을 더 구부리고 정면을 봐.

여 내 손 좀 잡아 줘. 무서워.

해설

인라인 스케이트를 가르쳐 주는 상황에 알맞은 대화를 고른다.

어휘

watch[watʃ] 주시하다, 조심하다 / step[step] 걸음 / ask for help 도움을 요청하다 / climb[klaim] 오르다 / stair[stɛər] 계단 / bend[bend] 구부리다 / look straight 똑바로 보다 / ahead[əhéd] 앞으로, 앞에

02 ②

Script

W On your right, you can see the bridge. It was built two hundred years ago.

M It looks wonderful. What about that palace?

W That was built three hundred years ago, but it was destroyed in the war in 1930. It was rebuilt 30 years ago. The king used to live there.

M I see. Excuse me, when do we have free time?

W From one to four.

해석

여 여러분의 왼쪽으로 다리를 보실 수 있습니다. 그것은 200년 전에 세워졌습니다.

남 정말 멋있네요. 저 궁전은요?

여 저것은 300백 년 전에 세워졌지만, 전쟁으로 1930년에 파괴되었어요. 그래서 그것은 30년 전에 다시 세워졌어요. 거기에 왕이 살았었죠.

남 그렇군요. 죄송하지만, 자유 시간은 언제인가요?

여 한 시부터 네 시까지예요.

해설

여자가 남자에게 관광지에 대해 설명해 주고 있는 상황으로 여자의 직업이 여행 안내원이라는 것을 알 수 있다.

어휘

bridge[bridʒ] 다리 / palace[pǽlis] 궁전 / destroy[distrɔ́i] 파괴하다 / rebuild[riːbíld] 재건하다, 다시 세우다

03 ⑤

Script

W Joseph, I need you to be home by seven. I'm going to meet my friend tonight.

M I don't think I can. I'm supposed to go to English class today.

W Then, what time can you be home by?

M It's a one-hour class, so I can probably be home by eight.

W I see. I should stay home and look after Sam then. I'll cancel my appointment.

해석

여 Joseph, 집에 7시까지 와야 해요. 저 오늘 저녁에 친구를 만나야 하거든요.

남 그렇게 안 될 것 같아. 오늘은 영어 수업 가기로 되어 있어.

여 그렇군요, 그러면 몇 시까지 올 수 있어요?

남 한 시간 수업이야. 그래서 아마도 집에 8시까지 올 수 있을 거야.

여 알겠어요. 그럼 제가 집에 있으면서 Sam을 돌봐야겠네요. 제가 약속을 취소할게요.

해설

I can probably be home by eight.라는 말을 통해 남자는 영어 수업에 갔다가 8시에 집에 들어올 것임을 알 수 있다.

어휘

look after 돌보다 / cancel[kǽnsəl] 취소하다

04 ③

Script

W It's thirty dollars and thirty cents.

M I'm sorry. It's more than I thought. I'm short just a little.

W How much do you have, then?

M Let me see. I have 30 dollars.

W That's OK. I'll cut down the price a little.

M Can you do that for me?

W Yes, but I will do it for you just this once.

해석

여 30달러 30센트입니다.

남 죄송합니다. 제가 생각했던 것보다 비싸네요. 돈이 조금 부족해요.

여 그러면, 얼마 가지고 계세요?

남 그게, 저에게 30달러 있어요.

여 괜찮아요. 제가 조금 깎아 드릴게요.

남 그렇게 해 주실 수 있나요?

여 네, 하지만 이번만 해 드리는 거예요.

해설

돈이 부족한 남자에게 여자는 할인을 해주겠다고 얘기하는 상황으로 남자가 느낄만한 심정을 고른다.

어휘

be short (돈이) 모자라다, 부족하다 / cut down 깎아 주다

05 ③

Script

M I can't open this door.

W Why not?

M You try it. I pulled and pushed the door, but it wouldn't move at all.

W I know why you can't open this door. You have to slide the door side to side.

해석

남 이 문을 열지 못하겠어.

여 왜?

남 네가 해 봐. 내가 당기기도 하고 밀어 보기도 했는데. 전혀 움직이지를 않아.

여 네가 왜 이 문을 못 여는지 알았다. 이 문은 옆으로 밀어야 해.

해설

You have to slide the door side to side.라는 여자의 말에서 남자가 열려고 하는 문이 미닫이문임을 알 수 있다.

어휘

pull[pul] 당기다 / push[puʃ] 밀다 / slide[slaid] 물건이 미끄럽게 움직이다 / side to side 옆으로

06 ①

Script

M Mommy, stop pushing the swing. I'm getting scared.

W Okay. Be careful when you get down from the swing. If not, you could fall down.

M I'll be careful. This swing looks easy to ride, but it's a little dangerous.

W Yes, it is. Unless you are careful, you can hurt yourself.

M Okay. Why don't we try the seesaw?

W Why not?

해석

남 엄마, 그네를 그만 밀어주세요. 저 무서워요.

여 알았어. 그네에서 내릴 때는 조심해야 한다. 그렇지 않으면 넘어질 수도 있어.

남 조심할게요. 이 그네는 타기엔 쉬울 것 같은데, 좀 위험해요.

여 응, 그렇단다. 조심하지 않으면 다칠 수도 있어.

남 알겠어요. 우리 시소 타요?

여 알았다.

해설

엄마와 아들이 그네와 시소를 타며 놀이터에서 노는 상황이다.

어휘

swing[swiŋ] 그네 / fall down 넘어지다 / unless[ənlés] ~하지 않는다면 / seesaw[síːsɔ̀ː] 시소

07 ④

Script

M Wow, your painting is really nice.

W Thanks. Can I see some of yours?

M Actually, I gave up.

W What happened?

M At first, I really tried hard, but I don't think I have any talent.

W That's not true. You just need more time. That's all.

M You and I started painting at the same time, but you are much better.

해석

남 와, 네 그림 정말 멋있다.

여 고마워, 네 것을 좀 보여 줄 수 있니?

남 사실, 나 포기했어.

여 무슨 일이니?

남 처음에는 정말 열심히 했는데 나에게 재능이 없나 봐.

여 그렇지 않아. 넌 단지 시간이 좀 더 필요할 뿐이야. 그뿐이라고.

남 너와 나는 동시에 그림을 그리기 시작했는데 너는 나보다 훨씬 잘 그리잖아.

해설

I don't think I have any talent.라는 남자의 말에서 자신이 그림 그리는 것에 재능이 없다고 생각하고 있음을 알 수 있다.

어휘

give up 포기하다 / at first 우선 / talent[tǽlənt] 재능 / at the same time 동시에

08 ②

Script

M Good morning, ladies and gentlemen. This is your captain speaking. Our traveling time from Busan to Fukuoka is about 3 hours, so our arrival time will be at 3 p.m. It is very dangerous to be on the deck because of high waves, so please be careful. Thank you.

해석

남 안녕하세요, 신사 숙녀 여러분. 저는 여러분의 선장입니다. 부산에서 후쿠오카까지의 여행 시간은 3시간이며 도착 시간은 오후 3시가 되겠습니다. 여러분이 갑판에 나가는 것이 높은 파도 때문에 매우 위험하오니, 주의해 주십시오. 감사합니다.

해설

high speed ship, deck, high wave라는 말에서 이 방송을 들을 수 있는 곳을 유추할 수 있다.

어휘

lady[léidi] 숙녀 / gentleman[dʒéntlmən] 신사 / captain[kǽptin] 선장 / traveling[trǽvliŋ] 이동하는, 여행의 / arrival[əráivəl] 도착 / deck[dek] 갑판 / because of ~ 때문에 / wave[weiv] 파도

09 ④

Script

W Will the flight from London be here on time?

M I'm afraid not. It will be delayed an hour.

W You mean it's going to arrive at 5, then?

M That's right.

W What's the reason for this delay?

M In fact, it left London late due to heavy fog.

W I see. My son is on that flight, so I'm worried.

M Don't be. There won't be any problems at all.

해석

여 런던에서 오는 비행편이 제 시간에 도착합니까?

남 그렇지 않습니다. 한 시간 연착될 것입니다.

여 그러면 다섯 시에 도착한다는 말인가요?

남 네.

여 연착된 이유는 무엇인가요?

남 사실, 비행기가 짙은 안개 때문에 런던에서 늦게 출발했습니다.

여 알겠습니다. 제 아들이 그 비행기에 타고 있는데 걱정되네요.

남 걱정하지 않으셔도 됩니다. 전혀 문제가 없을 것입니다.

해설

비행기는 한 시간 연착되어 5시에 도착할 예정이고 비행기 안에는 여자의 아들이 타고 있으며, 남자는 걱정하지 말라며 여자를 안심시키고 있다.

어휘

on time 시간을 어기지 않고, 정각에 / delay[diléi] 연기하다, 지연시키다; 지연 / due to ~ 때문에 / heavy[hévi] 짙은, 강한, 맹렬한

10 ①

Script

W Oh, dear! I dropped Mom's glasses on the floor because you pushed me. These are her favorites.

M What are we supposed to do? Can't we just throw them away and buy the same ones?

W No, we can't. We should tell Mom what happened.

M But I'm afraid that she will punish us.

W Let's tell her the truth and ask her to forgive us.

해석

여 아, 이런! 네가 밀어서 바닥에 엄마의 유리잔을 떨어뜨렸어. 이것들은 엄마가 좋아하는 것들이야.

남 어떻게 하지? 그냥 버리고 똑같은 유리잔을 사면 안 될까?

여 아니, 안 돼. 엄마에게 무슨 일이 일어났는지 얘기해야 해.

남 하지만, 엄마가 벌을 주실 것 같아서 무서워.

여 엄마에게 사실대로 얘기하고 용서를 구하자.

해설

Let's tell her the truth and ask her to forgive us.라는 여자의 말을 통해 여자가 정직하다는 것을 알 수 있다.

어휘

favorite[féivərit] 특히 좋아하는 것, 인기 있는 사람; 아주 좋아하는 / throw away 버리다 / punish[pʌ́niʃ] 벌주다 / truth[tru:θ] 사실 / forgive[fərgív] 용서하다

11 ⑤

Script

M Angela, look at these mirrors. Which one do you want to get?

W I'm not sure.

M Well, what about that heart-shaped one?

W No. That's a little old-fashioned, and so is the round one, too.

M Then, what about the square one? I mean the big one.

W It's too wide. What do you think about the long, narrow one?

M Maybe that one is the best. Let's get it.

해석

남 Angela, 여기 이 거울들 좀 봐. 어떤 걸 사고 싶니?

여 잘 모르겠어.

남 그럼, 하트 모양은 어때?

여 아니. 그건 좀 구식이고 둥근 것도 그래.

남 그러면 사각형은 어때? 큰 거 말이야.

여 너무 넓어. 길고 좁은 것은 어떠니?

남 그게 제일 나은 것 같아. 그걸 사도록 하자.

해설

길고, 가는 거울은 어떠냐고 묻는 남자의 말에 여자는 그게 제일 나은 것 같다고 말하고 있다.

어휘

mirror[mírər] 거울 / heart-shaped 하트모양의 / old-fashioned 구식의, 고풍의 / square[skwɛər] 사각형의 / wide[waid] 넓은 / narrow[nǽrou] 좁은

12 ⑤

Script

W ① The bus to New York arrives at one o'clock.

② It takes almost one day to go to Washington D. C.

③ It takes more than 10 hours to go to Philadelphia.

④ The bus to New York leaves at seven in the morning.

⑤ Traveling time to New Jersey is longer than to New York.

해석

여 ① 뉴욕으로 가는 버스는 한 시에 도착한다.

② 워싱턴 D.C로 가는 데 거의 하루가 걸린다.

③ 필라델피아 가는 데 10시간 이상 걸린다.

④ 뉴욕으로 가는 버스는 아침 7시에 출발한다.

⑤ 뉴저지로 가는 여행시간은 뉴욕으로 가는 시간보다 더 길다.

해설

뉴욕과 뉴저지까지는 6시간으로 여행 시간은 같다.

13 ②

Script

M I'm here to buy a pair of shoes.

W Are they for you?

M Yes, they are. I'm looking for some tennis shoes.

W Okay. What size do you wear?

M I wear size ten in dress shoes but ten and a half in sneakers.

W I see. These ones are size ten. Why don't you try them on?

M OK. (pause) I like the design, but they are a bit small for me. I think I should take a size ten and a half.

해석

남 신발을 사러 왔습니다.

여 손님이 신으실 건가요?

남 네. 테니스화를 찾고 있어요.

여 알겠습니다. 사이즈는요?

남 구두는 10사이즈를 신는데 운동화는 10 1/2사이즈를 신어요.

여 알겠습니다. 이게 사이즈가 10인데요. 한 번 신어 보세요?

남 네. 디자인은 마음에 드는데 좀 작네요. 저는 사이즈 10 1/2로 해야 할 것 같아요.

해설

남자는 사이즈 10 이 작기 때문에 10 1/2를 사겠다고 말하고 있다.

어휘

pair[pɛər] 한 쌍[켤레/벌] / a pair of 한 켤레의 ~ / dress shoes 구두 / sneaker[sníːkər] 운동화

14 ④

Script

W Today, we are going to meet the famous actor, Brian. Let's welcome him!

M Hello, everyone. I'm very happy to be here with all of you.

W You haven't been on TV for a long time. How have you been?

M I have been very busy acting in three movies.

W The movie that you played in is very popular these days. How do you feel?

M First of all, I would like to say thank you to all the movie viewers.

해석

여 오늘은 유명한 배우, Brain을 만나보겠습니다. 그를 환영해 주세요!

남 안녕하세요, 여러분. 오늘 여러분과 여기 함께 있게 되어서 매우 기쁩니다.

여 TV에 오랫동안 출연하지 않으셨는데요. 어떻게 지내셨어요?

남 세 편의 영화를 찍느라 바빴습니다.

여 출연한 영화가 요즘 매우 인기 있는데요. 기분이 어떠세요?

남 우선, 영화 관객들에게 먼저 감사하다는 말을 하고 싶어요.

해설

TV 쇼 진행자와 출연자가 인터뷰하는 상황이다.

어휘

famous[féiməs] 유명한 / welcome[wélkəm] 환영하다 / show up 나타나다 / be busy+-ing ~하느라 바쁘다 / play[plei] (영화 · 연극 등에서) 연기하다, 배역을 맡다 / first of all 먼저, 우선 / viewer[vjúːər] 시청자, 관객

15 ③

Script

① M Excuse me. You're not supposed to wear shoes here.
W Oh, I'm terribly sorry. I didn't know that.

② M I have two tickets for a concert. Would you like to come with me?
W I'm afraid I can't. I have some other things to do tonight.

③ M You shouldn't wear a cap in the classroom.
W Okay. I will put it on right now.

④ M Hi, Jeniffer. Can you come to my house this Saturday?
W I'm sorry. I have to go swimming.

⑤ M Can I use your cell phone?
W Sorry, my battery is dead.

해석

① 남 실례합니다. 여기서 신발을 신으면 안 됩니다.
여 아, 정말 죄송합니다. 그렇다는 걸 몰랐습니다.

② 남 나에게 콘서트 표가 두 장 있는데 나랑 같이 갈래?
여 안 될 것 같아. 오늘 밤에 다른 할 일이 있어.

③ 남 교실에서 모자를 쓰면 안 됩니다.
여 알겠습니다. 지금 당장 쓰겠습니다.

④ 남 안녕, Jennifer. 이번 토요일에 우리 집에 올 수 있니?
여 미안해. 나 수영장에 가야 해.

⑤ 남 네 휴대 전화 사용해도 될까?
여 미안한데, 배터리가 없어.

해설

③ 모자를 쓰지 말라는 남자의 말에 여자는 알겠다며 지금 당장 쓰겠다고 응답하고 있다.

어휘

terribly[térəbli] 몹시, 굉장히, 대단히 / put on 쓰다 *cf.* put off 벗다 / battery[bǽtəri] 배터리

16 ①

Script

W This is a daily record of what you do in a day. You write down things that happen to you each day. Some people just write this only on a special day like a birthday, a trip, and an anniversary. Someone also writes his or her secrets in this. Sometimes parents read it to find out whether their child is having any problems.

해석

여 이것은 당신이 하루 동안 무엇을 했는지에 대한 기록입니다. 당신은 당신에게 매일 일어나는 일들을 씁니다. 어떤 사람들은 생일이나, 여행 그리고 기념일과 같은 특별한 날에만 씁니다. 어떤 사람들은 또한 자신의 비밀을 거기에 씁니다. 때때로 부모님들은 자신의 아이들에게 문제가 있는지 알아보려고 그것을 읽습니다.

해설

당신이 하루 동안 무엇을 했는지에 대한 기록은 일기이다.

어휘

daily[déili] 매일의, 나날의 / record[rékərd] 기록; 기록하다 / anniversary[æ̀nəvə́ːrsəri] 기념일 / secret[síːkrit] 비밀 / find out 발견하다 / whether[hwéðər] ~인지, ~이든

17 ④

Script

M Hi, Kelly. What's up?

W Would you do me a favor?

M Sure, what do you want me to do?

W Can you drive me to the bank? I need to open a savings account.

M Sure, I can. I'm going to the library, and it's on the way, right?

W Yes. How nice of you!

해석

남 안녕, Kelly야. 웬일이니?

여 부탁 좀 들어줄래?

남 물론이야, 뭔데?

여 은행에 좀 데려다 줄 수 있니? 나 통장을 하나 만들어야 해.

남 당연하지. 나는 도서관 가려고 하는데 은행이 가는 길에 있지, 그렇지?

여 맞아. 넌 정말 친절해!

해설

Can you drive me to the bank?라는 여자의 말에서 정답을 알 수 있다.

어휘

drive[draiv] ~을 태워다 주다 / savings 저축한 돈, 예금 / account[əkáunt] 계좌 / open a savings account 통장을 만들다 / on the way 가는 길에, 도중에

18 ③

Script

M What time do you go to work?

W At around seven.

M Doesn't your company start working at nine?

W You're right. I just want to avoid rush hour. There are too many people on the subway if you go around 8. But before rush hour I can sit and rest on my way to work.

M That's true.

W The funny thing is people working with me think I'm a hardworking person because I go to work early.

M That's good.

해석

남 너 몇 시에 출근하니?

여 7시 정도.

남 회사가 9시에 업무를 시작하지 않니?

여 네 말이 맞아. 그냥 러시아워를 피하고 싶어. 8시에 나오면 사람들이 정말 많거든. 러시아워 전에는 앉아서 편하게 회사에 갈 수 있어.

남 그건 사실이지.

여 웃기는 건 내가 회사에 일찍 출근해서 나와 함께 일하는 사람들이 내가 근면한 사람인 줄 알아.

남 좋은데.

해설

① 무소식이 희소식이다.

② 늦더라도 안 하는 것보다 낫다.

④ 어려울 때 친구가 진정한 친구이다.

⑤ 뜻이 있는 곳에 길이 있다.

일찍 출근해서 러시아워를 피할 수도 있고 동료들이 자신을 근면한 사람으로 생각한다고 말하고 있기 때문에 '한 가지 일로 두 가지 이익을 얻는다.'라는 의미의 ③을 고른다.

어휘

avoid[əvɔ́id] 피하다 / rush hour 러시아워 / rest[rest] 쉬다, 휴식을 취하다 / hardworking[hɑ́ːrdwə̀ːrkiŋ] 열심히 일하는

19 ⑤

Script

M I'm going to visit my uncle this Saturday.

W You mean your uncle, Jack?

M Yes, do you still remember him?

W Sure, he used to teach us how to swim in the river.

M That's right. He runs a small jewelry shop. I'm going to help him.

W Please say hello to him for me.

해석

남 나 이번 주 토요일에 삼촌을 방문할 거야.

여 네 삼촌, Jack 말이야?

남 응, 너 아직도 그를 기억하니?

여 물론이지. 강에서 우리에게 수영하는 법을 가르쳐 주곤 했잖아.

남 맞아. 지금 작은 보석가게를 하는데, 삼촌을 도와주려고.

여 그에게 내 안부 좀 전해 줘.

해설

① 나도 그가 그리워.

② 그도 너를 기억하고 있어.

③ 그가 언제 도착하니?

④ 나는 보석 가게에 가는 중이야.

오래전에 자신들에게 수영을 가르쳐 주었던 삼촌을 만나러 간다는 남자의 말에 알맞은 응답을 고른다.

어휘

in fact 사실 / say hello to ~에게 안부를 전하다 / run[rʌn] 경영하다 / jewelry[dʒúːəlri] 보석류 / jewelry shop 보석 가게

20 ②

Script

W What are you doing now?

M My father is moving his office, so I'm helping him.

W Where is he moving?

M Home. He's going to use his study as an office.

W I see. You said your father is a writer.

M That's right. So he has a lot of books. Could you give me a hand?

W Sure, what can I do for you?

해석

여 너 지금 뭐 하고 있니?

남 우리 아버지가 사무실을 옮기고 계셔서 지금 그를 돕고 있어.

여 어디로 옮기는데?

남 집으로. 사무실로 아버지 서재를 사용하려고 하셔.

여 그렇구나. 아버지가 작가라고 했지.

남 맞아. 그래서 그는 책이 많아. 좀 도와줄 수 있니?

여 물론이야. 무엇을 도와줄까?

해설

① 그 일을 하는 건 쉽지 않아.

③ 미안해, 지금 그것들을 사용할 수 없어.

④ 난 괜찮아. 어서 해.

⑤ 괜찮아. 넌 그것을 모두 혼자 옮길 수 있어.

도와 달라는 남자의 요청에 알맞은 응답을 고른다.

어휘

by oneself 혼자, 혼자 힘으로 / office[ɔ́(:)fis] 사무실 / move into 이사 오다 / study[stʌ́di] 서재

- 시·도 교육청 공동 주관 중학교 영어듣기능력평가 기출 문제 완전 분석
- 최신 듣기평가 기출 유형이 100% 반영된 모의고사 16회분과 실전 영어듣기평가 2회분
- 잘 들리지 않았던 부분을 확실히 확인할 수 있도록 도와주는 회별 Dictation Test
- 기출 문제 유형 분석과 각종 핵심 표현을 총정리한 실전 대비 학습

중학 영어듣기

한 방에 끝낸다

AFTER SCHOOL Listening

애프터스쿨 리스닝 level 2

유형별 학습

NEXUS Edu

Part 1 그림 묘사

기출엿보기

1 **대화를 듣고, 남자가 선택한 쿠키를 고르시오.**

①  ②  ③  ④ 

Script

W I baked some cookies. Pick your favorite.

M Wow! Looks yummy. I'd like **a round** cookie, please.

W A round one? You mean the one with a star?

M No, I mean **the cookie with a bear on it**.

해석

여 내가 쿠키를 좀 구웠어. 마음에 드는 것을 골라.

남 와! 맛있겠다. 난 둥근 모양의 쿠키를 먹을래.

여 둥근 모양? 별이 그려진 쿠키 말이니?

남 아니, 위에 곰이 그려진 쿠키 말이야.

정답 ④

해설 남자는 모양이 둥글고 그 위에 곰이 그려진 쿠키를 고르고 있다.

2 **다음을 듣고, 그림에서 묘사되지 않은 사람을 고르시오.**

Script

W Two boys and two girls are cleaning the classroom. One girl is **dusting the wall**, and the other girl is **cleaning the window**. One boy is **picking up trash** and the other boy has slipped down onto the floor.

해석

여 두 소년과 두 소녀가 교실을 청소하고 있습니다. 한 소녀는 벽에 먼지를 털고 있고, 다른 한 소녀는 창문을 닦고 있습니다. 한 소년은 휴지를 줍고 있고, 다른 한 소년은 바닥에 미끄러졌습니다.

정답 ③

해설 ① 창문을 닦는 소녀, ② 벽의 먼지를 털고 있는 소녀, ④ 바닥에 미끄러진 소년으로 ③ 칠판을 닦고 있는 소년에 대한 묘사는 없다.

기출문장

인물 묘사

What does he **look like**? / **How** does he **look?** 그는 어떻게 생겼니?

She has **long curly**[**wavy**] hair. 그녀는 긴 곱슬머리이다.

She is **wearing glasses**[**hat**]. 그녀는 안경[모자]을 쓰고 있다.

He has **a mustache.** 그는 콧수염이 있다. / He is **bald.** 그는 대머리이다.

She is **shorter** than the girl **with straight hair**. 그녀는 생머리 소녀보다 키가 작다.

외모 beard 턱수염 heavy 뚱뚱한 skinny 마른 slender 날씬한

사물 묘사

Draw **five squares in a row.** 사각형 다섯 개를 일렬로 그리세요.

Fill in the square **with black ink.** 사각형을 검은색 잉크로 채우세요.

Color the second and fifth squares black. 두 번째와 다섯 번째 사각형을 검은색으로 색칠하세요.

Draw **a line under the fourth square.** 네 번째 사각형 아래 선을 그리세요.

What about this **plain** one? 이 무늬가 없는 것은 어때?

It has **a pocket** on the **outside.** 그것은 겉에 주머니가 있습니다.

무늬 & 모양 striped 줄무늬의 polka dot 물방울무늬 plain 무늬가 없는 checkered 체크무늬의 circle 원 square 네모 triangle 세모 line 선 round 둥근

위치 묘사

How can I **get to** the post office? 우체국에 어떻게 갈 수 있나요?

Go straight this way **for** two blocks. 이 길을 따라 두 블록을 직진하세요.

Turn right[**left**] at the corner. 모퉁이에서 오른쪽[왼쪽]으로 도세요.

It will be on **your left.** 그것은 당신의 왼편에 있을 겁니다.

It's the **second building on your right.** 당신의 오른쪽에 있는 두 번째 건물입니다.

The fire station is **around the corner from** the bank. 소방서는 은행에서 모퉁이에 있습니다.

The post office is **between** the church **and** the fire station. 우체국은 교회와 소방서 사이에 있습니다.

There is a bank **across from** the post office. 우체국 맞은편에 은행이 있습니다.

위치 & 거리 opposite[across from] 맞은편에 in front of 앞에 below 아래에 over 위에 in the middle of 중간에 between A and B A와 B 사이에 beside[next to, by] 옆에

상황 또는 동작 묘사

Two students **are talking** on the phone. 두 학생이 통화를 하고 있습니다.

Two students **are taking care of** a baby. 두 학생이 아기를 돌보고 있습니다.

A player **is waiting to hit** the ball. 한 선수가 공을 치려고 기다리고 있습니다.

A man **is trying to put** a ball. 한 남자가 공을 넣으려고 하고 있습니다.

동작 slip down 미끄러지다 wash the dish 설거지하다 clean the floor 바닥을 청소하다 water the garden 정원에 물을 주다 feed a squirrel 다람쥐에게 먹이를 주다

기출풀기

1 대화를 듣고, 여자가 사려고 하는 가방을 고르시오.

① 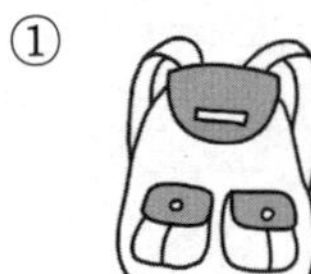

② 
③

④ 
⑤ 

2 다음을 듣고, 찾고 있는 아이의 모습으로 알맞은 것을 고르시오.

① 
② 
③ 
④ 

3 대화를 듣고, 남자가 찾는 곳을 고르시오.

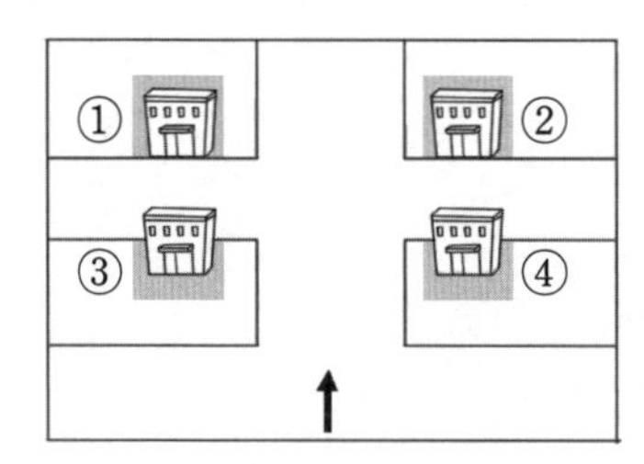

4 다음을 듣고, 그림의 상황에 가장 알맞은 대화를 고르시오.

① ② ③ ④

Part 2 장소, 직업, 대화자의 관계

기출엿보기

1 **대화를 듣고, 두 사람의 관계로 가장 적절한 것을 고르시오.**

① 점원 – 손님 ② 사장 – 직원 ③ 교사 – 학생
④ 가수 – 팬 ⑤ 수리기사 – 손님

Script

M Excuse me. I got this MP3 player for my birthday last week, and it doesn't work when I try to play music. **Could I exchange** it for another one?

W **You can exchange it** if you have **the receipt**. Do you have it?

M Yes.

W Here is a new MP3 player.

M Thank you.

W **Do you need anything else?**

M No, this will be all.

해석

남 실례합니다. 지난주에 생일 선물로 이 MP3 재생기를 받았는데 음악을 재생할 때 작동을 안 해서요. 이것을 다른 것으로 교환할 수 있을까요?

여 영수증이 있으시면 교환하실 수 있습니다. 영수증을 가지고 있으세요?

남 네.

여 여기 새 MP3 재생기입니다.

남 감사합니다.

여 더 필요하신 건 없으신가요?

남 네, 이게 다입니다.

정답 ①

해설 MP3 재생기가 작동하지 않아 교환을 원하는 손님과 점원의 대화이다.

2 **대화를 듣고, 두 사람이 대화하는 장소를 고르시오.**

① 미술관 ② 옷가게 ③ 우체국 ④ 도서관

Script

M Good morning. **May I help you**?

W I like the skirt on display. **Can you show me one**?

M Sure. **What size do you wear**?

W A size six.

M Here you are.

W **May I try this on**?

M Yes, you may. **The fitting room** is over there.

해석

남 안녕하세요? 도와드릴까요?

여 진열되어 있는 치마가 마음에 드는데요. 보여주실 수 있나요?

남 물론이죠. 어떤 사이즈를 입으시죠?

여 6사이즈요.

남 여기 있습니다.

여 제가 이것을 입어봐도 될까요?

남 네, 입어보실 수 있습니다. 옷 입어보는 곳은 저쪽에 있습니다.

정답 ②

해설 옷을 구입하려고 하는 손님과 점원의 대화로, 대화가 이루어지는 장소는 옷가게이다.

기출문장

장래희망 & 직업

What **do you do**? / What **do you do for a living**? 당신의 직업은 무엇입니까?

I **work for** World Travel. 저는 World Travel에서 일합니다.

I **want to be** a computer programmer. 나는 컴퓨터 프로그래머가 되고 싶어.

I **like to work with** computers. 나는 컴퓨터로 일하는 것이 좋아.

What **do** you **want to be** when you grow up? 너는 커서 무엇이 되고 싶니?

What **would** you **like to be in the future**? 너는 미래에 무엇이 되고 싶니?

I **have decided to become** a doctor. 나는 의사가 되기로 결정했어.

I'm interested in cooking. 나는 요리에 흥미가 있다.

Are you **interested in** stars and planets? 너는 별과 행성에 관심이 있니?

What are you **interested in**? 너는 무엇에 관심이 있니?

직업 salesperson 판매원 photographer 사진가 advisor 조언자 patient 환자 programmer 프로그래머 engineer 엔지니어 pilot 〈항공〉 조종사 flight attendant 승무원 tour guide 관광 가이드 firefighter 소방관 counselor 상담원 counselee 상담받는 사람 reporter 기자 repairman 수리공 secretary 비서 police officer 경찰관

장소 & 관계

⇨ [Hospital & Drugstore] doctor - patient, pharmacist - customer

What's **wrong**? / What **seems to be wrong**? / What **seems to be a problem?** 무엇이 문제입니까?

Do you **have a fever?** 열이 있나요?

I can **give** you **some aspirin**. 제가 아스피린을 드리겠습니다.

It will **ease** your **pain**. 이것이 통증을 완화시켜 줄 것입니다.

Take this **medicine**. 이 약을 복용하세요.

How should I **take this medicine**? 어떻게 이 약을 복용해야 하나요?

Do you **have any good medicine** for that? 거기에 필요한 약이 있나요?

Take this **pill two times a day**. 이 알약을 하루에 두 번 드세요.

I **have a runny nose**. 콧물이 납니다.

If you don't **feel better**, please **go to the dentist**. 낫지 않으면, 치과에 가십시오.

증상 fever 열 headache 두통 toothache 치통 sore throat 인후통 cough 기침; 기침하다 stomachache 복통 cavity 충치 temperature 체온 give a shot 주사를 놓다 check-up 검진 flu 독감 feel better 기분이 나아지다, 회복되다 go see a doctor 진찰을 받다, 병원에 가다 have an allergy to ~에 알레르기가 있다

⇨ [Restaurant] waiter / waitress - customer

What **would** you **like to have**? 무엇을 드시겠습니까?

Are you **ready to order**? 주문하시겠습니까?

How **would you like** your steak? 스테이크를 어떻게 해 드릴까요?

What **would you like for dessert**? 디저트로 무엇을 드시겠습니까?

What's **the today's special?** 오늘의 특별 메뉴는 무엇인가요?

I'd like **to have** a ham sandwich. 햄 샌드위치로 할게요.

For here or to go? 여기서 드실 건가요 아니면 가져가실 건가요?

⇨ [Hotel] clerk - customer

Do you **have a reservation?** 예약을 하셨나요?

How **many days** will you **stay** here? 여기에 며칠간 묵으실 예정인가요?

Can you **give** me **a wake-up call**? 모닝콜을 해주시겠어요?

I'd like to **check in[out].** 체크인[아웃]을 하고 싶습니다.

I'd like to **make a reservation.** 예약을 하고 싶습니다.

I need **a single room.** 1인실이 필요합니다.

⇨ [Department store & Store] clerk / salesperson - customer

May I **help** you? / **What can** I **help** you? 무엇을 도와드릴까요?

This is **on sale.** 이것은 세일 중입니다.

What size do you wear? 어떤 사이즈를 입으십니까?

I'**m looking** for a sweater. 스웨터를 찾고 있습니다.

I'**m** just **looking around.** 그냥 둘러보고 있습니다.

Can I **try this on**? 이것을 입어봐도 될까요?

I'd like to **get a refund.** 환불을 받고 싶습니다.

Do you have this **in a smaller size**? 더 작은 사이즈가 있나요?

Would you **like to exchange** them? 교환을 원하시나요?

상점 wrap up 포장하다 discount 할인; 할인하다 used 중고의 receipt 영수증 change 거스름돈

기타

⇨ Airport & Airplane

May I **have** your **passport**, please? 여권을 보여주시겠어요?

What's the **purpose of** your **visit** to Canada? 캐나다를 방문하는 목적이 무엇입니까?

How long are you going to **stay**? 얼마나 머무를 예정이십니까?

The flight will be **landing** soon. 비행기는 곧 착륙합니다.

The flight will be **taking** off in five minutes. 비행기는 5분 후에 이륙합니다.

비행기 seat 좌석 take off 이륙하다 land 착륙하다

공항 flight ticket 비행기 표 boarding gate 탑승구 passport 여권 immigration 입국 심사 be delayed 연기되다, 지연되다 be canceled 결항되다 one-way ticket 편도 티켓 round-trip ticket 왕복 티켓 available 이용 가능한

⇨ Post office & Bank

How do you want to **mail** it? 어떻게 보내고 싶으신가요?

I'd like to buy **some stamp.** 우표를 사고 싶습니다.

How long does it **take to get** there? 거기에 도착하는 데 얼마나 걸리나요?

I'd like to **send this package** to America. 이 소포를 미국으로 보내고 싶습니다.

I'd like to **open a bank** account. 신규계좌를 개설하고 싶습니다.

Can you **show me your ID**? 신분증을 보여주시겠어요?

은행 & 우체국 savings 저축 ATM 현금 자동 입출기 airmail 항공 우편 parcel 소포 postcard 엽서 teller (은행의) 출납계 open an account 계좌를 개설하다

기출풀기

1 대화를 듣고, 두 사람의 관계로 알맞은 것을 고르시오.

① 의사 – 환자　　② 경찰관 – 행인
③ 호텔 종업원 – 손님　　④ 스튜어디스 – 승객

2 대화를 듣고, 남자의 장래희망으로 가장 적절한 것을 고르시오.

① 천문학자　　② 조종사
③ 수의사　　④ 해양 과학자
⑤ 식물학자

3 대화를 듣고, 남자의 직업으로 알맞은 것을 고르시오.

① 의사　　② 경찰관
③ 소방관　　④ 축구 선수

4 다음을 듣고, 대화가 이루어지는 장소를 고르시오.

① 우체국　　② 도서관
③ 꽃가게　　④ 분실물 보관소

5 다음을 듣고, 방송이 이루어지고 있는 장소로 가장 적절한 곳을 고르시오.

① 백화점　　② 놀이공원
③ 동물원　　④ 야구경기장
⑤ 영화관

Part 3 주제 · 화제

기출엿보기

1 다음을 듣고, 여자가 설명하는 것으로 가장 적절한 것을 고르시오.

① cars ② foods ③ houses
④ clothes ⑤ umbrellas

Script

W These are **important things** for living. They **keep us from being cold** in the winter and hot in the summer. Inside them, we **can keep out of the wind**, and they **protect us** from **the hot sun**. When it rains, they **keep us from getting wet**. Also, we can **have a good time** watching TV, cooking food, or sleeping inside them. What are they?

해석

여 이것들은 우리의 삶에 중요한 것입니다. 그것들은 겨울에는 추위로부터, 여름에는 더위로부터 우리를 막아줍니다. 그것들 안에서 우리는 바람을 피할 수 있고, 그것들은 뜨거운 태양으로부터 우리를 보호해 줍니다. 비가 올 때, 그것들은 우리가 젖지 않게 해줍니다. 또한, 우리는 그것들 안에서 TV를 보고, 음식을 하고, 잠을 자면서 좋은 시간을 보낼 수 있습니다. 그것들은 무엇일까요?

정답 ③

해설 추위, 더위, 바람, 뜨거운 태양, 그리고 비로부터 우리를 막아주며, 그 안에서 다양한 활동을 할 수 있는 곳은 집(houses)이다.

2 대화를 듣고, 주제로 알맞은 것을 고르시오.

① 동물을 보호하자. ② 분리수거를 하자.
③ 자원을 절약하자. ④ 오염의 심각성을 알자.

Script

M I hear **many wild** animals like bears and elephants are **in danger**.

W Do you know why they are in danger?

M Well, I heard **people hunt those animals for money.**

W That's terrible. I think everyone **should try to protect them**.

M I agree with you.

해석

남 곰, 코끼리와 같은 많은 야생 동물들이 위험에 처해 있다고 들었어.

여 너는 왜 그 동물들이 위험에 처해 있는지 아니?

남 글쎄, 사람들이 돈 때문에 이 동물들을 사냥한다고 들었어.

여 끔찍해. 내 생각에는 모든 사람들이 그 동물들을 보호해야 해.

남 나도 네 말에 동의해.

정답 ①

해설 위험에 처한 야생 동물에 관한 이야기로 여자는 마지막 말에서 그들을 보호해야 한다고 이야기하고 있다.

기출문장

안내 방송

May I **have** your **attention**, please? 주목해주십시오.

Attention all shoppers! 모든 고객 여러분 주목해주십시오!

미아, 분실물 찾기

She is **looking for** her mom. 여자 아이가 엄마를 찾고 있습니다.

We're **looking for** a woman's bag. 여성용 가방을 찾고 있습니다.

We **have a lost child.** 미아를 보호하고 있습니다.

방송 lost child 미아 attention 주의

공항 & 비행기 안

In twenty minutes, we'll be **landing.** 20분 후에 착륙하겠습니다. / The flight will **take off soon.** 비행기는 곧 이륙합니다.

The flight will **be delayed** because of heavy rain. 폭우로 인해 비행기가 연착될 것입니다.

Please **put** your **seats into the upright position.** 좌석을 똑바로 해 주십시오.

Please **fasten** your **seat belts.** 좌석벨트를 매 주십시오.

Make sure you **have all your belongings with you** when you get off.
비행기에서 내리실 때 모든 소지품을 챙기셨는지 확인하시기 바랍니다.

비행기 & 공항 land 착륙하다 take off 이륙하다 delay 연기하다, 지연하다

세일 광고공항 & 비행기 안

We're **having a special sale** in our food corner. 식품 코너에서 특별 세일을 하고 있습니다.

Fifty **percent off**! 50% 세일합니다! / **Everything** is **half price** in the store. 상점 내 모든 제품이 반값입니다.

세일 miss out 놓치다 half price 절반 가격 have a sale 세일하다

동물

I have **no wings**. I **cannot fly**, but I **can swim.** 나는 날개가 없습니다. 나는 날지 못하지만, 수영을 할 수 있습니다.

I am **an insect** with **a yellow-and-black striped** body. 나는 몸에 노랗고 검은 줄무늬가 있는 곤충입니다.

I am **mostly white.** I **can fly**, but I **cannot swim.** 내 몸의 대부분은 하얀색입니다. 나는 날 수 있지만, 헤엄을 칠 수는 없습니다.

동물 묘사 wing 날개 beak 부리 fly 날다 swim 헤엄치다 in danger 위험에 처한 insect 곤충 sting 쏘다

기타

My job is to **protect you from** the rain. 내 일은 당신을 비로부터 보호하는 것입니다.

It **is similar to Thanksgiving** in the U.S. and Canada. 이것은 미국과 캐나다의 추수감사절과 비슷합니다.

Some students say it's **convenient and useful** when they need to call somebody or send a text message. 몇몇 학생들은 누군가에게 전화를 하거나 문자 메시지를 보낼 때 편하고 유용하다고 합니다.

We **should plant more trees** and **recycle more paper.** 우리는 더 많은 나무를 심고, 종이를 더 재활용 해야 해.

물건 & 특정일 holiday 연휴 national 국가의, 전국의 similar ~와 비슷한 traditional 전통적인

기출풀기

1 대화를 듣고, 무엇에 관한 내용인지 고르시오.

① 날씨　② 산불　③ 등산　④ 나무심기

2 다음을 듣고, 무엇에 관한 안내방송인지 고르시오.

① 분실물　② 할인판매
③ 컴퓨터 강좌　④ 도서관 이용방법

3 다음을 듣고, 무엇에 관한 내용인지 고르시오.

① 분실물 안내　② 할인판매 안내
③ 문화강좌 홍보　④ 비행기 탑승 안내
⑤ 미술관 관람 안내

4 다음을 듣고, 설명하는 대상으로 알맞은 것을 고르시오.

① 
② 
③ 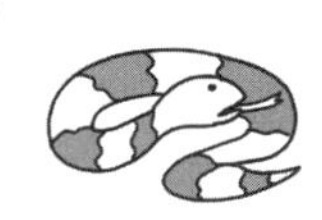
④ 

5 다음을 듣고, 무엇에 관한 설명인지 고르시오.

① 설날　② 단오　③ 추석　④ 동지

Part 4 특정 정보: 할 일·날씨·사려고 하는 것

기출엿보기

1 **전화 통화 후에 여자가 할 일로 가장 적절한 것을 고르시오.**

① 과학 숙제하기 ② 저녁식사하기 ③ 도서관 가기
④ Tom에게 전화하기 ⑤ 수업 준비하기

Script

[Telephone rings.]

W Hello. This is Sumi. Can I speak to Tom?

M Hi, Sumi. I'm afraid he is not at home now. Can I take a message?

W Thanks. I **am calling to ask if he can study with me** for the science test.

M He went to **study at the city library**, and he is going to **stay there until dinnertime**.

W Oh, really? When **did he go there**?

M He left home **right after breakfast**, at about 9.

W OK, I will **go to the library right away**. Thank you.

해석

여 여보세요. 저 수미인데요. Tom과 통화할 수 있을까요?

남 안녕, 수미야. 그는 지금 집에 없단다. 메시지를 남겨줄까?

여 감사해요. Tom이 저랑 같이 과학 시험 공부를 할 수 있는지 물어보려고 전화했어요.

남 그는 시립 도서관에 공부하러 갔는데 저녁시간까지는 거기에 있을 거라고 했어.

여 아, 정말이에요? 거기 언제 갔어요?

남 아침식사 바로 후, 9시쯤 집을 나갔단다.

여 알겠습니다. 지금 바로 도서관에 가야겠어요. 감사합니다.

정답 ③

해설 Tom이 도서관에 갔다는 말을 듣고, 여자는 지금 당장 도서관에 가야겠다고 말하고 있다.

2 **대화를 듣고, 오늘 남자가 이용하게 될 교통수단을 고르시오.**

① 버스 ② 자동차 ③ 지하철 ④ 자전거

Script

W Hi, David. What are you doing here?

M Hello, Ann. I'm going to work.

W Don't you usually **drive your car to work**?

M Yes. But think about the price of gas. **Taking the subway** or **the bus** is **much cheaper**.

W Oh, I see. Some of my friends go to work by bicycle if the weather is good.

M That's a good idea. Oh, **here comes my bus**.

해석

여 안녕, David. 너 여기서 무엇을 하고 있니?

남 안녕, Ann. 출근하고 있어.

여 너 보통 회사에 차를 운전하고 다니지 않니?

남 맞아. 하지만, 휘발유 가격을 생각해 봐. 지하철이나 버스를 타는 게 훨씬 싸.

여 오, 그렇구나. 내 친구들 몇 명은 날씨가 좋으면 자전거로 출근해.

남 그거 좋은 생각인데. 오, 저기 내가 탈 버스가 와.

정답 ①

해설 '저기 내가 탈 버스가 온다.'라는 남자의 말을 통해 남자가 이용하게 될 교통수단이 버스임을 알 수 있다.

기출문장

할 일 & 한 일

What did you **do** last weekend? 너 지난 주말에 뭐 했니?

Can you join me for lunch today? 오늘 나랑 같이 점심 먹을래?

How about going skating this Sunday? 이번 주 일요일에 스케이트 타러 가는 건 어때?

I'**m planning to go** hiking tomorrow. 나는 내일 하이킹하러 갈 계획이야.

Why don't we play tennis? 우리 테니스를 치는 건 어떨까?

I'**d better take a nap** after lunch. 나는 점심을 먹고 나서 낮잠을 자는 게 좋겠어.

I **have to stay home** and **do my homework.** 나는 집에서 숙제를 할 거야.

할 일 join 참가하다 stay home 집에 머물다 take care of ~을 돌보다 plan 계획; 계획하다 visit 방문하다

사려고 하는 것

What are you **going to buy**? 너는 무엇을 살 거니? / **What should** we **get** him? 그에게 무엇을 사줄까?

Which one do you **want for a present**? 너는 선물로 어떤 것을 원하니?

What are you **going to give** her? 너는 그녀에게 무엇을 줄거니?

I'm **looking for** a gift for my sister. 저는 여동생에게 줄 선물을 찾고 있어요.

How about buying her some dolls? 그녀에게 인형을 좀 사주는 건 어때?

사려고 하는 것 garage sale 차고 세일 present 선물 special 특별한 anniversary 기념일 birthday 생일

이용할 교통 수단

How do you **usually go** to Busan? 너는 보통 부산에 어떻게 가니?

How will you go there tomorrow? 너는 내일 거기에 어떻게 갈 거니?

Are you going to take the bus? 너는 버스를 탈 거니?

How do I get there from here? 여기서 거기까지 어떻게 가야 하나요?

You can **take a bus** from here, but the road will be very busy. 여기서 버스를 탈 수 있지만, 도로가 붐빌 거예요.

You can **take the subway**. Take line No. 3. 지하철을 타면 돼요. 3호선을 타세요.

교통 수단 express bus 급행 버스 traffic jam 교통 체증 station 역 bus stop 버스 정류장 transfer 갈아타다

날씨

Here is **the weather report** for tomorrow. 내일의 일기 예보입니다.

We've been having very **wet weather** for a couple of weeks. 2주 동안 날씨가 매우 습합니다.

Today it'll be **sunny with a 5% chance of rain**. 오늘은 비가 올 확률이 5%로 날씨가 화창하겠습니다.

The **weather forecast** said it **would rain** this afternoon. 일기 예보에서 오늘 오후에 비가 올 거라고 했어.

The **rain will continue until** this weekend. 비는 이번 주말까지 계속될 것입니다.

It's **getting windy**, too. We **might have rain.** 바람이 많이 불겠습니다. 비가 내릴 수도 있습니다.

날씨 report 보도 changeable 변하기 쉬운, 변덕스러운 expect 예상하다 heavy rain 폭우 wet 젖은 clear 맑은 forecast 예보 rainy 비가 오는 continue 계속되다 dark 어두운 foggy 안개 낀 lightning 번개 thunder 천둥 freezing 몹시 추운 chilly 추운 snowy 눈이 오는 temperature 기온 sunshine 햇빛 chance 가능성 humid 습한 shower 소나기

기출풀기

1 대화를 듣고, 남자가 사게 될 선물로 알맞은 것을 고르시오.

① 시계 ② CD ③ 손수건 ④ 요리책

2 세계의 날씨 예보를 듣고, 일치하지 않는 것을 고르시오.

①

Vancouver

②

Paris

③

London

④

Moscow

⑤

Singapore

3 대화를 듣고, 여자가 하게 될 봉사활동을 고르시오.

① 청소 ② 세탁 ③ 요리
④ 설거지 ⑤ 책 읽기

4 대화를 듣고, 여자가 오후에 할 일을 고르시오.

① 청소 ② 수영 ③ 낮잠 ④ 테니스

5 대화를 듣고, 여자가 이용할 교통수단을 고르시오.

① bus ② car ③ taxi ④ subway

Part 5 내용 일치·불일치

기출엿보기

1 다음을 듣고, 그래프의 내용과 일치하지 않는 것을 고르시오.

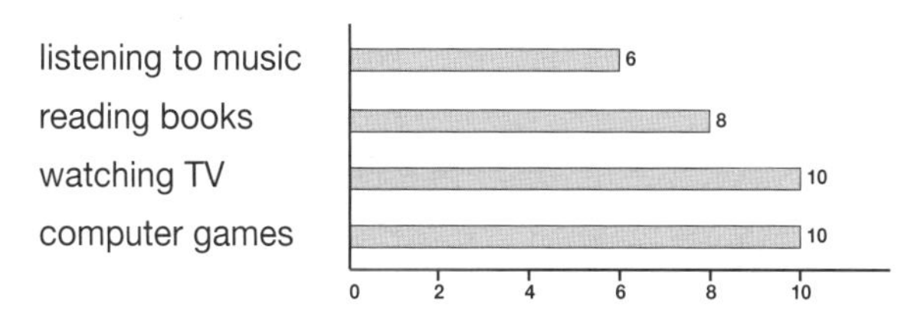

① 음악 감상　② 독서　③ TV시청　④ 컴퓨터게임

Script

M I asked my classmates about their hobbies. **Six students** are **interested in listening to music. Eight students** enjoy **reading books**, and the same number of students like **watching TV**. **Ten students** like **computer games**.

해석

남 저는 우리 반 학생들에게 그들의 취미에 대해서 물어보았습니다. 6명의 학생이 음악을 듣는 데 관심을 가지고 있었습니다. 8명의 학생이 책을 즐겨 읽고, 같은 수의 학생들이 TV를 보는 것을 좋아합니다. 10명의 학생은 컴퓨터 게임을 좋아합니다.

정답 ③

해설 TV시청을 좋아하는 학생이 10명으로 컴퓨터 게임을 좋아하는 학생들의 수와 같다.

2 대화를 듣고, 내용과 일치하지 않는 것을 고르시오.

① 호주는 겨울이고 약간 추웠다.
② 여자는 호주에 대해 관심이 많다.
③ 남자는 여름 방학에 호주에 다녀왔다.
④ 남자는 호주에서 여행을 많이 할 수 없었다.

Script

W Where did you go during the **summer vacation**?

M I **went to Australia**.

W Oh, wasn't it cold? **I heard it's winter there.**

M Yes, **it was a little cold**. But I could **enjoy lots of traveling** and **winter sports**.

W I wish I **could go there** next vacation. **Tell me more** about it.

해석

여 여름 방학에 어디 다녀왔니?

남 호주에 갔었어.

여 오, 춥지 않았니? 거기는 겨울이라고 들었어.

남 맞아, 조금 추웠어. 하지만, 여행도 많이 하고 겨울 스포츠도 즐길 수 있었어.

여 나도 다음 방학에 거기에 갈 수 있으면 좋겠다. 그곳에 대해 더 얘기해 줘.

정답 ④

해설 남자는 날씨는 추웠지만, 여행을 많이 할 수 있었다고 말하고 있다.

기출문장

수치

Ann is **as tall as** Maria. Ann은 Maria만큼 키가 크다.

Ann is **the youngest of** the three. Ann은 셋 중에서 가장 어리다.

John has **as many math classes as** Kate. John은 Kate만큼 수학 수업을 많이 듣는다.

John has **fewer** P. E classes **than** Kate. John은 Kate보다 체육 수업을 덜 듣는다.

Math is **the most popular** subject. 수학은 가장 인기 있는 과목이다.

English is **not as popular as** science. 영어는 과학만큼 인기 있지 않다.

Science is **more popular than** math. 과학은 수학보다 더 인기 있다.

The same number of students like watching TV. 같은 수의 학생들이 TV 보는 것을 좋아한다.

In my class, scientist was **the most popular job.** 우리 반에서 과학자는 가장 인기 있는 직업이었다.

The number one job is usually teacher or entertainer. 최고의 직업은 대개 선생님이나 연예인이다.

수치 & 그래프 same 같은 popular 인기 있는 most 가장 ~한/하게 least 가장 덜 ~한/하게 less 덜 ~한/하게 as … as ~ ~만큼 …한/하게

메모

Can I **take a message**? 메모를 남기시겠어요?

May I **leave a message**? 메모를 남겨도 될까요?

I'm **calling to change our appointment.** 약속을 변경하려고 전화를 했습니다.

When you get this message, please **call me back.** 이 메시지를 받으면 저에게 전화해 주세요.

She said she **would visit** you this Saturday afternoon. 그녀는 이번주 토요일 오후에 당신을 방문할 거라고 말했어요.

Please **tell him call me** back as soon as possible. 가능한 한 빨리 저에게 전화해 달라고 그에게 전해주세요.

메모 message 메시지 appointment 약속 change 변경하다, 바꾸다 cancel 취소하다

광고 & 안내문

The city library **is open from Monday to Saturday.** 시립 도서관은 월요일부터 토요일까지 문을 엽니다.

You **have to be quiet** in the library. 도서관에서는 조용하셔야 합니다.

The city library **opens at ten in the morning.** 시립 도서관은 아침 10시에 문을 엽니다.

You **shouldn't drink anything** inside the library. 도서관 안에서는 아무것도 마시면 안 됩니다.

Riding a bike keeps you healthy and slim. 자전거를 타는 것은 건강을 유지시켜 주고 날씬하게 해 줍니다.

Please **come and join us.** 오셔서 저희와 함께 해요.

Blue Sea Restaurant **opens every day.** Blue Sea Restaurant는 매일 문을 엽니다.

People can **have breakfast in the morning.** 아침 식사를 하실 수 있습니다.

Blue Sea Restaurant **is at 35 Park Street, New York.** Blue Sea Restaurant는 뉴욕, Park가 35번지에 있습니다.

People can **call the restaurant at 782-9567.** 782-9567번으로 전화하세요.

상점 open (상점, 은행 등이) 문을 연[영업을 하는]; 문을 열다 opening hours 영업 시간 closed (상점, 건물들이) 문을 닫은 closing time 문 닫는 시간(마감 시간)

기출풀기

1 다음을 듣고, 초대장의 내용과 일치하지 않는 것을 고르시오.

① ② ③ ④

2 대화를 듣고, 내용과 일치하지 않는 것을 고르시오.

Schedule for Vacation

① Season: Summer
② Place to visit: Paris
③ Transportation: Airplane
④ How long: 14 days
⑤ Place to stay: David's home

3 대화를 듣고, 대화와 일치하지 않는 것을 고르시오.

① Sally is Yumi's best friend.
② Sally has long hair.
③ Sally doesn't live near Yumi any longer.
④ Sally will come to see Yumi this weekend.

4 다음을 듣고, 잠을 잘 자기 위한 방법으로 제시되지 않은 것을 고르시오.

① 저녁에 커피 안 마시기
② 낮잠 자지 않기
③ 침실 조명 어둡게 하기
④ 따뜻한 우유 마시기
⑤ 밤늦게 TV 보지 않기

5 다음 대화에 나타난 여자의 증상이 아닌 것을 고르시오.

① 발열 ② 두통 ③ 콧물 ④ 기침

Part 6 숫자 – 날짜 · 시각 · 금액

기출엿보기

1 대화를 듣고, 남자가 받을 거스름돈으로 알맞은 것을 고르시오.

① $3 ② $4 ③ $5 ④ $6 ⑤ $7

Script

W May I help you?

M Yes, I'd like to order **a chicken burger** and a soda. **How much are they**?

W A chicken burger is **4 dollars** and a soda is **2 dollars**.

M Here's **ten dollars**.

W Here's your change.

해석

여 도와드릴까요?

남 네, 치킨버거 하나와 탄산음료 하나를 주문하고 싶습니다. 얼마예요?

여 치킨버거는 4달러이고 탄산음료는 2달러입니다.

남 여기 10달러 있습니다.

여 여기 거스름돈입니다.

정답 ②

해설 남자는 4달러짜리 치킨 버거와 2달러짜리 탄산 음료를 각각 하나씩 주문했고, 10달러를 점원에게 주었다.

2 대화를 듣고, 남자가 방문하기로 한 시각을 고르시오.

① 1:30 ② 2:00 ③ 3:00 ④ 3:30

Script

[Telephone rings.]

M Hello. This is ABC Computer. How can I help you?

W My computer is not working. Can you **send someone to check** it?

M I can come **this afternoon**. What is a good time for you?

W Can you come at two?

M Sorry. I **have appointments from one thirty** to three. How about **three thirty**?

W That's good. See you then.

해석

남 안녕하세요. ABC 컴퓨터입니다. 무엇을 도와드릴까요?

여 제 컴퓨터가 작동하지 않아서요. 점검을 위해 사람 좀 보내주시겠어요?

남 오늘 오후에 방문할 수 있습니다. 언제가 괜찮으신가요?

여 2시에 오실 수 있나요?

남 죄송합니다. 1시 30분부터 3시까지 약속이 있어서요. 3시 30분은 어떠세요?

여 좋아요. 그럼 그때 뵐게요.

정답 ④

해설 1시 30분부터 3시까지는 약속이 안 된다고 하고 3시 반에 방문하면 어떻겠냐는 남자의 말에 여자는 좋다고 말하고 있다.

기출문장

시간

What time does the movie **start**? 언제 영화가 시작하니?

When does it **end**? 그것은 언제 끝나니?

Why don't **we meet** at 6:10 at the restaurant? 식당에서 6시 10분에 만나는 게 어때?

We will be **landing** at Incheon International Airport in 10 minutes. 우리는 10분 후에 인천국제공항에 착륙하게 됩니다.

What time shall we **meet**? 우리 언제 만날까?

What time does it **leave**? 그것은 언제 출발하나요?

You only **have ten more minutes.** 너는 10분밖에 남지 않았어.

When does the next train leave for New York? 뉴욕행 다음 기차가 언제 출발하나요?

Do you have the time? 몇 시인가요?

It's **a quarter to eleven.** 11시 15분 전입니다.

How often does the bus leave for Gangneung? 강릉행 버스는 얼마나 자주 있나요?

It **leaves every thirty minutes.** 그것은 30분마다 출발합니다.

What is a good time for you? 언제가 편하니?

Can you make it at ten? 10시에 만날 수 있니?

시간을 나타내는 표현 o'clock 정각 quarter 15분 half 30분 end 끝나다 five to five 5시 5분전 ten to one 1시 10분전 ten after one 1시 10분 half past ten 10시 반 a quarter to ten 10시 15분전 noon 정오 midnight 자정, 한밤중

금액

That comes to 10,000 won. 10,000원입니다.

I **have a coupon for** 10% off. 저에게 10% 할인 쿠폰이 있습니다.

It's 50% off. 50% 세일입니다.

How much is **the fare**? 요금이 얼마인가요?

Here's your **change.** 여기 거스름돈이 있습니다.

They are **five dollars each.** 그것들은 각각 5달러입니다.

금액 How much is ~? ~ 얼마입니까? discount 할인; 할인하다 off 할인되어 coupon 쿠폰 change 거스름돈 fare 요금 cost 비용이 들다

날짜 & 요일

What date is it today? 오늘이 며칠이니?

What day is it today? 오늘이 무슨 요일이니?

We **have five more days until** the science test. 과학 시험까지는 5일이 더 남았다.

There are **two more days left.** 이틀이 더 남았다.

It's **the third Saturday of this month.** 이번달 셋째 주 토요일이야.

It's **next Saturday!** 다음 주 토요일이야!

날짜나 요일을 나타내는 표현 next Monday 다음 주 월요일 last Monday 지난 월요일 every weekend 매주 주말 on the 5th of May 5월 5일에 the day after tomorrow 모레 the day before yesterday 그저께

기출풀기

1 대화를 듣고, 두 사람이 만날 시각으로 알맞은 것을 고르시오.

① 6:20 ② 6:30 ③ 6:40 ④ 6:50 ⑤ 7:00

2 대화를 듣고, 여자가 남자에게 빌려준 금액을 고르시오.

① 15 cents ② 50 cents
③ 1.50 dollars ④ 2 dollars

3 대화를 듣고, 여자의 생일로 알맞은 것을 고르시오.

Sun	Mon	Tue	Wed	Thu	Fri	Sat
1	2	3	4	5	6	7
8	9	10	11	12	13	14
15	16	17	18	19	20	21
22	23	24	25	26	27	28

① 12일 ② 14일 ③ 21일 ④ 28일

4 대화를 듣고, 남자가 옷값으로 지불해야 할 금액을 고르시오.

① 10,000원 ② 20,000원
③ 30,000원 ④ 40,000원

5 대화를 듣고, 현재 시각으로 알맞은 것을 고르시오.

① 7:00 ② 7:10 ③ 7:20 ④ 7:30

Part 7 목적, 의도

기출엿보기

1 대화를 듣고, 여자가 남자에게 전화를 건 목적을 고르시오.

① 숙제를 함께 하려고 ② 설문조사를 하려고
③ 일자리를 제공하려고 ④ 책 반납일을 알려주려고

Script

[Telephone rings.]

M Hello?

W Hello, this is Rainbow Library. May I speak to David, please?

M Speaking.

W Hi, **the books** you borrowed from the library **are due today**. Could you **return the books today**?

M I'm not sure, but I think I can make it this afternoon. Thank you for calling.

W You're welcome.

해석

남 여보세요?

여 여보세요, 무지개 도서관입니다. David와 통화할 수 있을까요?

남 전데요.

여 안녕하세요. 도서관에서 대출하신 책이 오늘까지입니다. 오늘 책을 반납해주실 수 있으신가요?

남 확실하진 않은데 오늘 오후에 반납할 수 있을 것 같습니다. 전화 주셔서 감사합니다.

여 천만에요.

정답 ④

해설 the books you borrowed from the library are due today라는 여자의 말을 통해서 남자가 대출한 책의 대여기간이 오늘까지임을 알 수 있다.

2 대화를 듣고, 여자가 마지막에 한 말의 의도를 고르시오.

① 충고 ② 감사 ③ 칭찬 ④ 동의

Script

W Mike, how do you like your new school?

M It's very nice. The teachers are kind and the cafeteria is good. But it is a little far from my house.

W Do you walk to school?

M Yes, it **takes 30 minutes** and I'm always late.

W Then you **should leave earlier.**

해석

여 Mike야, 새 학교는 어떠니?

남 정말 좋아요. 선생님들도 친절하시고, 식당도 좋고요. 하지만, 집에서 조금 멀어요.

여 학교에서 걸어서 가니?

남 네, 30분이 걸려서 항상 지각을 해요.

여 그렇다면, 더 일찍 집을 나서는 게 좋겠구나.

정답 ①

해설 지각을 한다는 남자에게 집에서 일찍 출발하라고 충고하고 있다.

기출문장

목적

⇨ 예약

I'd like to **make a reservation.** 예약을 하고 싶습니다.

I'd like to **make a reservation** to go to Canada next Sunday. 다음 주 일요일 캐나다행을 예약하고 싶습니다.

⇨ 환불 & 교환

Would you like to **exchange** them? 저것들을 교환해 드릴까요? / I'd like to **have a refund.** 환불하고 싶습니다.

Do you **want** your **money back** or **would you like to exchange** it? 환불을 해드릴까요, 아니면 교환을 해드릴까요?

⇨ 요청 & 독촉

I ordered a pizza an hour ago, but it's **not here** yet. 한 시간 전에 피자를 주문했는데, 아직 도착하지 않았습니다.

I'd like to go volunteering. **Can you join** me? 나 봉사활동하러 가고 싶어. 너도 참여할래?

Can you **help** me? 저 좀 도와주세요. / **Can** you **come with** me? 나랑 같이 갈래?

⇨ 약속 변경 & 약속 취소

I want to meet him at seven o'clock, **instead.** 대신에 7시에 그를 만나고 싶습니다.

I'm afraid I **can't meet** you **tonight.** 오늘 밤에 너를 만날 수 없을 것 같아.

약속 & 예약 cancel 취소하다 change 변경하다 appointment 약속 make a reservation 예약하다 confirm 확인하다

의도

⇨ 요청

Will you bring me the book? 책을 좀 갖다 줄래? / **Do you lend** me some money? 나에게 돈을 좀 빌려 줄래?

Can you **give me a hand**? 나를 좀 도와줄래? / Would you **do me a favor**? 내 부탁 좀 들어줄래?

⇨ 위로 & 격려

That's too bad. 그거 안됐구나. / **I'm sorry to hear that.** 그 소식을 들어 유감입니다.

That's a pity. 안됐다. / **Don't worry. You'll be fine.** 걱정하지 마. 잘 될 거야.

I think you **can do it.** 나는 네가 할 수 있을 거라고 생각해. / **Cheer up!** 힘내!

⇨ 충고

Why don't you call the service center? 고객 센터로 전화를 해보지 그러니?

Maybe **you should** try another sport like swimming. 아마도 너는 수영과 같은 다른 운동을 해야 할 거야.

Then, **you should** leave earlier. 그렇다면 좀 일찍 떠나.

I think you **had better say** sorry to them. 나는 네가 그들에게 미안하다고 말해야 할 것 같아.

⇨ 동의

Me, too. So am[do] **I.** 나도 그래. / That's **fine with** me. 난 좋아.

I **agree with** you. 나는 네 말에 동의해. / That's **a good idea.** 좋은 생각이야.

⇨ 거절 & 사과

No, thank you. 사양하겠습니다. / **I'm sorry, but** I'm going to China next week. 미안한데, 나 다음주에 중국에 가야 해.

I'd like to, but I have to ask my mom first. 그러고 싶지만, 엄마한테 먼저 물어봐야 해.

I'm sorry. I didn't know that. 미안해. 모르고 있었어.

기출풀기

1 **대화를 듣고, 남자가 전화를 건 목적을 고르시오.**

① 약속 장소를 묻기 위해
② 약속 시간을 묻기 위해
③ 회의 불참을 말하기 위해
④ 도착 방법을 묻기 위해
⑤ 지각에 대한 양해를 구하기 위해

2 **대화를 듣고, 여자가 전화를 건 목적을 고르시오.**

① 식당 예약 ② 방문 약속
③ 음식 주문 ④ 차표 예매

3 **대화를 듣고, 여자가 하는 말의 의도로 알맞은 것을 고르시오.**

① 사과 ② 충고 ③ 축하 ④ 칭찬

4 **대화를 듣고, 여자가 하는 말의 의도로 알맞은 것을 고르시오.**

① 사과 ② 변명 ③ 충고 ④ 칭찬

5 **대화를 듣고, 남자가 편지를 쓰는 목적을 고르시오.**

① 초대 ② 사과 ③ 의논 ④ 감사

Part 8 심정, 이유

기출엿보기

1 **대화를 듣고, 남자의 심정을 고르시오.**

① 설렘 ② 걱정 ③ 놀람 ④ 부러움

Script

W So, you're **planning to go to Paris** this vacation?

M Yes, I'll visit my sister who is studying there and travel around Paris.

W What do you want to see there?

M I **want to see** the Eiffel Tower.

W You must **be excited**!

M **You bet**! **I can't wait**!

해석

여 그래서, 이번 방학에 너 파리에 갈 계획이니?

남 응, 거기서 공부하는 누나를 방문하고 파리에서 여행할 거야.

여 거기서 무엇을 보고 싶니?

남 에펠탑을 보고 싶어.

여 너 신나겠다!

남 그럼! 기다릴 수가 없어!

정답 ①

해설 남자는 이번 방학에 파리에 가는 것을 기다릴 수 없을 정도로 신난다고 말하고 있다. I can't wait!는 너무 기대돼 기다릴 수가 없다는 의미를 나타낸다.

2 **대화를 듣고, 여자가 집에 일찍 가는 이유를 고르시오.**

① 배가 고파서 ② 잠이 부족해서
③ 감기에 걸려서 ④ 손님이 오셔서

Script

W Mike, I want to **go home early** today.

M What's wrong?

W I **have a headache**.

M Do you **have a cold**?

W No. I stayed up late last night. I think I **need more sleep**.

M I see. **Go home and get some sleep**.

해석

여 Mike, 나 오늘 집에 일찍 가고 싶어.

남 무슨 일이니?

여 머리가 아파.

남 감기에 걸린 거야?

여 아니. 어제 늦게까지 깨어 있었거든. 잠을 좀 자야 할 것 같아.

남 그렇구나. 집에 가서 잠을 좀 자도록 해.

정답 ②

해설 여자는 어젯밤 늦게까지 깨어 있느라고 잠을 못 자 머리가 아프다고 말하고 있다.

기출문장

심정

⇨ 기쁨, 즐거움, 흥분

I'm **proud** of myself. 난 내 자신이 자랑스러워. / **Good for you**! 잘됐어!

That**'s amazing**. 굉장해. / I **can't wait**! 못 기다리겠어.

I'm really looking forward to it. 나는 그것을 학수고대하고 있어.

⇨ 걱정, 초조함, 두려움

What **should I do**? She will be really **mad at** me! 어떻게 하지? 그녀는 정말 나에게 화를 낼 텐데!

I have an English speech contest tomorrow, so I am **very nervous**. 내일 영어 말하기 대회가 있는데 정말 떨려.

I'm taking a test tomorrow, but I **haven't studied**. 내일 시험을 보는데, 공부를 안 했어.

I'm afraid that I will fail the exam. 시험에 떨어질까 봐 두려워.

I'm **so scared**. 나 정말 무서워.

⇨ 실망

That's too bad. I really want to see you. 아쉽다. 너를 정말로 만나고 싶은데.

He **can't come to** my party. 그가 내 파티에 못 온대.

⇨ 확신 & 희망

I'm sure our team will win. 나는 우리 팀이 이길 거라고 확신해.

I hope she gets well soon. 그녀가 곧 낫기를 바라.

⇨ 미안함

I'm sorry, but I can't go there with you. 미안한데, 나 너와 함께 갈 수 없어.

I made so many **mistakes**. 정말 많은 실수를 했어. / It's **all my fault**. 모두 내 잘못이야.

심정 & 태도

긍정 : excited 흥분한, 신난 pleased 기쁜, 즐거운 satisfied 만족한 happy 행복한 joyful 기쁜, 즐거운 glad 기쁜 funny 재미있는 interesting 재미있는 hopeful 희망에 찬 cheerful 쾌활한 grateful 고마운

부정 : worried 걱정스러운 disappointed 실망한 angry 화난 bored 지루한 lonely 외로운 sad 슬픈 surprised 놀란 nervous 초조한 depressed 우울한 upset 화난, 기분 나쁜 afraid 두려워하는 scared 겁먹은 annoyed 짜증난

이유

I'm very busy studying math on-line. 온라인으로 수학 공부하느라 매우 바빠.

Your school is not far. Just **walk to** school. 학교가 멀지 않으니까 그냥 학교에 걸어서 가거라.

I know they were laughing **because** I had my sweater on inside out.
그들이 왜 웃었는지 알겠어. 왜냐하면 내가 옷을 뒤집어서 입고 있었어.

⇨ 늦은 이유

There was traffic jam, **so** all the cars were going so slowly. 교통 체증 때문에 모든 차들이 천천히 움직이고 있었어.

I got up early, but **the traffic was heavy**. 일찍 일어났는데, 교통 체증이 심했어.

이유를 나타내는 표현 What happened? 무슨 일이 있었니? What's wrong? / What's the matter? 무슨 일이니? How come ~? 왜 ~?

기출풀기

1 **대화를 듣고, 여자의 심정으로 가장 알맞은 것을 고르시오.**

① 걱정됨　② 실망함　③ 미안함　④ 무관심

2 **대화를 듣고, 마지막 부분에서 두 사람이 느낄 심정으로 가장 적절한 것을 고르시오.**

① lonely　② happy
③ glad　④ disappointed
⑤ funny

3 **대화를 듣고, Jane이 학교에 오지 않은 이유를 고르시오.**

① 몸이 아파서
② 숙제를 못해서
③ 다른 학교로 전학을 가서
④ 웅변대회에 참가하러 가서

4 **대화를 듣고, 남자가 주말에 할아버지 댁을 방문하려는 이유를 고르시오.**

① 휴식을 취하려고
② 농장 일을 도우려고
③ 가족사진을 찍으려고
④ 할아버지 생신을 축하하려고

5 **대화를 듣고, 여자의 기분으로 알맞은 것을 고르시오.**

① angry　② happy　③ bored　④ scared

Part 9 조언, 속담

기출엿보기

1 **대화를 듣고, 관련 있는 속담으로 알맞은 것을 고르시오.**

① 뜻이 있는 곳에 길이 있다.
② 어려울 때의 친구가 진짜 친구다.
③ 로마에 가면 로마의 풍습을 따르라.
④ 낮말은 새가 듣고, 밤말은 쥐가 듣는다.

Script

W Would you take off your shoes?
M Excuse me? Do I have to **take off my shoes**?
W **Koreans do not wear shoes** in the living room.
M Oh, I'm sorry I didn't know that.
W Thanks for **understanding our custom**.
M You're welcome.

해석

여 신발을 벗어 주시겠어요?
남 뭐라고요? 제 신발을 벗어야 하나요?
여 한국인들은 거실에서 신발을 신지 않아요.
남 아, 죄송합니다. 그것을 몰랐습니다.
여 저희 풍습을 이해해 주셔서 감사해요.
남 별말씀을요.

정답 ③

해설 여자가 남자에게 한국인은 거실에서 신발을 신지 않는 풍습이 있다며 남자에게 신발을 벗으라고 요청하고 있다.

2 **다음을 듣고, 내용과 가장 관련 있는 속담을 고르시오.**

① Look before you leap.
② Better late than never.
③ Practice makes perfect.
④ Spare the rod, spoil the child.
⑤ Two heads are better than one.

Script

M Mr. Kim was a famous doctor. He made lots of money. But he was not happy because he was too busy. Thinking **it's never too late to change** his **job, he started to attend a cooking school**, and finally when he was 50, he became a chef. Now, he owns a restaurant and enjoys his job. He is happy now.

해석

남 김 씨는 유명한 의사였습니다. 그는 돈을 많이 벌었습니다. 하지만, 그는 너무 바빴기 때문에 그는 행복하지 않았습니다. 직업을 바꾸기에 결코 늦지 않았다고 생각하면서, 그는 요리 학교에 나가기 시작했고 마침내, 그가 50세가 되었을 때, 요리사가 되었습니다. 지금 그는 식당을 운영하고 있고 그의 직업을 즐기고 있습니다. 그는 이제 행복합니다.

정답 ②

해설 늦었다고 포기하지 않고 도전해 결국 직업을 바꿔 지금은 행복한 삶을 살고 있다고 말하고 있으므로 '늦더라도 안 하느니 보다는 낫다.'라는 의미의 속담 ②을 고른다.

기출문장

충고

Please **have breakfast.** 아침을 먹어라.

You **should take** some medicine. 약을 드셔야 합니다.

My advice is to take it easy and get lots of rest. 제 조언은 긴장을 풀고 푹 쉬라는 것입니다.

We **should save** water. 우리는 물을 절약해야 해.

Why don't you study harder in class? 공부를 더 열심히 하는 건 어때?

You **should not** drink coffee or tea in the evening. 저녁에 커피나 차를 마시지 말아야 한다.

You'**d better go** and see. 네가 가서 보는 게 낫겠어.

충고 & 조언 should ~해야 한다 had better ~하는 것이 낫겠다[좋다] why don't you ~? ~하는 게 어때? advice 조언

속담

Time flies. 시간은 빨리 흐른다.

Seeing is believing. 백문이 불여일견이다.

Even Homer nods. 원숭이도 나무에서 떨어질 때가 있다.

A friend in need is a friend indeed. 어려울 때 친구가 진정한 친구이다.

Time flies when you're having fun. 재미나게 보내는 시간은 빨리 흐른다.

When in Rome, do as the Romans do. 로마에 가면 로마법을 따르라.

No pains, no gains. 고통 없이는 얻는 것도 없다.

A stitch in time saves nine. 제때의 한 바늘이 뒤의 아홉 바늘을 던다.

A good medicine tastes bitter. 좋은 약은 입에 쓰다.

Walls have ears. 벽에도 귀가 있다. (낮말은 새가 듣고 밤말은 쥐가 듣는다.)

It's a piece of cake. 누워서 떡 먹기.

No news is good news. 무소식이 희소식이다.

Practice makes perfect. 연습이 완벽을 만든다.

Two heads are better than one. 백지장도 맞들면 낫다.

Don't judge a book by its cover. 표지로 책을 판단하지 마라.

Don't put all your eggs in one basket. 한 가지 일에 몽땅 다 걸지 마라.

Look before you leap. 돌다리도 두드려 보고 건너라.

Better late than never. 늦더라도 안 하느니 보다는 낫다.

Spare the rod, and spoil the child. 매를 아끼면 아이를 버린다.

The early bird catches the worm. 일찍 일어나는 새가 벌레를 잡는다.

The pen is mightier than the sword. 펜은 칼보다 강하다.

Where there is a way, there is will. 뜻이 있는 곳에 길이 있다.

It never rains but pours. (= Misfortune seldom comes singly.) 엎친 데 덮친 격이다.

Every dog has his day. 쥐구멍에도 볕 들 날 있다.

Well begun is half done. 시작이 반이다.

A little knowledge is a dangerous thing. 선무당이 사람 잡는다. (어설프게 아는 지식이 위험하다.)

기출풀기

1 **대화를 듣고, 남자에게 해 줄 수 있는 충고를 고르시오.**

① 직업을 자주 바꾸지 마라.
② 처음에 실패하더라도 너무 낙담하지 마라.
③ 학문에는 왕도가 없으니, 열심히 공부해라.
④ 외모를 보고 사람을 판단하지 마라

2 **대화를 듣고, 대화의 내용과 관계 깊은 속담을 고르시오.**

① No pains, no gains.
② A stitch in time saves nine.
③ A good medicine tastes bitter.
④ A friend in need is a friend indeed.

3 **다음을 듣고, 남자에게 조언해 줄 수 있는 속담으로 알맞은 것을 고르시오.**

① Walls have ears.
② It's a piece of cake.
③ No news is good news.
④ Practice makes perfect.

4 **대화를 듣고, 내용에 어울리는 속담을 고르시오.**

① 엎친 데 덮친 격이다.
② 백지장도 맞들면 낫다.
③ 쥐구멍에도 볕들 날 있다.
④ 어려울 때 친구가 진정한 친구다.

5 **다음 들려주는 내용과 의미가 가장 가까운 속담을 고르시오.**

① Birds of a feather flock together.
② A rolling stone gathers no moss.
③ When in Rome do as the Romans do.
④ Kill two birds with one stone.

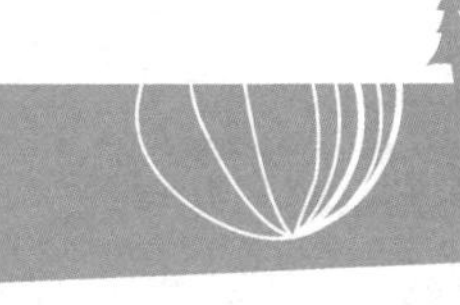

Part 10 상황·파악

기출엿보기

1 **대화를 듣고, 이어서 들려주는 질문에 알맞은 답을 고르시오.**

① 화가 ② 의사 ③ 변호사 ④ 마술사

Script

M What **do you want to be** when you **grow up**, Maggie?

W I want to **be an artist**.

M Who's your favorite artist, then?

W Picasso. How about you, John?

M I love magic, so I want to be a **magician**. But my parents want me to be a **doctor**.

질문입니다.

W What do John's parents want him to be?

해석

남 넌 커서 무엇이 되고 싶니, Maggie?

여 난 화가가 되고 싶어.

남 그럼 네가 가장 좋아하는 화가는 누구니?

여 피카소야. 너는, John?

남 난 마술을 좋아해서 마술사가 되고 싶어. 하지만, 내 부모님께선 내가 의사가 되길 바라셔.

정답 ②

해설 남자는 마술사가 되고 싶지만, 부모님께서는 의사가 되길 원하신다고 말하고 있다. 화가는 여자의 장래 희망이다.

2 **다음을 듣고, Tony가 할 말로 가장 적절한 것을 고르시오.**

① When can I talk to her?

② Don't worry. I'll call back.

③ Would you like to leave a message?

④ I'm afraid you have the wrong number.

⑤ Please tell her to call me when she comes home.

Script

M Tony **makes a phone call** to his classmate Sujin to ask her for some help. Sujin's father answers the phone and says **she is out**. He also says that he doesn't have any idea when she will come back. Tony really needs Sujin's help to finish **his homework** and wants her **to call him back** when she **gets home**. In this situation, what would Tony say to Sujin's father?

해석

남 Tony는 도움을 청하기 위해 자신의 반 친구, Sujin에게 전화를 겁니다. Sujin의 아버지가 그 전화를 받고, 그녀가 나갔다고 말합니다. 그는 또한 그녀가 언제 돌아올지 모른다고 말합니다. Tony는 자신의 숙제를 끝내려면 Sujin의 도움이 정말 필요했고, 그녀가 집에 들어오면 그에게 전화를 해주길 원합니다. 이 상황에서 당신은 Sujin의 아버지께 뭐라고 얘기하시겠습니까?

정답 ⑤

해설 Tony는 Sujin이 집에 돌아오면 자신에게 전화를 해달라는 말을 Sujin의 아버지께 해야 하기 때문에 그에 알맞은 영어 표현은 ⑤이 적절하다.

기출문장

상황을 묻는 질문 유형

In this case, what **would you say** to the teacher? 이런 경우에, 당신은 선생님에게 뭐라고 얘기하겠습니까?

In this situation, **what would** Tony say to Sujin's father? 이런 상황에서, Tony는 Sujin의 아버지에게 무엇이라고 말할까요?

What would you say to the student? 당신은 그 학생에게 뭐라고 말하겠습니까?

If you'd like to say something to him before the contest, **what would you say**?
대회 전에 그에게 무언가를 말하고 싶다면 당신은 뭐라고 말하겠습니까?

내용 확인을 확인하는 질문 유형

What does Linda **have to do** tonight? Linda는 오늘 밤에 무엇을 해야 하나요?

What is the woman **doing**? 여자는 무엇을 하고 있나요?

What are they **talking about**? 그들은 무엇에 대해 얘기하고 있나요?

What time did **today's first period start**? 오늘 첫 쉬는 시간은 언제 시작했습니까?

What's wrong with the restaurant? 그 식당은 무슨 문제가 있습니까?

What time will the man arrive in Busan? 남자는 언제 부산에 도착할까요?

How much is the watch now? 시계는 지금 얼마입니까?

Where is Mike **going to go this afternoon**? 오늘 오후에 Mike는 어디에 갈 예정인가요?

Why is Ji-hoon **going to the library**? 지훈이는 왜 도서관에 갑니까?

What time will John **go to bed**? John은 언제 잠을 잘 것인가요?

Where did the car accident **happen**? 어디서 자동차 사고가 발생했나요?

What did the woman **bring** to the shop? 여자가 가게로 가져간 것은 무엇인가요?

How much is it? 그것은 얼마인가요?

What do John's parents **want** him **to be**? John의 부모님께서는 그가 무엇이 되길 원하시나요?

기출풀기

1 다음을 듣고, 마지막 질문에 가장 알맞은 답을 고르시오.

① How long does it take?
② Can you help me, please?
③ What time shall we meet?
④ Can you show me the way?

2 대화를 듣고, 이어지는 질문에 알맞은 응답을 고르시오.

① a report ② a printer
③ a computer ④ a copy machine

3 대화를 듣고, 이어지는 질문에 대한 응답으로 가장 알맞은 것을 고르시오.

① hiking ② jogging
③ swimming ④ jumping ropes

4 대화를 듣고, 주어진 질문의 대답으로 알맞은 것을 고르시오.

Menu		
Pizza	Regular: $7	Large: $10
Coke	Small: $3	Large: $5

① $10 ② $12 ③ $13 ④ $15

5 다음을 듣고, 상황에 가장 알맞은 표현을 고르시오.

① Thank you. I have enough time.
② I have already finished it.
③ Can I have a few more minutes, please?
④ Excuse me, do you have the time?

Part II 어색한 대화

기출엿보기

1

대화를 듣고, 두 사람의 대화가 어색한 것을 고르시오.

① ② ③ ④ ⑤

Script

Number 1 W **How often** do you go to the cinema?
M **Once a month**.

Number 2 W **What** are you **going to do** this weekend?
M I went to Seoul last Saturday.

Number 3 W **How many subjects** do you study?
M I study **eleven**.

Number 4 W May I **help** you?
M Yes, I **want to buy** a laptop computer.

Number 5 W **What** do you **think** of **this concert**?
M It's **fantastic**.

해석

① 여 너는 얼마나 자주 영화보러 가니?
남 한 달에 한 번.

② 여 이번 주말에 너는 무엇을 할 거니?
남 나는 지난주 토요일에 서울에 다녀왔어.

③ 여 너는 몇 과목을 공부하니?
남 나는 11과목을 공부해.

④ 여 도와드릴까요?
남 네, 노트북 컴퓨터를 사고 싶어요.

⑤ 여 이 콘서트에 대해 어떻게 생각하니?
남 정말 멋져.

정답 ②

해설 여자는 이번 주에 할 일을 묻고 남자는 지난주에 한 일을 대답하고 있다.

2

다음을 듣고, 두 사람의 대화가 어색한 것을 고르시오.

① ② ③ ④

Script

Number 1 M **Would you get** me some milk?
W **Okay**, no problem.

Number 2 M **Why don't you** come camping with my family?
W I'd like to, but **I have to ask my** mom first.

Number 3 M Oh! I didn't **do well on** my English exam.
W I'm **sorry to hear that**. But you'll do better next time.

Number 4 M **How was** your trip to Europe?
W That's **fine** with me.

해석

① 남 저에게 우유를 갖다 주시겠어요?
여 네, 알겠습니다.

② 남 우리 가족과 함께 캠핑 가는 건 어때?
여 그러고 싶은데, 먼저 엄마께 여쭤 봐야 해.

③ 남 오! 영어 시험에서 잘 보지 못했어.
여 그 소식을 들어서 유감이야. 하지만, 다음번엔 잘할 수 있을 거야.

④ 남 유럽 여행은 어땠니?
여 전 괜찮아요.

정답 ④

해설 유럽 여행이 어땠는지 묻고 있는 질문에 알맞은 응답이 와야 한다.

기출문장

안부

Long time no see. 오래간만입니다.
How have you **been**? 잘 지내셨어요?
Where have you **been**? 어디 다녀오셨어요?
What's the matter with you? 무슨 일이니?
How was your **school** today? 오늘 학교에서 어땠니?
It's so **nice to see** you again. 다시 만나서 반가웠습니다.

경험

How was the musical? 그 뮤지컬은 어땠니?
What did you do **on the weekend**? 주말에 뭐 했니?
I didn't **do well on** my math test. 시험을 잘 보지 못했어.
Have you been to the new coffee shop? 그 새 커피숍에 가 봤니?
Have you heard about "The Summer Festival" at ABC park? ABC 공원에서 하는 '여름 축제'에 대해서 들어본 적 있니?
Have you seen Mr. Kim lately? 최근에 김 씨를 본 적 있니?

습관

How often do you exercise? 너 얼마나 자주 운동을 하니?
What do you usually do on Sunday? 너 일요일에는 주로 뭐하니?
What is your **hobby**? 네 취미는 무엇이니?
How do you get to school? 넌 어떻게 학교에 가니?
How long do you usually sleep? 주로 몇 시간 동안 잠을 자니?
How long does it take to go to school? 학교까지 가는 데 얼마나 걸리십니까?

취향 & 선택

What's your **favorite** subject? 네가 제일 좋아하는 과목이 무엇이니?
Which one do you **want** for a present? 생일 선물로 무엇을 받고 싶니?

약속

Can we **make it** at three? 3시에 만날 수 있을까?
Can you meet me at four o'clock at the library? 4시에 도서관에서 만날 수 있을까?
Let's meet at the bus stop at 5. 5시에 버스 정거장에서 만나자.
I **forgot** about the **appointment** to meet my friend. 내 친구 만나기로 한 약속을 잊어버렸어.

부탁 & 요청

Can I use your cell phone? 네 휴대 전화를 써도 될까?
Would you show me the way to City Hall? 시청 가는 길을 알려주시겠어요?
Would you turn down the music? 음악을 줄여주시겠어요?
Do you have this shirt in large? 이 셔츠 큰 사이즈로 있나요?
Where can I find the Harry Potter Books? 해리포터 책을 어디서 찾을 수 있나요?
Can I borrow your laptop computer now? 지금 네 노트북 컴퓨터를 빌릴 수 있을까?
Can you tell me where I am? 제가 지금 어디 있는지 말씀해주시겠어요?
Will you help me with the dishes? 설거지 하는 데 나를 좀 도와줄래?
Do you want some more cake? 케이크 좀 더 드시겠어요?
Would you like some more bread? 빵을 좀 더 드시겠어요?

이유 묻기

Why do you **look** so sad? 너 왜 그렇게 슬퍼 보이니?
Why have you **come** to Korea? 왜 한국에 오시게 되셨나요?

의견 구하기 & 제안하기

How about going to the concert? 음악회에 가는 건 어때?
Will you join us? 우리와 함께 가시겠어요?
Why don't you take a taxi? 택시를 타는 건 어때?
What do you think of this picture? 이 사진에 대해서 어떻게 생각하니?
Why don't we do our homework together? 숙제를 같이 하는 게 어때?

기타 질문

Are you **ready to order**? 주문할 준비되셨나요?
Help yourself to some cake. 케이크를 마음껏 드세요.
When is your birthday? 네 생일은 언제니?
How can I get there? 거기에 제가 어떻게 갈 수 있죠?
How much is this CD? 이 CD는 얼마인가요?
How many people are there in your family? 너희 가족은 몇 명이니?
Is it going to rain? 비가 올까?

기출풀기

1 다음을 듣고, 두 사람의 대화가 어색한 것을 고르시오.

① ② ③ ④

2 대화를 듣고, 자연스럽지 않은 것을 고르시오.

① ② ③ ④

3 다음을 듣고, 두 사람의 대화가 어색한 것을 고르시오.

① ② ③ ④

4 대화를 듣고, 두 사람의 대화가 어색한 것을 고르시오.

① ② ③ ④ ⑤

5 다음을 듣고, 자연스럽지 않은 대화를 고르시오.

① ② ③ ④

Part 12 알맞은 응답 파악

기출엿보기

1 대화를 듣고, 남자의 마지막 말에 대한 여자의 응답으로 가장 적절한 것을 고르시오.

① I didn't do anything to him
② I was so nervous.
③ My brother had a spare key.
④ Finally, I had a nice car.
⑤ My neighbor asked me a lot.

Script

M **Why** are you **so late**?
W I **couldn't open** my car.
M Oh, really?
W Yes! I **left the keys** in it.
M You locked them in the car?
W That's right.
M Then, **how did you get the door open?**
W ______________________

해석

남 왜 이렇게 늦었니?
여 자동차 문을 열 수가 없었어.
남 아, 정말?
여 응! 안에 열쇠를 두고 나왔었거든.
남 차 안에 그걸 두고 문을 잠갔다고?
여 맞아.
남 그럼, 어떻게 문을 열었니?
여 ______________________

정답 ③
해설 어떻게 문을 열었냐는 남자의 질문에 알맞은 답을 고른다.

2 대화를 듣고, 여자의 마지막 말에 이어질 남자의 응답으로 가장 적절한 것을 고르시오.

① She is very tall.
② Great! I will take it.
③ No, I don't like drawing.
④ Right. I have a daughter.

Script

W **How can I help** you, sir?
M I'm **looking for** something for **my daughter**.
W How old is she?
M She is 6 years old.
W Then, **what do you think about** this colored pencil set?
M ______________________

해석

여 무엇을 도와드릴까요, 손님?
남 제 딸에게 줄만한 걸 찾고 있어요.
여 따님이 몇 살이죠?
남 여섯 살이에요.
여 그러면, 이 색연필 세트는 어떠세요?
남 ______________________

정답 ②
해설 선물을 고르는 남자에게 색연필 세트를 딸에게 주는 건 어떠냐고 묻는 질문에 알맞은 답을 고른다.

기출문장

취향

A: **What kind of** movies do you like? 넌 어떤 종류의 영화를 좋아하니?
B: I love **romantic comedies.** 나 로맨틱 코미디를 좋아해.

A: Here's the **menu.** 여기 메뉴 있습니다.
B: **I'll have** chocolate ice cream. 저는 초콜릿 아이스크림으로 할게요.

A: **What** did you **think of** it? 그것은 어땠니?
B: I thought it was **interesting.** 응 그거 정말 재미있었어.

A: **How would** you **like** your steak? 스테이크를 어떻게 해 드릴까요?
B: **Well-done**, please. 바싹 익혀주세요.

경험

A: Did you **enjoy** it? 즐거웠니?
B: Yes, I **had a** really **good time.** 응, 정말 즐거운 시간을 보냈어.

A: **How long** will you stay here? 여기 얼마나 오랫동안 머무르실 건가요?
B: **For** one week. 일주일 동안이요.

A: **How often** do you send e-mail to your English teacher? 너는 너의 영어 선생님에게 얼마나 자주 이메일을 보내니?
B: **Once a month.** 한 달에 한 번.

A: **What kind of** movie did you see? 어떤 종류의 영화를 보았니?
B: We saw a **comedy.** 코미디를 봤어.

요청

A: **Could** you **say** that again? 다시 한 번 말씀해주시겠어요?
B: **Can** I **open** the window? 제가 창문을 열어도 될까요?

A: **Can** I **borrow** it later? 나중에 내가 그것을 빌려도 될까?
B: **Why not**? 그래.

A: I **beg your pardon**? 다시 한 번 말씀해주시겠어요?
B: Write your name and student number on this card. 이 카드에 이름과 학생 번호를 쓰세요.

A: **Can't** you **stay a little longer**? 좀 더 있다 가면 안되니?
B: **I'm afraid I can't.** 유감이지만, 안돼.

A: **Would you mind** spelling it for me, please? 철자 좀 말씀해주시겠어요?
B: Y-O-N-G-J-U-N. Y, O, N, G, J, U, N이에요.

A: Do you **have any good ideas**? 좋은 생각 있니?
B: Send them some money or clothes. 그들에게 돈과 옷을 보내.

위로

A: He fell down while riding his bike. 그가 자전거를 타다가 넘어졌어.

B: **I'm sorry to hear that.** 그 얘길 들으니 유감이다.

A: She broke her leg while she was skiing. 그녀는 스키를 타다가 다리가 부러졌대.

B: **I'm sorry to hear that.** 그 얘길 들으니 유감이다.

충고

A: I usually eat pizza and hamburgers. 나는 주로 피자와 햄버거를 먹어.

B: **You should not eat** junk food. 넌 정크 푸드를 먹으면 안 돼.

A: I'm really sleepy and tired. 나 정말 졸리고 피곤해.

B: **Why don't you** get some sleep? 잠을 좀 자지 그러니?

승낙, 거절

A: **How about going** to Gyeongbok Palace tomorrow? 내일 경복궁에 가는 게 어떨까요?

B: **That would be nice.** 그거 좋겠어요.

A: **Why don't we** go to the mall and look around? 쇼핑몰에 가서 둘러보는 건 어떨까?

B: **That's a good idea.** 그거 좋은 생각이야.

A: **Would** you **like to join** me? 너 나랑 같이 갈래?

B: Sure. **I'd be happy to.** 당연하지. 같이 가게 돼서 기뻐.

A: We **should try** not to waste water. 우리는 물을 낭비해서는 안 돼.

B: **You're right**! 네 말이 맞아!

A: May I **take a message**? 메시지를 전해드릴까요?

B: No, that's OK. I'll call again. 아니오, 괜찮아요. 제가 나중에 다시 전화할게요.

기타

A: **Where are you**? 너 어디 있니?

B: Sorry. I'm on my way. 미안해. 가고 있는 중이야.

A: **Isn't this** 458-2453? 458-2453번 아닌가요?

B: No. You **have the wrong number.** 아니오. 전화 잘못하셨습니다.

A: The doctor said I **would get well** soon. 의사 선생님이 내가 곧 나을 거라고 말했어.

B: I'm **glad to hear that.** 그 말을 들으니 기뻐.

A: I **won a prize** in speech contest today. 오늘 웅변대회에서 상을 받았어.

B: Good! You did a good job. 잘됐다! 정말 잘했어.

기출풀기

1 대화를 듣고, 여자의 마지막 말에 이어질 남자의 응답으로 가장 알맞은 것을 고르시오.

① OK. I'll tell her.
② Don't mention it.
③ I have a headache.
④ That would be nice.
⑤ It will take an hour.

2 대화를 듣고, 남자의 마지막 말에 이어질 여자의 응답으로 가장 알맞은 것을 고르시오.

① That's not mine.
② You're welcome.
③ No, thanks. I'm full.
④ Oh, I'm sorry to hear that.

3 대화를 듣고, 남자의 마지막 말에 이어질 여자의 응답으로 가장 알맞은 것을 고르시오.

① On business.
② For one week.
③ At the airport.
④ With my friends.

4 대화를 듣고, 남자의 마지막 말에 이어질 여자의 응답으로 가장 알맞은 것을 고르시오.

① The line is busy.
② Who's calling, please?
③ No, that's OK. I'll call again.
④ You have the wrong number.

5 대화를 듣고, 여자의 마지막 말에 이어질 남자의 응답으로 가장 적절한 것을 고르시오.

① You should not eat junk food.
② I don't like hamburgers, either.
③ I'm afraid I can't exercise with you.
④ Sorry to hear that. I also need to study a lot.

Answers

Part 1

1 ①

Script

W Wow! These bags are only $5 each. I want to buy one.

M Good. I'll help you find a nice bag. What about this plain one?

W Yeah, it's nice, but I already have a similar one. How about this square bag?

M I don't really like it. How about this bag? It has a pocket on the outside, so it is very useful.

W No. I really want to buy a bag that is a little bit bigger. I usually carry a lot of things.

M Oh, how about this bag with two pockets on it? It will be easy to carry, too.

W You're right. This bag is perfect for me.

해석

여 와! 이 가방이 하나에 5달러밖에 안 해. 하나 사고 싶어.

남 좋아. 네가 좋은 가방 고르는 걸 도와줄게. 이 무늬가 없는 가방은 어때?

여 응, 괜찮긴 한데 나한테 벌써 비슷한 게 있어. 이 네모난 가방은 어떠니?

남 그다지 마음에 들지 않아. 이 가방은 어떠니? 밖에 주머니가 있어서 매우 쓸모 있을 것 같아.

여 아니, 나는 그거보다 조금 더 큰 가방을 정말로 사고 싶어. 나는 보통 많은 것들을 가지고 다니거든.

남 아, 주머니가 두 개 있는 이 가방은 어때? 들고 다니기도 편하겠어.

여 맞아. 이 가방이 나에게 제일 알맞은 것 같아.

2 ①

Script

W May I have your attention, please? We are looking for a five-year-old girl. She has long curly hair. She is wearing a hat. She is also wearing a blouse and a skirt. If you see this girl, please call us at 987-6543 or come to the information center near the gate. Thank you very much.

해석

여 주목해주십시오. 다섯 살 된 여자 아이를 찾고 있습니다. 이 아이는 머리가 깁니다. 이 아이는 모자를 쓰고 있습니다. 또 블라우스와 치마를 입고 있습니다. 이 여자 아이를 보시면 987-6543으로 전화하시거나 정문 옆에 있는 안내소로 와주시기 바랍니다. 정말 감사합니다.

3 ③

Script

M Excuse me. Where's the post office?

W The post office? Go straight one block and then turn left. It will be on your left.

M So I go up this street one block, turn left and it'll be on my left?

W That's correct.

해석

남 실례합니다. 우체국이 어디인가요?

여 우체국이요? 한 블록 직진하셔서 왼쪽으로 도세요. 우체국이 왼편에 있을 거예요.

남 그러니까 이 길을 따라 한 블록 가서 왼쪽으로 돌면 우체국이 왼쪽에 있을 거라는 말씀이시죠?

여 맞아요.

4 ②

Script

① W When do we land?
M In two hours.

② W What would you like to have?
M I'll have the fish & chips.

③ W Can I try this on?
M Sure, the fitting room is over there.

④ W How much does it cost?
M A dollar fifty.

해석

① 여 언제 착륙하나요?
남 두 시간 후입니다.

② 여 무엇을 드시겠어요?
남 피시 앤 칩스로 하겠습니다.

③ 여 제가 이것을 입어봐도 될까요?
남 물론이죠. 옷 갈아입는 곳은 저기입니다.

④ 여 이것은 얼마입니까?
남 1달러 50센트입니다.

Part 2

1 ③

Script

M Good afternoon!

W Good afternoon! I'd like to check in.

M Do you have a reservation?

W No, but I need a single room.

M I see. Your name, please.

W Jeong.

M Sorry, can you spell it?

W J-E-O-N-G. Jeong.

M Oh, yes. Here is your key.

해석

남 안녕하세요!

여 안녕하세요! 체크인을 하려고요.

남 예약을 하셨나요?

여 아니요. 저는 1인실이 필요합니다.

남 알겠습니다. 이름을 얘기해 주십시오.

여 Jeong이요.

남 죄송하지만, 철자를 얘기해 주시겠어요?

여 J-E-O-N-G. Jeong이요.

남 아, 그러시군요. 여기 열쇠입니다.

2 ④

Script

M What are you doing here, Jane? It's late at night.

W I am watching the stars.

M Are you interested in stars and planets?

W Yes, I would like to learn about them. What are you interested in?

M I am interested in sea plants and animals. I want to study them because the sea can help solve food problems in the future.

해석

남 여기서 무엇을 하고 있니, Jane? 늦은 밤이야.

여 별을 보고 있어.

남 너 별과 행성에 관심 있니?

여 응, 나는 그것들에 대해서 공부하고 싶어. 너는 무엇에 관심이 있니?

남 나는 해양 식물과 동물에 관심이 있어. 해양이 미래에 식량문제를 해결하는 데 도움을 줄 수 있기 때문에 나는 그것들에 대해 공부하고 싶어.

3 ③

W Do you like your job?

M Sure. Sometimes it's very dangerous though. It's not easy to put out a big fire, but I feel happy when I save people's lives.

W Did you want to be a fire fighter when you were young?

M No, I didn't. I wanted to be a soccer player. But one day, I saw a fire fighter helping people, so I changed my mind.

해석

여 당신의 직업에 만족하시나요?

남 물론입니다. 가끔 매우 위험하지만요. 불을 끄는 것이 쉽지는 않지만, 사람들의 생명을 구할 때 행복합니다.

여 어릴 때 소방관이 되고 싶으셨나요?

남 아니오, 그렇지 않습니다. 저는 축구 선수가 되고 싶었어요. 하지만, 어느 날 한 소방관이 사람들을 도와주는 것을 보았고 제 생각을 바꾸었습니다.

4 ④

Script

M How can I help you?

W I left my bag on the train. Do you have it here?

M Let me check. What does it look like?

W It is red and has a flower print.

M Is this your bag?

W Yes. That's mine. Thank you.

M You're welcome.

해석

남 무엇을 도와드릴까요?

여 기차에 가방을 두고 내렸어요. 여기 있나요?

남 확인해 보겠습니다. 어떻게 생겼죠?

여 그건 빨간색이고 꽃무늬가 있어요.

남 이것이 당신 가방인가요?

여 네, 그것이 제 것입니다. 감사합니다.

남 천만에요.

5 ①

Script

W Hello, shoppers. We have a lost child. His name is Kim Min-su and he was found near the toy section of our department store. He is looking for his mom. He is 5 years old. He is wearing a red baseball cap, a white T-shirt and blue jeans. You can find him at the information desk. Once again! A 5-year-old boy named Kim Min-su is waiting for his mom at the information desk on the first floor.

해석

여 안녕하세요, 고객 여러분. 미아를 보호하고 있습니다. 아이의 이름은 김민수이고 저희 백화점 장난감 판매대에서 발견되었습니다. 아이는 엄마를 찾고 있습니다. 아이는 다섯 살입니다. 아이는 빨간 야구 모자를 쓰고, 흰색 티셔츠, 청바지를 입고 있습니다. 아이는 안내 데스크에 있습니다. 다시 한 번 말씀 드립니다! 김민수라는 다섯 살 난 남자 아이가 1층 안내 데스크에서 엄마를 기다리고 있습니다.

Part 3

1 ②

Script

M Did you watch the news last night?

W No. Did I miss anything special?

M There was a fire again in the mountains.

W That is terrible. It's been only 3 weeks since the last fire.

M That's true. The news said that it happened because someone was playing with matches.

W I think people should be more careful and responsible.

해석

남 너 어젯밤에 뉴스 봤니?

여 아니. 내가 뭐 특별한 뉴스를 놓쳤니?

남 산불이 또 발생했대.

여 그거 심각한데. 마지막 산불이 난 지 3일밖에 안 지났잖아.

남 맞아. 뉴스에서 그러는데 누군가가 성냥으로 장난을 쳐서 산불이 발생했대.

여 난 사람들이 좀 더 신중하고 책임감이 있어야 한다고 생각해.

2 ①

Script

W Attention all shoppers! We're looking for a woman's bag. It's small, blue and made of leather. If you find this bag, please bring it to the information center on the second floor. Thank you.

해석

여 모든 고객 여러분 주목해 주십시오! 여자 핸드백을 찾고 있습니다. 그 가방은 작고, 파란색이며 가죽으로 만들어졌습니다. 이 가방을 찾으시면 2층 안내소로 가지고 와 주시기 바랍니다. 감사합니다.

3 ⑤

Script

W Welcome to the L.A. Art Museum. My name is Mrs. Johnson and I will be your guide. This museum has three floors and contains many works from famous artists. First, we will go to the modern arts room. Then, we will see Picasso's paintings on the second floor. Please stay with me until the tour is over. Thank you for your attention. Let's go.

해석

여 L.A. 미술관에 온 것을 환영합니다. 제 이름은 Johnson이고 제가 여러분의 가이드입니다. 이 미술관은 3층으로, 유명한 화가들의 많은 작품을 소장하고 있습니다. 먼저, 우리는 현대 예술실로 갈 것입니다. 그런 다음, 2층에서 피카소의 그림들을 볼 것입니다. 관람이 끝날 때까지 저와 동행하셔야 합니다. 주목해 주셔서 감사합니다. 이제 가시겠습니다.

4 ②

Script

W I have a beak, and I like to catch fish with my beak. I am mostly white. I can fly, but I cannot swim. I like to fly around the sea. What am I?

해석

여 저에게는 부리가 있고, 저는 제 부리를 이용해서 고기 잡는 것을 좋아합니다. 저는 대체로 흰색입니다. 저는 날 수 있지만, 수영을 하지는 못합니다. 저는 바다 위를 나는 것을 좋아합니다. 제가 무엇일까요?

5 ③

Script

M This is one of Korea's greatest national holidays. It is similar to Thanksgiving in the U.S. and Canada. People wear traditional Korean clothes called 'Hanbok' on this special day. Also, they eat rice cakes and enjoy watching the full moon.

해석

남 이것은 한국의 가장 큰 휴일 중 하나입니다. 이것은 미국과 캐나다의 추수감사절과 비슷합니다. 사람들은 이 특별한 날에 '한복'이라고 불리는 한국의 전통 의복을 입습니다. 또한, 그들은 떡을 먹고 보름달을 보는 것을 즐깁니다.

Part 4

1 ①

Script

M What are you going to give Sarah for her birthday?

W I don't know. Maybe a CD. She loves listening to music.

M That's not a bad idea. What should I buy her?

W How about a watch?

M A watch?

W You know she's always late.

M You're right. I'll buy one for her.

해석

남 너 생일 선물로 뭘 Sarah에게 줄 거니?

여 잘 모르겠어. 아마 CD를 줄 거야. 그녀가 음악을 듣는 것을 좋아해.

남 안 좋은 생각은 아니네. 난 그녀에게 무엇을 사줘야 할까?

여 손목시계 어때?

남 손목시계?

여 그녀가 항상 늦는다는 거 너도 알잖아.

남 네 말이 맞아. 그녀에게 그것을 사줘야겠다.

2 ⑤

Script

M Good morning. Here is today's weather forecast. It will be sunny in Vancouver, but it will be cloudy in Paris. London will have lots of rain and Moscow will have heavy snow. There will be lightning in Singapore.

해석

남 안녕하세요. 오늘의 일기예보를 말씀드리겠습니다. 밴쿠버는 날씨가 맑지만, 파리는 흐리겠습니다. 런던에는 폭우가 내리고 모스크바는 많은 눈이 내리겠습니다. 싱가포르에는 번개가 치겠습니다.

3 ③

Script

M May I help you?

W Yes. I'm looking for some volunteer work. I would like to help people.

M We have many types of volunteer work. For example, we need volunteers for cleaning, washing, cooking, reading books and so on.

W Umm... I'm really good at cooking. Let me try that.

M Sounds good. You can start tomorrow.

해석

남 도와드릴까요?

여 네. 자원 봉사 일을 찾고 있어요. 저는 사람들을 도와주고 싶어요.

남 많은 종류의 봉사 활동이 있습니다. 예를 들면, 저희는 청소와 빨래, 요리, 책 읽기 등 많은 자원 봉사자가 필요합니다.

여 음, 저는 요리를 정말 잘해요. 제가 그것을 할게요.

남 좋아요. 내일부터 시작하세요.

4 ③

Script

M Susan, are you free this afternoon?

W I don't have any plans. Why?

M How about playing tennis with me?

W It's too hot outside.

M You're right. Let's go to a swimming pool.

W I'm sorry, I don't feel like it. I stayed up late last night.

M You should get some rest, then.

W Yeah, I think I'd better take a nap after lunch.

해석

남 Susan, 오늘 오후에 한가하니?

여 아무 계획 없어. 왜?

남 나랑 테니스 치는 게 어때?

여 밖이 너무 더워.

남 네 말이 맞아. 수영장에 가자.

여 미안한데, 수영할 기분이 아니야. 어젯밤 늦게까지 자지 않고 깨어 있었거든.

남 그럼, 넌 좀 쉬어야겠어.

여 응, 점심 먹고 낮잠 좀 자는 게 좋을 것 같아.

5 ④

Script

W Excuse me. I'd like to go to Gyeongbok Palace. How do I get there from here?

M You can take a bus from here, but the road will be very busy.

W Then what is the fastest way to get there?

M You can take the subway. Take line No. 3.

W I see. Could you tell me where the nearest subway station is?

M Sure. Just turn left at that corner.

W Thank you so much.

해석

여 실례합니다. 경복궁에 가고 싶은데요. 여기서 거기까지 어떻게 가야 하죠?

남 여기서 버스를 타면 되는데 도로가 많이 붐빌 거예요.

여 그러면 거기까지 가는데 가장 빠른 길이 무엇인가요?

남 지하철을 타면 돼요. 3호선을 타세요.

여 그렇군요. 가장 가까운 역이 어디인지 말씀해주시겠어요?

남 물론이죠. 저 모퉁이에서 왼쪽으로 도세요.

여 정말 감사합니다.

Part 5

1 ③

Script

① W The party is for Brandon.

② W Brandon's birthday party is on May 3rd.

③ W The party will be at Brandon's house.

④ W You must not tell Brandon about the party.

해석

① 여 파티는 Brandon을 위해 열리는 것이다.

② 여 Brandon의 생일 파티는 5월 3일이다.

③ 여 파티는 Brandon의 집에서 열릴 것이다.

④ 여 파티에 대해서 Brandon에게 말하면 안 된다.

2 ⑤

Script

W When are you going to take your vacation this year?

M In the summer, I'm going to Paris with my old friend, David.

W Really? That sounds great. How are you going to get there?

M By airplane.

W Oh, how long are you going to be away?

M For exactly two weeks.

W Great! Where are you going to stay?

M At my uncle's house.

W Sounds wonderful!

해석

여 올해는 휴가를 어디서 보낼 거니?

남 여름에 오랜 친구, David와 함께 파리에 갈 거야.

여 정말이야? 재미있겠다. 거기에 어떻게 갈 거니?

남 비행기로.

여 오, 얼마나 오랫동안 떠나 있을 거니?

남 정확히 2주 동안이야.

여 좋겠다! 어디에 묵을 예정이니?

남 삼촌 집에서.

여 좋겠다!

3 ②

Script

M What are you looking at, Yumi?

W Oh, I'm looking at a picture of my best friend, Sally. Do you remember her?

M Yes, I do. I remember her very well. She's pretty tall with short blonde hair. She used to live next door to you, right?

W Right. She's visiting me this weekend.

M Wow, that's great. I'd like to see her.

해석

남 너 무엇을 보고 있니, 유미?

여 아, 내 가장 친한 친구, Sally의 사진을 보고 있어. 너 그 애 기억하니?

남 응, 그래. 아주 잘 기억이 나. 그녀는 짧은 금발 머리로 꽤 키가 크잖아. 네 옆집에 살지 않았니, 맞지?

여 맞아. 이번 주말에 나를 방문한대.

남 와, 좋겠다. 나도 그녀가 보고 싶어.

4 ③

Script

W Do you sleep well? Here is some advice for you to sleep better at night. First, you should not drink coffee or tea in the evening. Second, don't sleep during the daytime. Third, watching TV late at night is not a good idea. If you want to have a good night's sleep, try to drink warm milk before you go to bed, or do some light exercises.

해석

여 잠을 잘 주무시나요? 밤에 잠을 더 잘 자기 위한 몇 가지 방법이 있습니다. 먼저, 저녁에 커피나 차를 마시지 말아야 합니다. 둘째, 낮 동안 잠을 자지 마십시오. 셋째, 늦은 밤에 TV를 보는 것은 좋은 생각이 아닙니다. 잠을 푹 자기를 원하신다면 잠을 자기 전에 따뜻한 우유를 마시거나 가벼운 운동을 하십시오.

5 ④

Script

M What's the matter?

W I have a terrible headache.

M Do you have a fever, too?

W Yes, I also have a runny nose and a sore throat.

M I think you have the flu. You should take this medicine and drink plenty of water.

해석

남 어떤 문제가 있으십니까?

여 두통이 심해요.

남 열도 있으신가요?

여 네, 콧물도 나고 목도 아파요.

남 독감에 걸리신 것 같네요. 이 약을 드시고 물을 많이 마시세요.

Part 6

1 ②

Script

M Hey, there's a free jazz concert tomorrow night.

W Oh, that sounds like fun. Where is it?

M At Green Lake Park.

W What time does it start?

M It starts at seven o'clock.

W OK. Why don't we meet at six forty?

M Well, they don't usually have a lot of seats, so ....

W Then, let's get there earlier. How about around six thirty?

M OK. Sounds good.

해석

남 이봐, 내일 밤에 무료 재즈 콘서트가 있어.

여 아, 재미있겠다. 어디에서 하니?

남 Green Lake 공원에서.

여 언제 시작하니?

남 7시에 시작해.

여 좋아. 6시 40분에 만나는 게 어때?

남 글쎄, 대개 좌석이 많이 않잖아. 그래서…….

여 그럼 거기에 일찍 가자. 6시 30분 어때?

남 알았어. 좋아.

2 ②

Script

M Kate, can I borrow some money?

W What for?

M I want a soda, but I don't have enough money.

W Okay. How much do you need?

M I have one dollar, but a soda costs one fifty.

W Okay. Here's fifty cents.

해석

남 Kate, 내가 돈 좀 빌릴 수 있을까?
여 뭐하게?
남 탄산음료를 마시고 싶은데, 돈이 충분하지 않아서.
여 좋아. 얼마가 필요하니?
남 나에게 1달러가 있는데, 탄산음료가 1달러 50센트야.
여 그렇구나. 여기 50센트야.

3 ③

Script

[Telephone rings.]

M Hello.

W Hello. May I speak to Sam?

M Speaking.

W Hi, Sam. This is Judy. Can you come to my birthday party?

M When is your birthday?

W It's the third Saturday of this month.

M Oh, it's next Saturday! That's great.

해석

남 여보세요.
여 여보세요. Sam 좀 바꿔주세요?
남 전데요.
여 안녕, Sam. 나 Judy야. 너 내 생일 파티에 올 수 있니?
남 네 생일이 언제니?
여 이번 달 셋째 주 토요일이야.
남 아, 다음 주 토요일이구나! 좋아.

4 ②

Script

W May I help you?

M Yes, please. I'm looking for a blouse for my mother.

W What size does your mother wear?

M Medium.

W Then, how about this pink one?

M I like it. How much is it?

W It was 40,000 won, but it's on sale today. It's 50% off.

M Oh, I'm lucky. I'll take it.

해석

여 도와드릴까요?
남 네. 제 어머니께 드릴 블라우스를 찾고 있어요.
여 어머니께서 어떤 사이즈를 입으시나요?
남 중간 사이즈요.
여 그럼, 이 분홍색은 어떠세요?
남 마음에 들어요. 얼마예요?
여 4만원인데, 오늘은 세일을 합니다. 50%요.
남 오, 전 운이 좋네요. 그걸로 사겠습니다.

5 ①

Script

W Peter, when does the soccer game start?

M Seven thirty.

W Then we only have half an hour before the game starts. Will we make it?

M We'll be there in 10 minutes.

W Are you sure? I don't want to miss the beginning of the game.

M Trust me. I'm sure.

해석

여 Peter, 축구 경기가 언제 시작하니?
남 7시 반이야.
여 그러면 게임이 시작하기 전 30분 밖에 안 남은 거네. 우리 시간 맞춰 도착할 수 있을까?
남 우리 거기에 10분 후면 도착할 수 있을 거야.
여 확실하니? 경기의 시작을 놓치고 싶지 않아.
남 날 믿어. 확실해.

Part 7

1 ⑤

Script

[Telephone rings.]

W Hello.

M Hi, Sumi. It's me, David.

W David! It's already 10 o'clock. You were supposed to be here by now!

M I know I'm running late.

W Everyone has arrived! You're going to be the last one here.

M Well, I'm stuck in traffic.

W OK. Try to get here as soon as possible.

M Alright. I'm sorry.

해석

여 여보세요.
남 안녕, 수미야. 나야, David.
여 David! 벌써 10시야. 지금쯤 여기 왔어야 하는 거잖아!
남 내가 늦었다는 거 나도 알고 있어.
여 모든 사람이 도착했어! 네가 여기 마지막 사람이야.
남 글쎄, 교통 체증으로 꼼짝도 못하고 있어.

여 알았어. 가능한 한 빨리 오도록 해봐.
남 알았어. 미안해.

2 ①

Script

[Telephone rings.]

M ABC restaurant. May I help you?

W I'd like to make a reservation.

M How many people?

W Five.

M What time, ma'am?

W At 7:30 this evening.

M What's your name, please?

W My name is Susan Kim.

해석

남 ABC 식당입니다. 도와드릴까요?
여 예약을 하고 싶습니다.
남 몇 명인가요?
여 다섯 명이요.
남 언제인가요, 부인?
여 오늘 저녁 7시 반이요.
남 성함이 어떻게 되시죠?
여 제 이름은 Susan Kim입니다.

3 ②

Script

W Why are you in such a hurry?

M What do you mean?

W You're pushing the close button as soon as the elevator opens.

M Am I? So what's the problem with that?

W Don't you know the price of oil is going up? If you don't wait for the door to close automatically, you'll waste electricity.

M Oh, I'm sorry. I didn't know that. I'll remember to wait next time.

해석

여 너 왜 그렇게 서두르니?
남 무슨 말이니?
여 엘리베이터에 타자마자 닫힘 버튼을 누르고 있잖아.
남 내가? 그런데 그게 무슨 문제라도 되니?
여 기름 값이 오르고 있다는 거 모르니? 자동으로 문이 닫히기를 기다리지 않으면 전기를 낭비하게 되는 거야.
남 아, 미안해. 그걸 모르고 있었어. 다음에는 기다려야 한다는 것을 기억할게.

4 ③

Script

W What happened to your leg?

M I fell over while playing soccer.

W Again? You had your leg broken a few months ago, didn't you?

M Yes, it's my second time.

W Maybe you should try another sport like swimming.

해석

여 다리가 왜 그러니?
남 축구를 하다가 넘어졌어.
여 또? 몇 달 전에 다리가 부러지자 않았니, 그렇지?
남 응, 이게 두 번째야.
여 아마도 너는 수영과 같은 다른 운동을 해야 겠다.

5 ②

Script

W Mike, you look serious. What are you doing?

M I'm writing a letter to Jane.

W But you just talked to her on the phone.

M I know. I wasn't very nice to her.

W What did you do?

M I said her new hairstyle looked funny.

W She must have been upset.

M Yes. So I want to say I'm sorry.

해석

여 Mike, 표정이 심각하네. 무엇을 하고 있는 중이니?
남 Jane에게 편지를 쓰고 있어.
여 하지만, 너 막 그녀와 전화 통화를 했잖아.
남 나도 알아. 나는 그다지 그녀에게 다정하지 못했어.
여 너가 어떻게 했는데?
남 그녀의 새 머리 스타일이 우스워 보인다고 말했어.
여 그녀가 틀림없이 화가 났겠구나.
남 응. 그녀에게 미안하다고 말하고 싶어.

Part 8

1 ①

Script

M You know what? Mary was in a car accident last night.

W Are you serious? Is she all right?

M Well, she broke her leg, so she is in the hospital right now.

W That's too bad. I hope she gets well soon.

해석

남 너 그거 알아? Mary가 어젯밤에 교통 사고를 당했어.
여 진담이야? 그녀는 괜찮니?
남 글쎄, 다리가 부러져서 그녀는 지금 병원에 있어.
여 정말 안됐다. 그녀가 곧 회복하길 바랄게.

2 ④

Script

W It's Sunday afternoon. Let's go out to the park and have fun.

M Good idea. We can pick up some Kimbab along the way.

W That sounds great. I'll buy something to drink at the supermarket.

M Okay. I will bring a mat to sit on.

W Very good. Oh, wait a second.

M What is it?

W I hear something. It sounds like thunder.

M Really? Oh, no. Some dark clouds are coming.

W That's too bad.

해석

여 일요일 오후야. 공원에 가서 놀자.
남 좋은 생각이야. 가는 길에 김밥을 좀 사자.
여 좋은 생각인데. 내가 슈퍼에서 마실 것을 살게.
남 좋아. 깔고 앉을 돗자리를 가져올게.
여 아주 좋아. 아, 잠깐만.
남 왜?
여 무슨 소리를 들었어. 천둥소리 같은데.
남 정말이니? 아, 안 돼. 먹구름이 몰려오고 있어.
여 정말 아쉽다.

3 ④

Script

M I haven't seen Jane today. Where is she?

W She didn't come to school today.

M Really? Why not? Is she sick?

W No, the teacher said that Jane went to participate in a speech contest.

M I hope she wins the first prize.

해석

남 오늘 Jane이 안 보여. 그녀는 어디 있니?
여 오늘 학교에 오지 않았어.
남 정말? 왜 오지 않았니? 그녀가 아프니?
여 아니, 선생님께서 Jane이 오늘 웅변대회에 나간다고 하셨어.
남 그녀가 일등을 했으면 좋겠어.

4 ②

Script

W Do you have any plans this weekend?

M Yes, I'm going to visit my grandfather.

W You went to see him last weekend for his birthday, didn't you?

M I did, but I should help him work on his farm. He's been very busy these days.

W What a good grandson!

해석

여 이번 주말에 계획 있니?
남 응, 할아버지 댁에 갈 거야.
여 할아버지 생신이셔서 지난주에 그를 뵈었지, 그렇지 않니?
남 그랬지, 하지만, 할아버지가 농장일을 하시는 걸 도와야 해. 요즘 정말 바쁘시거든.
여 넌 정말 착한 손자구나.

5 ①

Script

M How's your new apartment?

W At first, I liked it, but not any more.

M Why? Are there any problems?

W I can't sleep because the kids upstairs are running around every night.

M That's terrible. Do they make a lot of noise?

W Yes.

M Did you tell them about it?

W Yes, I did, but they didn't stop!

해석

남 네 새 아파트 어떠니?
여 처음에는 좋았는데, 이젠 아니야.
남 왜? 문제라도 있니?
여 윗층 아이들이 매일 밤 뛰어다녀서 잠을 잘 수가 없어.
남 안됐다. 많이 시끄럽니?
여 응.
남 그들에게 그것을 얘기해 봤니?
여 응, 그랬는데, 멈추질 않아!

Part 9

1 ④

Script

W I'm very proud of my friend, Julie.

M Why?

W She won the first prize in the math contest.

M Really? I'm a little surprised because she doesn't look so smart.

해석

여 나는 내 친구, Julie가 자랑스러워.
남 왜?
여 그녀가 수학 경시대회에서 우승했거든.
남 정말? 조금 놀랍다. 왜냐하면 그녀가 그렇게 똑똑해 보이지는 않거든.

2 ④

Script

W Did you hear the news?

M What news?

W During the summer vacation, Gi-ho's village was flooded because of the heavy rain.

M How terrible! Is he okay?

W Not really. He lost his books and clothes. So our class has decided to help him.

M That's a good idea! Can I help, too?

W Sure. That would be great.

해석

여 너 소식 들었니?
남 무슨 소식?
여 여름 방학에 폭우로 기호네 마을이 침수되었대.
남 정말 안됐다! 그는 괜찮니?
여 그렇지 않아. 책하고 옷을 모두 잃어버렸대. 그래서 우리 반은 그를 도와주기로 했어.
남 좋은 생각이야! 나도 도울 수 있을까?
여 물론이지. 그러면 좋지.

3 ④

Script

M I'm a middle school student. I enjoy music very much and I like to play the violin. I want to be a violinist like Sarah Chang. I play the violin every day, but I can't play it well. I make a lot of mistakes. What can I do?

해석

남 저는 중학생입니다. 저는 음악을 매우 즐기고 바이올린을 연주하는 것을 좋아합니다. 저는 Sarah Chang과 같은 바이올리니스트가 되고 싶습니다. 저는 매일 바이올린을 연주하는데, 잘하지는 못합니다. 저는 많은 실수를 합니다. 제가 어떻게 해야 할까요?

4 ①

Script

M What's the problem with your computer?

W It's not working at all since last night. I have a lot of work to do on it.

M Did you call the service center?

W Yes, but they are all on vacation.

M Oh, that's too bad.

해석

남 네 컴퓨터에 무슨 문제가 있니?
여 어젯밤부터 작동이 아예 안돼. 컴퓨터로 해야 할 일이 많은데.
남 서비스 센터에 전화해봤니?
여 응, 그런데 모두 휴가 중이래.
남 오, 그거 안됐다.

5 ④

Script

W During summer vacation, I work part time at the library. Some of my friends go traveling or visit their relatives, but I don't envy them. I'm very satisfied with working at the library. I can make money and at the same time, I can read a lot.

해석

여 여름 방학 동안, 나는 도서관에서 시간제로 일을 합니다. 내 친구들 중 몇 명은 여행을 가거나, 친척을 방문하지만, 저는 그들이 부럽지 않습니다. 저는 도서관에서 일하는 것에 매우 만족합니다. 저는 돈도 벌 수 있고 동시에 책도 많이 읽을 수 있습니다.

Part 10

1 ②

Script

W You want to enter the classroom, but the door is closed. You are holding a bag and some books in both hands. At that moment, a student is passing by you. What would you say to the student?

해석

여 당신은 교실로 들어가려고 하지만, 문은 닫혀 있습니다. 당신은 양손에 가방 하나와 몇 권의 책을 가지고 있습니다. 그때 한 학생이 당신 옆을 지나갑니다. 당신은 그 학생에게 무엇이라고 말하겠습니까?

2 ②

Script

M Good morning, miss. What can I do for you?

W I would like to return this printer.

M Oh! Is there something wrong with it?

W Well, yes. I tried to print my report, but it didn't work.

M I'm sorry, miss. Do you have your receipt?

W Yes, here it is.

질문입니다.

Q What did the woman bring to the shop?

해석

남 안녕하세요, 손님. 무엇을 도와드릴까요?

여 이 프린터를 반품하고 싶어요.
남 오! 그 프린터에 무슨 이상이라도 있나요?
여 음, 네. 제 보고서를 인쇄하려고 했는데, 작동하지 않았어요.
남 죄송합니다, 손님. 영수증 가지고 계세요?
여 네, 여기 있습니다.

질문 여자가 가게에 가져간 것은 무엇인가?

3 ②

Script

W You seem to have lost a lot of weight. Are you having any problems with your health?

M No, I exercise a lot.

W Do you go to the fitness center?

M I did, but not anymore. I just walk a lot everyday. I think jogging is the best way to lose weight.

질문입니다.

Q What does the man think is the best way of losing weight?

해석

여 너 살이 많이 빠진 것 같아. 건강에 무슨 문제라도 있는 거니?
남 아니, 운동을 많이 해.
여 헬스클럽에 가니?
남 그랬는데, 이제는 안 가. 그냥 매일 많이 걸어. 내 생각에는 조깅이 살을 빼는 데 가장 좋은 방법인 것 같아.

질문 남자가 살을 빼는 데 어떤 방법이 가장 좋다고 생각하는가?

4 ③

Script

W Can I help you?

M Yes, please. I'd like one large pizza and one small coke.

W For here or to go?

M To go, please.

W Okay. Anything else?

M No, that's all.

질문입니다.

Q How much is it?

해석

여 제가 도와드릴까요?
남 네. 피자 큰 거 하나랑 콜라 작은 걸로 하나 주세요.
여 여기서 드실 건가요, 아니면 가지고 가실 건가요?
남 가지고 갈 거예요.
여 알겠습니다. 다른 필요한 것 없으신가요?
남 아니오, 그게 전부입니다.

질문 얼마입니까?

5 ③

Script

W In English class, while you are taking a ten-minute quiz, the teacher says, "You have one minute left, so please hurry." However, you are not finished and you want more time. In this case, what would you say to the teacher?

해석

여 영어 수업에서 10분 쪽지 시험을 보는 도중 선생님께서 "1분 남았습니다. 서두르세요."라고 말씀하십니다. 하지만, 당신은 아직 시험을 다 보지 못했고, 시간이 더 필요합니다. 이런 경우에, 당신은 선생님께 뭐라고 말씀하시겠습니까?

Part II

1 ②

Script

W Number one

M What do you think of your English teacher?

W She is nice and friendly.

W Number two

M Why don't we go to the concert together?

W That's right.

W Number three

M May I ask you a question?

W Sure, what is it?

W Number four

M Will you help me with the dishes?

W I'm sorry, I can't. I'm so tired.

해석

① 남 네 영어 선생님에 대해서 어떻게 생각하니?
여 선생님은 다정하고 친절하셔.
② 남 우리 같이 콘서트를 보러 가는 게 어때?
여 맞아.
③ 남 제가 질문 하나 해도 될까요?
여 물론이죠, 뭔데요?
④ 남 제가 설거지하는 것을 도와주실래요?
여 죄송한데, 안 되겠어요. 전 너무 피곤해요.

2 ③

Script

W Number one

M How often do you play tennis?

W Twice a week.

W Number two

M How many pets do you have?

W I have three, two dogs and a cat.

W Number three

M How far is City Hall from here?

W It's a new building.

W Number four

M How long have you been in New York?

W About a month.

해석

① 남 얼마나 자주 테니스를 치나요?
여 일주일에 두 번이요.

② 남 애완동물 몇 마리를 가지고 계세요?
여 세 마리요. 개 두 마리와 고양이 한 마리예요.

③ 남 시청이 여기서 얼마나 먼가요?
여 그건 새 건물이에요.

④ 남 뉴욕에 오신 지 얼마나 되셨나요?
여 약 한 달쯤이요.

3 ②

Script

W Number one

M Where shall we meet?

W In front of the concert hall.

W Number two

M What's wrong? You look angry.

W Thank you for saying so.

W Number three

M Who's calling, please?

W This is Emily speaking.

W Number four

M How would you like your steak?

W Well done, please.

해석

① 남 우리 어디서 만날까?
여 콘서트장 앞에서.

② 남 무슨 일이니? 너 화가 난 것 같아.
여 그렇게 얘기해 줘서 고마워.

③ 남 전화 거신 분은 누구세요?
여 Emily입니다.

④ 남 스테이크를 어떻게 해 드릴까요?
여 바싹 익혀주세요.

4 ④

Script

M Number one

W Let's go to a concert.

M Sounds great!

M Number two

W How often do you watch TV?

M Almost every day.

M Number three

W How much is this?

M Just a minute, please. It's 2,500 won.

M Number four

W When is your final test?

M It's too difficult for me.

M Number five

W How about a glass of milk?

M Yes, please. Thanks.

해석

① 여 콘서트에 가자.
남 좋아!

② 여 너는 얼마나 자주 TV를 보니?
남 거의 매일.

③ 여 이거 얼마에요?
남 잠깐만요. 2,500원입니다.

④ 여 기말고사가 언제니?
남 그건 나에게 너무 어려워.

⑤ 여 우유 한 잔 어때?
남 네, 주세요. 감사합니다.

5 ①

Script

M Number one.

W Why are you late for class?

M Please get up earlier in the morning.

M Number two.

W How was school today?

M Not bad.

M Number three.

W I washed the dishes for you.

M How kind of you!

M Number four.

W Will you lend me an eraser?

M Sorry, but I don't have one.

해석

① 여 왜 수업에 늦었니?
남 아침에 더 일찍 일어나세요.

② 여 오늘 학교 어땠니?
남 나쁘지 않았어요.

③ 여 너 대신에 내가 설거지를 했어.
남 넌 정말 친절해!

④ 여 지우개 좀 빌려줄래?
남 미안해, 난 지우개가 없어.

Part 12

1 ④

Script

M Hello, Ms. Kim.

W Hi, how was the city tour?

M It was wonderful.

W I am glad you liked it. Seoul has many interesting places to visit.

M It has so many historical palaces.

W Yes, it really does. How about going to Gyeongbok Palace tomorrow?

M ______________________________

해석

남 안녕하세요. 김 씨.
여 안녕하세요. 시내 구경은 어땠어요?
남 좋았어요.
여 마음에 들었다니 기뻐요. 서울에는 가 볼만한 재미있는 곳이 많아요.
남 역사적인 궁전도 많고요.
여 네, 정말 그래요. 내일 경복궁에 가는 게 어떨까요?
남 ______________________________

2 ④

Script

W Can I borrow your camera this weekend?

M I'm afraid you can't. It's broken.

W What happened?

M I dropped it while I was riding my bike.

W ______________________________

해석

여 이번 주말에 네 사진기 좀 빌려줄래?
남 유감이지만, 안 돼. 고장 났어.
여 무슨 일이 있었니?
남 자전거를 타다가 떨어뜨렸어.
여 ______________________________

3 ②

Script

M Can I take a look at your passport?

W Sure. Here you are.

M Let me ask you a few questions.

W Yes.

M What is your reason for visiting Korea?

W Sightseeing.

M How long will you stay here?

W ______________________________

해석

남 제가 여권 좀 볼 수 있을까요?
여 물론이죠. 여기 있습니다.
남 제가 몇 가지 질문을 좀 하겠습니다.
여 네.
남 한국을 방문하는 이유가 무엇입니까?
여 관광이요.
남 여기 얼마나 머무르실 건가요?
여 ______________________________

4 ③

Script

[Telephone rings.]

W Hello. This is Liz. Can I speak to Steven?

M I'm sorry, but he can't come to the phone right now.

W When can I speak to him?

M I'm not sure. May I take a message?

W ______________________________

해석

여 여보세요. 전 Liz인데요. Steven과 통화할 수 있을까요?
남 죄송한데, 그는 지금 전화를 받을 수가 없습니다.
여 언제 그와 통화할 수 있을까요?
남 잘 모르겠네요. 메모를 남겨 드릴까요?
여 ______________________________

5 ①

Script

M Sandra, what's the problem? You look worried.

W I've been gaining a lot of weight these days.

M Do you eat a lot?

W No, I don't think so.

M What kind of food do you usually eat?

W I usually eat pizza and hamburgers.

M ______________________________

해석

남 Sandra, 무슨 문제가 있니? 너 걱정이 있어 보여.
여 나 요즘 살이 너무 쪘어.
남 너 많이 먹니?
여 아니, 그렇지 않은 것 같은데.
남 어떤 종류의 음식을 주로 먹니?
여 보통 피자나 햄버거를 먹어.
남 ______________________________